D1083067

Interdisciplinary perspectives on modern history

Editors
Robert Fogel and Stephan Thernstrom

From peasants to farmers

Other books in this series

Eric H. Monkkonen: *Police in urban America, 1860–1920*

Mary P. Ryan: *Cradle of the middle class: the family in Oneida County, New York, 1790–1865*

Ann Kussmaul: *Servants in husbandry in early modern England*

Tamara K. Hareven: *Family time and industrial time: the relationship between the family and work in a New England industrial community*

David Rosner: *A once charitable enterprise: hospitals and health care in Brooklyn and New York, 1885–1915*

Arnold R. Hirsch: *Making the second ghetto: race and housing in Chicago, 1940–1960*

Roy Rosenzweig: *Eight hours for what we will: workers and leisure in an industrial city, 1870–1920*

Hal S. Barron: *Those who stayed behind: rural society in nineteenth-century New England*

From peasants to farmers

*The migration from Balestrand,
Norway, to the Upper Middle West*

JON GJERDE

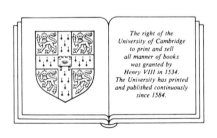

The right of the
University of Cambridge
to print and sell
all manner of books
was granted by
Henry VIII in 1534.
The University has printed
and published continuously
since 1584.

CAMBRIDGE UNIVERSITY PRESS

Cambridge
London   New York   New Rochelle
Melbourne   Sydney

Published by the Press Syndicate of the University of Cambridge
The Pitt Building, Trumpington Street, Cambridge CB2 1RP
32 East 57th Street, New York, NY 10022, USA
296 Beaconsfield Parade, Middle Park, Melbourne 3206, Australia

First published 1985

Printed in the United States of America

Library of Congress Cataloging in Publication Data
Gjerde, Jon, 1953–
From peasants to farmers.
(Interdisciplinary perspectives on modern history)
Bibliography: p.
Includes index.
1. Norwegian Americans – Middle West – Economic
conditions.   2. Norwegian Americans – Middle West – Social
conditions.   3. Balestrand (Norway) – Economic
conditions.   4. Balestrand (Norway) – Social conditions.   5. Balestrand
(Norway) – Emigration and immigration.   6. Peasantry – Norway –
Balestrand.   7. Farmers – Norway – Balestrand.   8. Middle West –
Foreign population.   I. Title.   II. Series.
F358.2.S2G54   1985   304.8'77'0483   84–21428
ISBN 0 521 26068 X

Contents

Tables .... *page* vii

Plates and figures xi

Preface xiii

1 Introduction 1

2 "The worlds we have lost":
  regional differences in trade, migration,
  and emigration in Norway 12

3 "The grass so fat it glistened":
  the social and economic structure
  of peasant Balestrand 25

4 "It will be man's fortune to see
  business extended": economic
  development of Balestrand, 1800–1865 56

5 Inheritance, marriage, fertility, and
  economic growth: social development
  of Balestrand, 1800–1865 85

6 The children of Askeladden: emigration
  from Balestrand to the United States 116

7 "They rushed from place to place":
  American settlement patterns among
  Balestrand's immigrants 137

8 "Norwegians . . . must learn anew": economic
  development of the American communities 168

9 "There is good moral fiber in the sons
  of the mountains": social development
  of the American communities 202

v

10 Conclusion 232

Notes 240

A note on secondary sources 295

Index 306

Tables

1   Annual population growth according to region, 1769–
    1875   *page* 15
2   Regions of most intense emigration, 1856–65   22
3   Farm units in Balestrand's parishes, 1825–65   61
4   Increase in arable land: Tjugum and Mundal parishes,
    1802–65   71
5   Annual increase in animal units and grain sown
    according to farmland type: Tjugum and Mundal
    parishes, 1723–1865   75
6   Annual imports and exports: Sogn, 1841–70   77
7   Servant and day laborer wages: Sogn, 1836–70   81
8   Relative cost of farms: Mundal parish, 1838–88   83
9   Conception of first child according to month of
    marriage of mother: Mundal parish, 1820–79   93
10   Age at first marriage: Mundal parish and a portion of
    Tjugum parish, 1820–79   99
11   Percentage and number ever married: Tjugum and
    Mundal parishes, 1801–65   100
12   Completed family size according to class and year
    married: Mundal parish, 1820–69   101
13   Illegitimate births in relation to total births and
    marriages: Balestrand, 1825–99   103
14   Conception of first child of fertile first marriage:
    Mundal parish, 1820–79   104
15   Conception of first child of fertile first marriage
    according to class: Mundal parish, 1820–79   105
16   Marriage patterns of indersts later classed as
    husmenn: Mundal parish, 1830–79   106
17   Frequency of celebration of communion: Tjugum
    parish, 1849–62   113
18   Emigration from Balestrand, 1844–1904   118
19   Migration to and from Balestrand, 1838–61   120
20   Destinations of emigrants from Balestrand, 1838–61   121

21 Class and unit size of Balestrand emigrant groups,
    1844–79   122
22 Emigration according to grend: Balestrand, 1844–69   133
23 County of birth in Norway for Spring Prairie, Norway
    Grove, and Bonnet Prairie church members, 1845–96   151
24 Birthplaces of marriage partners of Balestrand- and
    Leikanger-born: Norway Grove, Spring Prairie, Lodi,
    and Bonnet Prairie, 1850–74   152
25 Age-specific migration rates: Bandon, Camp, and
    Palmyra townships, 1885–95 and 1895–1905   162
26 Migration according to wealth: Bandon, Camp, and
    Palmyra townships, 1885–95 and 1895–1905   162
27 Residential stability according to wealth and church
    membership: Bandon, Camp, and Palmyra townships,
    1885–95 and 1895–1905   163
28 Age-standardized migration rates according to
    nationality, church, and sex (ages 5–59): Bandon,
    Camp, and Palmyra townships, 1885–95 and 1895–
    1905   164
29 Production of corn and wheat among Norwegians and
    non-Norwegians: Vienna township, 1849   173
30 Hired farm labor in Norwegian households, 1860,
    1880, 1900   174
31 Crop production among Norwegians and non-
    Norwegians: Vienna township, 1849   176
32 Nonwheat grains and potatoes produced by
    Norwegian-born and New England–born farmers:
    Vienna township, 1859 and 1869   177
33 Animals held per farm unit by Norwegian-born and
    all farmers: Vienna township, 1849, 1859, and 1869   178
34 Wheat production according to ethnocultural group:
    Vienna township, 1859 and 1869   180
35 Crop mix according to farm size: Vienna township,
    1859   181
36 Crop mix according to farm size and place of birth:
    Vienna township, 1859   182
37 Hay production according to ethnocultural group:
    Vienna township, 1859 and 1869   184
38 Variations between Norwegian farmers who remained
    in Vienna township after 1869 and those who left   186
39 Growth in livestock holdings among groups
    remaining in Vienna township from 1869 to 1879   188

40 Wheat as a percentage of crop yield: Arendahl and
    Camp townships and environs, 1859, 1869, and 1879   189
41 Nonmarket crops as percentages of total harvests:
    Arendahl Norwegians and Fillmore County farm
    units, 1859, 1869, and 1879   191
42 Nonmarket crops as percentages of total harvests:
    Camp Norwegians and Renville County farm units,
    1869 and 1879   191
43 Sex ratio of servants: Balestrand and Balestrand
    settlements, 1860–1900   196
44 Sex ratio of children aged 0–19 in households:
    Balestrand and Balestrand settlements, 1860–1900   197
45 Age at first marriage: Norway Grove, Spring Prairie,
    and Bonnet Prairie, 1851–96   204
46 Age differences between partners in first marriages:
    Norway Grove and Spring Prairie, 1851–96   205
47 Percentage ever married at given ages: Balestrand and
    Balestrand settlements, 1860–1900   206
48 Child/woman ratios: Balestrand and Balestrand
    settlements, 1845–1900   209
49 Child/married woman ratios: Balestrand and
    Balestrand settlements, 1845–1900   210
50 Age-standardized marital fertility: Balestrand and
    Balestrand settlements, 1860–1900   211
51 Illegitimate births according to year baptized: Norway
    Grove, Spring Prairie, Bonnet Prairie, and Arendahl,
    1851–1900   215
52 Conception of first child of marriage: Balestrand
    immigrants in Norway Grove, Spring Prairie, Bonnet
    Prairie, and Arendahl, 1850–96   216
53 Background in Norway in relation to conception of
    first child of marriage: Norway Grove, Spring Prairie,
    and Bonnet Prairie, 1850–96   218
54 Conception of first child of marriage according to
    place of parents' birth: Norway Grove, Spring Prairie,
    and Bonnet Prairie, 1870–96   219
55 Naming patterns for firstborn boys of first marriages:
    Balestrand and Norway Grove, Spring Prairie, and
    Bonnet Prairie, 1820–99   227

Plates and figures

Plates

1 A farmer using an ard to plow a field in mountainous
   Balestrand   *page* 31
2 The Langehaug støl in the Vetlefjord region of
   Balestrand   35
3 A typical hayfield near a Balestrand fjord   40
4 Cutting and bundling tree branches to be used as
   animal fodder   43
5 An elderly woman spinning outside her home   50
6 A cotter's wife making flatbread   66
7 A relatively late depiction of a Balestrand household
   showing the retention of a sexual division of labor   68
8 Land clearing to increase field size   70
9 Courtship was a private matter between young men
   and women   89
10 Members of a young cotter household from the
   Esefjord in Balestrand display their home   98
11 The cotter Ambjørn Bale sitting alone in front of his
   home   129
12 The home of a Balestrand immigrant family in
   Norway Grove   148
13 An austere Norwegian household in Norway Grove of
   the 1870s   175
14 A large, flat Norway Grove field of grain, probably
   wheat   179
15 Three men and one boy milking a relatively large
   herd of cows in the Norway Grove vicinity   198
16 Daughters spinning yarn under the direction of a
   stern mother   199
17 Young women sewing a quilt with a newfangled
   sewing machine   200
18 A Norway Grove extended family, engaged in various
   pursuits ranging from reading to spinning   208

xi

19   Two examples of increasing leisure, the melodeon and
     the newspaper   223
20   Croquet being played on an 1870s Norway Grove
     farmstead   224
21   A rare photograph of an interior displaying symbols
     of wealth   225
22   A large Norway Grove household displaying graphic
     evidence of its material success   237

Figures

1   Southern Norway   14
2   A Balestrand farmstead   29
3   Balestrand and environs   60
4   Frequency of celebration of communion: Tjugum
     parish, 1849–62   112
5   Quarterly wheat prices and emigration from
     Balestrand, 1844–75   127
6   Settlements in the Upper Middle West peopled by
     Balestrand immigrants   144
7   Nation of birth of landholders in Norway Grove–
     Spring Prairie region, 1861   146
8   Place of birth of Norwegian landholders in Norway
     Grove–Spring Prairie region, 1861   147
9   Place of birth of Norwegian landholders in Norway
     Grove–Spring Prairie region, 1874   149
10   Backgrounds of landholders in Arendahl township,
     1896   156
11   Backgrounds of landholders in Camp and southern
     Bandon townships, 1888   159
12   Land alienation according to ethnocultural group and
     land type: Arendahl township   172
13   Age-specific child/married woman ratios: Balestrand
     and Balestrand settlements, 1860–1900   212

Preface

This study, like all historical inquiry, is, in part, a personal search. Deep in my family's folklore are observations about the causes of emigration from Norway. But they are not necessarily consistent. On the one hand, my grandfather, when speaking of Sunnmøre, the region of his birth, said, "Sure it's beautiful there, but you can't live off beauty." Yet his brothers thought that he left "because you just couldn't keep Mons Peter down." Underlying these statements is the age-old question whether people were compelled to leave their European homes or were attracted by American opportunities. A second, broader question is the effects of the new American environment on the cultural development of rural immigrant communities. Put simply, how did people, my ancestors among them, adapt work roles, inheritance, marriage, and fertility patterns and the like to a new farming environment? Originating from similar cultural roots, Norwegian settlements in the United States differed markedly from Norwegian communities in Norway by 1900. And Norwegians and Norwegian-Americans even today are quick to note the cultural and behavioral differences of their counterparts, often to the disparagement of the other group.

By examining Balestrand, Sogn, and its American settlements, we can observe social and economic development of a region on the west coast of Norway; we can determine the underlying causes of its emigration; and we can analyze the process of cultural adaptation among its immigrants in the United States. Yet while I was considering aspects of my family's folklore, larger concerns of the nineteenth-century Europe and the United States of which most Americans' ancestors were a part became central. Rapid economic change and widespread geographical mobility were common features of life in the developing world economy of the nineteenth century. Migrations to European and American cities, to the American frontiers, and across the Atlantic, all of which were based on conditions at home and expectations of life in the new locations, resulted in radically different societies. This study examines one small slice of that process, a trans-Atlantic rural-to-rural migration continuing throughout much of the century, which can be adequately understood only by studying both the sending and the receiving areas. And as we will see, the Norwegian immigrant communities, building on a cultural tradition carried from Europe yet facing a new environment, evolved into a form much different from what had been left behind.

I owe a debt of gratitude to many people and institutions both in Norway and in the United States. I should first thank the American Scandinavian Foundation, the Emigration Fund of 1975, the Norway Fulbright Hays Committee, the University of Minnesota, and the California Institute of Technology for their financial support. In Norway Edgar Hovland, Jan Oldervoll, Rasmus Sunde, and Johannes B. Thue, as well as the staff at the Statsarkiv i Bergen, all were helpful. I want especially to thank Ingrid Semmingsen, for her assistance in delving into questions of Norwegian emigration; Gunnar Urtegaard, for his hospitality in and fine work on Balestrand and for his help with Norwegian photographs; and Ståle Dyrvik, who spent countless hours patiently counseling me on sources and trends in Norwegian historiography. In the United States there are also many, but I want to thank the editor and consulting editors of this series, Robert C. Ostergren, John G. Rice, Russell R. Menard, and especially John Modell, and my senior adviser, Rudolph J. Vecoli. All were generous with their time and incisive in their comments and suggestions. The staff of the Minnesota Historical Society and the State Historical Society of Wisconsin were also both helpful, and I am especially appreciative of use of the photographs granted by the latter. I am grateful for permission to use portions of my article "The Effect of Community on Migration: Three Minnesota Townships, 1885–1905," from the *Journal of Historical Geography*, 5 (1979):403–22, copyright 1979 by Academic Press Inc. (London) Limited. Finally, thanks to Heide Beccue for typing the final manuscript. In spite of such great assistance, all errors in the content and thesis of this study are my own.

Lastly, I would like to thank my family – my parents, aunts and uncles, and grandparents – for it is they who have bequeathed me my rich past. The book is dedicated to Ruth, who has demonstrated an ability to put up with and sometimes aid in a seemingly endless research project, and to Christine and Kari, who, in part owing to this book, we hope will treasure the ancestry we bequeath to them.

1   *Introduction*

The epic journey of the millions of people who crossed the Atlantic Ocean in the nineteenth century to settle in the United States has stirred the imagination of historians for decades. The homespun-clad peasants, whether they traveled in the creaking hull of a wooden sailboat or in the steerage of an iron steamer, disembarked in America to find a world very different indeed from the one they had left. Speaking Old World tongues, they entered ghettos in American cities or clung to land in the rapidly settling rural west. As Frank Thistlethwaite pointed out over twenty years ago, however, these journeys were only part of a worldwide process of urbanization, regional migration to Europe's "internal Americas," and international migration within Europe. Moreover, he challenged American historians to cut through the "salt water curtain" that checked understanding of that process by analyzing the effects of emigration both on the European communities and on the American settlements. Birgitta Odèn, echoing Thistlethwaite's contentions three years later, called for research that took both the country of immigration and the country of emigration into consideration, a method that was "feasible only if individuals are followed from their places of birth to their place of death."[1]

In spite of Thistlethwaite's influential suggestions, few historians have actually followed his prescriptions.[2] This failure is due in part to inadequacies in narrative and quantitative source materials in many regions of Europe that preclude tracing the migration process from its source to American settlements. The nature of migration itself, which encouraged its participants to disperse throughout the Western Hemisphere, also hinders such efforts. Certain areas in Europe and North America, however, possess ample source materials with which to describe social and economic development. Moreover, migration patterns on occasion worked to create strong trans-Atlantic linkages between sending communities in Europe and receiving settlements in the United States. In such cases we can extensively examine demographic, social, economic, and cultural

1

development in the community from which the migration commenced; the selection of migrants; the migration itself; and the cultural adaptations made by a circumscribed group of immigrants to the United States.

Norway, which encountered an unusually heavy trans-Atlantic migration, is one country blessed with ample source materials. Relatively unimportant to the major European powers in the seventeenth, eighteenth, and nineteenth centuries, Norway, through its administrative officials, quietly kept track of its population. Although the long, narrow Norwegian nation was situated on the northern rim of Europe, far away from major European power struggles, it remained shackled under the rule of its stronger Scandinavian neighbors until the twentieth century.[3] Beginning in 1661 Denmark-Norway was known as the Twin Kingdoms, with Copenhagen as the governmental and intellectual center of the realm. The outcome of the Napoleonic Wars led not to an independent Norway, as many of its increasingly nationalistic peasantry had wished, but to another union in 1814, this time with Sweden, a neighbor to the east. The emigrants who left before 1905 thus never lived in the independent Norway we know today, but as many were swept up in nationalist movements of the nineteenth century, they strongly asserted their allegiance to a nation of Norway that did not exist.

Undoubtedly of more concern than politics to the peasantry, however, was the day-to-day labor aimed at producing food on which to survive. Norway's population numbered a relatively insignificant 881,000 in 1800, was overwhelmingly rural, and was scattered throughout a terrain marked by mountains and fjords. The northerly clime permitted only a short growing season, as springs came late and winters early. Many along the vast seacoast relied on fish or on a combination of fishing and agriculture. The rolling valleys in eastern Norway and the region of Trøndelag provided a resource on which to base a substantial grain production. The wide tract of mountains that traversed the breadth of the long, narrow nation provided lumbering opportunities for some and work in mining for others, but for farmers demanded a transhumance system of agriculture based primarily on use of the rich mountain pastures. In spite of the inhospitable environment, the Norwegian peasantry was more successful economically than politically, and agricultural output kept pace with a rapidly growing population in the late eighteenth and early nineteenth centuries.

If Norwegian nationalists at one time lamented Danish and Swedish influences, today's historians and demographers can profit from a rigorous record keeping begun by the Scandinavian governments and state church. Parish priests were ordered by law to register births, deaths, and marriages in Norway from 1687 on, and the clergy was required to make annual reports to the central government concerning births and deaths as early as 1735. Moreover, the crown conducted agricultural censuses, with varying degrees of accuracy and completeness, outlining changing crop and animal production in Norwegian parishes. These censuses were increasingly thorough, so that by the nineteenth century the information recorded permits a decade-by-decade picture of agricultural development. Population censuses, taken in conjunction with the agricultural enumerations, further delineate Norwegian demographic, social, and economic development, especially in the 1801 and 1865 nominative censuses. Tax statistics, mortgage records, and land-transfer records augment the quantitative base provided by censuses and parish registers. A wide array of narrative materials complements the statistical sources in an important way. A comprehensive oral history of Norwegian rural society conducted in the early twentieth century, periodic reports from district officials to the king, community histories called *bygdebøker*, and observations by contemporary analysts such as Eilert Sundt, a pioneer sociologist, provide descriptive materials that flesh out the quantifiable framework of social and economic development.[4]

The collection of such abundant source materials occurred before and during an epoch of heavy emigration from Norway. Up to 1890 Norway maintained the highest per capita emigration in Europe, excepting Ireland, though this record was eclipsed by Italian emigration in the last decade of the nineteenth century.[5] Contemporary Norwegian statisticians were well aware of the massive volume of emigration. An 1890 report reckoned that while 1,893,000 Norwegians resided in Norway, 490,000 lived outside its boundaries – over one-fifth of living Norwegians.[6] The destination of most of the emigrants was the rapidly settling Upper Middle Western United States. Locating first in Illinois and Wisconsin, immigrants moved with the frontier into Iowa, Minnesota, and later the Dakotas. As late as 1910 half of the Norwegian-born in the United States lived in Minnesota, Wisconsin, and North Dakota.[7]

The Upper Middle West stood in stark contrast to the Norway the emigrants left. Instead of a landscape typified by mountains, fjords, and waterfalls, the settlers found in Wisconsin, Minnesota, and especially the Dakotas states that were relatively flat, blessed with vast expanses of fertile virgin prairies. Instead of a region inhabited for centuries, they discovered in the open land of the Middle West that could be claimed and purchased the means to a rapidly expanding, dynamic society. And instead of an agriculture that had been practiced for generations, they needed for the new land and its expanding market structure new methods and new crops.

Despite such glaring dissimilarities, the historian of the immigrant communities benefits from sources resembling those found in Norway. Pastors of the Norwegian-American churches usually retained the use of the parish registers to record the major life events of community members. Federal and state censuses mirror the Norwegian enumerations, and tax and land records, as in Norway, are also available in the United States. Norwegian immigrants, who were often quite self-conscious about their new settlements, left church histories, autobiographies, and accounts of travels throughout the Norwegian-American communities, all important narrative sources. Finally, letters between the United States and Norway often vividly expressed hopes and fears concerning life in America.

Almost invariably noted by the immigrants, the different circumstances in the Upper Middle West were often used to their advantage. Norwegians, particularly in the early stages of migration, tended to move to specific American rural regions, so that colonies consisting of kin and neighbors were fostered, and they thereby provided future researchers the second prerequisite for study of a migration-linked trans-Atlantic community. As the immigration continued, letters and remittances encouraged the development of a chain migration from a region in Norway to a settlement in the United States that closely tied together communities in the two continents.

Likewise, the vast expanse of open land during early settlement of the Upper Middle West provided immigrants the opportunity to own property and permitted Norwegian peasants to become American farmers. Thus, whereas the Norwegian emigration provides the parameters for studies according to Thistlethwaite's prescriptions, the rural settlement patterns among Norwegians in the United States work to fill yet another gap. Few recent studies of European immigration have been focused on rural areas.[8] Certainly immigrants tended increasingly to move to American urban opportunities; yet even in the later decades of the 1800s, one-fifth to one-quarter of foreign-born males cited agricultural occupations.[9] Norwegians were one of the most rural nationalities in American locations. Emigration that began when free land was available encouraged immigrants to take up farm settlement, and a larger percentage of second-generation Norwegians than of any other nationality group remained farmers in 1910.[10] As one Norwegian immigrant somewhat romantically proclaimed, "The farmer is the most typical representative of the Norwegians in this country . . . The struggles and opportunities of pioneer farming were exactly what appealed to him. He was longing for this very life and made a bee-line from the little plot of ground on a hillside in Norway to the princely 160 acres waiting for him in the west."[11]

The accessibility of rich sources in Norway and in the Norwegian-American settlement areas in the rural Upper Middle West therefore provide an opportunity for a microstudy of the great emigration. By choosing an emigration-prone district, we can examine the internal development of the area leading up to the emigration. And by following the emigrants to their major settlements in rural Wisconsin and Minnesota, we can analyze the adaptations of immigrants who, while residing in colonies composed largely of kin and acquaintances from home, entered an environment quite unlike the one they had left. This relatively small group of Norwegian immigrants obviously was only one segment of a gigantic movement across oceans and into American and European cities in the nineteenth century, and theirs certainly was not the archetypal experience of the migration: One does not exist. The cultural adaptations of the poor who drifted to Europe's cities, for example, undoubtedly differed. Yet this study does exemplify the experiences of a substantial portion of those immigrants who crossed the sea and enjoyed some measure of increased wealth as a result.

Balestrand, a county on the west coast of Norway, serves as a starting point for this saga. People began emigrating from this mountainous community, situated in the emigration-prone region of Sogn, in the mid-1840s. Within a couple of years a tradition of migration had developed that not only encouraged emigration but directed it to settlement areas in Wisconsin. The Norway Grove–Spring Prairie settlement in Dane County soon was dominated by people born in Balestrand and neighboring areas in Sogn. As open land became scarcer in Wisconsin, migration proceeded to areas farther west. Significantly, the ties to the mother colony often remained strong. New settlements in Minnesota that centered around the Arendahl Lutheran Church in Fillmore County and the Hauge's Lutheran Church in Renville County were also predominantly composed of Balestranders and Sognings, many of whom had lived in settlements to the east.

By isolating Balestrand and its settlements in the United States, we can compare the lines of development of both. Both changed. Not surprisingly, the American settlements that evolved in an environment strikingly different from Balestrand changed more rapidly. Varying family structures, farming patterns, and accumulations of wealth, to name only a few items, were influenced by the new American surroundings. Yet in spite of the environmental differences, the background in Balestrand must be examined if we are to understand the development in America fully. Immigrants carried patterns of behavior to the United States that were reestablished or transmuted in accordance with new concerns. The key to comprehending Norwegian-American development lies in the outcome of the tension between the old culture and the new environment.

Introduction: the emigration

Norwegian scholars have viewed the great emigration in the nineteenth century with ambivalence. In the early periods of professional historical research, emigration, a powerful force in Norwegian society, was on occasion totally ignored. The multivolume history of the country, *Norges Historie,* the last volume of which appeared between 1909 and 1913, contained no mention of it.[12] When Norwegians did begin to concern themselves with emigration, the relationship between population growth and emigration led historians to argue that resources had simply become inadequate to sustain the population. Indeed, as Norway experienced Europe's largest relative population growth in the half century after 1815, owing to such exogenous factors as peace, the introduction of the potato, and the increased practice of smallpox vaccination, the continual tension between population and food increased.[13] Historians contended that in areas with a constrained resource base, such as mountain communities encountering natural barriers, the relationship between the "population explosion" and limited land became increasingly precarious.[14] Swelling numbers of propertyless farmers cleared all available land up the mountainsides, so that further expansion was no longer possible in many rural areas. The boundaries had been reached,[15] regions had arrived at a saturation point in population,[16] and the poverty-stricken underemployed simply were forced to move. When the opportunity to emigrate to a fabled land of wealth swept through these communities, desperate people moved in droves.[17]

Implicit in this argument is the notion that agriculture was stagnant in Norway's mountain and fjord regions.[18] Much weight has been placed on upper-class contemporaries' observations that in addition to poor climate, "ignorance [ukyndighed]" and "adherence to old-handed down customs [vedhængen ved gamle nedarvede skikke]" hindered progress.[19] Høstingsbruk, the agricultural system in mountain communities such as Balestrand, has been particularly condemned as unproductive. Although it initially worked well with cheap supplies of labor, the resource boundaries had allegedly been reached by the middle of the nineteenth century, so that its productivity decreased and lower living standards resulted.[20] In short, as population increased, any growth was quantitative instead of qualitative; new land might be cleared, but production did not keep pace with population.[21]

Recent scholarship has undermined many of these older assumptions of economic development and has in turn cast serious doubt on the traditional explanation of emigration. There appears to have occurred a qualitative leap in agricultural productivity beginning in the 1700s and carrying over into the nineteenth century. Between 1800 and 1855, in the period of most rapid population growth, production of food kept pace with the added mouths to feed. Though the introduction of the potato was a factor in this agricultural development, the number of animals doubled at the same time, permitting an increased meat and dairy production.[22] Accordingly, calorie output per individual, estimated from agricultural production and grain imports in Norway, grew from around 2,040 per day in 1800 to around 3,260 by mid-century.[23]

An examination of agricultural development in Balestrand, as we will see, corroborates these findings. Increased inputs of labor, land, and capital worked to enlarge per capita farm production for the landed as well as the landless. With a growing population, households were motivated to work harder, invest more, and use techniques that permitted the application of more labor to feed the additional mouths.[24] Moreover, increasing outside demand for animal and crop goods produced in Balestrand at the same time created the means for development beyond the needs of subsistence. This export-led growth enabled the landed to specialize for the market in order to increase production, a development that in turn enlarged demands for labor and thereby raised wage rates for those who owned no land. If Balestrand not only sustained its households but enjoyed improving material welfare, in spite of a growing popula-

tion, the connections among population growth, agricultural production, and emigration are not alone adequate to explain the movement to the United States.

The decisions to migrate, then, were not based solely on fears of
declining material welfare. While Balestrand households altered
their economic patterns, they were forced to change social behavior
as well. Interconnections among inheritance customs, modified demographic behavior, and improved economic well-being created
sweeping changes in Balestrand society. In the first place, farms in
Balestrand were impartibly inherited, so that more and more individuals lived in landless status as population increased in the nineteenth century. Landlessness was certainly not new in Balestrand:
Cotters *husmenn*, as they were called in Norway, had been present
from the 1600s. Yet as larger segments of the landless ironically
enjoyed increasing opportunities, lower marriage ages and larger
households were the result. Not only were landless children denied
a future of landowning – a sign of prestige in the community – but
their greater numbers created uncertainty about their ultimate place
in the society. Land in the United States was a convenient solution
to the scarcity of landed futures, not only for the landless class but
also for those children of the landed who stood to inherit no land.

Secondly, as the society became increasingly landless, strategies
to permit household formation repeatedly came into conflict with
societal norms. Increasing rates of illegitimate births, for example,
were accepted by some segments of the society, whereas other
groups showed their displeasure through the formation of various
organizations. Upper-class leaders, such as the parish pastor, attempted to persuade people to accept the more urban, middle-class
courtship patterns by establishing clubs to work against traditional
behavior. Other groups, predominantly composed of Balestrand's
landless peasants, expressed a pietistic inclination and demonstrated their concerns about moral decline through prayer meetings
and greater activism within and without the church.

Emigration to American settlements was often predicated on the
availability of land there, but cultural concerns such as those expressed in pietism were also transferred to the United States. The
early emigrants, many of whom were landed farmers, based their
decisions to emigrate on calculations of comparative advantage,
weighing Balestrand and their conceptions of the United States but
limited, of course, by imperfect knowledge of the latter. Foremost in
their minds were the large tracts of land supposedly just waiting to
be claimed by land-hungry immigrants. Early emigrants were leav-

ing a society of increasing landlessness and, by moving to places where open land was available, attempting to preserve principal aspects of their social fabric that were disappearing in Balestrand. By traveling in groups or entire households and usually settling in small rural communities in the United States, they hoped to enjoy both greater material wealth and a reestablishment of old values in the New World.[25] These two motives, far from being mutually exclusive, were in the emigrants' eyes compatible with one another.

Introduction: the immigration

In spite of settling in compact communities of kinsmen, in spite of possessing a rich cultural tradition, and in spite of hoping to reestablish that tradition, the immigrants from Balestrand were compelled to adjust to the new American environment. The process of immigration, some have argued, was so wrenching that it led to community disorganization, but the Balestrand immigrants behaved in a manner similar to that clearly portrayed by Virginia Yans-McLaughlin in her study of urban Italian-Americans.[26] Participating in a continual adaptation where old values interacted with new situations, facing the constant dialectic between environment and culture, the rural Norwegian-Americans produced by their behavior a curious mixture of tradition and change.

Since Balestrand's residents had adapted to a dynamic society at home before emigration became common, it is not surprising that its immigrants readily adjusted to conditions across the sea. Early Balestrand immigrants moved to a locality that was rich in arable land. They quickly learned that new crops, such as corn, were productive and that some others which had been used sparingly in Norway, such as wheat, were marketable. And as land in initial Balestrand colonies was taken up, children of early settlers or later immigrants formed new communities to the west.

Mobility among the Balestrand settlements in America compelled further adaptations. Growing scarcity of hired hands in the United States, a reversal of the land/labor ratio in Balestrand, forced the nuclear family to become the most reliable source of labor in the settlements. Increased fertility produced the necessary workers within the family, but it also obliged women to take on heavier duties in raising children and reduced their roles in farm production. Likewise, the limited number of available workers encouraged immigrant farmers to focus on farm operations requiring less labor input. Crops such as grains, traditionally men's work, were emphasized, especially as demand for wheat expanded, while animal production, traditionally women's work, decreased.

Balestrand communities continued to be based on strong Old World linkages among the immigrants, but they encountered a new environment that encouraged change. Kinship ties were retained and often augmented through marriages. Past patterns of courtship and marriage continued, although the frequency of illegitimate births declined. And each community was organized around a rural church that often stressed theological inclinations similar to those emphasized by the pietistic movements of Balestrand. Yet adaptations to new circumstances in some instances in conjunction with maintenance of traditional patterns in others, generated further modification. Migration, for example, was often based on an attempt to realize the customary livelihood upon which to base a marriage. Internal migration, however, decreased the availability of labor and compelled additional change. The combination of labor shortages and traditional gender roles in farm work encouraged yet greater alterations in work roles according to sex and age. Although the Balestrand communities were tightly knit, then, there were such unintended modifications as an increasingly important nuclear family and great changes in the sexual division of labor.

When farmers realized greater wealth as the wheat boom reached its height, cultural change became even more apparent. Courtship patterns were modified so that not only illegitimate but also prenuptially conceived births diminished; women left outside farm work to an even greater degree; and the church came to play a dominant role in promoting such social change. As Balestrand farmers were swept into the vortex of a market economy and as their resources grew, they began to imitate patterns of bourgeois behavior they had observed in Norwegian cities before the emigration, as well as in the United States. Nonetheless, the Balestrand immigrants fashioned a bourgeois behavior uniquely their own, a behavior deeply colored by the pietist attitudes permeating their settlements.

Balestrand immigrants thus experienced considerable cultural change in their new homes in the United States. The adaptations, however, were not so much the result of new concepts of behavior as the outcome of familiar concepts functioning under new conditions. The interaction between tradition and change, which transformed the Balestrand immigrants from peasants to members of the bourgeoisie, generated modifications that began to disguise peasant pasts but were consonant with the immigrants' cultural experiences nevertheless. And a few decades after the immigrants experienced sweeping cultural changes that led to bourgeois behavior, analogous developments occurred in Balestrand as well.

The large bonnets worn by immigrant women to church each Sunday, the pianos in the parlors of their white frame houses, and the fine carriages in late nineteenth-century rural immigrant communities literally and figuratively were a world apart from the roughhewn log buildings that had been left behind in Norway. Yet the cultural tradition of Balestrand provides keys to the development that occurred across the sea in the immigrant communities.

2 "The worlds we have lost": regional differences in trade, migration, and emigration in Norway

The emigration from Norway to the United States, which began in 1825 and reached significant proportions in the 1830s, was often attributed to an "America fever" that afflicted the common peasant. Those who opposed the migration, of course, used the term in the pejorative sense. Norwegian nationalist poet Henrik Wergeland, for example, in 1843 called it "the most virulent disease of our times, a national bleeding to death, a true madness, since those whom it possesses will listen neither to their own nor others' reason, they scorn all examples, they toss aside the present in favor of a still more threatening, uncertain, darkling future, and let themselves be driven into a maelstrom of unknown sufferings."[1] For others, particularly those who moved, the "madness" of emigration was based on expectations of a more prosperous future. The hopes for material improvement, moreover, were often reaffirmed by those who had already taken the fateful step. Few could be unmoved when they read in a letter from America that "every poor person who will work diligently and faithfully can become a well-to-do man here in a short time."[2]

Migration and trade within preemigration Norway

However one felt about it personally, the great migration to the United States was a powerful force in Norwegian society. Only Irish emigration per capita exceeded that of Norway in the nineteenth century.[3] And just as rates of emigration differed nationally, so did they vary within countries. Dissimilar regional emigration rates were in part due to a tradition of migration that developed in certain communities, but they were related more to varying social and economic patterns within Norway. While some regions were typified by high fertility and outmigration, others were characterized by a controlled fertility that obviated large-scale mobility.[4] Demographic patterns were often influenced by methods of inheritance, which in turn were related to the ecological structure of the region. Districts

12

that were well suited for cattle farming, for example, often practiced impartible inheritance, creating a large landless class that further influenced demographic patterns. On the other hand, coastal regions dependent more on the sea than on the land could divide estates, a practice that in turn affected the society. The presence of these different ecotypes has led David Gaunt to stress that instead of speaking of the world we have lost, historians should study the *worlds* we have lost, each with their distinctive patterns of life.[5]

The presence of diverse ecotypes, however, did not mean that Norway's regions were isolated from one another. Indeed, a large natural increase in certain inland areas was predicated on the opportunity to migrate to the coast.[6] In fact, emigration to the United States was only one of the migration streams throughout the Norwegian countryside, and a relatively late one at that. Internal migration, common at least from the 1750s, became even more widespread by 1818, when migration was permitted if one registered with and received permission from the parish priest.[7] The volume of movement within Norway is difficult to determine, since only net migration figures are available. Still, three major trends of internal migration are traceable from the mid-eighteenth century to the eve of the great migration to America.

Beginning in the 1750s, a stream of migrants in search of property began moving from land-poor districts in south Norway to the northern areas of Trøndelag and north Norway. By 1789 colonists continued to find land in these "internal Americas" of Norway's north (refer to Figure 1 for regions of Norway throughout the chapter). After the movement had slowed in the beginning of the nineteenth century, another, weaker wave began in the 1830s, when people from eastern Norway began the long move north.[8] This colonization continued even after emigration was common, particularly among migrants who could not afford the price of passage to the United States but who could manage to migrate internally.[9]

A second direction was the drift to the coast from inland regions, which occurred for two essential reasons. On the one hand, people migrated to the coast as early as the 1700s because disease-related mortality near the sea was higher than inland: The free farmsteads and occupations pulled individuals there – one man's death was another man's bread.[10] On the other hand, the combination of fishing and farming provided a surer livelihood than agriculture alone, and the exploitation of two enterprises furnished greater work opportunities.[11] Migration to the coast became increasingly significant in the second half of the nineteenth century, so that by the final

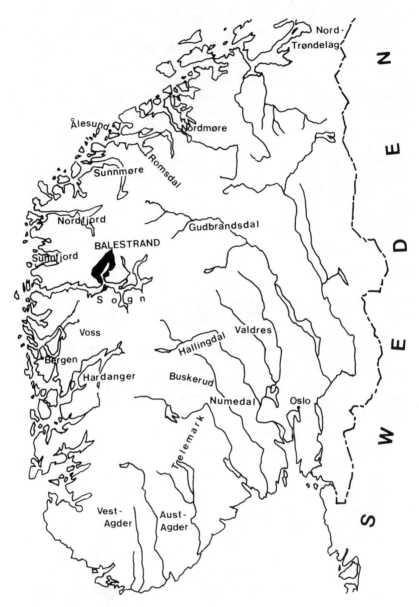

Fig. 1. Southern Norway

Table 1. *Annual population growth according to region, 1769–1875 (%)*

	1769–1801	1801–45	1845–75
Mountain districts	0.53	0.86	0.31
Lowland districts	0.58	0.78	0.55
Fjord districts	0.72	1.01	1.21
Coastal districts	0.65	0.97	1.50
Agricultural districts	—[a]	0.88	0.48
Forestry districts	—	0.84	0.74
Fishing districts	—	0.80	1.37
Shipping districts	—	1.03	1.47
Industrial districts	—	0.88	1.53

[a]Dashes indicate no data.
Source: A. N. Kiær, *Oversigt over de Vigtigste Resultater af de Statistiske Tabeller Vedkommende Folkemængdens Bevegelse, 1866–1885* (Christiania, 1890), pp. 28–29, 32–33.

third of the 1800s, not only mountain and fjord districts but other agricultural districts as well were tapped in this movement.[12] The net growth of Norway's regions reflects this migration. Between 1769 and 1875 coastal districts, despite their lower fertility and higher mortality, grew over 50% faster than their mountain district counterparts. Between 1801 and 1875 districts relying on agriculture increased only about two-thirds as fast as fishing districts, and in the final thirty years of the period fishing districts saw an annual growth of 1.37%, compared to the yearly agricultural population growth of only 0.48% (see Table 1).[13]

Although Norway experienced late industrialization and urbanization, movement to the cities provided a third alternative for internal migration. The grim reality of life in the city probably made this the least inviting choice. Yet between 1769 and 1845 urban growth kept pace with population increases in general, and afterward cities grew more rapidly than the rural areas. Burgeoning towns, moreover, developed in spite of a negative natural growth. In Bergen, for example, the 10,500 fewer births than deaths between 1735 and 1800 were more than offset by the 32,500 people who moved in from rural areas. Thus the records of a Bergen church in 1809–10 indicate that only 27% of those dying at over fourteen years of age were born in the town itself.[14] As the pace of industrialization increased, growth of the cities accelerated. Between 1845 and 1875 the industrial communities were the most rapidly increasing areas of Norway's population, with an annual growth of 1.53% – more than three times that of farming regions.[15]

Permanent internal migration was supplemented by seasonal movement that provided temporary work opportunities. For three months out of the year the fisheries in Nordland attracted male migrants who fished while the women remained at home tending the farms.[16] In some areas of Sogn, Hardanger, Gudbrandsdal, Telemark, and Numedal – all inland mountain and fjord regions – men worked as cattle dealers, and other itinerant traders traveled Norway's roads throughout the year. Young men from Numedal, for example, sold wares throughout the land and reportedly returned on occasion with enough wealth to buy farms.[17] Finally, people moved about in search of servant work, especially in difficult times. Even during normal circumstances, however, traditions of migrating servants took hold. Balestrand, for instance, annually attracted servants from specific counties in Sogn.[18]

Varying wealth and knowledge of migration opportunities influenced the destinations of migrants. Those with greater resources moved to land in the north while the more destitute drifted to the cities. In either case, the migration strongly indicates that characterizing Norwegian peasant society as a stagnant, monolithic world shackled by custom is unwarranted.[19] An even more salient demonstration of the interaction among Norwegian peasant communities was the widespread trade throughout the land. Officials of the state, upper-class bureaucrats stranded in rural peasant communities, often reflected their sense of exile by stressing the isolation of the agricultural regions and their backward farming methods. Historians have used these assertions as evidence that the old society was indeed static and closed. The officials, however, overemphasized the isolation by ignoring a growing commerce that, at least by the beginning of the nineteenth century, worked to create an improved living standard for the peasant population through a regional division of labor. Fish, timber, meat, dairy products, or grain were traded between areas deficient in one facet but with surpluses in others. By growing a surplus of fairly easily produced goods to exchange for those necessary foodstuffs more difficult to raise in one's own region, households could improve their material wealth. In addition to trading for food, farmers used surpluses to create cash to pay taxes and buy necessities such as salt and iron. And the wealthy could buy goods they would rather purchase than make, as well as luxuries like tobacco, coffee (which came into customary use in the latter part of the 1700s), tea, sugar, and brandy.[20]

The regional division of labor was facilitated by trade at fairs that began as early as the sixteenth century. The autumn fair at Lærdal, for example, began in 1693 and by 1761 was attracting shopmen from Bergen and traders from Valdres and Hallingdal, areas across the mountains of Norway.[21] Mountain areas in Gudbrandsdal relied on trade, especially when their grain froze. Traveling up and down the long central valleys, the traders also met at the Romsdal fair in Veblungsnes – like Lærdal, an area where the end of the fjord met the rising mountains – which began in 1533.[22]

Direct trade between regions and between city and farm eventually displaced the fairs. An expanding boat traffic tied rural areas on the west coast to Bergen. The most substantial trade occurred along the coast between Nordland and Bergen. In the 1750s alone merchants from Sunnmøre, a region between Bergen and Ålesund, owned forty boats with capacities ranging from 40,000 to 120,000 pounds, which made four to five tours to Bergen yearly.[23] In addition, boat-owning farmers up and down the west coast made semiannual trips to Bergen in order to trade wood and dairy products for food grain, herring, and salt. Reports of trade between Sogn and Bergen are documented as early as 1820. The number of boats and their capacities increased throughout the first two-thirds of the nineteenth century, so that by 1869 the 102 larger trading boats in Sogn could carry five to seven times as much cargo as the ships used in 1820.[24] Traders also operated between rural regions with different production emphases. For example, farmers from Vik, an inland county on the Sognefjord, exchanged potatoes for fish from households in coastal fishing communities as early as the 1830s. Likewise, cattle and sheep from the mountain areas were shipped to eastern communities in Norway that specialized in grain production.[25]

While internal migration better allocated labor resources, the considerable trade, which was substantial three centuries before the advent of emigration, distributed food produce. As early as 1743 the priests of Vik, Leikanger, Sogndal, Hafslo, and Lyster in the inland Sognefjord region of which Balestrand was a part complained that they lived in the best agricultural district in the area, yet it was not self-sufficient in grain. As officials of the clergy, they did not understand that small grain harvests were due not to an inability to produce enough but to a realization among the peasant farmers that it was simpler to trade other goods for grain.[26]

Regional variations within Norway

Social interaction through trade and migration did not, however, create a homogeneous Norwegian society. Indeed, the regional division of labor actually worked to enhance dissimilar social and economic regional patterns. In addition to the basic rural–urban differences, Eilert Sundt, the pioneer Norwegian sociologist of the mid-nineteenth century, stressed the presence of distinct local cultures throughout the narrow fjords, deep valleys, and relatively isolated mountain communities of the Norwegian countryside.[27] Relics of the lost peasant past point to the heterogeneity, especially in the mountain and inland regions that underwent heavy outmigration. Not only did the *bunad,* elaborate formal dress worn in the peasant communities during times of festivity, have regional designs, but each community fashioned nuances on the costume that set it off from others. On a larger scale, the folk art that survives to this day reflects the dissimilar styles inherent in the regional traditions. Rosepainting (*rosemaling*) is still separated into the flowery Telemark style and the more symmetrical Hallingdal style, among others.[28] Building customs and the design of the Norwegian farmstead provide yet another example of regional variation. Not only were different methods of construction common, but the simple placement of the farm structures varied remarkably, from types on the west coast with buildings clustered to buildings in the east and in Trøndelag that were designed in a rectangular fashion.[29]

The farmstead differences reflect the importance of the environment, which influenced regional variations in Norway. The clustered farmstead types were found in mountainous areas where farmers could not have used the geometrical patterns of the east even if they had wished. These ecological differences not only created the basis for the regional division of labor that facilitated trade but also influenced the economic and social structure within each region. The most basic geographical division within Norway separated relatively flat expanses of grain land in eastern Norway and Trøndelag from the mountain and fjord regions of the west that took sustenance from the sea and the higher pastures. Since farms were large and land was rich in the east, landowners were more clearly set apart from their workers as population increased in the nineteenth century. The farm-owning family segregated itself from the servant class; strategies of inheritance, which placed a premium on marriage within the farm-owning class, in turn greatly restricted interclass courting. The landless, on the other hand, became more and more reliant on rural wage labor throughout the 1800s.[30]

But even within the west coastal districts, the area on which we focus here, sharp regional variations were apparent. Most important, certain localities were able to rely on economic activities in

addition to agriculture, activities that not only lengthened the work
year but created a greater security in the event of crop failure. In
areas near the sea a booming fishing industry in the nineteenth
century provided additional work and income for the peasants. In
Agder, a southern Norwegian region, seafaring and shipbuilding
furnished other occupations to supplement farming. These incomes
outside agriculture enabled peasants to rely less on farming and
made it possible for them to subsist on smaller landholdings. Accordingly, beginning in the sixteenth century, farms in these areas
were often divided among heirs.[31]

West coastal regions in the mountains and valleys with neither
the expansive cropland of the east nor the outlet to the sea engaged
in yet another method of production. In addition to growing grain
and potatoes, by the beginning of the nineteenth century farmers
directed much of their labor toward producing animal and dairy
goods by exploiting the vast mountainsides. Reliance on animal
husbandry, an operation more efficient with larger units of production, furnished the basis of yet another pattern of land and labor
use. Farmers in rural regions such as Sogn did not divide their farms
in response to the growing population, as did those who relied on
fish. Instead, as population increased many youths were forced into
cotterhood and others worked as day laborers on the large farms.
The units of production in Sogn that remained large in both land
and labor resulted in greater social inequalities and more whole-year
laborers than were the norm in the west.[32]

Patterns of land, labor, trade, migration, and emphases in production in turn influenced social patterns in western Norway. Cultural practices, such as marriage, courting, and sexual customs, varied from community to community. Eilert Sundt, in his exhaustive
study of "morality" in the mid-nineteenth century, found regional
variations in regard to the peasant custom of "bundling" and the
consequent frequencies of premaritally conceived births. Not surprisingly, it was in regions such as Sogn and Gudbrandsdal, where
the farms were large and the means of creating a landed livelihood
were constrained, that prenuptial births were most common. In a
detailed examination of the neighboring regions of Sunnfjord and
Sogn, Sundt found two completely dissimilar systems of courtship,
marriage, and fertility. Marriage in Sunnfjord was constrained by
parental demands; fertility was lower owing to delayed marriage
and separation of husband and wife for labor activities; and the
frequency of illegitimate births was low, especially when compared
to neighboring Sogn. In Sogn, on the other hand, the custom of

bundling and the placing of marital decisions more firmly in the hands of the young caused rates of illegitimacy much too high for Sundt's taste. The different sexual practices in Sogn and Sunnfjord were strikingly illustrated by one of Sundt's examples. In the small Sunnfjord community of Vik, the first illegitimate child in fifteen years was brought to the church for baptism in 1865. Unfortunately, the woman had taken service in a community in Sogn the year before.[33]

The worlds we have lost in Norway were reflected not only in varying patterns of land use, farm size, class division, and marital and sexual practices, but in emigration as well. In general, regions that provided the greatest economic opportunity were least likely to experience large-scale emigration either to America or to other Norwegian localities. Areas with close ties to places of opportunity in the cities or on the seacoast were more likely to undergo an internal migration than a movement to the United States. Influenced by economic patterns at home and by access to certain channels of information about migration opportunities, some regions became typified by internal migration to the cities or the coast while others predominantly chose agricultural opportunities in the north of Norway or America. In such an emigration-prone region as Sogn, for example, 840 people moved to America and 220 to northern Norway between 1846 and 1850, whereas only 57 went to closer seacoast opportunities in the region of Møre. In the following ten years, when 4,258 people were emigrating to the United States from Sogn, only 16 left for America from the neighboring regions of Sunnfjord and Nordfjord, with their constrained fertility, greater economic opportunities, and closer ties with Bergen.[34]

Emphases of production in the rural communities that created different land and farm patterns also provide the key to the regional differentiation in emigration. Fishing and other activities that could give employment without the use of land created a base that militated against migration. It was said in coastal regions such as Romsdal that cod were an America for the people. Helgeland, another fishing region to the north, illustrated the effect of fishing opportunities on emigration patterns. The district relied on both fish and agriculture; the result was a food source that could also be traded and one that rarely failed in both areas in one year. People ate "herring and potatoes the first day and potatoes and herring the next" – a stable, if boring, diet. Although many preferred the exciting and often lucrative gamble of fishing for *havets sølv* (the silver of the sea), and many began to see farm work as "slave labor," the two opportunities acted as complementary economic activities late into the nineteenth century. But disappearance of the herring around 1878 created a violent crash in the economy. Poor relief led to increasing taxes, which in turn ended in many foreclosures on the land. Although the opportunities in the United States had been known for decades, it was not until this time that emigration became a major factor in the peoples' lives.[35]

In addition to fishing, such other activities as shipping, boatbuilding, and lumbering also provided alternatives to migration. The late emigration from Agder, a region in the extreme south of Norway, reflects another windfall from the sea. Although Agder experienced a heavy early period of emigration in the 1850s, the movement slowed to a trickle for the following thirty years. A burgeoning shipbuilding industry that created a golden period, with abundant job opportunities for residents of the southern coast, made the United States less inviting. By approximately 1880, however, when Agder's wooden ships faced competition with the steamship, the overexpanded economy went into a tailspin and emigration became widespread.[36] Like those of Helgeland, Romsdal, and Agder, residents of other places with booming economies felt little need to emigrate until economic difficulties occurred or until the call of America and its alleged greater opportunities became too inviting.[37]

If one wishes to focus on the locations of early intense emigration from Norway, regions in the cattle-producing areas near the west coast and in central mountain valleys provide the arena for this rapid depopulation of the countryside. Ironically, regions with the most traditional folk cultures, cultures with which folk art today is still identified, were also areas of innovation in emigration. Hallingdal, Valdres, Telemark, and Sogn in the mountain and fjord districts, which had long experienced an internal outmigration, supplied the bulk of early Norwegian emigrants across the seas (see Table 2). Since emigration from these areas began so early, a tradition developed. Flows of information in the form of letters or returned travelers from the American communities created aspirations to share in the opportunities of the New World, and prepaid tickets often provided the means. Areas of intense emigration, on the other hand, had relatively few internal migrants. The people from these isolated peasant areas preferred to move to the United States, where groups of family and friends, ample land, and opportunities for new wealth awaited.[38]

Balestrand, a central district in the Sogn region, is an illustration of a mountain area that underwent a heavy emigration prior to the

Table 2. *Regions of most intense emigration, 1856–65*

	No. of emigrants	Annual emigrants per 1,000 population
Sogn	6,430	17.2
Valdres	3,144	15.6
Hallingdal	2,248	15.2
Hardanger and Voss	2,011	9.0
Upper Telemark	2,143	8.4
Numedal	895	6.8
Sunnhordland	2,200	6.7
Ryfylke	3,112	6.6
Lower Telemark	1,138	5.8

Source: Andres A. Svalestuen, "Om den Regionale Spreiinga av Norsk Utvandring før 1865," in Arnfinn Engen, ed., *Utvandringa – Det Store Oppbrotet* (Oslo, 1978), p. 77.

U.S. Civil War. Although Sogn was not the scene of the earliest large-scale emigration, it quickly became an area typified by movement to America. Between 1836 and 1845, during the first wave of extensive migration from Norway, the mountain districts of Telemark and Buskerud by far outstripped Sogn in migration; the latter provided only 8.6% of the total. The first emigrant from Sogn in fact did not move from his home until 1839, and it was partly due to his letters home that the first large wave of 461 emigrants left Sogn between 1843 and 1845.[39] After that time, America fever diffused throughout the region and emigration rates exploded. Between 1846 and 1865 the 7,500 emigrants who moved from Sogn constituted about one-eighth of all Norwegian emigration (and between 1856 and 1860, Sogn contributed one-sixth of the total). From 1856 to 1865 Sogn was the region of most intense per capita emigration for all Norway, with 17.2 emigrants leaving the country yearly per 1,000 people. In spite of the migration tradition that developed in Sogn, the heavy outmigration up to the end of the American Civil War reduced the intensity of postbellum emigration in comparison with that from other regions more recently touched by America fever. Although 14,350 people left Sogn for America between 1865 and 1895, they were only 3.5% of the total from Norway.[40]

Balestrand, like the other districts of Sogn, is a mountainous area; it comprises more than 626 square kilometers bordering the Sognefjord. Also like the rest of Sogn, Balestrand had its most intense emigration in the earliest stages. Although the first emigrant did not depart from Balestrand until 1844 – five years after the first Sogning emigrant – 871 people had moved to America by 1865, nearly 45% of all who would emigrate from Balestrand up to 1904. Moreover, America fever was most contagious in those twenty years: 21.4 people per 1,000 emigrated annually between 1846 and 1855 and 20.6 in the following decade. Just as Balestrand was situated midway between the inland mountains and the sea, then, so were its emigration patterns typical of Sogn's.[41]

If Wergeland was correct in his interpretation of the America fever, Sogn and Balestrand were inhabited by those who possessed little reason. A more dispassionate inquiry into the causes behind the mass migration, however, points to a strong correlation between the type of agriculture practiced in a locality and the propensity of its residents to move to the New World. The intricate connections among the economic base of the cattle- and sheep-producing region, its inheritance patterns, and its demographic behavior created a socioeconomic structure that promoted a migration substantially larger than that of other areas. Historians have often placed considerable emphasis on a faltering agricultural structure. The peasant, particularly in mountainous regions of animal husbandry, has been portrayed as a primitive farmer practicing methods in the same backward way year after year. If strange weather or natural pests caused bad times, the "Malthusian scissors" cut the population down to levels that could be fed until another crisis occurred and another tragedy again regulated the number of people. The peasants, in this scenario, did little to alter their environment; they did little to adapt to changing conditions. Historians have further contended that the farmers reached the boundaries of land use as population grew in the early nineteenth century because of exogenous factors including smallpox inoculations and the introduction of the potato. All available land had been drained, production had been moved up the mountainsides as far as the climate permitted, and the living standards of the population as a consequence began to decline.

The next two chapters examine the agricultural system of Balestrand that developed down through the centuries, focusing especially on the adaptations made in the nineteenth century when the great population growth allegedly caused the limits of growth to be reached. Just as trade created a structure that allowed a more rational allocation of resources among the regions, so did agricultural practices adjust to changing conditions. In short, by intensively examining an example of one world we have lost – the inland cattle- and sheep-farming region of Norway – we will recognize that the widespread emigration did not occur because the bounds of economic development had been reached. Indeed, the agricultural system in Balestrand was flourishing; if anything, the lack of labor was a greater problem for landowners than lack of food was for the landless.

If the economic base was enlarging, however, inheritance patterns and demographic behavior in conjunction with a growing economic base ultimately encouraged emigration from the mountain regions. As already noted, whereas farms were divided among heirs in the fishing regions along the coast, they were impartibly transferred from generation to generation in Balestrand. Ironically, larger segments of the society lived in landless status, but their economic opportunities were increasing. Decisions of marriage and fertility, reflecting increasing opportunities, resulted in earlier marriages and larger families. The United States, where "every poor person who [worked] diligently and faithfully [could] become a well-to-do man," was a solution to a dilemma that was bequeathed to each generation. Whereas internal migration remained moderate in the decades leading up to the emigration, a reflection of stable economic circumstances, the emigration to America, predicated on an attempt to escape knotty questions of inheritance for the present generation and the next, eventually reached a fever pitch in cattle regions.

3 "The grass so fat it glistened": the social and economic structure of peasant Balestrand

The landscape of Balestrand recalls stereotypes of Norwegian beauty or images of the fairyland in Norway's deep folk culture. Snow-tinted sugarloaf mountains erupt from the blue-green water of the Sognefjord, Norway's longest on its west coast. Waterfalls plummet thousands of feet, dancing over rocks through wooded valleys and eventually finding the fjord. Situated where the fjord divides, Balestrand's narrow fjord arms point to the ice-covered glaciers that peak between the towering mountains. Yet the beauty that one admires today created difficulties for the peasant farmer of the past. The steep mountains precluded extensive flat cropland; the dense forests were troublesome to clear, demanding exploitation in other ways; and natural disasters such as periodic avalanches – one reportedly so large that it formed a bridge over the fjord – tested the people's will to survive.[1]

Despite the parsimonious land, Balestrand's residents traditionally relied on agriculture as their main economic activity. After the Black Death ravaged Balestrand in the fourteenth century, the population slowly increased from 174 in 1522 to 938 by 1666 as new farms were settled on the best land near the fjord. The earliest farms were also the largest, for colonization moved away from the central area to less desirable regions as population growth continued.[2] New families formed from this growing population had two options in creating a livelihood: clearing a new farm or dividing an old one. Before 1647 clearing occurred more often, but the period between 1647 and 1666 witnessed an increased division of farms, especially of those that had been cleared early. By 1666 the clearing of new farms was over in Balestrand; henceforth, division of an existing farm was the only means of adding to the ranks of landholding farmers.[3] At this time a new social class began to develop. Those who could not own part of a divided farm were forced to become cotters (known as *husmenn* in Norway), people who owned no land but rented small parcels from a landowning farmer in exchange for labor duties.

Throughout the centuries of agricultural expansion after the Black Death, a cultural complex of farm structure, production methods, and strategies of land and inheritance developed. This system, the backbone of the peasant economy well into the nineteenth century, was the basis for maintenance of the rural society. It undoubtedly evolved through trial and error, with successes and failures transmitted orally from generation to generation. By the nineteenth century ideal sowing and harvesting dates had been defined for proper crop maturation. Moreover, mechanisms of insurance, such as alternative types of forage for animals in poor hay years, had been developed to avoid the danger of inadequate crops.

The agricultural system developed within a framework of limited market activity and corresponded to behavior found in other traditional peasant economies.[4] The principal economic function of farm work was to produce goods that fed and protected the farm people. The corresponding burden was the labor needed to produce these goods. Hence the number of hours worked – what A. V. Chayanov called the degree of "self-exploitation" – was dependent on the uneasy equilibrium between the demands of the people for sustenance, on the one hand, and the "drudgery of labor itself," on the other.[5] Put simply, the people worked until the equilibrium was reached: Any extra labor after that point was superfluous, for it meant extra work without additional gains. With a centuries-old knowledge of weather conditions in relation to crop growth and the capacity to lengthen the work day if greater output was needed, the farm folk could minimize the uncertainty of life in a difficult environment.

The economic structure of Balestrand, however, existed in a process of continual change and development. Farm households constantly were adjusting to varying supplies of labor. As population grew in the nineteenth century, more cotters and servants were available. Likewise, improving networks of trade permitted greater use of available labor, augmented wealth, and increased specialization. Farm production then took on a different character, with an enlarged output that departed from Chayanov's equilibrium of labor and output. Yet amidst these changes in farm size, landowner/cotter ratios, and amount of trade there was a well-founded system of agriculture that optimally exploited Balestrand's resources. The description of farm structure, agricultural methods, and cultural practices in this chapter serves as a basis for analysis in the next of conditions of nineteenth-century economic development.[6]

Farm organization in Balestrand

The *gard*, the unit of production around which Norwegian peasant life evolved, was an "inseparable unit of people, animals, house, and land." Schematically, it was centered around the *tun*, a cluster of buildings that housed the people and animals and stored the personal property. Surrounding the farmyard were a variety of land types generally more improved the nearer they were to the tun. Closest was the *innmark*, or infield, a fenced-in area of crop fields and meadows markedly cut off from the surrounding land. Beyond the innmark lay the *utmark*, the area between the farm and the mountain woods. This seemingly useless region, which was neither cultivated nor extensively manured, was an essential place for summer grazing and a source of hay and other forage.[7]

The gard structure took shape during the repopulation of Norway after the Black Death. As the population on a single farm grew, the larger supplies of labor and increased need for food induced greater use of tilled and untilled land. If the gard was divided among heirs into multiple farm units (*bruker*), the farm families working the parceled land lived on the same farmyard complex. Throughout the division, attempts were made to assign each family a similar quality and quantity of land and to distribute the buildings equally. The law of field division practiced in western Norway, based on Gulating law, which dated from the Middle Ages, demanded that each parcel of land be subdivided so that the good and poor land was distributed equally among the farmers. The infield was thus often stripped, so that farm households living on the same tun had numerous adjoining strips.[8] Subdivision at times resulted in crowded farmyards and small innmark fields.[9] In order to maintain peace within such confined conditions, the boundaries between the strips of land were sacred, and violation of them was the greatest sin one could commit. The penalties for breaking the law were illustrated by the spirit of the boundary violator, who according to traditional belief was forced to carry heavy marking stones ceaselessly after death because he had dared to move them while alive.[10] Customs also developed to bind the farm folk together and force cooperation among workers when a gard was divided. Households worked together through an arrangement (*skipnad*) built on customs and rules, often unwritten, often imprecise, that provided for the smooth functioning of the farm.[11]

The tun organization in Balestrand was typically a cluster style with farm buildings seemingly placed helter-skelter within the yard (see Figure 2).[12] The apparent lack of order, however, was illusory. The tun was designed so that each farmer had his cluster of buildings, together with the outbuildings that were always on the fringes of the cluster or on lower ground, so the dunghills ran away from the buildings.[13] Unlike the American farm, the tun had numerous houses with specific functions. Three essential inhouses (*innhus*) – the *stove* (living room), *eldhus* (baking and washing room), and *stabbur* (storeroom) – were supplemented by other buildings, ranging from the bathhouse to the woodshed. The outhouses (*uthus*) consisted of the *løe* (the haybarn divided into three rooms, the middle of which was used for threshing) and specific buildings for horses, cows, sheeps, goats, and pigs.[14] Farmyards had different arrangements of the houses, which varied in quality and quantity, and whereas many farms might not have each type of building, others might have multiple examples.[15] Since Balestrand households rarely divided their farm units, however, the crowding on the tun and the miniaturization of fields was not as widespread there as in other Norwegian regions.

The tun in Balestrand was often placed on inferior land in order to permit use of the better soil for crops. By the nineteenth century most of the infields in Balestrand, typically divided into strips and plots, were devoted to crops. Between this cultivated innmark and the utmark was a belt of uncultivated land, the *natural eng* (meadow), which as late as 1863 was difficult to distinguish from the utmark because of stones, underbrush, bushes, and knolls within it. On its outskirts was the *hamnehage*, an enclosed pasture used for grazing, which was of yet poorer quality than the innmark and natural eng, but still better than the utmark.[16]

Although it was the wildest and most remote part of the Balestrand farm, the utmark was of central importance. Here, as noted, animals grazed during the summer months and fodder was collected for the winter. Here also the *støl*, the base of operation of the summer pasturage, was located. Containing buildings similar to those on the home tun, the støl was the summer home of women servants who cared for the animals. Although the utmark was less demarcated than the innmark, rights of use were clearly defined, and as animal products took on greater and greater significance in sections of Norway, the struggle for støl pasture could erupt in litigation.[17]

Food production was based on numerous tasks performed throughout the year. Patterns of work followed the rhythms of the

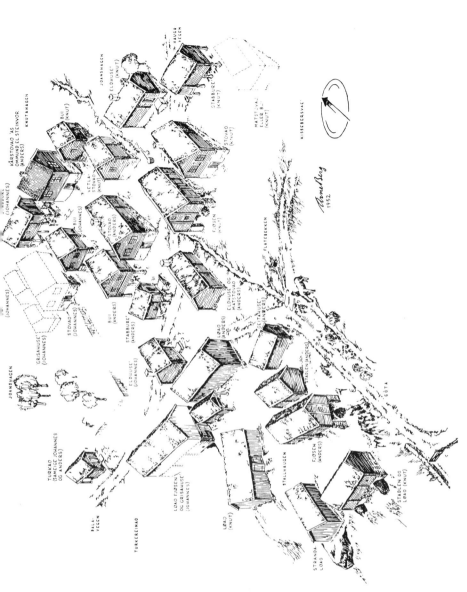

Fig. 2. A Balestrand farmstead. *Source:* Arne Berg, *Norske Gardstun* (Oslo, 1968), p. 160

day, the week, and the year. Labor per day was also cyclical: Difficult times followed the less onerous. Summer days, which would begin with the sun around four o'clock each morning and end at nine in the evening, were succeeded by long, dark winter days that demanded less work. And there were weekly periods of rest throughout the year, on Sundays and also on Saturdays after three o'clock. An elderly woman affirmed that work ended at three on Saturday "because then all of Heaven's bells rang," a belief dating from the Gulating law, which declared Saturdays holy.[18]

Since Balestrand did not contain large expanses of arable cropland, much of the farm labor was directed toward creating animal products for trade and consumption. The need for manure for fertilizer and hay for feed, however, created a symbiotic relationship between crop and animal production, neither of which could be practiced without the other.[19]

Crop production patterns in Balestrand

Grain was generally planted on the best arable land near the farmyard. Norwegian infields were often on the sunny side of the valley, and stones were not always removed from the soil. An official from Øvre Numedal as late as 1860, for example, wrote that people sowed their grain between the rocks. The lack of stone removal was less a failure to improve the land than the reflection of a belief that more grain was harvested when stones remained in the fields to warm the soil during the day and radiate heat during the night.[20] Although fields had been divided between hay and grain at one time, the infields on Balestrand farms were used almost entirely for grain crops by the mid-nineteenth century.[21]

Crop production in Balestrand consisted of four major tasks throughout the year: preparation of the fields, planting, harvesting, and threshing. Since it was essential to get the seeds in the ground as early as possible, a concern reflected in the saying that "a day in the spring did more than a week in the fall," late springs caused anxiety.[22] Yet farmers did not want to sow so early that the seeds froze or rotted in the ground. One method used throughout much of Norway to facilitate an earlier planting involved putting sand or ashes on the snow: Both were dark and absorbed the heat of the sun to melt the snow more quickly. The advantage of sand was its greater density, which caused it to work as a better radiator, but ashes were easier to transport and used more often in Balestrand.[23]

To prepare for planting, the fields first were evened out and the

Plate 1. The ard, a primitive hoelike plow, was the implement most often used in breaking the soil in the spring. Here a farmer is seen plowing a hilly field in mountainous Balestrand. *Source*: De Heibergske Samlinger-Sogn Folkemuseum; photographer unknown

margins between the strips improved. Manure was then moved to the fields from the cowbarns. In places where the terrain was relatively flat and horses were available, the manure was carried in wagons. Otherwise, men carried it in baskets weighing up to sixty kilograms.[24]

After the land had been satisfactorily leveled, the earth had to be readied for planting. In Balestrand the common implement for turning the soil was the *ard*, a wooden hoelike plow with an iron blade. In other areas of Sogn the ground was spaded by hand.[25] Although the ard appeared primitive, its use actually increased from the 1770s to the mid-nineteenth century because of its maneuverability in the smaller fields. The first iron plow did not appear in Balestrand until 1850, when one was imported from eastern Norway.[26] The farmer, who used the ard to plow up the earth and create furrows, was followed if necessary by two men with hoes to break clumps further apart (see Plate 1). Next a wooden harrow was used to remove loose stones and to even the earth. The field was then ready for planting.[27]

Years of experience had taught the farmer when the grain should be sown in order for a crop to mature by fall. Since methods of speeding up snowmelt had been developed, each farm had an ideal fixed date for planting. Natural signs of springtime, however, such as size of the tree leaves or of snow drifts in particular areas of the mountains, were closely monitored.[28] Late springs brought added work, but the fixed sowing day, ranging from May 12 in the deep fjord areas to May 25 elsewhere, was usually met.[29] The sower relied on skill in evenly casting the grain, but because planting was a holy act, appeals were made to God to provide a good harvest. Accordingly, the sower worked bareheaded and prayed "i Jesu navn," or urged "kom atte, kom atte [come back, come back]."[30] As a rule, the sower tried to cast the grain so that only three seeds would fall in an area the size of a horse's hoof. After the seed had been sown, it was pushed down with a smaller ard, especially where the soil was loose, or with a harrow with spikes called a såhorv.[31] Finally, the manure that had been carried out earlier was spread over the newly sowed field. All the cultivating, sowing, and manuring was done for each field in a sequence, since the workers did not want to prepare a field that they could not plant the same day.[32]

Whereas oats were the principal grain in Outer Sogn and barley was the major one in Inner Sogn, Balestrand, in the middle of the region, produced a mixture. The great innovation of potatoes was first reported in Sogn in 1765 at Lyster; by 1808 they were grown in all parishes of Sogn except Borgund and parts of Lærdal.[33] Because potatoes are a root crop, they were planted somewhat differently. A furrow was formed, using a broad ard, and the potatoes were placed about four inches from each other. Another furrow was then made about two feet from the first, and the process was repeated. When weeds came up the field was harrowed, but after the potato plants appeared it was only plowed between rows.[34] Planting of potatoes permitted crop rotation; pure barley (klårkorn) was sown in fields that had been potato acreages the year before.[35]

The season of harvest, like the time of sowing, was tied to natural signs as well as distinct dates. The disappearance of snow spots on the mountains, for example, was an indication that the summer was warm enough for the grain to mature. Of course, it was only when the grain was adequately ripe that the farmers could decide when to begin the harvest. If all was on schedule, August 20 was a usual date for the cutting to begin.[36] All members of the farm had their distinct roles in the harvest. Cotters, for example, had work obligations to the farmer; day laborers could do piecework to earn extra goods, such as wood for fuel. The harvest had to be completed quickly, so in addition to full utilization of available labor within the farm and the hiring of workers from without, impromptu competitions were encouraged. Youths often attempted to cut around the head farmer to make him appear foolish on an island of grain (*sett på holme*). Pieceworkers who completed their work early gained free time or could work for additional pay.[37] As the grain was cut, it was moved to *staur*, stakes in the ground on which the grain was set to dry. All other work except daily chores ceased while the grain was moved to the grain barn (*løe*) in the farmyard, either by horse or by manpower, after it had dried. Even the contribution of small children, who followed picking up loose spikes of grain and laying them in small bundles, reflects the importance of collecting the entire valuable harvest.[38]

Threshing, the final task in the yearly grain production cycle, was delayed until other outside work had been completed. Often it did not begin before November, and it could last the whole winter on larger farms. It was performed by hand: Two workers faced each other with a flail, one threshing while the other was in his backswing. After the grain had been threshed, it was raked up, put into sacks, and carried to the storeroom, where it lay until it was taken to the grinding house.[39] Hand threshing lasted well into the nineteenth century; the first threshing machine did not come to Balestrand until 1862, and they were uncommon until the 1890s.[40]

The production of grain in Balestrand was thus steeped in customs, both secular and religious, that had provided successful results in the past. Although farmers had learned which grains prospered in which fields and even used primitive methods of solar energy to facilitate warmth, grain production was still considered a miracle. Once the seed was planted, it was in God's hands.[41]

In spite of well-defined knowledge of optimal grain production methods, Balestrand – and Sogn as a whole – has remained a grain-importing region throughout its history. Only in bountiful years, such as 1853, when 100 barrels (*tønder*) of grain were sold by farmers in the Sogn counties of Hafslo, Lærdal, and Leikanger, were harvests large enough for exports.[42] If greater grain production had been needed, the fields could have been enlarged and improved, as they were in the 1800s when population growth demanded more foodstuffs. Yet since Balestrand and its ecological structure were better suited to cattle production, farmers found it to be advantageous to rely on exports of animal products to offset the deficit in grain production each year.[43]

Animal production patterns in Balestrand

Just as the grain production was dependent on the manure from animals, so did animals rely on the forage collected to sustain them throughout the year. A centuries-old pattern of animal care evolved in the cattle areas of Norway. Axel Smith, a priest in Trysil, a county in extreme eastern Norway, criticized the method in the mid-1700s: The cattle grazed from July to the end of the summer, but they were forced to feed off hay and forage substitutes during the winter, until they were released the following spring sometimes too weak to stand.[44] This priest, in addition to many other members of the official class, lamented the primitive aspects of this method, called *høstingsbruk*.[45] The administrator of Sogn argued that the yield per animal was far less than should have been expected because of poor winter feed. The labor-intensive nature of forage collection was too expensive, he continued, and as a whole the advantages of høstingsbruk were really *"illusorisk."*[46]

Yet the raising of animals through this method, in spite of the criticisms of the wealthy, was the major source of both income for Balestrand farmers and important proteins for the peasant diet. By supplementing hay cut in the meadows of the innmark and utmark with leaves, bark, twigs, and moss, farmers could maintain larger herds. Moreover, although farmers knew that forage substitutes did not contain as much food value as hay, the supplements gave the animals a more diverse diet, worked against diseases from vitamin deficiencies, and improved milk and meat quality. Accordingly, the quality of a farm was based not only on arable land but on good hayfields and an abundant leafy forest as well. Farmers with good resources in the utmark often paid large tax bills, a reflection of the value of uncultivated land. Likewise, it was in demarcating rights and responsibilities concerning the utmark that contracts between farmers and their cotters had the strongest specifications – again a reflection of the importance of animal production.[47] Since the animals could easily live through the summer, the problem was to maintain them through a long, dark Norwegian winter. Given the circumstances of the peasant farmer, høstingsbruk was a rational attempt to utilize resources at hand to sustain large herds.

Animal husbandry in Balestrand consisted of two distinct operations. One was the direct care, feeding, and milking of the animals throughout the year; the other comprised harvesting and collecting of the forage that fed the animals through the winter. The animals were cared for each day by the *budeie* (milkmaid), usually a hired

Plate 2. The Langehaug støl in the Vetlefjord region of Balestrand was a busy mountain workplace. The barns were situated at lower places on the hill; the *sel* on the crown of the hill was the dwelling of the milkmaid, where cheese and butter were made. *Source*: Norsk Folkemuseum, Oslo; photographer unknown

woman servant but at times a daughter of the farm owner. Owing to Balestrand's climate, her work year was divided into two very different seasons based on the availability of fresh forage. The winter was a period when poor feed was used to maintain the animals in the dark barns in the farmyard. The summer that followed offered halcyon days when fresh feed grew on the lush pastures of the mountainside. As a rule, the summer period began when the sheep were let out of the barns after the birch trees had *musøyra,* that is, after the leaves had grown as big as mouse ears. The cows were released later, when the alders had musøyra.[48]

The summer feeding system was based on the støl, the place of operation in the mountain pastures where the animals were cared for and milked (see Plate 2). Fundamental to this system was the migration of the animals farther up the mountainsides through the summer as the snow melted in higher altitudes and new grass appeared. Each farm in Balestrand had two, sometimes three, støls. The *vårstøl* (spring støl) was used in spring before the animals could

be moved up to the *fjellstøl* (mountain støl). As early autumn sig-
naled the approach of winter, they migrated back to the vårstøl. The
tenure in each støl was dependent upon the weather. Støls could
not be utilized until the vegetation was adequate. A late spring
precluded use of the vårstøl, and a cold period in the fall with
snowfall or heavy rain could force an early return.[49] Usually, however, the animals in Balestrand moved to the spring støl around July
7 and grazed there for three to four weeks. They then climbed to the
mountain støl, where a stay of five to six weeks preceded the return
to the vårstøl near the beginning of September. The animals then
migrated back toward the farmyard around Michaelmas (September
29), grazing there until they were put into the barns for winter.[50]

The milkmaid, the animals, and large packs of equipment and
food did not move to the støl until the fences had been repaired
there in the spring. The animals usually knew the way, arriving long
before the milkmaid and her pack animals. As a rule, all grazing
animals were sent to the støl, but large farms or farms with many
small children or old people who needed a "home cow" provided
exceptions.[51]

The milkmaid received wages that varied greatly according to her
age, the help she had at the støl, and the length of time she was
there. At times a herdsman, often a young boy from a cotter household or from a family with many children, aided the milkmaid in
looking after the animals. The herdsman was usually paid in food
and lodging, but if he had worked before he might receive some
wages.[52]

Most støls in Sogn included barns either dug into a hill or made of
wood, only a few of which had manure cellars. The manure was
usually thrown out a window to an open place protected from wind
and weather. Early in the summer, as in the grainfields, the manure
was spread over the pastures. The day began on the støl around five
o'clock, but if the animals became impatient to get out into the
pasture, they were milked as early as four o'clock in the morning.
Cows and goats were milked again in the evening, but the sheep's
afternoon milk was left for the nursing lambs. Milking, however,
was only one of the tasks of the milkmaid. She watched over the
animals if a shepherd was not present and made butter and cheese
from the milk. During seasons of haying and forage collection, she
also had to help with "rush work." The milkmaid's diet consisted in
part of dairy products made on the støl, but she also ate other goods
brought to her when the remainder of the milk products were carried down to the farm, about every two weeks.[53] After a busy sum-

mer, the animals and equipment were again taken home, and plans were made for the long winter ahead.

The first day of winter was traditionally considered October 14 – *vinternatti*, as it was called. About a week later the animals were led to the barns, where they would remain for seven months. During that time the milkmaid kept close track of the forage supplies. If the fodder was being depleted too rapidly, more was collected, but late springs could cause anxious days before the animals were again released. Various strategies were used to relieve the animals' hunger in winter and early spring. The barns were kept dark, since it was commonly believed that darkness would lessen hunger. In many places the animal barns were separated from the haybarn, so that the milkmaid had to carry the hay longer distances. This practice, it was believed, saved hay, because the worker would tend to carry as little as possible, but transporting the hay through the tun also had magical effects that helped keep friendships intact. Most cows calved in February – an event of great celebration – but the foremost time of festivity was around May 20, when the animals were let out.[54]

The rigorous work of caring for the animals in the winter again fell on the milkmaid, who, according to one letter from America, "housed and fed them as if they had been half-brothers."[55] The chores were similar from farm to farm even if different types of forage were used. The milkmaid went to the barn around six o'clock in the morning, where she shoveled manure, gave the cattle some hay, and milked them. After her breakfast, she returned with a bundle of twigs or leaves, watered the animals, and gave them the final morning bundle. Around six o'clock in the evening, the milkmaid returned to feed the cows *sørpa* (a mush made of leaves and water), milk and water them, and give them their final hay or twigs. Preparations took much of the rest of the day. Up to thirty-eight buckets of water for the sørpa were carried daily from the brook to the cookhouse (eldhus), where they were warmed and carried to the barn.[56] It is said that the milkmaid talked with the animals during this arduous time, and the thought was always the same: "Oh, don't mourn about winter, my cows. The Lord will certainly send back the spring."[57]

Forage production patterns in Balestrand

As vital to the animals' well-being as the milkmaid's care was the labor-demanding collection of forage throughout the year for winter feed. Grain was too valuable to be used as animal feed, but, as noted, other types of forage were gathered to provide a diverse diet. The most obvious fodder source was the hay cut on the meadows near the farmyard and in the utmark. Contemporaries determined that a cow or horse needed 60 to 100 våger (2,370 to 3,950 pounds) of hay to be fed through the winter, although on farms where pastures were good only 40 våger were needed. The hay was collected at various places, depending on a farm's resources. One farm in Balestrand, for example, cut only 600 våger of hay from the utmark, although it had 4 horses, 2 young horses, 36 large cattle, 16 young cattle, and 120 sheep. The 150 to 200 mål (37.0 to 49.4 acres) of natural pasture near the farm made up the difference. At the other extreme was a farm that fed 2 horses, 1 young horse, 55 large cattle, 15 young cattle, and 170 sheep without any natural pasture. The hay came almost entirely from the rich, uncultivated utmark on the mountainsides near the farm.[58]

The harvesting of hay was coordinated with other field work. After the spring planting (våronna), workers moved to the meadows to begin clearing. In some places the twigs and leaves covering the fields were burned; in others they were carried home to be used as floor covering for the animal barns. If excess manure remained after fertilizing the fields, it was spread in the meadows near the farm. The cutting of hay commenced in early July, beginning, as a rule, on the fenced-in meadows (bø) near the farmyard. Although the amount secured from these pastures varied from farm to farm, the harvest generally was quite small. Only the larger farms did not have to take most of their hay from the utmark; on some farms the innmark meadows of the bø fed only the horses.[59]

The utmark therefore played another essential role in addition to sustaining the animals through the summer at the støl. If the farmer expected to nourish his herds reasonably through the winter, he had to harvest hay in the utmark.[60] The cutting of hay had to be combined with the migration of the herds so that neither would affect the other adversely. Theoretically, the animals were given priority in their grazing. As the herds were sent out to the pastures in the spring, moving up into the mountains as the winter receded in the higher altitudes, the farm folk were readying themselves for the cutting that would take place later in the summer. Men went to the pastures to set up hesja (hay-drying racks) while the animals still grazed there. Farms had more than 100 such racks and sometimes as many as 130, most of them needing repairs. Other workers followed carrying material that was not already available in the utmark.

Women retied the racks and cleaned up the wood around any hesja that was no longer in use. The old wood from racks that were not too distant was carried to the farmyard and used as firewood.[61] After the animals had grazed the lower støl and moved up to the mountain støl around the beginning of August, workers began to cut the stølsgjerde, fenced-in meadows in the spring støl situated on flatland or south slopes, which provided good growing conditions. The harvest was finished well before the animals returned from the higher altitudes; after their return they ate the grass remaining between stones and bushes and that which had grown up after the cutting.[62]

The hay harvest, which could last from June to October, was a season of heavy work demanding efficiency (see Plate 3). The fields were often divided into the number of days of work, so the farmer knew if the cutting was on schedule. More important to the workers, the fields were divided according to the wages payable for cutting them.[63] The payment was based on the size of the field without consideration of difficult terrain. Nonetheless, the names tåreslåtten and jammerdalen (the hayfield of tears and the vale of lament), two sections in Fjærland, indicate that some fields were more troublesome than others.[64] With consistent field divisions and payments for the harvest, farmers could easily determine the progress of the cutting and the amount they would have to pay in wages.

The harvest was designed to provide for efficiency and speedy completion of the work. The sexual division of labor was strongly defined in haying, a practice that fostered a specialization of work. The women raked and put the hay on the racks while the men reaped, one woman working with two men. So prescribed was the division that it was thought a shame for a man to rake or stack the hay.[65] The haying was also a season when servants could earn extra wages. Any work beyond their prescribed duty was considered friarbeid, piecework that was paid in wages. This incentive to complete the work quickly provided the farmer an assurance that the haying would be finished in time. Finally, cotters had responsibilities to work for the farmer in the cutting season. In general, greater numbers of hayfields were offset by greater numbers of cotters on the farm.[66]

Refinements through the centuries created improved methods for the arduous labor with scythes. The dott (a broomlike instrument) was used to keep the grass upright so the scythe could better cut it.[67] Each worker had his place in the field; if one shifted, forcing others do his part of the work, he was called a teigaskit (a good-for-

Plate 3. A typical hayfield near a Balestrand fjord. Note that rocks and hills are not removed and that the grasses are naturally growing rather than planted, a common feature before 1860. The building is a barn where the hay was stored until it was moved to the farmstead in winter. The fencelike structures are hesja, made of branches and strips of birch bark, on which the hay dried. *Source*: Norsk Folkemuseum, Oslo; photographer unknown

nothing in the hayfield). The men threw what they had cut behind them while the women raked. When the men were finished, they moved to another field; the women set the hay on racks, which were usually situated at the lower end of the field.[68] The first hayracks were built as early as 1752. Before then, the hay was dried flat on a hill, a method that was continued in rocky areas where poles could not be put in the ground.[69]

After the hay had dried, it was moved to haybarns in the utmark or in the farmyard. On large farms, up to twelve such barns were located in the utmark to store hay. Eventually, of course, all the hay was moved to the farmyard where the animals wintered. Depending on terrain and the farmer's wealth, the hay was either carried or driven down to the farmyard. Poorer farmers and cotters often had to carry the hay on their backs in bundles of about thirty-six kilograms from altitudes of seven hundred meters above sea level.[70] More fortunate were those who used horses and sleds to drive the hay down, in loads of about one hundred kilograms, over the snow in winter.[71]

Haying was an efficient system for providing forage for the wintering animals without interfering with their summer grazing. Labor was divided according to task to create greater efficiency, and workers were given pecuniary encouragement for a speedier completion of the seasonally defined work. Moreover, the grass resources were used to their maximum, first as pasture in the spring and then as hayfields in the autumn.[72] Even so, the reliance on animals in Balestrand demanded the acquisition of greater reserves of fodder. Other forage types, in addition to providing for a fuller, more diverse diet, also could be obtained in less busy periods of the year. Winter was a principal season for gathering forage, not only because there was less work to be done then but because farm folk could judge how much additional forage was needed as the resources were being depleted in the animal barns.

As already noted, the herds came down from the mountains in the fall to graze on the pasture near the farmyard until they were set in for the winter. Amazingly, the cows had been out in the pastures for only about five months, the sheep a little longer. The hay was by then at the farmyard or in barns throughout the utmark, and farm folk seriously debated how good a hay year they had had and how many animals they could feed through the winter. Since animal care was a female task, the wife often decided. The goal was to feed as many animals as possible through the winter. Those that could not be kept alive until spring were slaughtered or sold, in some places

reducing the herds by about one-tenth. The collection of such naturally growing fodder as leaves, twigs, and bark provided an insurance against poor hay years. Although gathering such forage
throughout the winter was difficult work, and there were limits on
how much could be amassed, constraints on the willingness to work
among the peasant group circumscribed the collection more than
the absolute availability of the fodder, especially in Balestrand, with
its extensive deciduous forest.[73]

Collection of forage other than hay was a regular practice throughout cattle-producing Norway. The types used, however, varied according to the ecological structure of the area. Leaves were gathered
throughout Norway; kelp and seaweed were important along the
seacoast; moss was used in the mountain communities; and bark and
twigs were collected in many other areas.[74] The amount of fodder
gathered varied greatly from place to place and depended on the
abundance of the hay harvest and the size of the animal herds.
Around Oslofjord, for example, leaves were collected only in difficult
years. In Gausdal, a mountain area in southern Gudbrandsdal, a
large farm gathered seventeen thousand bundles of leaves because of
a poor hay year in the 1870s.[75]

The leaves and small twigs from one of the richest deciduous
forests in Norway provided Balestrand farmers with a primary fodder. For hundreds of years Balestrand was famous for its dense
deciduous forests. It was said that Mundal's valley had once possessed such a dense forest that it was impossible to go through with
ease. When a man from a Mundal farm tried to cut a path through
the forest with horse and sleigh, no trace of him was ever re-
covered.[76] The most valuable tree was the elm, especially abundant
on the east side of Fjærlandsfjord. As early as 1668 complaints were
registered regarding the allocation of elm forests on the Ese farm,
and by 1814 the division of a farm in Distad prompted one farmer to
say that he had received less of the good land but more elms than
the other party.[77] Apparently he was satisfied. Four years earlier a
book had advocated the planting of an elm tree stand, described as a
"grove of safekeeping [biærings Lund]," as insurance.[78]

The collecting of leaves often began before the cutting of hay. In
Balestrand the weeks between St. John's Day and St. Swithun's Day
(June 24 to July 12) were the customary starting days, and they were
called the busiest of busiest times, especially for the women.[79] After
the haying, the gathering often continued as long as there were
leaves on the trees. The usual method of collecting leaves involved
cutting bundles of branches (see Plate 4). Workers took the branches

Plate 4. Both women and men laborers spent many hours in Balestrand's mountainous terrain cutting and bundling tree branches used as animal fodder throughout the winter. *Source*: Picture collection, University Library of Bergen; photograph by Knud Knudsen

with their left hands and cut until they could grip no more. This made one bundle, and because of different grasps each fagot varied in size. (On occasion, workers would get reputations for making their bundles too small. These undersize fagots were called *lambadrepa* – lamb killers – since sheep were fed by the bundle and the young would not get an adequate amount of feed.) After the branches were cut, the *snil* (the cutting instrument) was held in the laborer's mouth while the bundle was bound. As in the hay harvest, work was done according to task. Adult male workers were required to cut 180 bundles a day; women, 120; and the part-time leaf worker, the milkmaid, 80. Each person was done with the day's work when the daily quota was reached.[80] The farm folk were careful not to overcut the trees. Trees that had stood for many years were used cautiously, and at times a piety developed toward them that took on an almost religious character.[81]

In addition to bundling branches with leaves, women and child laborers also ripped off handfuls of leaves and collected them in baskets.[82] Yet another source was those leaves raked up in autumn.[83] The entire collection of leaves was taken – often hand carried – down to the farmyard in the fall and stacked in the storeroom. A man in Balestrand was expected to carry twelve bundles on each trip, although there were reports of up to twenty taken at a time in other Norwegian regions. The leaves that fell from bundles as they were transported were raked and placed in sacks for later use.[84] The farmer or his wife, by utilizing fixed labor requirements and developing formulas for feeding, could determine how many animals could be fed through the winter with the collected leaves.[85]

The leaves could be gathered only in summer and fall, but twigs and bark provided another source of forage available throughout the winter. If the farm folk calculated that the hay and leaves were being depleted too quickly, they could increase collection of this third source. Likewise, if the spring was late in arriving, gathering could continue until the danger of starvation disappeared. The use of these forage substitutes was reported early in Norwegian animal production areas: Hans Møller recorded examples of the use of bark and twigs cut in the winter in 1793 in Gudbrandsdal.[86] In nineteenth-century Balestrand the system had already matured to the point at which holidays were used to measure the amount of twigs to be collected. Before Candlemas (February 2), four bundles of twigs were collected per person per day; between Candlemas and Annunciation Day (March 25), the figure was five bundles; and after Annunciation Day, it was six.[87] The dependence on twigs varied from farm to farm, and in later times some farms did not use twigs until after Candlemas. Holidays, especially Candlemas, were also used as gauges for the nearness of spring: One man, when he attended church on Candlemas, checked the extent to which the icicles were dripping from the church. If there were no drips, he returned home to collect twigs, but if the icicles were melting, he stayed after church and celebrated, certain of an early spring.[88]

The festive spirit this man felt when he endured the winter without collecting twigs is easily understood. Since they were one of the last types of forage gathered in the winter, twigs were at times indispensable in keeping the animals fed. The work, however, was extremely arduous and occasionally dangerous. Men often went to the elm forests in the darkness so early in the morning that they had to bite the branches in order to find elms. The long work days occurred during seasons of instable weather in remote places that at times were the scene of avalanches. In the 1850s one worker was killed by avalanches on the Fjærlandsfjord. Though death was rare, workers still faced long, demanding days on difficult terrain.[89]

Shavings of bark, moss, and roots were additional sources of forage collected in different seasons. The *skav* (bark shavings) were taken mainly from elm, aspen, mountain ash, ash, and willow, but the bark of hazel was at times fed sheep and goats.[90] The milkmaid collected moss for winter use on fair weather days at the end of August, when the milk from the cows decreased and she was not as busy making cheese and butter. The moss was carried home to the støl, packed in a corner, and taken to the farmyard for the winter.[91] At times farm folk also dug up fern roots found on the borders in early spring before the snow had completely melted. The roots were carried home in sacks, washed, and cut up for the animals, a treat of fresh forage.[92]

The utmark therefore played an indispensable role in ensuring the welfare of the farm. The wealth of forage on the mountainsides created a flexibility that lessened the risks of animal husbandry. Pastures in the utmark – described by nationalist poet A. O. Vinje as "grass so fat it glistened" – were vital if farms were to enlarge their animal holdings. Almost unlimited tree leaves provided another source that could be collected at a time when the quality of the hay harvest could be assessed. Collecting of twigs and bark, more arduous work still, was a further insurance against loss of animal life as forage supplies were monitored through the late winter. If resources were low or the spring was late, otherwise idle workers trudged out to the inhospitable utmark to claim more forage supplies. Inordinately poor weather conditions may have increased the workers' burdens, but the well-developed knowledge of resources and climate militated against significant property loss.

Nonagricultural production patterns in Balestrand

Life on the farm was oriented toward creating food upon which to live. Animal and crop production, however, was not the sole work activity of farm folk. Tools, houses, and clothing had to be made, additional nonagricultural sources of wealth had to be exploited, and the all-important trading journeys had to be conducted. Owing to the seasonal nature of agricultural work, the less busy times were used for these activities. Much of the domestic work was completed during work periods at night in the winter. *Kveldseta* work, as it was called, began on All Saints' Day (November 1) and ended at Annunciation Day (March 25). Work for the farm generally lasted from six to nine o'clock in the evening, after which time servants could work for themselves.[93] The women made and mended clothes, but worked mainly on the carding and spinning of wool. This community work included nearly everyone; the young did the easier tasks, but girls learned to spin early, at least by the time of confirmation at around age fifteen. The men did skaving work, taking the bark off branches for animal feed. They also carved wooden shoes, made rakes, patched shoes, and wove baskets. The poorer households used winter months to make goods for sale to supplement their incomes.[94] Despite long work hours in the summertime, slack days were used for collecting birch bark for roofs, willow twigs for binding, and rush, the marrow of which was used for wicks. Finally, trapping and fishing supplemented the diet. In the utmark weasel, martin, and even bears were hunted or trapped, and fish were taken from the fjord.[95]

Despite such wide-ranging manufacture of goods in the home, farmers traded to obtain products cheaper to create elsewhere or unproducible on the farm, thereby easing their work requirements. In Balestrand farmers usually journeyed to Bergen twice each year, once in the spring and once in the fall. In the spring wood cut in the winter was traded for grains and spring herring. The autumn journey involved the exchange of milk products made in the summer for salt used in the slaughter in late fall. Meat was not a component in the trade; animals were usually sold, if at all, in Sogn on the hoof.[96]

In sum, the agricultural year in Balestrand was long and the work was not easy. Moreover, a constant threat of too much rain, late springs, and snowy winters confronted the farm folk. But the people withstood these difficulties and developed a secure method of production in spite of the obstacles. An inhospitable season might have forced people to work far harder from time to time than many would have liked, but farm production year after year created harvests adequate to sustain the community.

Social patterns in Balestrand

As agricultural methods evolved to exploit the land, legal and social norms developed to tie the land to kin groups and kin groups to larger social groupings. Likewise, folk beliefs influenced behavior during the important events – the rites of passage – binding individuals closer to the society of which they were a part. Deep-seated folk traditions coupled custom with social mechanisms to regulate behavior, set norms, and create a smoother functioning of farm life.

Land in Balestrand was the main source of wealth, and strict laws were designed to transfer that wealth from generation to generation. Partly because of its importance, land was inextricably tied to the family through a line of descent called *ætt*, which descended through the oldest living son or, if no sons were living, the oldest daughter. Through the allodial right (*odelsrett*), fixed by law from the Middle Ages, members of the lineage could repurchase the land for a fixed period of time if it had been sold outside the ætt. The legal rationale was quite simple: The land was the property of the lineage, past and present, and not of the particular individual who had forsaken it.[97]

The relationship between the line of descent and its land reached far back in the oral tradition, and written laws only acknowledged what was already common practice. Through this tradition the family line increased in importance, and the ancestry at times became almost magical. One sign of prestige was the number of generations the farm had been *i ætti* – within ownership of the line. Farm folk spoke nobly of the first owner of the farm in the lineage. The *nisse* (the mythical elf who dwelled in the farmhouse) was actually a supernatural personage who represented the founder of the ætt. Consistent with the prestige of the lineage, anyone who sold the farm outside the line of descent was disgraced, and some believed that it was a crime against one's ancestors. When one farmer on a Balestrand farm sold a part of his holdings, it reputedly gave his father-in-law such a shock that he hanged himself. Obviously, for many it was urgent to buy the farm back into the lineage if it had gone into different hands.[98]

The line of descent solidified the authority of the male head of the household (*husbond*). The husbond was the owner of the *odelsgard*, a position of prestige and responsibility. He was nearly always married and head of a household that consisted of his family and other persons connected to the farm – servants or members of the extended family. The vital role of female work on the farm, however, extended the influence of the farm wife. The two-parent household was so important in the leadership of the farm that if a man or woman was widowed and did not remarry, he or she usually gave up the farm even if the inheritor was female.[99] The husbond made most decisions concerning the farm's operation, but his wife controlled domestic labor and work in the cowsheds. The farm couple oversaw their servants. They made sure that the servants arose early in the morning, the husbond waking the men, his wife the women. They also controlled the social behavior of the servants, all of whom had to ask permission to go out in the evening except during the free night, Saturday.[100]

Because individuals were tied to their lineage and the lineage to the farm, naming patterns followed strictly defined rules that reused the names of ancestors. Such customs were not meant merely as remembrances, however: Those bearing names of the dead also bore their spirits. The saying "The same name does the same good" illustrates a belief in deep connections between persons and names. According to the naming custom, the firstborn son, who probably would inherit the farm, was named after his father's father; the second son bore the name of his mother's father. When the wife had inherited the farm, the order was reversed. This naming pattern was almost universally used. In Mundal parish of Balestrand between 1810 and 1879, for example, 90.5% of the firstborn boys in initial marriages were named after one grandfather.[101] The tradition was so strong that when both grandfathers had the same name, the first two boys could bear identical names. When a widower or widow remarried, the first child of the corresponding sex received the name of the former spouse. Finally, if a child died the parents often gave the next baby of the same sex the same name.[102]

In view of the importance of the farm in relation to the lineage, intergenerational transfer of the estate was an event of great significance. Symbolically, the son (or daughter) destined to carry on the lineage often received power over the land when he (or she) was permitted to marry. Changes in life expectancy and fertility, however, forced alterations in inheritance procedures. Since life expectancy was low in the eighteenth century, the son customarily took over the farm at the death of the father. But by the mid-1700s reduced mortality and a considerable growth in population created the need for the father to retire in order for the son to marry by mid-life.[103] Later still, sons began to marry before the farmer retired and to live within the household with their wives and children.[104]

With the increasing incidence of retirement, contracts were drawn that stipulated the responsibilities of the son to his parents. *Kårbrever* or *kårkontrakter*, as they were called, designated the food and care the older couple should receive in retirement (*kår*). They were always written and were often drafted at the same time as the written contract of sale or deed.[105] Written into all kårkontrakter were basic conditions such as ownership of animals, land, and grains and provisions for baking, painting, and care. The retired couple cared for their animals as long as they were able, but farm workers often took responsibility when the pensioners became too old. Usually the retired people were given two to three cows and four to five sheep, and when the herds were at the støl they were given a fixed quantity of milk daily, usually one-half liter of unskimmed milk. Upon retirement, the pensioned usually chose the cattle and sheep they would keep, but when the animals were slaughtered, they were forced to accept lesser-quality dressed meat if it was offered. When they kept their own animals, the retirees had their own pastures as well. In addition, they were given the same piece of arable land year after year, plowed and fertilized by farm folk but sowed by the retired man himself. Wood was also provided the couple, but the man often cut the wood himself and carried it into the house. His wife kept busy spinning, weaving, and knitting, in addition to sewing all their clothes (see Plate 5). When the retirees could no longer perform their work, the farm folk took over the duties.[106]

One kårkontrakt from the Våtevik farm of Balestrand in 1840 illustrates how specific the clauses could be. The couple received 711 pounds of the best grain from the farm, in addition to 7 sheep and 2 lambs, and 1 *mæle* of land (1,000 square meters) that would be plowed and fertilized. They received a free house, firewood and light, baking, brewing, and care, especially in sickness. If one of the pair should die, the survivor would get 5 sheep, 434.5 pounds of grain, and two-thirds of the fields.[107] Beneath this legal exterior, however, the contract could be used by the old couple to retain some control over the functioning of the farm. The stipulations within the contract at times were not taken at face value, but provided a legal safeguard against intergenerational conflict. If the retirees were not treated fairly, the contract allowed them to take the young to court. In one place, for example, a kårkontrakt stipulated that the pensioners be furnished 30 pounds of coffee a year. The coffee was probably never given in such large quantities, but if unfair treatment occurred, the youths knew that they would be liable. In other cases the old man deeded over the farm but kept all personal property in his hands, to retain some input in the farming decisions.[108] Finally, the kårkontrakt itself was burdensome to the young farmers, taking from one-quarter to one-third of the farm's production, and it could be used as a weapon to keep the farm within the lineage. Potential buyers often lost interest in a farm

Plate 5. When an elderly couple retired, they still continued to work. Here an older woman is seen spinning outside her home. Spinning was specifically women's work, done by old as well as young. Servant women often received a part of their wages in raw wool, from which they made their own clothes. *Source*: Norsk Folkemuseum, Oslo: photographer unknown

when they were told of the kårkontrakt responsibilities that would be transferred as part of the sale.[109]

As sons increasingly often in the nineteenth century were married before they took control of the farm, parents would try to purchase another farm for a son, a step that gave the father control of two farms.[110] Since the parents were rarely able to own two farms, however, the young couple usually married and lived in their own sleeping room on the farm. At times they received a part of the farm and owned their own cattle until the whole farm, with its burdensome kår responsibility, was transferred to them.[111]

Despite the importance of the lineage, people on a farm were not isolated from other farms and families in the valleys and dales of Balestrand. Indeed, a rich social life based on festive celebrations and co-work knitted farms into strong, strictly defined neighborhoods. Varying neighborhood divisions were based on standing rules of self-help and social obligation that developed between farms. The smallest division was *granne,* a close relationship between neighboring farm units. Farms related to one another could be situated in the same farmyard or only have hayfields bordering one another in the outlying meadows and woods. Yet although farms with *grannelag* were separated by varying distances, they usually were the closest possible neighbors.

Because of its small size, the obligations and fellowship within the grannelag were only less intimate than those within the farm itself. The term *nabo* (neighbor) symbolized someone related through grannelag, and people clearly differentiated between such a neighbor and another person from the region.[112] The practical purpose of the grannelag was the exchange of labor during times when a farm needed more workers to complete a task. Social occasions were also essential, the most noteworthy being the grannelag gathering during the Christmas season. The festivities included gifts of cake and liquors to the servants who gathered to celebrate yet another religious occasion. Cotters were also invited, but sometimes they preferred their own, less ostentatious, parties within the grannelag. This Christmas celebration was so fixed that no invitations were sent to members of the grannelag. Moreover, the custom was so old that elderly members of the community in 1850 said, "Such has it always been," and it has been speculated that the gathering at Christmas dated from the Middle Ages.[113]

Somewhat larger geographical units were *grend,* with corresponding social groups called *bedlag.* Like the grannelag, the bedlag was a source of collective labor, but it was noted more for its social gatherings. Each bedlag contained a group of farms defined by natural boundaries and often named after a prominent farm in the neighborhood or after the fjord on which the group lay.[114] The entire region was divided into grend, and although population shifts in later times caused some minor changes in grend boundaries, the main boundaries remained strictly defined.[115]

Grend gatherings celebrated the important rites of passage in the community, especially marriage and burial, and represented one of the most colorful examples of Norwegian folk life. Often depicted in the paintings of Norwegian romantics in the late nineteenth century, the community, dressed in colorful folk costumes, enjoyed the festivities for days on end. Preparations for an event began with the invitation of all who belonged to the grend. Rules of inclusion were quite strict: The complaint "Why is he invited? He doesn't belong to the grend" was heard on occasion at grend celebrations. Weddings were held at the home of the bride. If the groom was from another grend, only his friends, family, and close neighbors were invited.[116] The guests were invited to grend gatherings by an honored near relative or respected man, often a brother of the bride or bridegroom. The inviter went from farm to farm and was served food and a dram of aquavit or beer. Not surprisingly, he was in "high spirits" when he had completed his duties.[117] Since grend gatherings could be quite large, guests brought most of the food, their contributions determined by a well-established set of customs. Donations varied according to the occasion, one's relationship to the party giver, and one's financial standing.[118]

Since large work projects at times exceeded available labor on a farm, bedlag and grannelag members also traded labor through a *dugnad* (collective work arrangement) when it was needed. The amount of labor needed determined whether the bedlag or the grannelag was called, but the character of the work was strictly governed by custom. Overly large projects were not "covered" by this work insurance, and neighborhood members never requested workers for major undertakings.[119]

The rites of passage in the Balestrand community, celebrated so vigorously by the grannelag and bedlag, not only extended social networks through marriage and childbirth but governed patterns of inheritance that largely determined wealth in the agrarian community. Like the economic activities of Balestrand, the rite of passage was based on a system of age-old custom that contained mechanisms for creating a dynamic, yet smoothly functioning, system.

Marriage was a momentous life event. Not only did it determine one's spouse for life, but it defined the economic position for which one was destined. Not surprisingly, many omens and beliefs evolved in Balestrand with regard to courtship and marriage. Courtship was most successful during the waxing of the moon, especially around Candlemas (February 2). If a maid wished to know her future husband, she went out to a crossroads the first time she saw the moon in February. There she would turn around three times and say "Tell me the name of the man I shall get." She then returned to the farmyard and did not move until an unmarried man's name was mentioned. He would be her husband. Once an engagement was contracted, she could also determine her material prospects with her betrothed on Christmas Eve. She put three bowls on the table, one with beer, one with milk, and one with water. At midnight her fiancé came into the dark room and drank one of the bowls. If he drank the beer, he would be a drunkard; if he drank the water, he would be poor; but if the milk was drunk, he would be rich.[120]

The marriage itself, however, was not subject to omens but was a complex set of agreements and meetings. When a marriage was proposed, near relatives, usually the fathers, acted as spokesmen for the youths. Two proposers, the bridegroom and often the brother of the bride, went and officially asked for the bride's hand. The engagement (*truloving*) was often contracted in the winter, with the wedding usually taking place the following summer.[121] The wedding was often celebrated around Midsummer's Day because it was between the periods of heavy work and occurred when good food was available. The celebration, which was attended by the *bedlag*, could continue for a week but usually lasted only three days.[122]

The protracted negotiations that determined marriage partners and thus created a household were dependent on acquisition of a livelihood upon which to subsist. Since farm ownership or cotterhood were traditionally the sole means of acquiring livelihoods in Balestrand, a mechanism was created that adjusted the frequency of marriage and number of fertile years a woman lived in wedlock. The custom that prohibited marriage before a livelihood was procured forced poorer members of the society to marry later. As a rule, for example, brides of cotters were older than their farmer counterparts, so that they had fewer years in which to bear children. Again custom adjusted society by creating a powerful limit on reproduction of the economically weakest part of the population.[123]

Omens also played a prominent role in the precarious and mysterious pregnancies and birthing of children, the future heirs of the farm. Poor hygiene caused the birth of a child to be a dangerous affair for both mother and child. Women observed many "don'ts" throughout pregnancy in order not to harm the fetus. They were not to look a hare in the mouth, lest the child be a harelip; they were not to take part in the slaughter, lest the blood that hit the woman be reflected in birthspots on the corresponding part of the baby. During a difficult birth, acts of sympathy eased the delivery. All knots in the house were loosened and the hair of the woman was untied to facilitate the child's exit from the womb. If the birth became extremely difficult, the husband destroyed a sled, plow, or other implement in sympathy, which assisted in a safe delivery. If all was lost, however, the woman could take solace in the fact that all who died in childbirth went to heaven.[124]

Death, like birth, was a crucial event in peasant society. Before the extensive use of kår contracts, the household head's death occasioned the transfer of the farm. Death was thus central to the operation of the old peasant society; it stood in the middle of life just as the graveyard lay in the middle of the community.[125] Folk beliefs again played a significant role in the final rite of passage. After the last rites, the corpse was washed and carried out of the house. The straw on which the dying person had lain was burned so that the deceased could find peace in the grave and not return.[126]

One of the central events in Norwegian history, however, was that death began to take a less dominating place in the society. Whereas the average age at death for men in the 1820s was still only forty-five, by the mid-eighteenth century mortality had begun to decline among infants and children from around 250 per 1,000 in 1750 to about 200 per 1,000 in 1800.[127] The corresponding yearly growth rates increased from 0.38% between 1701 and 1750 to 0.70% between 1750 and 1814. After the crises of the Napoleonic Wars, the growth rate exploded to nearly 1% per year during the mid-nineteenth century.[128] Norway's population grew faster than that of most European countries between 1815 and 1855, although the mid-nineteenth century saw decreased growth owing to emigration.[129] Balestrand also enjoyed this population boom. Between 1769 and 1801 the population grew 1.03% annually; in the following fifty-four years, the yearly increase was 0.80%.[130]

Increasing life expectancy and less frequent loss of infants contributed to a death rate in Norway that was consistently among Europe's lowest from the eighteenth century onward. On the other hand, as networks of trade developed, an increased demand for labor permitted more new cotters to marry and expanded the value of children, encouraging greater fertility. In both cases growing population placed increased demands on the cultural systems of food production, land structure, and intergenerational transfer of wealth. Whereas this chapter has described an agricultural system in a continual process of change that adjusted to altered seasonal demands, the next explores the responses to the population growth that forever changed the old peasant society. As we will see, farmers and cotters in Balestrand were actually creating a larger per capita agricultural wealth as the nineteenth century progressed. Emigration from Balestrand, contrary to the arguments of many historians, was not due to underemployment of a rural population in a society whose limits of growth had been reached.

4 "It will be man's fortune to see business extended": the economic development of Balestrand, 1800–1865

Høstingsbruk was a malleable system of agriculture in which labor-demanding tasks could be expanded when necessary to create additional food sources. If the hay harvest was poor, further work in the utmark enlarged the collection of other types of forage. The rapidly increasing population, however, forced Balestrand households to expand their farm operations permanently. Historians have often painted a bleak picture of the region's ability to adjust to population growth and agricultural extension. "By the middle of the 1800s," one historian of Sogn writes, "farmers and cattle dealers had used all the mountain pastures. There were seters [støls] and cattle pens everywhere . . . The communities now had not only reached the outer boundaries of the whole expansion in economic life, but there was overpopulation as well."[1] "Around the middle of the nineteenth century," another writer concurs, "the population [of Middle and Inner Sogn] had reached a boundary." This "overpopulation," he continues, was the "principal reason behind the emigration from the rural communities."[2]

Other observers have been more sanguine about the consequences of the population growth. Eilert Sundt noted in the 1850s that

> certain writers in political economy continually assert and stress the proposition that in old states, in countries where people have lived and worked for a long time, nearly all the fertile spots and all other fruitful places of work are fully occupied. It is therefore difficult for the growth of the economy to keep in step with the continued increase in the size of the population. Thus there always arises the danger of overpopulation. Now this proposition is combatted by another, which I myself prefer to believe, namely that with morality and industry it will be man's fortune, under normal circumstances, to see business extended to the extent of the needs of the expanding population.[3]

Sundt, a keen observer of Norwegian peasant society, described a process that dovetails with recent social scientific research.[4] As

56

Julian L. Simon writes, "The relationship between technological progress and population growth is *not* a race between two independent forces but rather a system in which technological progress is to an important degree a function of population growth."[5] As populations increase, households and societies in general are compelled to adopt new agricultural techniques that increase output. The innovations demand greater expenditures of labor but create larger harvests per land unit to feed the growing population.[6] In the long run, moderate population growth has a more positive effect on the standard of living than a stationary population. Although an additional child burdens the child's parents and society in the short run, the long-term benefits of additional work input by parents, greater industrial investment, and economies of scale create an improved standard of living.[7]

The economic development of Balestrand reflects much more closely the arguments of Sundt, Ester Boserup, and Simon than those of historians who have cited underemployment owing to a limit of resources. In spite, perhaps because, of rapid population growth, production per capita was rising among all social classes in Balestrand throughout the nineteenth century. For as population was increasing, landowning farmers were benefiting from expanded opportunities for trade. Larger urban markets and better transportation facilities inspired an export-led growth that encouraged even greater agricultural production. Increased profits from trade tempted the landed to increase output through longer work periods and encouraged a more intensive *and* extensive use of land and capital. Though farmers profited most from the expanded trade, landless laborers secured more work at higher wages: After all, land had to be cleared or improved, more fodder had to be collected, additional grain had to be sown and harvested, and larger herds had to be tended.[8]

The changing economic patterns in the society were filled with irony. Although the landless enjoyed an increasing well-being as the nineteenth century progressed, they found themselves further removed from the landed households, which controlled even more wealth. Likewise, although the landless controlled greater resources, a larger proportion of households owned no land. Yet economic development certainly occurred, both from a growing population that spurred internal growth and from an enlarging trade infrastructure that stimulated still further expansion. In the end, simple underemployment or lack of resources simply cannot be considered adequate to explain the massive emigration from Balestrand.

Resources, population growth, and structural changes

Strategies of growing European peasant communities for raising output varied from expanding the agricultural work year to diversifying work into nonagricultural activities. Though additional work often decreased output per man-hour, output per man-year increased so that an enlarging population could be sustained.[9] Growing demand for industrial goods at times created paths for labor more lucrative than traditional agriculture. The "protoindustrialization" of the countryside lengthened a work year constrained by the seasonal rhythm of nature and provided for an enlarged population without a corresponding increase in arable surface. In many areas, moreover, a fruitful symbiosis between agriculture and the putting-out industry allowed expansion in both areas. A "brave and worthy farmer" in eighteenth-century Switzerland, for example, cultivated "only one-eighth of the holding of his grandfather and yet [was] living happily and well."[10] Agriculture's importance declined as opportunities for industrial activity created additional wealth in a growing population.[11]

Regions without markets for industrial goods expanded the work year by exploiting resources in the sea, forests, or mines, in addition to farming. Norway remained an agricultural land well into the nineteenth century, but in no single area was farming the only important source of income. Fish was a major resource for trade and consumption in the north, along the west coast, and even in inner fjord areas; by 1850, 75,000 fishermen lived in Norway.[12] Forestry was more critical than farming in various eastern Norwegian communities, and most regions gained some income from it. Timber could be cut in autumn and early winter after the heaviest farm work or in the summer between the spring labor and the haying.[13] Trade in such crafts and natural resources as fish, salt, iron, hemp, grains, linen, glass, ropes, millstones, tobacco, and liquor attests to the significance of commerce throughout the Norwegian countryside.[14]

Agricultural work rhythms were coordinated with new economic pursuits if the latter increased in importance. When demand for fish grew, for example, farmers altered their land structure, work patterns, and sexual division of labor to enable the yearly labor increases.[15]

As in other areas, households in Balestrand adapted their ecological and market opportunities to create individual combinations of production activities. Household industries for export were rare in

Balestrand. Women were able seamstresses and weavers, but their work was used mainly at home. As late as 1870 households still commonly made their own clothes, furniture, and simple farm implements. Male craftsmen, however, often were hired within the community. Shoemakers, carpenters, and tailors moved about, staying in people's homes to do their work, although even these crafts were at times performed by household members.[16]

Without large markets to which to sell finished goods, the Balestrand economy relied on farming, lumbering, and trade throughout the nineteenth century. The ecological structure of areas within Balestrand, however, brought about two very different regional patterns. The parish of Vangsnes did not have deciduous forests with which to feed animals but contained instead large groves of coniferous trees suitable for boatbuilding. In addition, the good wind conditions in Vangsnes facilitated seafaring in the fjord (see Figure 3).[17] People in Vangsnes therefore directed their energies toward trade and adapted their agriculture to fit seafaring activities. Fewer labor-intensive crops were planted, and goods that demanded less labor were produced. Potatoes fitted particularly well into a farm and seafaring system: They were less labor-demanding than animals, and because the harvest date was less crucial than that for grain, the traders gained flexibility. Vangsnes households also lumbered, produced small amounts of grain, and owned a few animals. They traded their potatoes and wood with coastal regions for fish and grains, in addition to profiting from transport.[18]

The parishes of Tjugum and Mundal responded differently to population growth. Geographically unfit for sea trade and lacking large markets for protoindustrialization activities, these two parishes concentrated on increased production of food products for consumption and trade. Farms in Mundal and parts of Tjugum were endowed with large elm forests well suited for increased animal husbandry. Other areas in the two parishes placed the underutilized expanse of flatland in crop production. As trade increased, the farms specialized in operations for which their land was best suited.

The combination of growing population and different ecological structures in Vangsnes and in Tjugum and Mundal led the parishes toward dissimilar social structures. Shipbuilding and seafaring created outside employment opportunities in Vangsnes, so that farms could be divided among heirs who increasingly apportioned their work between potato growing and sea trade.[19] Between 1825 and 1865 the estate division that created 47.6% more farm units forced fewer children into landlessness when they entered adulthood (see

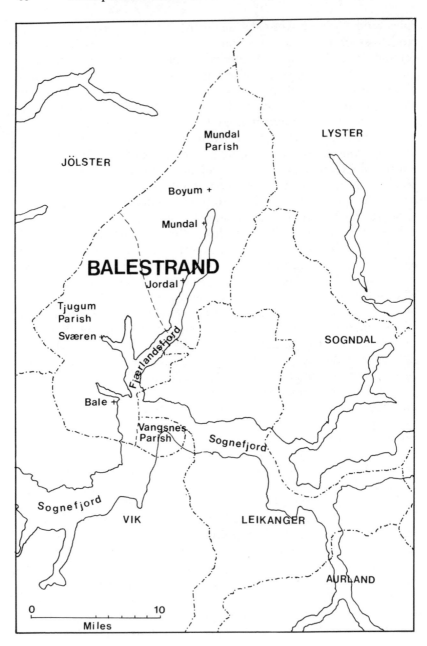

Fig. 3. Balestrand and environs

Table 3. *Farm units in Balestrand's parishes, 1825–65*

	Tjugum and Mundal	Vangsnes	Total Balestrand population
1825	112	21	1,702
1865	109	31	2,205
% change	−2.7	47.6	29.6

Sources: Balestrand manuscript population censuses, 1825, 1865.

Table 3). Farm structures were less complicated, and the nuclear family became the norm on the smaller Vangsnes farms.[20]

Unlike those in Vangsnes, the farms in Tjugum and Mundal were rarely divided, so that between 1825 and 1865 the number of farm units actually decreased. Enlarged animal herds that demanded year-round care, coupled with the extension of the work year, created an economy of scale that made larger units of operation more productive. Farms of this region were larger than those not only of Vangsnes but of other inland communities in western Norway. Tjugum and Mundal farms, for example, had more individuals per farm unit than those in Voss to the south or in Sunnmøre and Nordmøre to the north.[21] Although the maintenance of large farms fitted the production needs of the area, however, a larger proportion of households were forced to live in landless status in Tjugum and Mundal than in Voss and Møre, not to mention Vangsnes.

Such farm division patterns influenced the intensity and direction of migration. Ultimately, emigration from Vangsnes never reached the extent of that from Tjugum and Mundal. Farm division in Vangsnes, by providing land for more of its inhabitants, militated against emigration. Also important, however, was the greater likelihood of movement within Norway: Since people from Vangsnes had commercial contacts with the coast and Bergen, they were likely to be aware of opportunities there and to move to them. Between 1889 and 1915, for example, more migrants from the relatively isolated parish of Mundal than from Vangsnes went to America.[22] Since the parishes of Tjugum and Mundal represent a høstingsbruk region that engendered a widespread overseas emigration, their economic development is closely analyzed here.

Just as regions with dissimilar ecological structures exploited their environments differently, with varied economic patterns as a result, so did social groups utilize their resources in a distinct fashion according to their needs and abilities. The principal social division in Tjugum and Mundal was between the landed (farmers) and the landless (cotters, day laborers, and servants). Although both groups were a part of an economic structure that was enlarging throughout the nineteenth century, each faced different risks, constraints, and opportunities. Farmers were much more closely tied into a money economy. They were forced to borrow money in order to buy their farms, they paid wages, and they marketed their goods in Bergen and with traders throughout Sogn. Since farmers controlled the majority of the wealth in the area, they emphasized production for the market, specializing in certain agricultural products and trading for goods difficult to produce at home. Farm operations among the landless were based less on market activities. They produced food upon which to subsist and supplemented their incomes with day labor or piecework, usually for farmers. Farmers therefore concentrated on marketing agricultural goods in order to pay debts and accrue profits, whereas cotters used their products at home, worked for wages, and produced nonagricultural goods for the local market.[23]

Because the farmers had greater access to capital and land, they retained a greater relative share of the increasing wealth of the area. By 1802, 54.5% of the land in Balestrand was owned by farmers who worked it, an increase from 8.7% in 1647, when the crown and church were the principal landowners. Moreover, farmers in the very agriculturally inclined parishes of Mundal and Tjugum owned 63.0% and 57.3%, respectively. The purchase of land in Balestrand accelerated after 1765, and farmer ownership outstripped that in neighboring regions of Sunnfjord and Nordfjord, where farmers owned 11.3% less of the land. Increased ownership of land among Balestrand farmers possibly was due to the greater efficiency of their larger scales of production, which effectively used the nonlandholding sectors of the population as a ready source of labor. With increasing landed wealth, farmers became more class conscious in the nineteenth century. If a farmer paid day laborers more than was customary, for example, he was reprimanded by other farmers.[24] As the landed became economically stronger, the social divisions increased.

In spite of the greater class divisions, landless households also gained greater wealth throughout the nineteenth century. Larger inputs of labor, a vast clearing of new land, and additional crops, especially the potato, expanded agricultural output. Day labor, transporting work, and handwork, especially blacksmithing, augmented the welfare of the poorer segments of society. While farmers successfully concentrated on agricultural production, cotters and others filled out the occupational hierarchy by completing necessary tasks both in- and outside agriculture.[25] By piecing together a number of activities, the landless could create livelihoods that would have been impossible if they had concentrated on only one.

Changing labor, land, and capital inputs

The growing agricultural production can be better understood by examining the inputs of labor, land, and capital used by the farmers and cotters to enlarge their operations. Relatively complete agricultural statistics reveal the material growth more fully than the changes in nonagricultural livelihoods, so the adaptations of farmers, who controlled the land, are simpler to identify. Cotters and wage-earning classes, however, also made changes in their use of land, labor, and capital, even if they were less dramatic.

The landed farmer class employed the bulk of the labor in the community. The Balestrand farmer household in 1801, for example, averaged 3.9 nonconjugal family members, most of whom were servants, compared to an average of 0.4 in cotter households. In the same year farmer households composed of family and servants made up 77.5% of Balestrand's population. As population grew and markets increased throughout the nineteenth century, paid labor increased in farmer households. Yet as cultivation became more intense and gathering moved higher into the mountains, return per labor unit was less. Farmers thus were forced to consider financial returns of production in relation to outlays of paid labor. For households without land, the relationship between labor and output was not as complicated. Cotter households hired few paid laborers and enlarged work within the family to create the necessary foodstuffs upon which to survive.[26] Because farmer units were larger and employed more paid labor, their changing labor inputs involved greater change.

Landed farmers increased and improved their labor inputs in two ways. First, not only were more laborers hired, but they worked longer hours to broaden exploitation of the land both qualitatively and quantitatively. As greater expanses were used, tasks took longer to perform simply because resources were more distant. Second, and more important, greater efficiency was obtained through a better organized and more specialized work force. Larger groups of workers permitted farmers to devise a more intricate division of labor.[27]

Greater labor demands on year-round servants, who were paid annually, or on cotters, whose work obligations occurred only sporadically, are reflected in the increased needs of the farms. To feed their animals in 1865, for example, Balestrand farmers required 736,440 leaf bundles, which equaled 5,200 days of work merely to collect the leaves. The larger herds in the nineteenth century forced workers to gather the leaves in even more remote places and increased the labor demands still further.[28] As the amount of work increased, even children were more fully employed in farm households. While grain was cut and carried down to the tun, youths followed behind and picked up lost grain shoots.[29] Likewise, they helped carry manure to the fields and dug up fern roots to feed the animals in the spring. The small tasks children could perform reduced work demands on hired help and decreased the amount of labor their parents had to hire. Indeed, a close correlation between the size of the farm operation and the number of children remaining in the household reflects the importance of work by the whole farm family.[30]

In addition to working longer days, however, each Balestrand farmer hired a different mix of laborers to suit the production possibilities of his particular operation. Farms in Balestrand can be divided into two types according to the extent of their infield areas. Those situated on fjord bottoms, in the valleys, and on *nes* (promontories), such as the farms of Tjugum, Bale, and Vangsnes, had extensive flatland that made larger infields possible. Farms located along fjords where the land shot up out of the sea contained limited flat croplands.[31] The shoreline farms, since they lacked flat arable fields, relied more on the rich resources in the utmark and specialized in animal products.[32] The flatland farms, on the other hand, depended on increasing grain and potato production throughout the century.

As farm operations produced different mixes of crops and animals, their labor needs varied. Grain production embraced short periods of heavy labor and long periods of idleness. The grain was sown in the spring and cut in the fall, both periods of arduous labor, but the work slowed down considerably in between. Animals, on the other hand, demanded year-round attention. Cows and sheep were milked daily and continually tended; their winter forage had to be collected; and dairy products, such as cheese and butter, had to be made. On the basis of varied labor needs owing to the dissimilar crop and animal mixes, farmers efficiently exploited different types of workers to create their farm goods with the least expense.

The different work responsibilities of cotters and year-round servants corresponded well to duties of crop and animal production,
respectively. Cotters, who performed an annual obligation of about
three weeks' work for the farmer, were used during the planting
and harvesting of grain. The farmer did not have to feed the cotter
households, and in slack work periods when there were no obligations, cotters could labor toward their own subsistence. Year-round
laborers, on the other hand, satisfied animal producers. Though
servants were paid by the farmer, the wages, especially for women,
were not high. Whole-year laborers thus increased rapidly on
shoreline farms between 1802 and 1865, as animal holdings demanded their work, whereas cotters tended to live on flatland farms
where there were greater seasonal work duties and more flatlands
upon which to set up cotters' places. Between 1802 and 1865, fifty-
three of the eighty-seven new cotter places in Balestrand (61%) were
founded on flatland farms.[33]

For most of the year, the cotter worked on his small plot of land
rented from the farmer. The cotter's rent was paid through a combination of money and work duties performed during the busy
planting and harvesting periods. The duties and rights of the cotter
were made clear in a written *festekontrakt* that enables analysis today
of typical cotter performance in the nineteenth century.[34] The six
surviving cotters' contracts reveal a pattern of typical responsibilities. All cotters were required to work for the farmer at specified times, averaging about seventeen days. Work responsibilities
consisted mainly of help with the spring planting and the grain and
hay harvests in the fall. Only in one contract written in 1901 was
gathering of leaves included.[35]

During the spring the cotter and his wife typically were required
to work one day in the planting. He also maintained the fences in
certain areas, built hayracks (hesja), and removed stones from fields
while his wife did baking work (see Plate 6). More important were
responsibilities during the harvest. Though work requirements
often varied in hay cutting, the cotter generally cut one *dalarteig* –
about four and one-half days' work.[36] The duties were so fixed that
hayfields were often named after the cotters who harvested them
year after year. The cotter could cut the field at any time within
certain limits. In one agreement, for example, he had to begin by
seven weeks before Michaelmas and finish within five weeks.[37]
Grain harvest labor was also an important autumn cotter responsibility. A cotter usually agreed to cut a grain field, which averaged
about fourteen thousand square feet and took about six days' work.

Plate 6. Among the duties of the cotter's wife was a period of baking. Here a woman is seen making flatbread, a typical food of the region. *Source*: Picture collection, University Library of Bergen; photographer unknown

Finally, the cotter and his wife worked for two days in the potato harvest.[38]

The landed enjoyed considerable support from their cotters' labor. Assuming the average responsibility of each cotter was 17 days each year, the 145 cotters in Tjugum and Mundal in 1865 performed 2,465 days of work, or 22.5 days of work per farm unit annually. These duties, moreover, were fulfilled almost exclusively in periods when rapid, efficient work was essential. Finally, the farmer paid no direct wages, since the work served as part of the rent for the cotters' use of small parcels of land on the farm. Indeed, the cotters' contribution to production was so essential that historians have argued that in view of their increasing numbers, they were a basic reason for the productive growth in the 1800s.[39]

Although cotters performed their work on nearly every farm, they were, as already observed, relatively more important on the flatland farms containing ample land upon which to grow crops. On shoreline farms it was servants who played the larger role. Servanthood was usually a life stage among children of local cotters and farmers. It typically lasted from age fifteen to age thirty, although it could begin very early and continue well into middle adulthood if no marriage opportunities intervened. Girls usually began servanthood at an earlier age than boys, and although they generally married younger, women were more likely than men to serve throughout their adult lives.[40] In 1801, for instance, 11% of women servants in Balestrand were under age fifteen and 36% were over age thirty, compared to 8% and 17%, respectively, of the men. The growing population in the nineteenth century, however, did not result in extended periods of servanthood. In Balestrand servant work clearly was more a life's work in 1801 than in 1865, especially for women.[41] In addition to local people, migrants from the east – Valdres and Hallingdal – as well as from neighboring parishes served in Balestrand.[42] Servants' wages were low and often in kind, but servanthood provided a means of providing for oneself, accumulating some capital or a dowry, and gaining valuable work experience.

Whereas cotters' work involved grain production and was mainly performed by men, servant responsibilities were likely to consist of year-round animal work, primarily a woman's duty. In view of the increasing importance of animals in Balestrand, women's work with the animals was of extreme consequence in the farms' operations.[43] Women servants were advantageous to farmers not only because they performed essential animal work, creating products that were increasing in importance, but also because their wages were lower. Ideally, each farming unit had one male servant, one female servant working on domestic tasks, and one milkmaid (budeie). This rule, of course, varied with the size of the farm, but it illustrates the very clear dependence on the labor of female servants and children. In 1865 servants and children over twelve (deemed working members of the community) employed in Tjugum and Mundal numbered 353 men and 483 women (58% female). Moreover, throughout the nineteenth century women servants became more numerous in relation to men servants. In Tjugum, for example, the men per farm unit increased only 7%, compared to a 47% leap among the women.[44]

Clear distinctions were made between men's and women's work among the servants (see Plate 7). In general, women were responsible for the animals and domestic chores and the men for the fodder and the crops. Women performed all work in the cattle barns, including shoveling manure, milking, and carrying water for all the animals. In the fall they clipped the sheep and during the slaughter took care of the blood and entrails. The domestic servants took care of the male workers' needs, including daily food preparation and the care and making of clothes. Men's work was more seasonal.

Plate 7. This relatively late depiction of a Balestrand household shows the retention of a sexual division of labor. The farmer stands proudly in front of his new hay wagon and farm; the male servants are ready to cut hay, while their women counterparts have rakes in hand. *Source*: De Heibergske Samlinger-Sogn Folkemuseum; photographer unknown

They sowed and reaped, set up hayracks, carried the hay down to the tun, leaved the trees, cared for the implements, and built the houses.[45] Activities such as leafing, collecting bark and twigs, and cutting hay were performed by both sexes, but with strict sexual divisions of labor.[46] Although their work was less arduous, women servants worked longer hours than the men. Men took hour-long breaks for dinner; the women cooked and did evening work, such as spinning and carding, that further lengthened the day. And care for the animals – with the shoveling of manure and the carrying of water – often could be very hard work.[47]

When farmers needed workers in addition to their cotters and servants, they hired day laborers. Oftentimes these day laborers were cotters who had completed their obligations to the farmer and were engaged in "free time work" (friarbeid). One cotter might cut an extra four *marketeig* of hay – about six days' work – and receive a ton of herring. Another might harvest grain for about three days and be paid firewood for his efforts.[48] Servants could also work for extra goods after their primary responsibilities to the farmer had been completed – an incentive to get the cutting responsibilities done quickly in order to leave time for extra work.[49]

Farmers increased labor inputs by using cotters primarily in the grain work, servants particularly in animal work, and wage workers when the need arose. Although wage bills increased throughout the century, each farmer could still adjust his costs to his own production emphasis. The cotter households, for example, would have been far too expensive to have been maintained as year-round labor. But since they provided an additional source of labor during busy times in the crop cycle and cost the farmer little, cotters undoubtedly enlarged farm output. The division of labor according to class and sex, moreover, helped to increase worker efficiency. The servants, whose roles became more specialized, became more capable in their work. The milkmaid concentrated on animal tasks, the domestic servant became well versed in inside work, and male servants were more effective in their forage collection and grain labor.

Landless households had fewer options for improving their use of labor. Cotters rarely, if ever, hired laborers to work on their small plots or to collect forage for their limited animal herds. The complex arrangements used by farmers to utilize different types of labor to their fullest were impossible for cotters. Cotters and day laborers had to content themselves instead with increased labor within the household as the primary means of improving output. The landless, however, enjoyed greater opportunities to choose between working on their rented land and laboring for wages as the century progressed.

As farmers enlarged operations, they employed the work force so fully that continual complaints were heard about labor shortages. Even in the 1820s and 1830s farmers had difficulty finding cheap labor, and by 1835 Jacob Aall noted many complaints about the lack of labor, complaints that were reiterated some years later by the official from the district of which Balestrand was a part.[50] The greater demand for labor was largely due to an increased market for the farmers' goods, which encouraged greater production. This, in turn, stimulated a broadened use of land in the area.

The landed were the principal group to increase land, as well as labor, input in Balestrand, not only because market opportunities encouraged an enlarged production but simply because farmers owned the land. Various methods were used to increase and improve their land resources.[51] First, farmers altered their patterns of

Plate 8. Land clearing was one means of increasing field size. Although the work was usually undertaken by servants or cotters, the land owner ultimately benefited most. *Source*: Picture collection, University Library of Bergen; photograph by Knud Knudsen

arable land use. By placing greater emphasis on the wild pastures (utmark) as a source of forage, farmers were able to plant more productive crops in the infields. The innmark in Balestrand became used solely for grain fields as one-time natural pastures near the tun were converted into arable land. The utmark was utilized more and more as a source for naturally growing hay and other types of fodder until eventually almost all forage was gathered there. As often is the case, the more labor-intensive work was offset by a greater wealth of food than had existed earlier.[52]

The second means of creating additional grain fields was related to the first: clearing of new land (see Plate 8). Land, such as natural pastures near the tun, was rid of stones and planted, a step that placed even greater reliance on the utmark as a source of forage. The amount of cultivated land rapidly increased in Norway between 1723 and 1855, with this clearing being particularly important in the nineteenth century as population swelled.[53] Between 1835 and 1845, for example, 208,000 mål (51,400 acres) were cleared in Norway.[54]

Table 4. *Increase in arable land: Tjugum and Mundal parishes, 1802–65*

	Total cropland (mål)	Annual increase (mål)	Land per individual (mål)
1802	1,462.1	—	1.11
1845	2,256.7	18.5	1.30
1855	2,741.6	48.5	1.49
1865	2,845.5	10.4	1.50

Sources: Balestrand manuscript population censuses, 1801, 1845, 1855, 1865; Balestrand land-tax rolls, 1802.

Farmers in the parishes of Tjugum and Mundal participated in this massive clearing of land. According to census reports, land in grain and potato production was enlarged in varying amounts throughout the nineteenth century. In the early years of the century, cropland increased by 18.5 mål (4.6 acres) annually. During the good crop years between 1845 and 1855, land in use rose by 48.5 mål (12.0 acres) per year; the growth lessened in the next ten years to only 10.4 mål (2.6 acres) per year (see Table 4). In spite of an uneven increase, the amount of arable land not only kept pace with the swelling population but actually grew faster. Whereas the area per individual in 1802 was 1.07 mål in Tjugum and 1.17 in Mundal, by 1865 the figures had risen to 1.33 and 1.70, respectively.[55]

Furthermore, reports at mid-century indicated that clearable, un-cropped land still existed in Tjugum and Mundal, but had not yet been improved. According to the *matrikkel* of 1863 (part of a study that changed the tax base), 62.6% of the farm units contained additional land that could have been set into crop production. The land on the one-third (19 of 56) of farms that both asserted the possibility of crop extension and disclosed the amount of land that could be cleared totaled between 429 and 460 mål, about 110 acres.[56] If the other two-thirds had similar quantities of clearable land, the total for Tjugum and Mundal would have been well over 300 acres. In arable land availability in Balestrand, then, the boundaries of development had not been reached by 1863. Because of the massive emigration, little of this clearable land was ultimately put into production. Yet the capacity to augment arable fields reflected a capability to increase production still further if the need had arisen.

The land already in use could also be improved to enlarge the harvest. Such land intensification is difficult to document, but two indicators provide some evidence that it did occur. For one thing, cotter contracts typically specified stone removal as a work responsibility; either land was being cleared, then, or already cropped fields were being improved. Second, the ratio of crops harvested to seed sown remained even throughout the nineteenth century in spite of the clearing of less-productive land. Apparently, improved land and seed varieties offset the poorer land put into production.[57]

Increases in arable land were based on an extension of nonarable sources of fodder. As hayfields were converted into grain land near the tun, the utmark was utilized even more extensively.[58] The greater reliance on the utmark did not overextend resources in Balestrand: Retention of the right to own as many creatures as one could feed through the winter in the common pasture indicates that utmark resources remained adequate.[59] Although farmers could take each other to court over misuse of the utmark, the rich hay and leaf sources apparently obviated any remarkable conflict in Balestrand.[60]

Land use was altered in the utmark as well, in a way that ultimately increased labor efficiency. The spring and mountain støls were lowered so that the higher areas went out of use for grazing around the middle of the century. The lower støl was set around one to two hundred meters above sea level and the mountain støl around three to six hundred meters above sea level – hundreds of meters lower than earlier. By moving the støls closer to the farmstead, farmers got better and longer growth of grass in the spring støl and were able to use the old mountain støl for harvest of winter fodder. Possibly more important, the farmer could use the milkmaid's labor more efficiently by having her nearer the tun. When times of busy activity occurred, she could move more easily from her støl abode to areas of work where her help was needed.[61]

As usual, cotters and other landless households faced greater constraints in increasing land inputs. The farmer, of course, owned the land on which the cotter worked, so he had to give his consent before the cotter could begin land clearing. Yet since farmers could in this way increase their arable land resources without adding any labor input of their own, they often permitted their cotters to extend their lands. One cotter in Mundal parish, for example, had a "rubbish place [*harka plass*]" where he at first got only dry hay but where he eventually had a potato field of one hundred square meters.[62] Unlike the landed, however, cotters had to determine whether their labor was better employed working for wages or clearing additional land that ultimately would belong to the farm owner. Often they chose the former course.

Farmers were also the principal users of capital, the third input. Although their personal property did not include large-scale ownership of major implements such as threshers or reapers until late in nineteenth-century Balestrand, farmers significantly altered their use of less capital-intensive properties.[63] The ard remained the most important plowing implement in Balestrand, even gaining importance from the 1770s to the 1850s because of its maneuverability in the smaller strips on the farms.[64] Yet while official reports noted use of the ard, they also commented on the increased use of plows, harrows, and sowing machines in the early nineteenth century. Especially when prices were good, as in the early 1850s, farmers were able to mechanize their operations to a greater degree.[65] These changes continued as plows and iron harrows were used in place of the ard beginning in the 1860s. Improved use of fertilizer also enlarged production.[66]

More significant still was an increased reliance on harrows and especially wheeled vehicles between 1800 and 1850. In a sample of probate records on a number of farms in Sogn, the assessed value of plows, harrows, and wheeled vehicles increased 123% in the fifty years to an average worth of 5.8 *speciedalars* (or about $6.30; the speciedaler [spd.], the main monetary unit in Norway from the early sixteenth century until the mid-1870s, was worth 120 skillings [skill.], 1 of which equaled about $0.009). Fartein Valen-Sendstad has argued that because implements improved between 1800 and 1850 throughout Norway, the country's agriculture had reached a transitional stage by 1800 in which improved means of production yielded larger returns and laid the foundation for new standards.[67]

The farmer class, through trade of its crop and animal product surpluses, also accrued supplies of capital that could be invested – for instance, in improved implements. Although Norway's first savings bank was not founded until 1822, Balestrand had its own by 1847.[68] The bank became an institution that helped temper poor years and provided capital for investment in good ones. Between 1856 and 1860, for example, when the land prices rose as a result of the good harvests, the amount in the Balestrand savings bank increased 42.9%, from 15,287 to 21,846 speciedalars. As with labor and land, farmers were the major beneficiaries of increasing capital resources. With property that was mortgageable, they had greater access to loans that they could invest in improvements, whereas the cotters continued to rely on their subsistence agriculture. Moreover, farmers, possessing capital reserves, had insurance against disasters that could befall their increasingly specialized operations.[69]

Changing strategies of production among landed and landless

The farming class that controlled the landed wealth in Balestrand thus visibly enlarged its inputs of labor, land, and capital to increase farm production. By hiring additional workers, expanding the use of arable and nonarable land, and investing in better implements, farmers increased production of goods that fed the household and, more important, were also traded. These landholders augmented their wealth throughout the nineteenth century as they exported more goods from Balestrand. The landless classes faced greater constraints on enlarging inputs of labor and land on their small rented plots. Yet they were often able to choose between paid labor for landholders who needed their services and work on their home fields. Apparently they increased both, as cotter production per capita grew and wage labor and craft specialization were extended as well. Landed and landless households varied their production strategies in response to these constraints and opportunities. Farmers raised goods that both were in demand as exports and produced well on their particular farms. Cotters, who by and large did not trade their agricultural products, raised the animals and grew the crops that provided the greatest return.

Landowning households realized that an expansion of crops had to be accompanied by additional animals that would supply necessary fertilizer.[70] Owing to Balestrand's reliance on cattle for both shoreline and flatland farms, however, the increased land was amply fertilized.[71] Balestrand shoreline and flatland farms were therefore able to create strikingly dissimilar crop and animal patterns by the nineteenth century. Between 1723 and 1802 the growth in animal units (*kyrlag*, units that weigh the various animal types according to their consumption of forage and thus allow comparisons of whole animal holdings: ½ horse = 1 cow = 4 hogs = 6 sheep) and grain sown in both farm types paralleled one another (see Table 5). Only in Mundal parish was the increase in animal units significantly larger in shoreline farms. In the first six decades of the nineteenth century, however, a pattern of greater specialization developed. The flatland farms in both Tjugum and Mundal increasingly relied on grains, whereas the shoreline farms owned larger herds of animals. Farmers concentrated on goods best suited

Table 5. *Annual increase in animal units and grain sown according to farmland type: Tjugum and Mundal parishes, 1723–1865 (%)*

	Tjugum				Mundal			
	Shoreline animal	Shoreline grain	Flatland animal	Flatland grain	Shoreline animal	Shoreline grain	Flatland animal	Flatland grain
1723–1802	0.40	0.41	0.42	0.44	0.67	0.44	0.49	0.38
1802–65	0.25	0.02	0.32	0.92	0.68	0.28	0.68	1.66

Source: Derived from Gunnar Urtegaard, "Jordbruksdrift og Sosial Lagdeling i Balestrand frå 1500 til 1865" (major thesis, Universitetet i Bergen, 1980), pp. 151–52, 160–61.

to their resources while they exploited the labor types that most closely fit their production needs. Accordingly, servants increased rapidly on shoreline farms, and flatland farms used cotters to a greater degree.[72]

By specializing according to their land resources, farmers concentrated on the goods best suited to increase productivity of their land. Census reports indicate that they were successful in increasing production. In Tjugum parish, for example, grain produced per farm unit annually increased from 19.9 to 28.1 hectoliters between 1802 and 1865 – a growth of 41.2%. In Mundal the expansion was an even greater 58.3%, as grain production per unit grew from 21.6 to 34.2 hectoliters. The number of animal units per farm showed a similar increase of 30.2% in Tjugum, from 19.2 to 25.0, and of 56.5% in Mundal, from 21.6 to 33.8. Equally important, output per household member was also growing, albeit at a slower clip, ranging from 16.8% to 33.1% annually in grains and from 6.9% to 32.1% in animal units.[73] By 1865 this increased production had created an estimated calorie output for crops alone, per household member per day, ranging from 3,356.9 in Tjugum to 3,842.0 in Mundal, an ample food supply for the working population. The total output, however, was not consumed by the farm population. Although household members were probably provided with adequate nutrition, much of the produce was traded to create additional income for the increasingly wealthy farming class.[74]

Trade had been essential to the Balestrand economy decades before the beginning of the nineteenth century.[75] Throughout their history, neither Balestrand nor Inner Sogn as a whole had produced enough grain to feed the people, despite growing populations of farmers. Food grains were acquired by trading excess dairy goods, potatoes, and wood at market or in Bergen. With greater production, however, grain imports to Sogn decreased in the nineteenth century (see Table 6).[76] Farmers could exchange more of their surpluses for luxuries or sell them for cash.

As grain imports declined, exports of potatoes, animal products, fruit, and wood increased rapidly. Potato exports remained consistent throughout the middle of the nineteenth century but had become quite large by the late 1860s. Likewise, though the export of live animals remained steady and even declined in some instances, animal product exports were rapidly increasing by the mid-nineteenth century. Fruit and wood were also developing as export goods at this time. Although apples were widely reported as exports by the 1830s, export of fruits greatly expanded in the middle of the

Table 6. Annual imports and exports: Sogn, 1841–70

Period	Grain imports (tønder)	Potatoes (tønder)	Fruit (value in spd.)	Exports						
				Horses (head)	Cattle (head)	Sheep/goats (head)	Pigs (head)	Butter (bismerpunder)[b]	Tallow (bismerpunder)	Cheese (bismerpunder)
1841–45	10,000	6,000	—	480	4,000	1,500	—	8,000	3,500	3,500
1846–50	10,000	4,000	1,000	500	4,000	4,000	—	10,000	3,500	—
1851–55	8,000	6,000–7,000	2,000	300	2,500–3,000	4,000	500	9,000	3,500	3,000
1856–60	6,000	—	3,000–4,000	400	2,500	3,500	400	20,000[c]	6,000[c]	8,000[c]
1861–65	—[a]	—	—	200	2,800	4,000	—	20,000	10,000	4,000
1866–70	8,400	24,000	—	250	1,600	—	—	33,000	—	4,000

[a]Dashes indicate that data are missing from reports.
[b]One bismerpund equals approximately twelve pounds.
[c]Figures are for both Sogn and Fjordane.
Source: Amtmannsberetninger (the five-year reports from the district of which Sogn was a part).

century.[77] Wood was the safety valve for poor crop years. Although Balestrand households did not possess the rich supplies of wood found in other areas, they cut burning and building wood for trade as well as home use. The prominent role the wood trade could play in a local economy is illustrated by neighboring Leikanger, which had a rich wood source. A Leikanger official in 1865 valued the yearly export of wood at around 5,250 spd., nearly equal to the combined export values of animal products, worth 2,100 spd., and animals, worth about 4,260 spd.[78] Poor crop or animal years were partially recouped by increased cutting and trade of wood resources. Balestrand's totals surely did not near those of Leikanger, but the trade in wood between Sogn and Bergen that began as early as 1820 was still thriving in the 1870s.[79]

Not only were Balestrand farmers enjoying greater trade, but prices were improving to their advantage. Meat and, to a lesser extent, animal product prices were rising in the cities.[80] Changes in the 1850s increased returns on food up to 100% in four years in spite of increasing outputs.[81] While prices of farm goods were rising, those of wares purchased by farmers declined between the 1830s and around 1850. Industrial goods were cheaper, and salt and sugar, as well as other grocery items, also fell in price.[82]

Because landless households did not possess the resources to produce goods for trade, they attempted to feed themselves as well as possible with their own farm products and to supplement them with outside work. Cotters were the most fortunate landless group, but even their rights to the farm's resources were strictly limited in the contract with the farm. Anders Nilsen of Thue farm in Tjugum parish, for example, could crop the land around the house he built. He was allowed to use two small fields on which in 1865 he sowed about one-fifth *tønne* of barley (about eighteen kilograms) and one-half *tønne* of potatoes (about fifty-eight kilograms). He also received an area for hay, the right to leaf one hundred baskets of birch leaves, and the rights to the wood he could find. His animals could graze on the home pastures before they went to the støl in the spring, and they could use the farm's spring and mountain støls during the summer.[83] This strictly defined use of resources continually placed the cotter in a less enviable situation than the farmer. When gathering forage in the utmark, for example, cotters had to go higher up in the mountains, a procedure that was more laborious and also provided less rich fodder resources.[84]

Cotters faced other limitations to enlarging production in addition to those placed on them by their farmers. Many cotters, even if they did receive permission to enlarge their fields, did not have adequate capital to create a production apparatus for an expanded scale of operation. A cotter without horses, for example, was forced to rely on his farmer, who would lend out his animals when they were not needed.[85] Since they lacked mortgageable property, cotters had difficulty in obtaining credit if they wished to expand.[86]

Because of their constrained situation, cotters emphasized animals and crops different from those preferred by farmers. Like the landed, they had to use both arable and nonarable land in order to produce an animal and crop mix. But cotters raised products that were either prolific or suited to poorer resources, a practice that led them to concentrate on sheep and potatoes. Not only were sheep cheaper to buy, but they could be raised on greater proportions of leaves and twigs than cattle. In 1865, 21.3% of the sheep in Balestrand were held by cotters, compared to only 12.1% of the cattle.[87] Likewise, cotters planted potatoes instead of grains. Potatoes were particularly advantageous since they were resistant to frost, could be grown higher up on the hillsides and in less fertile lands than grains, and were more prolific per land unit than grains. Moreover, since potatoes could be harvested for longer periods, the cotter's responsibilities to the farmer during the grain harvest were less likely to interfere with his own harvest. Whereas the harvest ratio of grain and potatoes was around 1:1 in farming households, it was 1:6 in those of cotters.[88] The cotters used the little area they controlled to create as much food as possible, food that was consumed at home. As late as 1900 a Leikanger medical report noted that "it is the same traditional diet again and again, day after day, herring (or fish), potatoes, and flatbread served in the same mode."[89]

In spite of the emphasis on sheep and potatoes, the cotters' production was rising in all respects in the nineteenth century. The number of cotter households in Balestrand increased from 71 to 160 between 1802 and 1865, yet grain production rose from 1.25 hectoliters per household in 1802 to 1.95 in 1865. Animal units per household increased even more, from 2.77 to 4.51; and potato production, not reported in 1802, provided an additional 10.3 hectoliters per place by 1865. Production per individual expanded as well, with an increase in grain from 0.30 hectoliters in 1802 to 0.41 in 1865, in addition to the 2.2 hectoliters of potatoes per individual by 1865. The number of animal units rose from 0.65 per individual in 1802 to 0.88 in 1865. Cotters in Tjugum and Mundal parishes experienced even more rapid growth than those in Vangsnes. Animal units per cotter household member in Mundal, for example, doubled in these sixty-three years. Although landholders' production was growing faster than that of cotters, cotter households still enjoyed greater production than in the past, in spite of their increasing number.[90]

Despite their greater self-sufficiency in agriculture, the independence of the cotters must not be overstated. In 1865 the nutritional value of home food production per cotter household member averaged only around one thousand calories and forty grams of protein per day, much below the minimum standards needed to survive.[91] Cotter household members supplemented food production by hunting and fishing, but more important were wage labor opportunities that also were expanding in the nineteenth century.

Cotters had traditionally worked as wage laborers in the Balestrand society. They often performed additional summer agricultural labor for the farmer when their duties had been fulfilled or expanded their work year into the winter by cutting wood, a task for which they were usually paid in kind.[92] Throughout the nineteenth century, however, not only did opportunities for wage labor increase, but craft work became an increasingly important part of many cotters' incomes. Traditionally, crafts had largely been the cotter's domain, but greater wealth and specialization among farmers created an even greater demand for cotter handicrafts throughout the nineteenth century. While some cotter craftsmen created much of the church art, others concentrated on more functional crafts, such as coopering, carpentry, or basketmaking, which were usually more lucrative.[93] When farmers repaired their buildings, talented cotter carpenters were often hired. Cotter coopers traded grain for barrel work and were paid well, receiving the volume of grain their barrels would hold. The opportunities for craftwork are illustrated by the situation of a cotter who became frustrated with the heavy demands of his work obligations to a farmer and quit to go full time into carpentry, a decision he subsequently wished he had made earlier.[94]

Cotter households were increasing their crop outputs throughout the nineteenth century, but if we assume that 2,600 calories per day is a normal level of nutrition, over 60% of the cotters' calorie intake had to come from outside their own food production. Most of the added nutrition was obtained through extra labor to farmers and through increasingly important crafts. The number of full-time handworkers in Balestrand grew from eleven to thirty-three between 1801 and 1835, but many cotters were part-time craftsmen in

Table 7. *Servant and day laborer wages: Sogn, 1836–70*

	Yearly servant wages (in spd.)		Daily day laborer wages (in skill.)	
	Men	Women	Men	Women
1836–40	6–10[a]	2–4[a]	24	16
1841–45	13–19	6–8	24	16
1846–50	15–20	8–12	24–34	—[b]
1851–55	16–24	10–15	20–34	—
1856–60	20–30	12–16	30–48	18–20
1861–65	20–30	12–16	30–48	18–20
1866–70	20–30	10–20	36–60	—

[a]Plus clothes.
[b]Dashes indicate no data.
Source: Amtmannsberetninger.

occupations with growing opportunities throughout the nineteenth century.

Day laborers, "cotters without land [*husmenn uten jord*]" (a class developed by 1845, the members of which rented only the houses they lived in), and "shore-sitters [*strandsidderer*]", all of whom were without land to farm, were totally dependent on the greater wage labor in Balestrand. After working in these capacities for a number of years, they often became cotters with rented land, acquiring a more certain future. Yet with increasing utilization of land and need for labor, even these classes enjoyed an improved well-being in the nineteenth century. Although Sogn's administrative official wrote that the district was overpopulated in 1845, he also noted farmers' complaints that there were not enough servants.[95] Wage statistics for day laborers in Sogn confirm the farmers' grievances (see Table 7). The average day labor wages for both men and women increased steadily throughout the century. The one surviving report from Leikanger listed wage rates similar to those offered throughout Sogn.[96] The need for labor continued; the Sogn official called emigration one of the three major problems for the communities in the late 1840s.[97] The farmers' dilemma – how to create an adequate labor force – benefited the landless laborers, whose wages increased and who could expect longer periods of work.

Servants were also enjoying improved circumstances throughout the nineteenth century. The age structure of servanthood indicates that by 1865 fewer people worked their whole lives in service than in 1802.[98] Men and particularly women were leaving this transitional life stage in larger percentages to work in adult occupations as farmers, cotters, or day laborers.[99] Specific wage data for servants are difficult to find for Balestrand, but reports from the officials of Sogn indicate that wages were rising from the earliest reports in the 1830s well into the 1870s (see Table 7). Moreover, as the demand for women servants increased, their wages rose faster than those of men servants.[100] A relationship might exist between shorter periods of servanthood and higher pay: Since they worked to gain dowries or accumulate a little capital, servants with increased wages may have reached their goals sooner and been able to marry earlier.

Conclusion

Both landless and landed groups experienced better, more certain standards of living throughout the first two-thirds of the nineteenth century. Owning large farms, the landed were able to exploit augmented trade opportunities by improving the use of additional labor in order to increase production.[101] As the farms grew larger, the landless enjoyed expanded opportunities for wage labor. Cotters increased not only their wage incomes but their harvests as well. Certainly work was more strenuous and hours were longer, but the improved well-being that resulted offset greater labor input. The large emigration from Balestrand thus was not simply due to an overextension of resources and underemployment, as many historians have claimed.

Emigration occasionally was an escape for landed farmers whose farming operation had failed. Just as the landed and landless utilized varying strategies for material improvement, they faced varying risks. The poor crop years that occurred in 1825, 1847, 1869, and 1879, as well as inflammatory sicknesses among cattle and a potato blight, reduced farm production.[102] For the landless, smaller harvests had to be supplemented by additional wage work. If rents were not paid, cotters could lose their places, or, worse yet, ultimately end in poor relief. Farmers, however, faced greater pecuniary risks from economic setbacks, especially as the nineteenth century wore on. Farm transfers in a fifty-year period in the mid-nineteenth century, for example, indicate that purchasers of farms in Mundal parish were paying nearly twice as much per tax unit at

Table 8. *Relative cost of farms: Mundal parish, 1838–88*

	Price paid per taxable unit[a]		
	Mean	Median	N
1838–48	1.45	1.25	15
1849–58	1.81	1.72	29
1859–68	2.20	2.05	16
1869–78	2.69	2.50	18
1879–88	2.75	3.08	14

[a]The measure is derived by dividing the price paid (in spd.) by the taxable value of the farm (in *skill.* of *skyld* [tax]).
Source: Panteregister (list of mortgages).

the end of the period (see Table 8).[103] Just as mortgages increased owing to these higher land prices, individual farm owners also paid large retirement obligations to former owners (kår) and increasing wages to workers. The farmers' burdensome responsibilities at times strained their abilities to meet all their expenses.[104] And the greater speculation that frequently accompanied increased market activity did little to reduce financial difficulties when poor crop years occurred.[105]

Some farmers emigrated to avoid economic difficulties. One early emigrant not from Balestrand, for example, as first son was entitled to one of the best farms in his community. "But it was encumbered with a debt of fourteen hundred dollars . . . It was obvious that I would assure myself a hopeless future by taking charge of the farm with its heavy indebtedness, buying out my brothers and sisters . . . and, finally, providing a pension for my father."[106] Instead, he emigrated.

Isolated instances of economic failure, however, were not the underlying cause of the widespread emigration from Balestrand. In spite of increasing wealth and opportunity, structural changes that encouraged emigration were occurring. Just as the economic system was undergoing a period of transition, so were social configurations adapting to different conditions. The landed and landless, who used dissimilar economic strategies, also altered their patterns of courtship, marriage, and household formation within their different parameters of opportunity. It was these changing equations in the complex interrelationships among inheritance, economic activity, and fertility, as we will see in the next chapter, rather than simple economic factors, that made emigration inviting. Many from the farmer, cotter, and laboring classes ultimately judged it to be comparatively advantageous to leave Balestrand for the vast stretches of open land in the American Middle West.

5 Inheritance, marriage, fertility, and economic growth: social development of Balestrand, 1800– 1865

An American tourist happened upon a momentous series of events for the Husum farm in Borgund, Sogn, in 1871. Following a family dinner shortly after the death of the wife of the household head, discussion around the table became subdued as the eldest son tried to convince his father that it was time to give up the farm. The father first remonstrated and finally acquiesced after the other children sided with their brother. Henceforth the heir would sit at the head of the table, and he and his wife would decide the important issues of farm production. The legal background of this transfer, however, was more complicated. The eldest son had married in 1860, at which time he received half of the farm. He and his wife worked this half for a trial period, a common practice in Norway before the whole farm was transferred. Six years later the kårkontrakt was drawn up to define the conditions when the transfer occurred. It was only in 1871, when the mother died and another head woman was needed to run the female activities of the farm, that the older man – still only fifty-three years of age – was forced to relinquish his position of leadership. After eleven years the son finally got full control; he finally sat in the seat of prestige at the end of the table; and the kårkontrakt finally went into effect.[1]

This example is rare only to the extent that it was so well documented. Generations reaching back to 1315, when the first kårkontrakt was drafted, and especially after the mid-eighteenth century, when lengthened life expectancy increased the need to transfer the farm before the father's death, had participated in this emotional passage that bequeathed prestige as well as property.[2] The process, moreover, was common not only throughout Norway but in much of northwestern Europe as well. In the European Middle Ages it was customary for old people to give up their land to an heir before they died; they surrendered their authority but expected their keep from the land.[3] This arrangement, which became institutionalized in the kårkontrakt in Norway, also played a powerful role in reducing the length of marriage and the possibility of children. In general, the time of the heir's marriage was dependent on the land's being turned over to him. In a system of primogeniture, his siblings were even more constrained: They could be nourished and remain on the farm, but they could not marry until they acquired livelihoods that would sustain new families.[4]

The inextricable interrelationships between inheritance and marriage thus created a tendency toward later marriage ages, which in turn shortened the period during which a fertile woman was married. A systematic restraint on fertility was intricately tied to the transfer of estates. Ideally, during periods of economic stress, when opportunities for livelihoods became more rare, marriage ages rose and lifelong celibacy increased; fertility was thereby lowered. Conversely, in times of opportunity, marriage age would decline, more children would be born, and population would increase.[5] In times of high adult mortality, children usually inherited estates sooner and married younger, whereas a rising adult life expectancy, on the other hand, would delay marriage.

Changing conditions in Balestrand in the eighteenth and nineteenth centuries encouraged dissimilar patterns of marriage and inheritance among varying segments of the society. Demographic pressures from lower infant mortality and increasing life expectancy forced adjustments. The kårkontrakt was utilized more often as household heads lived longer. Its use allowed children to take control of the farm and marry while parents who continued to live were cared for. If heirs had been forced to wait until parental death, their household formation might have been delayed so long that some would probably have relinquished their inheritances in order to marry.[6]

Likewise, as a greater proportion of children reached adulthood, more livelihoods upon which to base marriages had to be created. Since farms usually remained intact throughout intergenerational transfer in Balestrand, many sons and daughters of the landed became cotters, remaining unmarried until a place opened or until one was cleared. The children of cotters, like their parents, also had to find places within the occupational structure that would feed their families before marriage was permitted.

The growing economic structure, however, which allowed an increasing population to be fed, also created an additional wealth of livelihoods upon which to base marriages. The conjunction of a greater availability of livelihoods with the traditional patterns of household formation among the increasingly large landless group altered mechanisms that had maintained a high marriage age, especially among the economically weaker segments of the society. Earlier marriage in turn tended to enlarge the size of increasingly numerous landless households. Although the paths chosen by the landless were rational in the short term, they created potentially less sanguine futures for their children.

The combination of new economic and demographic realities thus led to changing strategies of household formation, especially among the landless. Just as they had to create their places in society, the landless had to find and court suitable mates. Parents of landless youth, who bequeathed a small legacy, had less control over their children than landed parents. Courting and marriage among the landless proceeded as quickly as livelihoods could be patched together. Traditional methods of courting, which included bundling, often resulted in children born outside wedlock.

Dissimilar economic strategies among the landless and landed were thus replicated in the social sphere. The outcome of changing social norms among the landless exacerbated cleavages within the community. Greater incidence of illegitimate births, for example, resulted in moral and legal arguments – led primarily by the landed – against their increasing occurrence. Other moral divisions developed within the landless group itself, which experienced both religious awakenings and the creation of subcultures with behavior antithetical to customary local Christian peasant patterns. The adaptations among the landless were adjustments to new social realities. But they resulted in concern about future livelihood possibilities and in strains within contemporary society, both of which ultimately encouraged emigration and affected patterns within the American immigrant communities. In order to understand the developing social structure and its relation to emigration, we must first examine traditional strategies of courtship, marriage, and inheritance.

Traditional patterns of courtship, marriage, and household formation

A peasant marriage, which was based on the availability of an occupation, served both as a contract between a man and a woman and as an intergenerational transfer of wealth tying two family lineages together through legal and religious sanctions. Choice of marriage partners was agreed upon by the individuals who married and by their parents, who transferred the wealth. The influence of either group in determining the potential spouse varied, but ultimately the parents' power was based on their control of wealth.

Even in areas such as Balestrand, where youth were instrumental in courtship, marriage was probably based less on romantic love than on wealth or abilities. A Swedish vicar in the 1840s looking back noted that in Sweden, as in Norway,

> similarities in wealth rather than in ideas or personal preferences was the foundation of marriage among peasants in those days. Least of all beauty and grace decided the outcome. Terms like these did not even have equivalents in peasant idiom . . . I have heard talk of a charming horse and even a charming pig, but never yet of a charming girl.[7]

Marriage was also a contract between two members of different work groups essential to the functioning of a household. The sexes had very basic labor responsibilities and different patterns of life, such as birthing, that set men and women apart yet created a mutual need. Note that the transfer of the Husum farm occurred when the wife died and a female head was needed in the household. Indeed, "the material progress of the family," according to Sundt, "depended as much upon the wife as upon the husband."[8]

Even if love was not the primary factor, courting was important for finding partners whose wealth and skills would improve the couple's prospects after marriage. Since peasant custom strongly constrained open affection in public, the courting custom of bundling developed not only in Norway, including Balestrand, but in much of Europe as well.[9] Young men visited women in their rooms on Saturday, the single night when they were free to leave their farm homes. Courting could begin as young as one's early teens, but only older servants considering marriage became sexually intimate. Eventually, "night courting [*nattfrieri*]" relationships might mature to the point at which the man would spend the night with his female host. Suitors often visited servant women for years without marriage plans coming to fruition. Only when there were prospects of a livelihood and marriage could engagement and sexual intercourse be considered. Night courting thus provided some privacy for avoiding the ridicule and jokes that were directed at a young couple who showed too much affection in public, and thereby laid the foundations for marriage (see Plate 9).[10]

The character of the night courting depended on the intimacy of the couple and upon the regional culture in which they lived, but its course was quite structured. Sundt, in a detailed explication of one typical example, pictured the courtship process. After four Saturday visits, the man woke the woman late at night and they talked outside her room. The next visit they entered her chamber and conversed on a bench "whilst a couple of girls and a boy [snored]

Plate 9. Courtship was a private matter between young men and women. Open displays of affection were frowned upon, and privacy, as the presence of the young boys in this photograph attests, was difficult to find. Night courting thus was a solution. *Source*: Picture collection, University Library of Bergen; photograph by Knud Knudsen

around them in the room." By the sixth Saturday, the two sat or lay on her bed, but on the seventh, he "[flung] his arms about her neck, [repeated] all his good promises, [got] her consent and [fell] asleep." These visits continued until the couple eventually was privately engaged, but, Sundt added, the secret could not be "kept secret very long" – undoubtedly a euphemism for her pregnant state. The custom, Sundt argued, was the only way young people of the servant class became "acquainted," and it was "completed in all modesty and faithfulness"; it was a mistake to assume that "girls who take to their lovers in this way are girls without modesty."[11]

Night courting patterns could vary widely from region to region. One youth who was about to get into bed with a woman took off his coat and shoes according to his village's customs. The woman was from another region with different norms, however, and cried, "if you're going to take off your coat, next will be your trousers," as she ran from the room.[12] Servanthood remained a time for finding a partner while working to establish some economic basis for marriage. As couples became "acquainted," many women became pregnant, a state that was legitimized by marriage.[13]

Balestrand, as a part of Sogn, was within a region famous for its permissive night courting practices. As early as the mid-eighteenth century, the Norwegian theologian Erik Pontoppidan visited Inner Sogn and complained about disorder in the cowbarn, a euphemism for night courting, and the objectional practices (*uskikk*) that resulted.[14] Well into the nineteenth century accounts concerning Balestrand remained the same. On July 9, 1819, a government report noted the basically faultless (*ulastelige*) moral behavior, arguing that the single disorder was the old custom of young men visiting women at nighttime, which was improper (*uanstaendigt*) and clearly would lead to licentiousness (*ryggesløshet*). That same year Edvard Quale wrote the bishop about the common night courting in Sogn. Quale was afraid that ridding the region of the custom would be very difficult because night courting was so old and deep-rooted that youth continued to consider it harmless (*uskyldig*).[15]

Night courting patterns were facilitated by the lack of supervision of servants. Female servants throughout Norway generally slept in the cowbarn loft in the winter and moved out to sleep in the haybarn (*løa*), the *støl*, or the storehouse beginning in May.[16] In Balestrand both male and female servants slept in the cowbarn loft or in the *fjøskammers* (rooms on the *fjøs* [cowbarn] floor) beginning in November. These rooms had two beds – one for the servant girl and one for the boy. Well into the 1880s grown children of the farm owner also slept in the loft. Lodging quarters in the fjøs provided warmth during winter and better supervision of the cows who had begun to calve. But the custom was unsanitary, and the absence of parental supervision of the youth left the clergy in a state of dismay.[17]

In the summer men moved up to cut the hay and often stayed on the støls. After the milkmaid had helped with the daily cutting, she returned to the higher mountain støl. Very often she invited one of the men to the støl in the evening in order to "help her with the animals," and he obviously slept there with her that night.[18] The official class became more concerned about night courting as the nineteenth century wore on and often blamed the sleeping arrangements for its presence. Sundt wrote of a farmer who had recently built a new cattle house with four bunk beds. When Sundt asked him if he had eight milkmaids, he was incredulous when the farmer answered no, the girls slept on the bottom and the boys on the top so that each could keep watch on the other's behavior.[19]

The community and family intervened in the courtship process, especially if wealth would be transferred through the marriage. When people thought it was time for a couple to marry, they held a *bjølleleik,* a ringing of bells to bother the couple when the suitor was with the woman.[20] The sanctions of the parents, who would provide their children with inheritances, were obviously more binding. Fathers exercised their rights to give away children – especially daughters – at times without their acquiescence. Children often lamented, but usually accepted, their parents' choice of marriage partners. In Telemark, for example, after a boy had become engaged to a widow from the region of Hallingdal, his father set up a marriage to a wealthy widow in his home community. The defiant boy said to his fiancée on the day of the settlement, "To you I have given my hand, but my heart lies back in Hallingdal." The song of another youth who also complied against her wishes reiterated the complaints of the boy: "How does it help to have farm and land, when I must have one I grudge; how does it help to have fields and pasture, when I whimper each night in bed?"[21]

Although such intergenerational conflicts could occur, parents and children usually agreed upon the mate. After the decision to marry had been made, there began a complex set of negotiations between families. The most important agreement was the engagement, the truloving, which was usually contracted during a festive holiday such as Christmas or Easter. The bride- and bridegroom-to-be, together with two witnesses, were recorded in the church book, where the date of the truloving was often given greater emphasis than that of the marriage itself. Marriage usually followed at midsummer about three to six months later, for when the truloving had been contracted, few engagements were broken.[22] And because the engagement was so binding, sexual relations between the engaged couple were sanctioned.[23]

Night courting and the interval between the truloving and marriage both resulted in a significant incidence of prenuptially conceived children, but the nature of premarital sex in the two cases was quite distinct. On the one hand, premarital sexual relations and prenuptially conceived children among engaged couples were legitimized by the marriage that occurred before the child's birth.[24] Sexual relationships were not a stage in the search for a mate, but rather began only after the search had been completed. Likewise, the bride did not marry because she was pregnant but allowed herself to become pregnant because she was about to marry.[25]

On the other hand, illegitimate children, resulting from night courting among suitors who had no livelihoods and could not marry, were more troublesome. Although elaborate engagements pre-dominated among the landed, prenuptial births occurred more often among servants from landless groups. Yet attempts were made in eighteenth-century Norway to legitimize children through later marriage. In Etne, for example, 170 of the 220 premarital pregnancies between 1715 and 1797 were eventually followed by marriage.[26] The strong demand for legitimacy based on Christian theology created a means for society to safeguard itself from unwanted births as well as to protect the potential marriage partners.[27] So long as livelihoods were attainable and intimate night courting was ultimately based on marriage, parents worked to legitimize their offspring.

Typical patterns of marriage had built-in mechanisms that worked to reduce the incidence of illegitimacy. Ideally, the wedding was held around St. Hans' Day (Midsummer Day). Between heavy work periods, midsummer featured good weather, long days, abundant food, and empty cowbarns, since the cattle were at the støl.[28] The truloving, as a rule, had occurred three to six months earlier and the bride was often pregnant, but few June brides had already delivered babies.[29] Of the marriages in Etne between 1715 and 1801, for example, only 14% of the women having June–July marriages had had children before the ceremony, though an additional 42% were pregnant.[30] In Balestrand, between 1820 and 1839, June was the only marriage month for which more first births of the marriages were legitimate than illegitimate or prenuptially conceived (see Table 9).[31]

Conception, however, occasionally occurred before the engagement was contracted, an event that disrupted the marriage pattern. Couples in this situation were pressured to marry. Marriages in October and November – a period when conditions were less desirable than the early summer days of June and July – indicate pregnancies that began in the summer months without proper truloving. Though marriage partners would probably have preferred a June wedding, their child would have been born before the summer came. The November wedding served as a safety valve, an accommodation to the demands of the Christian church by sexually active youth in a peasant community in which marriage properly regulated sexuality.[32]

Whereas certain mechanisms legitimized firstborn children, others contributed to the creation of larger households among the more wealthy than among the poor. Most obviously, poorer men tended to choose older women, partly because they were more experienced

Table 9. *Conception of first child according to month of marriage of mother: Mundal parish, 1820–79 (numbers of children)*

	1820–39		1840–59		1860–79	
	Legit.	Illegit./ prenup. conc.	Legit.	Illegit./ prenup. conc.	Legit.	Illegit./ prenup. conc.
Jan.	0	2	0	1	2	4
Feb.	0	4	1	3	0	1
Mar.	0	0	1	0	0	0
Apr.	1	8	4	10	2	6
May	1	1	5	6	10	4
June	15	12	21	24	11	8
July	8	8	13	3	8	4
Aug.	0	0	0	0	0	0
Sep.	0	0	1	0	0	1
Oct.	3	6	1	8	4	0
Nov.	2	2	1	5	2	0
Dec.	0	1	0	4	0	1

Note: Illegitimate births were those that occurred before the parents married. Prenuptially conceived births were those taking place less than nine months after marriage.
Source: Balestrand church records.

in work but also because, as one cotter said, "I thought that when I took such an old woman, the crowd of young ones would not be so great, for it is difficult for one who is in small circumstances to feed so many."[33] In addition, however, prospects of wealth inclined well-to-do women to marry sooner than those without means. Since a landed family's child would eventually inherit a portion of her parents' wealth, she was valued more highly in the marriage market. Hence the marriage age of a woman who would probably wed a landed farmer tended to be lower than that of a woman destined to be a cotter's wife. Farmers' wives in Balestrand were married 4.3 years younger than cotters' wives on the average in the 1820s, and those in eighteenth-century Etne were 4.7 years younger.[34] By marrying later, cotters' wives had around five fewer years in which to conceive children, and the delay thus provided a powerful check on the economically weaker segments of the population.[35] The ties among courtship, marriage, and inheritance, then, helped to maintain a relatively egalitarian peasant world in Balestrand.

*Changing patterns of courtship, marriage, and household formation in
the nineteenth century*

The accelerating population growth in nineteenth-century Balestrand directly affected the relationships among courtship, marriage, and inheritance. As life expectancy increased and infant
mortality decreased, more occupations upon which to form households had to be created or fertility had to be reduced.[36] If we accept
the thesis that "families tended to use every demographic means
possible to maximize their opportunities and to avoid relative loss of
status,"[37] we see that behavior in Sogn and a neighboring district
displayed two very dissimilar patterns to adjust to the changed circumstances. Eilert Sundt, in his work on "morality" in Norway,
extensively examined the adjacent regions of Sogn and Sunnfjord,
which confronted the modified demographic realities of the nineteenth century with different strategies. At one time, according to
Sundt, households in the two areas employed similar systems of
courtship, marriage, and inheritance. But by the middle of the nineteenth century, when Sundt made his investigations, he perceived
the "boundary between Sunnfjord and Sogn" as "a point where
two very different cultural [*folkelive*] conditions meet."[38]

Families in Sunnfjord practiced methods absent in Sogn to control
fertility and assure marriage and a good livelihood for each heir.
One Sunnfjord custom, for example, separated married couples
when the wives went to Bergen to work as wet nurses and thereby
increased intervals between births. Parents, because they had fewer
offspring, could retain greater control over the marital decisions of
their children. Courtship was conducted by an *omtalsmænd* (spokes-
man), but parents had complete command over marriage partners
and timing in their efforts to assure desirable livelihoods for their
children.[39] Such circumstances decreased and sometimes obviated
the importance of night courting. When marriages were arranged
for children at a young age, for example, night courting could not
proceed. Other negotiated settlements that planned marriages further precluded bundling. *Heimdabyte* (home exchange) was a ma-
neuver in which a daughter was married to the heir of a farm on the
condition that her brother, as heir to the second farm, eventually
marry her new sister-in-law. In this way, through planned marriage, two children were assured landholding livelihoods.[40]

Although Sundt judged that parents in Sogn had the same wishes
for their children as those in Sunnfjord, he wrote that they merely
let their sons and daughters try their own luck at courtship. With

this placing of greater control over courtship and marriage in the hands of the youths, the importance of night courting increased. Sundt marveled at the lack of modesty (*blufærdighed*) among the common folk in Sogn. If an unmarried man reached a farm late at night while traveling, according to Sundt, he could go into the cow-barn and sleep with a girl, even if his dialect indicated that he was from far away. It was even worse among the local youths. "When the community's own boys go around at nighttime," Sundt wrote, "visiting the girls in one or another fjøs (cowbarn), they immediate-ly get permission to cast off their coat and shoes and lie and spread themselves under the cover with the girl and spend the entire night."[41]

The consequences of these patterns, according to Sundt, were varying levels of happiness in the two regions. In Sunnfjord parents had such control over their children's destinies that many weddings married "dissimilar" couples of differing ages, a practice that eventually caused much unhappiness. Sundt concluded that Sunn-fjord people were more lethargic than the lively Sognings.[42] Yet the young age at marriage in Sogn and the great number of children born created a large class of cotters, *indersts* (farm servants living together as couples and waiting for cotters' places), and strandsid-ders, who Sundt thought had too many children. Their quick and thoughtless actions, Sundt argued, caused Sogn communities to become overpopulated, so that the only way out was for many to move to America – something that did not happen so often in Sunn-fjord.[43] Finally, the emphasis on night courting led to many un-wanted and illegitimate children in Sogn. Sundt determined that Sogn had nearly the highest occurrence of night courting in Norway and a correspondingly low level of "morality."[44] His distinctions were verified in the 1855 census: 4.0% of all births in Sunnfjord were illegitimate, compared to 13.5% for Inner Sogn and 10.9% for Outer Sogn, of which Balestrand was a part.[45]

Though Sundt argued that these dissimilar paths of development caused divergent patterns of land ownership, they were also the result of varying socioeconomic structures. In Balestrand and Sogn the flourishing agricultural sphere that demanded cotters largely offset the need for additional livelihoods and modified efforts to control fertility and the destinies of the offspring. The large families, however, forced many of the next generation into landless status. In Indre Holmedal, a county in Sunnfjord, for example, there were 32 cotters with land and 24 cotters without land for every 100 farmers in 1855. When these numbers are compared with the Balestrand figures of 123 and 15, or with the extreme case in Sogn of Lærdal, where the figures were 251 and 82, the success of the Sunnfjord farmers in retaining land for their heirs is obvious.[46]

In essence, the expanding agricultural opportunities created contradictory demographic pressures on the peasant population of Balestrand. Though the economic base was enlarging, the proclivity for practicing impartible inheritance of land, owing to the economies of scale in cattle production, forced most children of farmers and cotters into landless status. Yet greater opportunities also created a broadened source of livelihoods based on landlessness. Growth in the landless class, coupled with increasing occupational possibilities, worked to alter the strategies of household formation and inheritance for many in the nineteenth century. As more households held no land, constraints on marriage age based on inheritance became less important. With little property and no land to inherit, the children of cotters had to fend for themselves and form households when they were able. Increasing occupational opportunities for the landless actually enabled them to marry younger than previously, a practice that in turn increased their total fertility.

Two very distinct subcultures of the landed and the landless confronted changing opportunities for household formation throughout the nineteenth century and developed differing measures and behavior in response to them. Within the landed farm household, the eldest son's future was decidedly preferable to that of his siblings. Barring physical or mental defects, he would inherit the status and wealth of the farm. He had little doubt about his prospects, since his inheritance was assured. In keeping with the traditional nature of the farm transfer, the heir had to wait for his father to retire before assuming control of the land and marrying.[47] In Balestrand the eldest son typically received the farm in increments until the kårkontrakt went into operation and the burden and benefits of managing the household fell on him.[48]

The marriage date for the heir was quite constrained by the prescribed nature of the youth's position. He could not wed until he had procured a livelihood, that is, not until his father relinquished at least a part of the farm. The parents had the decisive word on not only when the marriage would occur but with whom the boy would marry. If he married without permission to a member of the lower class, he risked being turned away by his parents.[49] The eldest son's age at marriage therefore was largely determined by parental decisions concerning retirement, so that circumstances within the household, such as the father's age, were more important in determining time of marriage than outside economic considerations. In any case, the heir was certain of a propertied marriage at some time in his life. Following traditional patterns of marriage, the heir's wife was usually years younger than her husband, the result of property considerations that paired those with greatest wealth in the community (see the previous section of this chapter).[50]

Although farmer's children other than the heir did inherit a portion of the estate, their future was constrained by the lack of land opportunities in Balestrand, so different strategies had to be devised. Such children received a portion of the farm's value, the sons getting double shares, when the land was transferred to the heir. Since they did not inherit land, these youths had to use their assets to create viable livelihoods. Usually they stayed at home and worked until they married, often after accumulating a small number of cattle or learning a craft such as carpentry. The most useful strategy, however, was to use their wealth and status as landed children to court farm-owning widows or women who stood to inherit their fathers' farms, a tactic that allowed them to escape descent into landlessness. Some chose spouses who possessed farms but lacked other qualities. One son is said to have stated, "Before I will become a husmann, I'll even marry Britha" – apparently not the most desirable spouse – a step he did take around 1830.[51] Most children of farmers were forced into landless status, and many settled down on their fathers' farms as cotters working for their brothers.[52] As cotters, the children of farmers faced the task of finding livelihoods without the amenities of their fathers' status. The farther they were removed from landed status, the more they were forced to use the strategies of the landless.

Children of cotters behaved quite differently in creating livelihoods and forming households. Whereas the farmer's oldest son and, to a lesser extent, his other children inherited positions of status and wealth, children of the landless had to create places in the society through their own skills. Very rarely did they experience mobility into the landed class, and property inherited from their parents was usually limited, if there was any at all.[53] A cotters' child usually worked as a servant until a cotter's place was vacated or a farmer gave permission to clear a new one (see Plate 10). Household formation among cotters therefore was based less on the situation within the family than on the economic opportunities and each cotter's own abilities. The increasing demand for servants and cotters in the nineteenth century provided the means for many to patch together livelihoods, marry, and begin new landless households.

Plate 10. Members of this young cotter household from the Esefjord in Balestrand display their home, to which they probably have only recently moved. *Source*: Picture collection, University Library of Bergen; photograph by Knud Knudsen

Higher wages allowed servants to accumulate money for dowries or beginning capital, and the need for cotters also permitted formation of additional households.

With little prospect of any inheritance, cotters' children also had less cause to defer to their parents' wishes regarding marriage time or choice of spouse. As youths, they were left to court whom they wished and marry when they could. This removed an important constraint in the peasant society that worked to delay marriage, a constraint fewer individuals faced as a greater portion of the population entered adulthood in landlessness. With little reason to delay marriage, landless youths married as soon as they acquired farming abilities, accumulated investing capital, and received permission to clear or assume cotters' places. Despite the increase in landless households, the demand for cotters and the capacity to create additional viable livelihoods in the nineteenth century actually led to a lowered age at marriage for cotters (see Table 10). Landless men were married at an average age of over thirty between 1820 and 1839, but age at marriage began to decline in the 1840s and remained below thirty, on the average, for the next forty years. In one period

Table 10. *Age at first marriage: Mundal parish and a portion of Tjugum parish, 1820–79*

	Men		Women	
	Farmer	Cotter	Farmer	Cotter
1820–29				
Mean	28.5	30.3	24.9	29.2
Median	26	30	23	28
N	15	20	15	20
1830–39				
Mean	27.7	31.0	25.8	28.0
Median	24	30	23	28
N	6	20	6	20
1840–49				
Mean	26.7	26.7	23.7	25.3
Median	26	26	23	24
N	22	32	22	32
1850–59				
Mean	27.6	29.7	25.5	26.8
Median	27	28	25	26
N	19	22	19	22
1860–69				
Mean	30.4	27.7	26.3	27.6
Median	31	27	26	27
N	13	23	13	23
1870–79				
Mean	25.2	24.8	23.1	24.8
Median	24	25	22	24
N	8	20	8	20

Source: Constructed from results of family reconstitution for the parish of Mundal and three selected farms in Tjugum.

(1860–79) the cotters' age at marriage was actually lower than that of men who inherited farms. Landless women in Mundal experienced a decreased age at marriage throughout the nineteenth century as well, so that by the 1840s they entered married life at an age similar to that of farmers' wives.

Not only were the constraints that encouraged delayed marriage diminished, but it was often in the interests of landless youth to take over or clear cotters' places as soon as possible. For in spite of increased opportunities, youths continued to face the possibility of lifelong celibacy (see Table 11). Larger proportions of the younger

Table 11. *Percentage and number ever married: Tjugum and Mundal parishes, 1801–65*

	Age 20–29		Age 30–39		Age 40–49		Age 50–59		Age 60–69	
	%	N	%	N	%	N	%	N	%	N
1801										
Men	16.0	100	75.0	72	92.6	54	93.1	58	92.3	39
Women	25.5	98	62.7	110	76.5	81	78.8	52	86.0	43
1845										
Men	22.1	145	63.1	103	93.4	91	87.3	79	95.1	41
Women	29.3	147	63.6	118	89.2	93	97.0	67	86.8	53
1855										
Men	26.6	139	80.2	106	79.5	83	90.4	73	79.1	43
Women	27.1	181	70.2	131	75.6	86	84.3	89	77.5	40
1865										
Men	17.8	129	80.5	113	95.2	84	85.9	64	96.3	54
Women	25.5	165	73.3	116	82.9	111	77.5	71	89.7	58

Sources: Balestrand manuscript population censuses, 1801, 1845, 1855, 1865.

age groups were married through the middle of the nineteenth century, but a significant segment of the population remained unmarried throughout. Once a mate was found and prospects of a livelihood certain, marriage followed quickly.

The lowered marriage age that demonstrated greater opportunities, however, also created the potential for added distress in the next generation. Cotters in Mundal married one to two years later on the average than farmers throughout the period, but, more important, the traditional pattern of much higher age at marriage for cotters' than for farmers' wives was being reduced.[54] Although cotters' brides remained older than those of landowners, their average age was falling from near thirty in the 1820s to around twenty-five fifty years later. But in choosing to marry earlier as greater opportunities arose, they were also implicitly choosing larger households that would ultimately put increasing stress on their abilities to provide food and clothing, not to mention the needs of the more distant future.[55]

Although Balestrand cotters were behaving rationally in forming households when opportunities presented themselves, the declining age at marriage owing to increased opportunities undermined

Table 12. *Completed family size according to class and year married: Mundal parish, 1820–69*

Year of marriage	Farmer	Husmenn, other landless
1820–29		
Mean	6.7	4.6
Median	6	4
N	15	23
1830–39		
Mean	5.9	4.5
Median	6	4
N	10	11
1840–49		
Mean	7.8	6.9
Median	7	7
N	19	13
1850–59		
Mean	8.2	6.3
Median	8	6
N	16	16
1860–69		
Mean	6.4	6.5
Median	7	7
N	9	12

Source: Family-reconstitution forms, Mundal parish.

one of the most powerful fertility checks in the preindustrial society: Because they married earlier, cotters' wives bore more children throughout the century (see Table 12). Completed family size among cotters increased from around four children between 1820 and 1839 to six or seven in the periods following, a rate of increase much greater than that of the farmers. The larger families were successfully fed by enlarged production, and as labor input increased throughout the century, additional children might have been beneficial to the cotters' or farmers' operations. Still, the more numerous offspring would face the same obstacles as their parents in finding livelihoods when they reached adulthood. Moreover, as the number of children in each family became larger, the openings within the society inevitably would become more scarce.

Opportunities in the United States provided a solution for both farmer and cotter families with children, as well as for individuals in search of livelihoods. An official's report during the early stages of the emigration from Sogn emphasized these causes for movement to America. Though "overpopulation" was noted as a cause of emigration, it was overpopulation not from common underemployment (*næringsløshed*) but from what the writer termed "irresponsibly established marriages," marriages that were judged irrational in the long run, however sensible they seemed to the actors involved.[56] Anticipation of livelihoods in America also worked to lower marriage ages. Youths wed before emigrating with the expectation that the livelihood upon which to base their marriage would be found in the United States. Indeed, the lower marriage ages throughout the 1800s were in part due to these trans-Atlantic strategies for procuring employment.[57]

Further ramifications of changing strategies of household formation

While the strategies of the landless created the potential for future economic difficulties, they also laid the groundwork for a discord that developed between the landless and the landed and among landless segments in Balestrand. Illegitimate births, a common result of night courting, were at odds with moral teachings within the society. Yet as parental wealth decreased for most and the choice of spouse was based more on talent than on inheritance, night courting increased. Balestrand, like the rest of Sogn, where most youths were landless, remained an area of widespread night courting. Visiting church authorities continually noted with concern the presence of courting put largely in the hands of youths. In 1834 one complained that *nattesværmen* (night romance) among servants had not diminished and that only with painstaking supervision (*omhyggelige tilsyn*) by household heads could it be reduced. Apparently the household heads were not supervising properly, because six years later another bishop reported that night courting still was a social abuse (*uskikk*) that demoralized the community. Yet another account in 1855 used the large number of illegitimate children as evidence that night courting unfortunately was still common.[58]

Illegitimacy that resulted from night courting often placed youths in difficult positions. Because they lived as servants and slept in accessible cowbarns away from the supervision of adults, pair bonding often occurred before livelihoods had definitely been secured. Moreover, though many new livelihoods were fashioned in the nineteenth century, their underpinnings were more often unstable and insecure than in the past, and economic prospects on occasion

Table 13. *Illegitimate births in relation to total births and marriages: Balestrand, 1825–99*

	(A) Illegitimate births	(B) Total births	A as a % of B	(C) Total marriages	A as a % of C
1825–29	35	124[a]	8.1[a]	49	71.4
1830–34	32	273	11.7	39	82.1
1835–39	38	257	14.8	41	92.7
1840–44	38	309	12.3	50	76.0
1845–49	38	317	12.0	67	56.7
1850–54	52	387	13.4	71	73.2
1855–59	60	367	16.3	67	89.5
1860–64	28	358	7.8	80	35.0
1865–69	20	369	5.4	66	30.3
1870–74	32	352	9.1	69	46.4
1875–79	28	328	8.5	64	43.7
1880–84	12	318	3.8	49	24.5
1885–89	10	297	3.4	61	16.4
1890–94[b]	8	281	2.8	53	15.1
1895–99[b]	9	257	3.5	52	17.3

[a]Total births and illegitimacy ratio based on 1827–29 period only.
[b]Vangsnes parish missing.
Source: Balestrand church records.

failed to materialize.[59] As the landless groups were becoming a larger segment of the population, nattfrieri, with its concomitant possibility of conceiving children, became an increasingly dominant method of courtship. And prenuptial births that resulted from night courting rapidly increased in the nineteenth century. In Leikanger (of which Balestrand was a part until 1847) the illegitimacy ratio – 4.2% between 1796 and 1805 – exploded to 11.0% in the 1830s.[60] The rates for Balestrand were even higher between 1830 and 1860: By the late 1850s every sixth child was born out of wedlock (see Table 13).[61]

Not only was illegitimacy more frequent, but marriages in Mundal parish were increasingly more likely to be performed after the birth of the couple's first child throughout most of the mid-nineteenth century (see Table 14). The behavior of the landless, furthermore, represented by the cotters, remained distinct from that of the landed farmers at least from the 1820s onward (see Table 15). Growing proportions of cotter marriages were preceded by prenuptially born or prenuptially conceived children, whereas the first child of farmer

Table 14. *Conception of first child of fertile first marriage: Mundal parish, 1820–79*

Year of marriage	Legitimate	Prenuptially conceived	Illegitimate
1820–29			
%	33.3	51.3	15.4
N	13	20	6
1830–39			
%	42.1	50.0	7.8
N	16	19	3
1840–49			
%	43.3	35.0	21.7
N	26	19	13
1850–59			
%	39.6	35.4	25.0
N	19	17	12
1860–69			
%	47.4	18.4	34.2
N	18	7	13
1870–79			
%	60.7	28.5	10.7
N	17	8	3

Source: Family-reconstitution forms, Mundal parish.

households increasingly was born more than nine months after marriage. Other children were born to parents who did not marry one another and, in many cases, did not marry at all.[62]

The increasing incidence of prenuptial births was due in part to the capriciousness inherent in acquiring livelihoods. But it also must be at least partly tied to the evolution of courtship and marriage patterns within a swelling propertyless class that developed norms deviant from past mores. As noted, courtship placed more in the hands of the youths and based on night courting resulted in many pregnancies outside marriage. If a pregnancy occurred after a couple decided to wed, they sought permission from a farmer to clear a cotter's place, to assume a vacant one, or to patch together some combination of work to justify their marriage. On occasion, couples lived together and the woman became pregnant in anticipation of a livelihood on which to base their household formation. The interval between pregnancy and livelihood acquisition might be long

Table 15. *Conception of first child of fertile first marriage according to class: Mundal parish, 1820–79*

	1820–29[a]		1830–39		1840–49		1850–59		1860–69		1870–79	
	%	N	%	N	%	N	%	N	%	N	%	N
Farmer												
Illegitimate	11.1	2	0	0	9.1	2	12.0	3	20.0	3	0	0
Prenuptially												
conceived	39.9	7	60.0	6	22.7	5	36.0	9	12.3	2	37.5	3
Legitimate	50.0	9	40.0	4	68.2	15	52.0	13	66.7	10	62.5	5
Cotter												
Illegitimate	41.2	7	27.8	5	39.4	13	41.2	7	52.9	9	25.0	4
Prenuptially												
conceived	35.3	6	50.0	9	52.5	17	47.1	8	29.4	5	37.5	6
Legitimate	23.5	4	22.2	4	9.1	3	11.8	2	17.6	3	37.5	6

[a]Year of marriage.
Source: Family-reconstitution forms, Mundal parish.

enough so that the child was born out of wedlock, an example of "marriage frustrated" by uncertainty.[63] In Mundal parish between 1820 and 1879, for instance, 28.7% of the 174 illegitimate births were followed by the marriage of the couple. Others who intended to become married, yet were without livelihoods, used another strategy for household formation. Throughout the nineteenth century, more couples married and remained indersts until permission to operate cotters' places was given. The man worked as a servant and the woman as the milkmaid on a farm that needed their labor.[64] As age at marriage declined among indersts, this tactic was used more frequently (see Table 16).

On other occasions, however, men could not find adequate livelihoods or were unwilling to enter wedlock. Their partners, who bore illegitimate children without marrying, were forced to remain in less enviable positions. In 1801 unmarried women who had given birth to illegitimate children, usually conceived while the women were in service, tended to live in the homes of parents or brothers.[65] They remained in a milieu that continued to demand night courting as a means to marriage. Peter Laslett has argued that increased illegitimacy was due to a subsociety of illegitimacy-prone individuals whose fertility rose faster in periods when general fertility was also rising.[66] Many of the repeaters were such women who,

Table 16. *Marriage patterns of indersts later classed as husmenn: Mundal parish, 1830–79*

	Marriage age		Frequency	
	Mean	Median	N	% of all marriages
1830–39	34.8	34	5	6.5
1840–59	29.5	26	11	10.2
1860–79	27.1	27	11	16.7

Source: Family-reconstitution forms, Mundal parish.

according to Sundt, had "fallen once" and whose lives were "such that they would fall again and again." Though men bore most of the guilt for the first illegitimate child a woman mothered, Sundt argued that a woman became vicious after having been once seduced and continued to seduce other men in the hope of finding a mate.[67] The subsociety discovered by Laslett was at least partly this group of women, who were using their resources to gain matches.

Possibly because women played such an important economic role in Balestrand, their status permitted relatively frequent repetitive bastard bearing and the formation of single-parent families.[68] Yet the marginal status in which women lived after bearing children out of wedlock, and the Christian strictures against such behavior, placed them under stress they otherwise would not have experienced.[69] Although a constant percentage of women would eventually wed throughout the nineteenth century, those who bore illegitimate children without marrying faced decreased marriage possibilities and greater likelihood of distress. Moreover, their children could lay no claim to paternal inheritance, a fact that did little to improve their already marginal status.[70]

In spite of the misery that at times ensued, contemporary observers believed that prenuptial births were becoming the rule rather than the exception among large segments of the population. Balestrand's priest in the early 1860s wrote that immorality resulting from improper interaction (*letferdige overgang*) between the sexes had become the norm, so that children accepted and learned the custom; they grew up in this defilement (*besmittelse*), he argued.[71] Such interaction occurred at prolonged gatherings during marriages and burials, where youths at the earliest ages followed their parents and took part in the festivities.[72] Some observers believed that the custom was so deep-rooted that youth felt themselves to be guiltless in night courting.[73] Much of the displeasure of these upper-class critics was directed toward the landowners of rural society, who did little to hinder night courting.[74] All attempts to end night courting and illegitimacy would ultimately be fruitless, Balestrand's priest agreed, so long as the farm folk permitted both male and female servants to sleep in the same room.[75]

Peer pressure within the servant group to engage in night courting was powerful. Arne E. Boyum, a servant who ultimately would emigrate, "found pleasure in the goblet of sensuality" of night courting in Balestrand, as "prayer and meditation on the Word of God were laid aside" and "games and play with friends of both sexes in what the world calls fun, occupied my mind entirely." Among the many servant activities, "worst of all was the pernicious running around at night . . . a pool of vice into which many a youth of those districts fell." Boyum became a servant at age sixteen and entered his new surroundings "young and not steadfast, and as it is always easy to learn evil, what happened to me here was that I gradually became more and more a friend of frivolous young people, and became of like mind and behavior with them."[76]

In spite of apparent indifference within the farmer class and considerable peer pressure among the servants, increased night courting and illegitimate births began to create discord within Balestrand society. Farmers who had to defray the expenses of poor support looked askance at illegitimate births, which often bred poverty and thereby increased their taxes. Likewise, some segments of the landless began to resist the dominant courtship practices. More fundamental, however, were the contradictions between illegitimacy and Christian morality regarding children and marriage. Although compromises between peasant practices and moral sanctions were frequent, movements that developed throughout Balestrand society among both the landed and the landless emphasized Christian standards and moral propriety. Since they ultimately profoundly influenced the course and tone of American settlements, they are considered here in greater detail.

Moral and religious movements within mid-nineteenth-century Balestrand

Norwegian society traditionally made firm distinctions between illegitimate and legitimate children. The silver wedding crown worn by brides the entire first day of the wedding celebration graphically illustrated this differentiation. First used toward the end of the Middle Ages, the crown represented the Virgin Mary, queen of heaven and virgins, and could be worn only by the seemingly virgin bride. The pregnant bride wore a piece of cloth between the crown and her head to avoid direct contact. If the bride had already mothered a child, in places such as Sunnfjord she had to wear a cloth crown that strongly resembled a fool's cap.[77]

Barriers against improper behavior in Balestrand were nowhere near so strict as those in Sunnfjord, but dissimilar courtship patterns related to class did create behavioral divisions within society.[78] Such divisions were reflected in varying premarital sexual conduct among the landless and the landed. Indeed, if Balestrand had had marriage customs similar to Sunnfjord's, fully two-fifths of landless women would have worn the fool's cap between 1840 and 1859, compared to less than one-tenth of the landed (see Table 15). Yet if courtship and marriage behavior patterns remained distinct, the downward mobility of farmers' children into cotter status, which had traditionally helped maintain a more egalitarian society in Balestrand, was retained. Even though larger segments of the society were remaining landless for generations, social divisions continued to be based more on geographical division of neighborhood than on land ownership. Farmers' children still danced with servants during summer festivities. The farm family, including servants, continued to eat at one table, and the important holidays were celebrated by the grend, rather than according to social class.[79] Likewise, social distinctions that did develop, such as in seating at church, were due more to lack of space than to social differentiation.[80]

This social interchange was instrumental in the attempts by the landed to curb the custom of night courting. Sundt believed that he was observing the disappearance of night courting among farmer families, especially those that had connections with city folk. He expressed the hope that the changing behavior would percolate down from the "better farmer families" to the servant class, which might be expected to follow the farmers' examples.[81] Concerted attempts were made in Balestrand to end the night courting customs. Pastor Sverdrup of Balestrand used his authority to establish clubs that worked against the custom in the mid-nineteenth century. He first organized a group of farmers who pledged to inform on night courting activities so that fines and punishments could be made. According to Sundt, only a few were "upstanding enough" to appear with such reports. Later, in 1860, a voluntary club to end night courting was organized. The bylaws noted that night courting was a social abuse difficult for people to oppose individually, whereas a club could more effectively stand against the deeply rooted custom. Individual members pledged to try to bring an end to night courting and to report it if it occurred; household heads vowed to provide separate sleeping quarters for boys and girls. The second organization, less coercive than the first, was more successful; by 1861 there were 386 members. Illegitimacy rates in Balestrand did begin to decline in the 1860s, an indication of success among the second organization (see Table 13).[82]

Equally important were pietistic movements among the propertyless that stressed the moral and religious implications of illegitimacy. One servant, who lived in the mileau of night courting, asked,

> But did I find peace therein? No, no! I knew well that I had departed from God, from the covenant of my baptism, and from my confirmation promise. I had no peace, my conscience was disturbed, yea, I was often so anxious and uneasy that in order to quiet the inner voice, I diligently sought peace where there was frivolity and so-called fun. But when I then again was alone, I was as uneasy and disturbed as before. O what wailing and misery, that one so defiantly shall resist God's calling Spirit and grace.

This man added, "Alas! Alas! how deplorable that the children of God and the members of Christ shall be torn out of the fellowship with God, and become members of a harlot, and the habitation of the unclean Spirit! It is tragic that such a custom can exist in the midst of Christendom."[83] The strong undercurrent of religious propriety thus placed stress on those members of the landless subculture who chose to court although they were made uneasy by moral teachings against the practice. It was in such situations that religious awakenings attracted portions of the community.

Religious rites in Balestrand had usually been a harmonious aspect of social life. Although they sat apart according to sex and social station during the church service, those who worked together on a farm usually went together to church. On Sundays when no service was performed, devotion and prayer meetings were held at home, and Scriptures were read throughout the week. Many were deeply pious: For example, a woman servant born in 1813 went across the fjord to church and, because of fasting, nearly fainted when she returned the long distance home after the service.[84]

Changes in the religious structure occurred in the mid-nineteenth century, however, when a pietistic movement that one historian called "a darker Christianity," which "ended the easy tones in work and free time," extended over Balestrand.[85] Voluntary groups of "readers," those who valued reading the Scripture among themselves, gathered at meetings independent of the state church.[86] The first pietistic awakening began in Balestrand when Ingebrigt Mundal moved to Mundal parish in 1846 and began to organize meetings. Other lay preachers soon worked throughout the Balestrand area.[87]

The reader movement created internal divisions within Balestrand society. Some ridiculed the movement from the beginning, with men sarcastically inquiring if they should bring *hæresekk* (course sacks of pig hair) to meetings to dry their tears and women facetiously asking if they should bring their knitting.[88] Others entered the readers' fellowship and readily accepted the puritanical doctrines that challenged certain widely accepted practices. One reader, for example, refused to serve alcoholic drinks during traditional gatherings such as Christmas celebrations. His efforts were not popular with many; after the reader's death, his son reinstated the traditional Christmas intemperance.[89]

Few sources from Balestrand explicate the internal tensions people felt when pietistic teachings conflicted with traditional peasant conduct. That is why the reminiscences of Arne Endresen Boyum, who first became aware of the readers in his fifteenth year, are so revealing. After attending religious meetings for several years while he was working as a servant, Boyum decided the readers were "right." His parents wanted correct outward behavior, but they were not emphatic "regarding daily prayer to God for strength and grace to walk in the footsteps of Christ, and to deny everything that is not in accord with the Word and example of Christ." During "an extensive spiritual awakening in the district" in 1851, when Arne was eighteen, several youths "were reached by the working of God's Word and Spirit," although only a few were "wholly transformed." Arne also was "powerfully drawn by God's call" but was "afraid of being pointed out as one who accepted the views of the so-called readers." Still attempting to avoid the "noisy and frivolous young people" who had a "fascinating power" over him, he did not have the "courage and boldness" to speak against sin.[90]

Boyum never made the complete break to join the readers, and like "the seed that fell on the rock," his pietistic inclinations "soon withered away and bore no fruit." Others like him, who were "powerfully" drawn to God, "gradually fell back into the same worldly mind and being, and became, if anything, worse than they were before." The Devil kept telling Boyum that it would be "sour and dreary" if he joined the readers and that he should become "again happy in the delights and pleasures of the world." Eventually, "the inner admonitions were stifled more and more, and by degrees my mind became so worldly and vain that I began to find pleasures in the goblet of sensuality." He knew that this was the "wrong way," but Satan "whispered that it was too early for conversion, there would surely be a more convenient time later."[91]

Boyum's was probably not the typical case, but his experiences do illustrate the internal conflicts. Closely related to moral questions of propriety, contradictions between correct behavior and customs such as night courting apparently troubled many. The sum of the individual decisions also created the potential for divisions within society, even among families and friends, as Boyum implied. A good indication of the cleavages that developed in Balestrand is the frequency with which individuals celebrated communion. Communion was a holy sacrament that was customarily administered in the spring and fall to members of the community but that could be requested by communicants at any church service. Annual patterns of communion therefore provide a good indication of religious divisions in the society. In some years members of the community celebrated communion as a group, participating in the sacrament around the same number of times each year. In other years, however, people individually chose to break from custom by requesting communion many times throughout the year, indicating self-doubts distinct from the concerns of the majority of the community.

A rare *communikant register* from Balestrand between 1849 and 1862 reveals an undulating pattern of tension between the normal group patterns in some periods and increasing requests for communion among a group of readers in others (see Figure 4 and Table 17). The number of communions celebrated annually by each person in Tjugum parish increased during the awakening around 1851 noted by Boyum, but especially in the early 1860s (by which time Boyum had emigrated). Not only did the portion of the community taking the sacrament frequently increase at times, but larger segments of those not taking it at all increased simultaneously. Apparently questions of morality and religiosity that troubled many were not shared by other segments of the society, who reacted negatively to the pietists' concerns and as a result avoided communion. Questions of moral propriety and pietism obviously helped create and also reflected divisions within Balestrand society.

% of individuals celebrating
     communion:

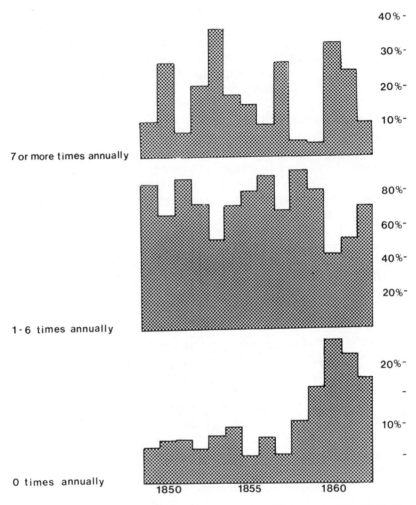

Fig. 4. Frequency of celebration of communion: Tjugum parish, 1849–62.
Source: Kommunikant register, Balestrand

Table 17. *Frequency of celebration of communion: Tjugum parish, 1849–62*

	No. of communions for each individual annually					
	0	1–2	3–4	5–6	7–8	9+
1849 (N = 488)						
No.	32	92	133	183	48	0
%	6.6	18.9	27.3	37.5	9.8	0
1850 (N = 524)						
No.	39	100	80	159	139	7
%	7.4	19.1	15.2	30.3	26.6	1.3
1851 (N = 510)						
No.	39	84	156	197	34	0
%	7.6	16.4	30.6	38.6	6.7	0
1852 (N = 530)						
No.	32	77	86	222	99	14
%	6.0	14.5	16.2	41.9	18.7	2.6
1853 (N = 549)						
No.	48	56	84	156	190	15
%	8.7	10.2	15.3	28.4	34.6	2.7
1854 (N = 504)						
No.	48	60	58	244	88	6
%	9.5	11.8	11.5	48.4	17.5	1.2
1855 (N = 507)						
No.	26	61	124	215	79	2
%	5.1	12.1	24.6	42.4	15.5	0.4
1856 (N = 522)						
No.	42	82	182	174	39	3
%	8.0	15.7	34.9	33.4	7.5	0.6
1857 (N = 496)						
No.	26	55	51	228	128	8
%	5.2	11.0	10.3	46.0	25.8	1.6
1858 (N = 478)						
No.	51	94	216	97	20	0
%	10.7	19.6	45.2	20.2	4.2	0
1859 (N = 599)						
No.	97	118	244	121	13	6
%	16.2	19.6	40.7	20.2	2.2	1.0
1860 (N = 596)						
No.	143	23	126	113	126	65
%	24.0	3.8	21.1	18.8	21.1	10.9
1861 (N = 561)						
No.	120	67	83	155	83	53
%	21.4	12.0	14.8	27.6	14.7	9.4
1862 (N = 483)						
No.	83	69	136	151	38	6
%	17.2	14.3	28.1	31.3	7.8	1.2

Source: Kommunicant register, Balestrand.

Conclusion

The emigration to America has been viewed as flight by impoverished farmers and destitute cotters from the bleak prospects of Norwegian rural life. Even Sundt argued that conditions in the 1840s created a great demand for bread (*rift om brødet*) that contributed to such societal ills as increasing illegitimacy, emigration, internal migration, and criminality.[92] Yet, as we have seen in Balestrand, a region whence a widespread emigration would originate, a broadening economic structure provided more certain sources of food and created greater work opportunities, manifested in lower ages at marriage among landless youths.

The combination of a growing population, impartible inheritance of land, and the improved well-being itself, however, provided fewer immediate landed positions for farmers' children. Likewise, as the larger households placed more youths in the livelihood market when they reached adulthood, there existed the possibility that marriage and household formation would have to be delayed in the future if additional livelihoods could not be created. Although youths by the mid-nineteenth century were able to patch together livelihoods with greater ease than before, they faced the possibility that the basis for marriage would disappear after cohabitation and family formation had begun. Moreover, as more landless youths entered adulthood with fewer defined opportunities, night courting led to rapidly increasing incidences of prenuptial births that were not followed by marriage. Such behavior created social cleavages reflected in attempts by the landed to reduce night courting and in religious movements among the landless. The pietistic awakenings, which attempted to reconcile the community's moral teachings with present realities, divided in particular the landless, the group most intensely influenced by the ambiguities of the changing society.

There is no reason to believe that the community would not have adapted to the conditions that were transforming Balestrand into a primarily landless, wage labor society.[93] Internal changes, such as fertility control similar to that practiced for years in Sunnfjord, might have evolved. Indeed, anti–night courting organizations appear to have succeeded in reducing the incidence of prenuptial births. The opportunities in America, however, intervened. The rich, cheap land and higher wages in the United States provided an abundant source of livelihoods – especially landed livelihoods – that relieved the pressure developing in Norway. As settlement in

America continued, people in Balestrand began to base their futures on opportunities not only at home but across the sea as well.

Just as American opportunities profoundly affected Balestrand society, so did conditions in Balestrand powerfully influence development of communities in the United States. Land-hungry emigrants from both propertied and unpropertied classes set out for the expanses of farmland that awaited in the Middle West, carrying cultural traditions to their new settlements. The American colonies were influenced by the pietistic thought that swept through Norwegian society as well as by social change that was filtering down from what Sundt called the "better farmer families." In a very real sense, emigrants from Balestrand were attempting to use uniquely isolated, vast expanses of land to preserve their social fabric in an environment that was more conducive to economic growth.

Patterns of migration, as we will see in the next chapter, reiterate the notion that opportunities in Balestrand were adequate. Migrants could have left for other regions with greater opportunity throughout Norway if conditions had been unsuitable in Balestrand. Only when information about the vast openings in the United States filtered into the community did widespread migration commence. Likewise, the initial migrants represented the wealthier elements, who were not forced from Balestrand but instead chose to exploit the comparative advantage of life in the United States. As parents followed sons and daughters or as wives followed husbands, a folk migration developed to exploit the unique opportunity of open land in an environment where traditional social relationships could be maintained.

6   *The children of Askeladden: emigration from Balestrand to the United States*

Accounts about America and its abundance drifted through Norway's mountains and valleys in the 1830s and 1840s. It is fascinating today to imagine the frenetic discussion that must have permeated remote peasant communities when the vast opportunities of a strange, faraway land came to light. Many denounced the promise as a hoax. "In the mountain districts in those days [of early emigration]," Svein Nilsson reported in 1868,

> the strangest stories were told about America and the dangers of a trip across the ocean. Some of the mountain people had heard that skippers often sold emigrants as slaves to the Turks; others maintained that the ocean swarmed with horrible monsters capable of devouring a whole ship – cargo and all. But according to some accounts, an even worse fate awaited those who were not swallowed by sea beasts or crushed between towering icebergs. In America, so the stories went, the natives commonly captured white men and ate them on festive occasions to the glory of their gods. These and similar tales circulated in the mountain valleys and many of the inhabitants crossed themselves in sheer amazement at the reckless daring of the emigrants.

Not surprisingly, early emigrants were viewed by some "with suspicion and pity. . . . The emigrants were considered foolish daredevils," Nilsson continued; "it was even hinted that they acted upon the inspiration of the Evil One himself who thus sought to lead them to destruction."[1]

Yet as the more daring took the fateful step of emigration, the information about America and its opportunities became more detailed and widespread. Letters written by hands that could be trusted recounted the wealth of land awaiting across the sea. In some places a prevailing strong desire to leave Norway created an America fever. "For a time," one early immigrant remembered,

> I believed that half of the people . . . had lost their senses. Nothing else was spoken about than the land which flows with milk and honey. Our minister . . . tried to cure the fever. Even from

116

the pulpit he urged the people to be discreet and pictured the hardships of the voyage and the ferocity of the American Indians in most forbidding colors. But this was merely pouring oil on the fire.[2]

The America fever diffused through the valleys and over mountains as accounts were spread. Mobile traders, who had many contacts throughout the mountain communities, circulated news of American opportunities from place to place. One trader who visited a farm that had received an American letter said, "When I heard of it I was very anxious to see the letter or hear its contents." The letter portrayed vast American wealth, and "from that time forward," he remembered, it "was frequently in my thoughts, and I reasoned that there must be some places in the world where opportunities were greater than here." Upon returning home, he soon emigrated – after spreading news of the United States and creating an America fever in his home community.[3]

The path of information about America spread throughout the Norwegian west coast and eventually reached Balestrand, but only after a handful of venturesome local people emigrated and disseminated information through letters did America fever grip the community. Early emigrants from the regions of Rogaland and Hordaland were numerous, and the inland area around Voss soon experienced heavy emigration as well. Niels Knudsen Røthe was the first Vossing emigrant in 1836, and largely as a result of his reports, 507 people from Voss left for America over the next eight years. Like the early emigrants from Balestrand, many of the early Vossings were what an official called "wealthy folk who owned good farms." This district governor believed that the emigrants who forsook their farms left mainly because of the overdrawn reports about the wealth that could easily be obtained in the United States.[4]

Among the landholder emigrants were members of the Skjervheim farm in northern Voss. Upon their urging, a sister of one of them and her husband, Per Iversen Unde, a farmer in Vik, in 1839 became the first emigrants from the district of Sogn.[5] Like the emigrants from Voss who preceded them, Unde and his brother wrote a letter in 1841 that recounted the bounty of the American Middle West and spread the America fever to Sogn.[6] In 1843, 93 people left Vik, to be followed by an additional 147 in the next two years.[7] America fever diffused rapidly throughout Sogn, particularly in counties near Vik. Leikanger saw 45 people leave for America between 1843 and 1845; Aurland, 44; Sogndal, 39; and Balestrand, 34.[8] In the following decades counties further inland on the Sognefjord,

Table 18. *Emigration from Balestrand, 1844–1904*

	Total Balestrand population	No. of emigrants	Percent of total emigrants 1844–1904
1845	1,983		
1855	2,122		
1865	2,204		
1876	2,188		
1891	2,282		
1900	2,187		
1844		6	0.4
1845–49		219	11.1
1850–54		206	10.4
1855–59		216	10.9
1860–64		221	11.2
1865–69		191	9.6
1870–74		128	6.5
1875–79		110	5.5
1880–84		114	5.7
1885–89		169	8.5
1890–94		186	9.4
1895–99		106	5.3
1900–04		109	5.5
Total		1981	100.0

Sources: Balestrand population censuses, Balestrand church records; Bergen immigrant protocol.

such as Lærdal and Lyster, became the most intense emigration districts.[9] Sogn as a whole was the Norwegian region of most intense emigration from 1836 to 1865. Between 1856 and 1865, for example, 1.7 people per 100 left Sogn for the United States every year.[10]

Balestrand, situated near the initial impulses of America fever in Vik, experienced a relatively early emigration. The first emigrant left Balestrand in 1844, but large yearly totals began four years later, when 102 emigrated following a poor crop year (see Table 18). In the five-year period between 1846 and 1850, emigrants from Balestrand constituted 27.9% of the Sogn total. The emigration from Balestrand ebbed and flowed, but as more people moved from the inner regions of Sogn in the following years, Balestrand lost its prominent place as a center of America fever. People continued to leave Balestrand for North America, however, and by the turn of the century

1,872 people had emigrated, the high points in absolute numbers coming in 1856 and 1861, when 151 and 153 people left, respectively.[11]

Patterns of migration from Balestrand

Patterns of emigration, including the destinations of the migrants, the composition of the emigrating group, and the intensity of the migration, reinforce the notion that it was the wealth of American opportunity rather than deteriorating economic conditions in Balestrand that generated America fever. Emigration intensity varied greatly from region to region. Between 1851 and 1855, for example, emigration frequency from the more inland areas of Sogn stood in stark contrast to that from places near the sea. Whereas 237 people moved from Aurland, 308 from Vik, 332 from Sogndal, 282 from Lyster, and 372 from Lærdal – all inland areas – only 4 left from Kinn, 7 from Innvik, and 3 from Davik – all counties near the sea.[12] The dissimilar opportunities provided by differing ecological structures largely explain the contrasts. With more openings for landed farmers, people near the sea had less reason to move. Emigration from Balestrand and other emigration-prone areas, as already noted, helped avoid longer deferral of inheritance, of acquisition of livelihoods, and of household formation, areas that might have created future problems. Yet emigration from Balestrand was a phenomenon quite unlike past internal migration, both in scale and in composition. Certainly America provided a rich source of land upon which livelihoods could be based. But unlike locations on the coast and in the cities, it also created an opportunity for the migrants to maintain their social fabrics, which included a deep-seated value of landholding.

Sognings had migrated to places such as Nordland, Romsdal, and urban areas for decades. Internal migration from Balestrand increased somewhat at mid-century, but its magnitude was nowhere near that of the emigration to America by the mid-1840s (see Tables 19 and 20). Moreover, internal migration was more likely to be a short-distance relocation to another Sogning community with a similar ecological structure than the more radical departure to the city, the seacoast, or the frontier north. For those leaving the region, the United States became the principal destination, and only when the knowledge of abundance in America diffused did the floodgates of emigration open.[13]

Many among this flood of emigrants were members of the land-

Table 19. *Migration to and from Balestrand, 1838–61*

| | No. of emigrants | | |
	Within Norway	To America	No. of immigrants
1838–40	8	0	9
1841–43	13	0	9
1844–46	28	65	26
1847–49	31	160	58
1850–52	30	78	48
1853–55	31	138	47
1856–58	7	206	43
1859–61	16	192	71
1838–61	164	839	311

Source: Balestrand church records.

holding farmer class. The first decade of emigration, when well over one-fifth of all emigrants leaving Balestrand before 1900 moved, was dominated by the farmers and their children (see Table 21). And throughout the first thirty-six years, farm family members represented 44.6% of the total emigration, a figure proportionate to the landowning population in Balestrand in 1855.[14] Those with greater wealth and status in the peasant society certainly were not forced out, but instead chose to move their capital resources to an area with greater opportunity.

The members of the farmer class composing nearly two-thirds of the total emigration in the first five-year period not only were landed but were among the wealthier landed elements of the society. The 1845 manuscript census for Tjugum parish provided more complete information than usual and thus makes it possible to compare the well-being of emigrant households in relation to that of farms as a whole for the parish. The eleven farm families who left between 1845 and 1854 were well above average in wealth when the census was taken. For example, the households of Ole Olsen Thorsnes and Truls Hermundsen Meel, both of which would settle in Wisconsin, each contained 25 members. On the average, the eleven farms had 16.3% more workers than average, including more male servants, children at home, cotters, and day laborers. The greater need for labor was reflected in personal property, since animal holdings were 21.6% larger and the planting of grains also exceeded the average by 32.0%.

Table 20. *Destinations of emigrants from Balestrand, 1838–61*

	N	% of total
Elsewhere in Sogn	69	7.1
Seacoast	22	2.3
Bergen	24	2.5
North Norway		
(Nordland)	12	1.2
America	839	86.9
Total	966[a]	100.0

Source: Balestrand church records.
[a]Destinations of 37 internal immigrants unknown.

Landowning farm households dominated the early stages of emigration in other areas of Norway as well. In Vik, across the fjord from Balestrand, landowners were both relatively and absolutely the largest migrant group. The early emigration, between 1839 and 1855, saw the heads of fifty-nine farms, nearly one-quarter of the total number of farm units in Vik in 1845, leave the community.[15] Only 25.8% of all the emigrants to the United States from the parishes of Rollag and Veggli in Numedal were from the cotter class, and as in Vik and Balestrand the percentage was an even smaller 17.1 in the early years of the emigration, between 1841 and 1860.[16] In Tinn, Telemark, though more from the cotter class would emigrate, only 13% of the emigrants between 1837 and 1843 and 29% of the total emigration were of cotter background.[17] As was the case in Balestrand, the early farmer emigrants were men of considerable wealth. According to an official in the region, emigrants from Nedre Telemark between 1841 and 1845 left with an average of 2,000 to 4,000 spd. per family, a sum equal to about $2,200 to $4,400. An official from Stavanger reckoned that emigrants possessed around 50 spd. ($55) on the average, excluding their tickets.[18]

Children of landholders moving alone or in groups were also a significant segment of the early emigration from Balestrand. Using the capital they received from their inheritance, young sons and daughters who would not inherit any land at home could emigrate in hopes of living as landed farmers across the sea.[19] Youths at times left with significant sums of money; one farmer's son from Tinn, Telemark, carried 600 spd. with him when he emigrated in 1843.[20] Like farmers' families, farmers' children were most notable early in the emigration from Balestrand (see Table 21). In the first two five-

Table 21. *Class and unit size of Balestrand emigrant groups, 1844–79*

	Farmer families	Cotter families	Farmers' children	Cotters' children	Kårmenn[a]	Others[b]
1844–49						
Total	100	43	45	20	7	5
%	45.4	19.5	20.5	9.1	3.2	2.3
Ave. unit size	5.3	3.6	2.0	1.5	7.0	1.7
1850–54						
Total	62	44	59	26	4	0
%	31.8	22.6	30.3	13.3	2.0	0
Ave. unit size	5.6	3.1	1.9	1.2	1.3	—
1855–59						
Total	40	91	23	44	1	8
%	19.3	43.9	11.1	21.3	.5	3.9
Ave. unit size	5.7	4.8	1.8	1.3	1.0	2.7
1860–64						
Total	30	121	26	26	2	4
%	14.5	57.9	12.4	12.4	1.0	1.9
Ave. unit size	5.0	4.5	1.9	1.7	1.0	4.0
1865–69						
Total	54	82	22	15	1	1
%	14.5	57.9	12.6	8.6	.6	.6
Ave. unit size	4.9	4.6	2.2	1.4	1.0	1.0
1870–74						
Total	6	59	17	27	0	14
%	4.9	47.9	13.8	21.9	0	11.4
Ave. unit size	6.0	5.4	1.7	1.3	—	3.5
1875–79						
Total	23	10	21	34	0	0
%	26.1	11.4	23.9	38.6	0	0
Ave. unit size	3.8	5.0	1.2	1.1	—	—
1844–79						
Total	315	450	213	192	15	32
%	25.9	36.9	17.5	15.8	1.2	2.6

[a]Pensioners.
[b]Servants, strandsidders, craftsmen.
Source: Balestrand church records.

year spans of emigration they constituted one-fifth and three-tenths of all emigrants, respectively. Like their parents, farmers' children were innovators who possessed the means to move across the sea and claim the rich lands that awaited.[21]

If the wealthy were so attracted to America that they created a migration unprecedented in its magnitude, what made America so alluring to them? First of all, people who took the fateful step of emigration repeatedly stressed an improved future for their offspring as a primary motive. Johan Reinert Reiersen, who wrote an early "America book" that provided information about conditions in Norwegian settlements in the United States, asked the essential question in the introduction of his report: "What made the emigrant decide upon this serious and virtually irrevocable step?" Since the individual motivations for the massive movement were vital to Reiersen, the question was one of the first things he asked immigrants in their new American homes. The "most important" motive, he felt, was the "gloomy prospects parents foresee for their children in Norway . . . besides the hope of laying a foundation in America for the next generation's independence and good fortune. Everyone," he continued, "recognizes in some fashion or other that in Norway the place is too narrow, the area is too crowded."[22]

Priest Houge of Vik, across the fjord from Balestrand, echoed Reiersen's contentions. Taking a more compassionate view of emigration than most of his colleagues in the clergy, Houge noted the arduous conditions of agriculture in Vik when compared to the reports of excellent prospects in America. Future expectations, however, were of prime importance. "Anxiety about the future," he wrote, "hope of gentler conditions and less difficult days, wishes for reunions with earlier emigrants, and above all, the thoughts about obtaining a successful future for their children, which I have often heard said as a main motive of my people who have left their homes, is motive enough."[23]

Letters from the immigrants themselves also emphasized the hope for a better future for children in the United States. Anne Johnsdatter Einung, one of the earliest emigrants from the Telemark community of Tinn, emphasized, "I am moving not for myself, but for my children." She had a good farm, but only one of her seven children could have inherited it.[24] A letter to Dovre noted the difficult work in the United States but added that the people were happy "for their children's sake [for børnenes skyld]" that they had moved to America. "When the children have it so good," the writer added, "we no longer think about our drudgery and toil [slik og slæb]."[25] Yet another man considered opportunities in America a blessing: The best inheritance parents in poor condition could give their children, he believed, was to bring them to America, where they could live as free people.[26]

Calculations for the future, once based on opportunities within Balestrand, became more complicated when emigration to the United States became an option. For those concerned about prospects for land and easy accessibility to livelihoods, emigration was a compelling choice. One writer analyzing a household's options came to an obvious conclusion:

> A man with one thousand dollars and five children reasons as follows: One thousand dollars divided among five children amounts to little or nothing here in this country. But if I go to America, where there is plenty of fertile land to be had for next to nothing, my little capital, combined with the industry of myself and my children, is sufficient to furnish all of us an independent and satisfactory position.[27]

The "oft-expressed hope of winning 'a better future for my children'" was often fulfilled. Years later, an immigrant reflected that "our father's hope that he would prepare a better future" had been accomplished and concluded, "We can never thank God enough for the fact that he gives us our daily bread."[28]

People from cattle-producing communities with impartible inheritance, in addition to seizing the chance to procure landed futures, also were encouraged to move by reports of immediate improvement in material well-being. Families without land, according to some accounts, could quickly become landed, and those with smaller parcels in Balestrand could acquire large expanses of property simply by moving to America. One American observer argued that a Norwegian immigrant arriving in *"det Store vesten* [the great West]" could use his wages for one year to save $120. After two years he could thus buy forty acres of land for a total of $50 and use the remainder of the capital to purchase houses, animals, and implements, so that "at the end of two years he has become an independent man and is in the position to marry without having to worry himself or his family."[29]

Reports from government officials concerning emigration repeatedly emphasized the pull of America's wealth as another primary cause of the movement. The district official from Sogn and Fjordane, after the first decade of heavy emigration, wrote that it was based on the hope of a better position in life in the United States.[30] In the 1860s the causes were the same; the official believed that the large

number of emigrants was due to the "expectation of better conditions for them and their children."[31] Balestrand's minister was more
specific in his report written the same year: He believed that the
widespread emigration was "exclusively" due to the search for
"easier access to earning capital that America" offered. Moreover,
the "steady information" to this effect that people received from
formerly emigrated relatives and friends made the possibilities all
the more alluring.[32]

The letters from family and friends that frequently observed greater opportunities for children also often graphically portrayed the
economic advantages of life in the United States. Some observers
argued that the letters were exaggerated and created a too rosy
impression of conditions in America.[33] This they well might have
done: Reiersen, who advocated emigration, said nonetheless that
most emigrants had idealized conceptions of what they would find.
Letters, however, often contained concrete examples of wealth that
documented the available opportunities.[34] Some, such as Anders
Viig in 1841, put the advantages quite simply: "Every industrious
and abled bodied person," he asserted, "will make a better living
here than in Norway." Others vividly portrayed their feeling of
release from the arduous work in Norway. One immigrant from
Agder said in 1850, "My brothers and sisters and I have all acquired
land, and we are happy and content. This year we have produced so
much foodstuff that we have been able to sell instead of having to
buy, and we all have cattle, driving oxen, and wagons. I feel very
sorry that you have to work your youth away in Norway," she
concluded, "where it is so difficult to get ahead."[35]

The bountiful land, high wages, and opportunity for enormous
material wealth were also emphasized in the letters. One writer
stressed, "Here the food is overflowing and we get to drink as much
sweet milk as we desire; when the milk becomes sour, it is thrown
out to the pigs" – a practice of waste unheard of in Norway.[36] A
woman from Hallingdal likewise did not regret having left Norway,
especially when she remembered the burdens of which she was
relieved in the cattle stalls in the winter and during the arduous
collection of leaves and grass. "Here," she added significantly, "one
does not need to be thrifty with the hay."[37] The theme of easier
cattle husbandry was reiterated by another letter writer in 1860. He
was satisfied that he had moved to America, recalling the "heavy
burden" from which he had escaped. "I feel very glad about it all,"
he wrote, "when I remember moving to the støls, the plight of the
cattle in winter, the difficulty of getting hay . . . From all this, with

God's help, I regard myself as freed."[38] Not only was farm work less arduous, but wages were higher. One man urged his brother to emigrate; "You can earn more in two months," he figured, "than you can earn in Norway the whole year" – a compelling argument even without the additional opportunity to become landed.[39]

If letter writers tended to exaggerate, to what degree were circumstances actually better in the United States? When someone in Balestrand received a letter recounting wages and land opportunities, how did the possibilities really compare with those at home? Many letters contained specific data on wage levels and the availability, fertility, and cost of land, in addition to the value judgments. The wage rates in Sogn bear out Reiersen's argument that wages were "twice – yes, three or four times – as high as they are in Norway." Men, for example, could expect a daily wage equal to 244.3% of what they received in Sogn, whereas women could get 47.1% more on a daily basis. The disparity between yearly rates was even greater, ranging from 465.6% more pay for men to 400.0% more for women. Reiersen also reported that the cost of living in America was about half that in Norway and that work in America was relatively abundant.[40] A journalist, discussing the pros and cons of emigration in 1869, contended that because of the higher wages and lower living costs, land could indeed be obtained through labor in the United States. Although laborers in Norway could work year after year without accruing much capital, a man in America "in two to five years can become owner of farmland large enough to support a family."[41]

As already observed, information about opportunities for land in the letters, like wage data, also made emigration enticing. Land ownership was within reach for the propertyless, Reiersen stated, because a good worker, after "consulting those of his countrymen who arrived before him" to find work, could earn 75 cents a day in Wisconsin and save 50 cents of it. After one hundred days' work, the $50 saved could be used to acquire a 40-acre farm.[42] Those with capital, of course, were more fortunate, since they could immediately purchase cheap government land. In the years to come, the landed immigrants could buy a yoke of oxen, cows, and some sheep and swine, as well as the necessary machinery. Reiersen estimated that by beginning with $500, a Norwegian farmer who was frugal and hardworking could enjoy an increase in wealth of $935 after three years.[43] How did these examples compare to wealth in Balestrand? In 1863 the most valued farm in Balestrand had 32½ mål of land in grain and potato production.[44] Yet if the reports from America were

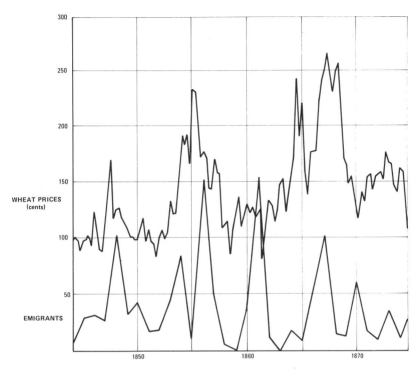

Fig. 5. New York wheat prices per bushel and emigration from Balestrand, 1844–75. *Sources*: Data from Balestrand church books; John Giffin Thompson, *The Rise and Decline of the Wheat Growing Industry in Wisconsin*, Economic and Political Science Series (Madison, Wis., 1909), p. 226.

true, the immigrant could acquire 40 acres of land with ease – equal to 162 mål. With such fantastic accounts of wealth and mobility in America, it is not difficult to understand why government officials believed that the reports were exaggerated.

In spite of an improved well-being in Balestrand throughout the nineteenth century, then, the knowledge of greater opportunity in America resulted in a large emigration led by the wealthier segments of the society. After comparing conditions at home and across the sea, many chose to exploit the abundant openings in the United States. When conditions did prove to be more favorable in America, emigration increased. A close relationship exists, for example, between the prices of wheat in New York, representing economic conditions in the rural Middle West, and emigration from Balestrand (see Figure 5). When wheat prices rose, an increase in emigration usually followed a year or two later, especially in the early periods. People in Balestrand became keenly aware not only of conditions in Norway but of wages and prices across the sea as well.

Diffusion of emigration from Balestrand

That wealthy farmers led the early emigration from Balestrand indicates that initial movement was a decision between opportunities in America and those in Norway among segments of society that would have been comfortable in either place. The early emigrants were usually the well-to-do, the innovators, the leaders in society – those who were most aware of opportunities in the United States and elsewhere.[45] The emigration, however, rapidly diffused to all segments of society and soon profoundly influenced all elements in Balestrand, whether they emigrated or not (see Plate 11).

As the emigration continued, the reduced availability of labor benefited the landless. Farmers continued to use labor-intensive høstingsbruk, and they needed to adjust to fewer available laborers. Depleted labor supplies forced higher wages, on the one hand (see Table 7 in Chapter 4), and increased mechanization, on the other.[46] Complaints of labor shortages were common from the beginning of emigration, as expanded farms still required workers.[47] This increased demand for their labor permitted the landless to profit from threats of emigration as leverage to improve their situation at home.[48] It is little wonder that they considered America a blessing.

Farmers faced the changing labor structure from the other side of the fence. American opportunities worked to increase their labor costs but also created greater options for use of capital. With emigration as a possibility, the landed could weigh the pros and cons of farming in their home parish and in the United States. Emigration could bail out farmers who encountered adverse conditions, and after poor crop years the propensity to migrate increased. But even in good times the option of America was used as a safety valve that reduced risk and allowed increased speculation. One diary from Lesja, Gudbrandsdal, for example, stated that the 1860s were a period of economic prosperity when many young farmers lived beyond their means. By 1864, when speculation caught up with them, many salvaged what money they could and emigrated. Because of this trend, the writer claimed, "people approached the optimistic reports in letter and newspapers from America as a sign from God."[49]

The very awareness of America, whether one emigrated or not, worked to alter one's place in the social structure in Balestrand. As

Plate 11. Ambjørn Bale, who lived as a cotter on the Bale farm in Balestrand, sits alone in front of his home. Though he did not move to America, he was nonetheless affected by the phenomenon, since most of his children did. *Source*: Norsk Folkemuseum, Oslo; photograph by J. Finne

emigration sapped labor supplies, the landless who remained enjoyed improving conditions. Reports about economic circumstances in Sogn indicated an apprehension that falling land prices and increasing wages would cause continued emigration by the landowning farmers. Yet by mechanizing and paying higher wages, farmers adapted to the changing conditions. Servants were increasingly lured to Balestrand from the outside by higher wages.[50] By the 1860s an official disclosed that although landowners continued to leave Balestrand, they were smaller farmers. Ironically, though emigration bettered the welfare of the landless in Balestrand, it was these poorer elements who became the major emigrant group by the 1860s, as information about the United States diffused and as strategies for paying transportation costs evolved.

Two prominent barriers to emigration, access to information about conditions in the United States and the wherewithal to defray the costs of passage, were surmounted with varying speed by the poor. Though information diffused rapidly through all segments of society, the ability to pay for transportation was limited to certain groups. An early, substantial emigration from Balestrand, however, soon enabled many from the poorer segments of society to move to the United States as well. First, earlier emigrants often needed labor in their new settlements, a need in part remedied by providing passage to youths in Balestrand in exchange for work duties. Second, and more important, kin networks developed strategies that permitted family members without capital to emigrate. Typically, passage was provided for one family member, who worked in the United States to earn money that was sent home to enable additional kin to leave. Family members were thus often essential in providing both information and capital; the ensuing folk migration resulted in settlements in the United States based on Old World ties.

Accounts about opportunities in America were made available through a number of sources. Newspapers gave frequent – often unfavorable – accounts of emigration, which books sought to counter with "accurate" narratives of life in the United States. Since shipping companies profited from emigration, agents representing the various lines actively promoted it throughout Norway. In 1881, for example, the thirteen main agencies registered in Oslo had 6,254 underagents spread throughout Norway, 8 of whom worked full time in Sogn at one period.[51] Undoubtedly the most influential sources of information, however, were the letters from friends and relatives who had already emigrated to the United States.[52] Reports of government officials consistently stressed these letters as a primary cause of further emigration.[53] One wrote quite succinctly, "America is no longer an unknown land," owing to the lively correspondence between the home community and emigrants in most households.[54]

Because most letters were sent to kin remaining in Norway, those who emigrated as a result often moved to join the family whence the letters came. Correspondence thus worked not only to enlarge the volume of emigration but to influence its destination as well.[55] As emigration continued, the increasing volume of letters multiplied the available information on conditions in America. More and more people emigrated partly as a result of letters and then sent back their own reports, spurring still more to emigrate. As the movement progressed and the migration diffused, letters were sent more often even to the landless, so that scarcely any households in Balestrand had no near relatives in the United States.[56]

Even though some contended that the letters exaggerated opportunities in America, few could argue that money sent home was not a vigorous confirmation of wealth across the sea. Many letter writers also offered assistance for passage to the source of this wealth, in the form either of money or of prepaid tickets.[57] Data on the number of prepaid tickets from Balestrand have been retrieved from emigrant protocol lists. Although the data are spotty, they are complete for two periods: Nearly half (47.0%) of the 168 emigrants between 1880 and 1885 and well over two-thirds (72.3%) of the 137 between 1899 and 1904 traveled with prepaid tickets.[58] Similar patterns have been discovered in other areas throughout Norway. For example, travelers with prepaid tickets constituted, between 1875 and 1915, 38.9% of those from Vik in Sogn and 38% of those from Brønnoy and Vik in Helgeland; between 1871 and 1907 such travelers made up 44.9% of those from Tinn and Telemark and 51.9% of those from Dovre.[59] Moreover, research on Tinn has confirmed that prepaid tickets were especially important to poor emigrants. Whereas 87% of the cotter class traveled by prepaid tickets between 1881 and 1907, only 45% of the tenant farmer class (those who did not own their land but were more independent than cotters) and 33% of the farmer class used them.[60]

Letters and remittances underscore the value of kinship ties in enabling emigration. The nuclear family was the principal unit of emigration of the earliest emigrants, and particularly of the earliest farmers. From the beginning of emigration through 1849, 48 families constituted 89.3% of emigrants leaving Balestrand, compared to a mere 24 unattached individuals.[61] People moving individually, however, were often part of long chains that would ultimately lead the whole family from Balestrand to America. Between 1845 and 1854 only 28.6% of the emigrants traveling singly already had other nuclear family members in the United States. But in the following twenty years 65.3% of the 95 single emigrants from Balestrand already had siblings, parents, children, or spouses in the United States.[62]

Cotter's son Sjur Iversen Rømoren, for example, moved to Wisconsin in 1845 at age twenty-one, becoming the first person to leave Mundal parish. Three years later, brother Zacarius Iversen, his wife, and their two children followed. Yet another seven years intervened before Anne Iversdatter, at age thirty-five, became the only woman in the nuclear family to emigrate from Balestrand, where she had been an unmarried servant. Frequently found among the landless, this pattern suggests that remittances from earlier family emigrants had enabled additional kin to move to America. A different cotter family from Boyum farm, one generation removed from

the farming class, used strategies, ranging from reliance on wealthier relatives for passage to emigration of single family members, that
ultimately brought the whole household to America. In 1848 Brithe
Arnesdatter Boyum was able to move to Wisconsin, traveling with
her uncle, a farmer. Five years later her younger brother and sister
joined her when they emigrated with a maternal uncle, also a farmer. The youths were able to pay the fares of remaining family members in 1856. The entire household settled first in Norway Grove,
Wisconsin, before moving to southeastern Minnesota. The decision
to emigrate was an economically wise one. All the children eventually owned land, ranging up to 537 acres, something they undoubtedly would have been denied in Balestrand.[63] Other studies
have also emphasized the role of kinship in increasing the volume of
emigration. Of the 147 groups of emigrants from Dovre between
1866 and 1914, for example, 85% had at least two persons who were
near relatives in the group. Of the 123 individuals who emigrated
between 1891 and 1895, 63% had near relatives among earlier
emigrants.[64]

Just as nuclear family ties were important in emigration, the less
easily discovered or verified ties of extended family, farm, and even
neighborhood were also crucial. The stereotypical rich American
uncle who sent passage and the group of siblings who with their
families and parents settled in the Upper Middle West were both a
part of the migration tradition. Hans Hansen Mundal, for instance,
was the first child of cotter Hans Olsen to emigrate, moving with his
wife, children, and younger brother and sister to Wisconsin in 1849.
Nine nephews, five nieces, and two sisters left Balestrand between
1856 and 1870. Ties among unrelated farm members also at times
provided opportunities to move to America, the most extraordinary
example in Balestrand being that of farmer's widow Bothilda
Gjerde. After her husband died, Bothilda resolved in 1856 for one
reason or another to move to the United States. In addition to her
own passage, she paid the fares of all cotters and their families on
the Gjerde and Grøneng farms, totaling over twenty people. This
step, she believed, would protect her from homesickness.[65]

Just as kinship ties influenced emigration patterns, so did those of
neighborhood. The first emigrant from Balestrand left Vangsnes in
1844, but the inland valleys of the Sværefjord, Vetlefjord, and
Fjærlandsfjord rapidly became the most intense emigration regions.
Well over one-third of the residents in the neighborhood around
Sværefjord, for example, had left Norway up to 1849 (see Table 22).
Likewise, the neighborhoods of Boyum farm (*Boyagrendi*) and Mun-

Table 22. *Emigration according to grend: Balestrand, 1844–69*

	1840–49			1850–59			1860–69		
	No. emig.	Pop. 1845	%	No. emig.	Pop. 1855	%	No. emig.	Pop. 1865	%
Tjugum par.									
Balagrendi	9	115	7.8	6	121	5.0	27	165	16.4
Eitorngrendi	2	100	2.0	10	90	11.1	9	93	9.7
Fjærstagrendi	8	100	8.0	8	123	6.5	20	130	15.4
Sværefjordgrendi	70	184	38.0	66	222	29.7	16	218	7.3
Tjuagrendi	0	197	0	46	228	20.2	40	200	20.0
Tusgrendi	3	71	4.2	25	70	35.7	4	80	5.0
Vetlefjordgrendi	38	209	18.2	69	218	31.6	19	241	7.9
Mundal par.									
Boyagrendi	24	181	13.3	32	191	16.7	28	175	16.0
Jordalsgrendi	20	201	9.9	70	196	35.7	69	203	34.0
Mundalsgrendi	41	282	14.5	49	298	16.4	84	302	27.8
Vaateviksgrendi	3	78	3.8	19	70	27.1	22	63	34.9
Vangsnes par.									
Vangsnesgrendi	7	210	3.3	27	253	10.7	64	259	24.7
Garadngrendi	0	49	0	2	34	5.9	0	43	0

Source: Balestrand church records.

dal farm (*Mundalsgrendi*) in Fjærlandsfjord and Vetlefjord (*Vetle-fjordgrendi*) experienced relatively heavy early emigration.[66] Economic misfortunes possibly caused emigration to be concentrated in these districts. Of the eleven farmers who left Tjugum parish in the ten years after 1845, ten came from the flatland farms in the Vetle-fjord and Sværefjord neighborhoods.[67] Yet since the emigrants included relatively wealthy farmers leaving rich land, it is more likely that they moved because of information from others who had already emigrated. Letters from the Wisconsin settlements that described opportunities in America rapidly disseminated throughout the grend.[68] The closely knit neighborhood frequently celebrated marriages, burials, and annual holidays, gatherings that undoubtedly served to spread the news about America rapidly once it arrived in Balestrand.[69] Although information about emigration infiltrated into certain neighborhoods first, it soon diffused so that all but one area was eventually affected by movement to the United States (see Table 22).

The landless did not possess resources of information or capital to lead the emigration, but, as noted, they eventually became the largest emigrant segment leaving Balestrand (see Table 21).[70] The increasing trans-Atlantic networks among kin and friends, a "tradition factor" that increased the volume of emigration, were especially salient in the old emigration districts like Balestrand, which developed strong bonds with the United States. The intricate networks of kin that connected Norway and America made it scarcely more difficult, possibly easier, to find family and friends in Minnesota than in Bergen.[71]

Conclusion

America had a profound effect on Balestrand residents. Children in the mid-nineteenth century were raised with the alternative of moving to the United States. They could weigh the economic advantages and social satisfactions of the United States and Norway and move accordingly. Moreover, the sum of these individual decisions changed the entire socioeconomic structure of Balestrand. The pervasive tradition of migration to the United States also brought people in Balestrand to look outside their community for betterment increasingly often. An old farmer in 1860 noted, "Folk today are not satisfied eating bark as our parents did"; instead they desired the things that were attainable in America. "Why ought we not also aspire to better livelihoods," he added, "just like tax collectors [*fut*] and priests here in the land?"[72] These aspirations, what one historian called "demanding mentality" and a "new spirit of the times," forced employers in Balestrand to pay higher wages in order to retain labor supplies.[73] But they were also an integral part of the emigration itself, a legacy carried from Balestrand by the emigrants who were forming settlements in the Upper Middle West.

At the same time, however, emigration was often based on conservative attempts to recreate traditional aspects of life in the new American communities. Districts that, like Balestrand, were typified by emigration often possessed Norway's most traditional folk cultures as well. For hundreds of years migrants had moved from the inner communities toward the coast or into the cities. It was in these more cosmopolitan areas, where pressures to give up old folkways were strongest, that much of the regional folk culture was abandoned. Accordingly, a barrier developed between the conservative, traditional inland communities and the areas on the coast and especially in the cities. An American writer noted the conflict between city and farm on a boat trip from Bergen to the Sognefjord. "There is one thing," he wrote in 1881,

that a bonde (farmer) will never do, no matter how rich he may
be, and that is to buy a first class ticket . . . Not that he is mean,
for he is far from it . . . He has not the slightest inclination to
mingle with the people of the cities, many of whom, here as
elsewhere look down on these tillers of the soil, making fun of
their clothes and manners, and refusing to mix with them . . .
Besides if a farmer were inclined to take a first class ticket, he
would refrain from doing so, lest he should be ridiculed by his
friends, who would think that he was putting on airs and wanted
to appear like a herre (gentleman).[74]

It is important to note that America provided not only ample land
and higher wages but a location where a relatively isolated agricultural framework permitted Balestrand emigrants to retain parts of
their social fabric under more sanguine conditions. As knowledge of
the openings in the United States diffused, a migration tradition
developed.[75] The more traditional regions often became the hotbed
of America fever. People from Vangsnes parish, for example, with
their ties to the coast, were more likely to migrate internally around
the turn of the century, whereas those from the more isolated areas,
such as Mundal parish, tended to emigrate.[76] As Ingrid Semmingsen writes, "One might say that paradoxically rural conservatism prompted [the emigrants] to make a radical decision. Gradually the number of fellow dalesmen in America became so large that
it seemed less strange to join them than to move to other places in
Norway. They were perhaps trying to defend and protect an old
pattern of life by emigrating."[77]

In short, emigrants from Balestrand carried a rich cultural tradition with them to America. Among the cultural components, however, were innovations as well as long-standing norms. The Balestrand immigrant settlements became pervaded by the "new spirit
of the times," but more specifically they were influenced by the
pietistic movements within their old society and by efforts of the
official classes, such as the clergy, to implant middle-class propriety
in the community. Although the prairies of the Upper Middle West
seemed an ideal location to preserve the cultural tradition, then, it
should not be forgotten that the cultural tradition to be preserved
had been in a continual process of flux.[78]

The dissimilar environments in Balestrand and the settlement
areas of the Upper Middle West precluded the complete transplantation of many cultural components. Rolling woodlands and prairies
in America stood in stark contrast to the massive mountains and
blue-green waters of the fjords. Likewise, the divergent ratios of

land and labor, the greater opportunities to own land, and the developing market structure radically altered patterns as Balestrand immigrants began to settle in Wisconsin and Minnesota in the 1840s. It has been argued that these environmental differences of cheap land and expensive labor changed behavior patterns and "simplified" European cultures overseas.[79] Yet as we shall see in the remaining pages, the adaptations to American conditions were produced through a tension and interaction between old cultural norms and new environmental configurations. The immigrants remained active participants in this interplay and introduced changes that were compatible with both elements.

In the following chapters we will examine the adaptation of emigrants who built new homes on the prairies of the Middle West in settlements dominated by people from Balestrand. A myriad of social, economic, demographic, and cultural changes occurred as the farmers adjusted to American conditions. Such adaptations were closely related to the new farming patterns and increasing wealth that the immigrants enjoyed. Like the other adjustments made by the immigrants, however, these were consonant with the cultural traditions carried from Norway and developed within the Norwegian-American settlements. Well-to-do Norwegian-Americans, who often returned around the turn of the century to the modest peasant homes they had left thirty, forty, or fifty years before, were striking examples of the cultural adaptations in the United States. One wealthy returnee led a writer from Aurland, Sogn, to exclaim, "Such it could go when poor boys got air under their wings. Then they were part of an adventure just as remarkable, just as grand, and just as thrilling as that told about Askeladden, the princess and the kingdom."[80] It is to this adventure that we now turn.

7   "They rushed from place to place": American settlement patterns among Balestrand's immigrants

The journey to the United States often was not the final experience of geographical mobility for the Balestrand immigrants. Open land to the west continued to beckon many immigrants, who after moving once migrated again. A Norwegian-language newspaper remarked that "the 'America fever' has raged in many places in old Norway and it is not always quieted by the establishment of a home in the New World. Those who live in the old settlements learn that great reaches of fertile and free land are to be had to the westward, and so they again turn toward the new and the unseen."[1] An immigrant years later concurred. "It was hunger for land," he wrote, "which drove the first and the most to America. They threw themselves at the earth and slaved on it and never could get enough. The history of the first settlements shows how they rushed from place to place always looking for land, and when they found some, they left it to look for something better."[2] Repeated migration created a glaring break from the experience in Norway previous to the emigration, one that profoundly influenced the spatial organization of Balestrand immigrants as well as strategies of farm tenure and family structure.

Young immigrants often led westward migrations in the Upper Middle West. In 1873, for instance, a caravan of Norwegian-born immigrants left the group's first American residence in southeastern Minnesota and northwestern Iowa for yet another new home to the west, eventually settling in eastern South Dakota. For many, the "weary journey" was a "honeymoon trip," according to a local historian. Young men and women newly married had left an area with few land opportunities for the open prairies in the Dakotas.[3] Likewise, some years later a letter written to Norway observed, "It is common here in America that when a locality is settled, young people, especially young married couples, will move on to new districts where there is either free or at least cheap land. If they are lucky and find good land and in addition are industrious and sensible, they soon will acquire an independent position."[4]

137

The pattern of young married couples' leaving home had not begun in America. Emigration from Balestrand often followed soon after marriage, since household formation had been based on land and labor opportunities anticipated in the United States. Of the thirty-four couples between the ages of twenty and twenty-nine who emigrated from Balestrand through 1860, for example, 44.1% had married within six months and an additional 17.6% had wed within a year of departure. Certainly the linkage between marriage and migration was partly because the decision to stay at home or to seize on new opportunities elsewhere was often made at about the time when youths married.[5] But a household formation was also frequently based on a livelihood awaiting in the United States that would sanction the marriage.

As noted in the preceding chapter, the migration from Balestrand to the United States, which was often followed by additional journeys to the west, was deeply influenced by the flows of information arriving from the United States. Settlements peopled by immigrants from Balestrand and neighboring areas of Sogn therefore dotted the Upper Middle West. Moreover, just as they settled together, the immigrants also tended to migrate to the west in groups, enjoying the same advantages of community. Mobility was thus not necessarily the antithesis of community stability. Some immigrants from Balestrand retained the benefits of remaining in a region peopled not only by Norwegians but by people of similar background and theological inclinations as well. Others found it to their advantage to move again, often among colonizing groups that replicated the benefits of community enjoyed by those who stayed.

A moving community was a logical compromise between the desire to own land and the advantages of group settlement. But migration also tended to increase the importance of the nuclear family. The nuclear family became the principal unit of migration even after emigration. Moreover, great opportunities to migrate increased the cost of labor and placed yet greater emphasis on the family in farm production. The presence of land and the frequency of migration thus became central components of the changing conditions to which immigrants were forced to adapt.

Rural Norwegian settlement patterns in the United States

Marcus Lee Hansen, in his seminal essay "Immigration and Expansion," suggested that nineteenth-century immigrants to the United States behaved very differently from their Yankee neighbors when buying and selling land, migrating, and "pioneering." Europeans, it seems, were "surprised, even shocked," at the "sacrilegious attitude of agriculturalists toward the 'holy earth.'" Old Americans had a different attitude toward the land they were claiming. "The farms hewn from the wilderness," Hansen continued, "were not to be the homes for untold generations of descendants; they were sources of income with which the owners would willingly part if they scented a speculative gain in the transaction. They traded farms in the same lighthearted spirit that they swapped horses." This frenetic trading of land, which also resulted in widespread mobility, varied from immigrant strategies. The ambition of the German-American father was "to see his sons on reaching manhood established with their families on farms clustered about his own." The American father, conversely, made no such effort on behalf of his offspring, for "to be a self made man was his ideal." Each new generation would create its place in society just as its predecessor had done.[6]

Hansen also argued that "neither by experience nor temperament was the immigrant fitted for pioneering." Only a few of the immigrants who ventured into the "wilds" became successful; the majority drifted "back to civilization" with emphatic advice: "Let the Americans start the clearing, they alone possess the specialized techniques." In short, "by nature and habit the American was restless . . . the immigrants were the 'fillers-in.'"[7] Hansen thus posited a dichotomy of behavior. The American moved, exploited opportunities for cheap land, and wheeled and dealed in order to become a self-made man. The immigrant was less mobile, owing to his ingrained love of the land, which he would not exploit sacrilegiously. He stayed put, increased his holdings, and measured his success by the degree to which his dream of creating farms around him for his offspring was realized.

Yet as Hansen himself stressed in the same essay, the immigrant communities did participate in the westward migration. Communities that were established inevitably faced a closing out of land opportunities, and

> relief was found only when the colony sent out a subcolony or, more often, half a dozen. Young men who had reached maturity in America, fathers who had become infected with the prevailing restlessness, established themselves elsewhere, usually not more than a score of miles away . . . When this large settlement in turn became crowded, colonies were sent out to more distant regions, perhaps across state boundaries. The migration often assumed

the form of a joint enterprise. A caravan of a hundred or more wagons departed and took possession of a township. Additional immigrants, however, usually continued to seek the old communities, where they were told that ampler opportunities awaited them in the newer settlements. So they resumed their journey, generally with more hardships; and the story of surprise arrivals and enforced charity was repeated. A decade passes and again the social organism divided, losing perhaps a little of the regional homogeneity at each division.[8]

The root of Hansen's ambivalence about immigrants' community stability and mobility seems to be the incongruity between the two patterns: some people settling in homogeneous communities based on Old World cultural ties and others moving about, seemingly in a reflection of a mobile, individualistic American society.[9] Norwegians often emigrated, settled, moved again, and resettled within a framework of ties originating in Norway. Stability within Norwegian colonies was due not so much to an emotional attachment to the soil as to benefits derived by the immigrants from compact settlement. Mobility was not necessarily symptomatic of an individualistic society but might be an attempt among segments of the settlements to realize better circumstances to the west. Fluid settlement patterns were a logical attempt to exploit American resources within the context of Norwegian immigrant confines.

Norwegian immigrants often moved to the Upper Middle Western settlements that already were primarily Norwegian.[10] Kristofer Janson, while traveling in the United States in the 1880s, marveled that "the Norwegians succeeded in secluding and bunching themselves together in colonies and in maintaining their Norwegian memories and customs. I often had to pinch my arm to realize that I really was in America . . . One heard nothing but Norwegian speech and it never occurred to me to address people on the road except in Norwegian."[11] The settlements, however, were often focused on even more specific Norwegian regional ties. Because of the chain migrations from Norway, immigrants from single valleys and dales often settled together.[12] Nearly half (47.5%) of the household heads in Koshkonong, one of the major early settlements in Wisconsin, had been born in Telemark. The Coon Prairie settlement, also in Wisconsin, consisted of two major groups from Upland and Rogaland that settled near, but remained distinct from, each other.[13] The crazy-quilt pattern of nationality groups on the land, therefore, was further subdivided into smaller, more culturally distinct groups with common pasts, a subdivision that created even more cohesive communities.[14]

The spatial divisions between regional communities within larger Norwegian settlements were often consciously perceived by their residents. One member of the Beaver Creek settlement in Wisconsin described a ten-mile stretch along a road in which his own Hardanger group was dominant. Just beyond the borders of his father's farm, however, was a "solid patch of 'Strilar,' fishermen from the outer fjords, with whom the Hardanger group felt they had little in common." Settlements in the United States were often distinguished with reference to former spatial relationships in Norway. One section of the Blue Mound area in Wisconsin was called *vestmannsbatomen* (the Westman's Bottom) by people from Valdres because Telemarkings, whose home in Norway lay to the west of Valdres, lived there. "Nordmenn" were those from Sogn, since they came from north of the mountains, again a regional distinction originating in Norway.[15]

In addition to spatial differentiation, cultural and social divisions, based on regional settlement, could lead to discord. In a northern Iowa settlement, for instance, Vossing children mocked those from Røros. One informant remembered that as a child "we used to come home and cry because they made fun of our speech, and then mother said to us, 'that's nothing you need to cry about, just talk Norwegian the way you do here at home, for your speech won't shame you unless you shame yourself.'" Courtship between youth from differing regional groups was at times condemned. A Sogning who had courted a girl from Nordfjord overheard two Nordfjording women talking about the end of their affair. "Oh well," one of the women said, "maybe Anna is just as well off, for he's nothing but a lousy Sogning anyway!"[16]

Varying moral standards were also occasionally identified with regional backgrounds. The people in the Beaver Creek settlement of Wisconsin were from Hardanger and from areas to the south that were known in the settlement for their piety. When a house was raised by a "southerner," four skilled fiddlers from Hardanger asked permission to hold a housewarming dance. "But he didn't like this," an informant noted. "He looked at them awhile and then he answered: 'No,' he said, 'we're not like the Hardanger people with dancing every evening!'"[17] Certainly Norwegian regional groups interacted among one another, as the courtship just noted attests. But parochial barriers remained a factor influencing community development that is often understated by historians today.[18]

Though the regional groups squabbled, the ties within groups based in Norway tended to settle people together and worked to enlarge settlement size. A contemporary observer noted the intense desire among Norwegians to acquire land. When they succeeded, he wrote, "the price of land in and around the Norwegian settlement rises. As their neighbors of other nations frequently find it to their account to sell out to them, the Norwegian settlements commonly enlarge."[19] In spite of this desire to enlarge settlement, however, land availability was often exhausted with amazing rapidity. Land in Koshkonong was quickly claimed after colonization began in 1842. "People came streaming into this place from all directions," according to an early account, "and as a result all the tillable land here was snapped up in an unbelievably short time. 'We scarcely had time to orient ourselves in our new home,' says one of the first settlers of the town of Dunkirk, 'before we were surrounded by neighbors on all sides.'"[20] As early as 1844 a Norwegian traveler who had passed through Dane County, Wisconsin, believed that little room remained for newcomers; by 1848 Ole Munch Ræder wrote that "the whole prairie" of the Rock Prairie, Wisconsin, settlement "is bought except for a few undesirable parts, so that now one must pay considerably more than government prices."[21] Instead of paying higher prices, many Norwegian immigrants moved to land farther west as it became available.

As early as 1854, three years after Indian treaties had opened land for white settlement, the *Daily Minnesotan* reproduced a *Madison Argus* report "that not less than 300 Norwegan [sic] parties have recently sold their farms in that vicinity and started for Minnesota."[22] Often the migration parties were large. One group in 1850 consisted of more than one hundred men, women, and children, their wagons, oxen, horses, two hundred head of cattle, some hogs, and sheep.[23] Nineteen years later another caravan of forty-two families with teams, five hundred cattle, and two hundred sheep set out from northeastern Iowa for west-central Minnesota.[24]

Just as these groups of migrating Norwegian immigrants were often based on Old World ties, they frequently used settlements along the way with similar bonds as stopping-off places. Old Norwegian settlements served as resting places for the new immigrants, who paused to acclimate themselves to the American conditions or to accumulate capital as laborers.[25] One resident of the Koshkonong settlement contended in 1869:

> Immigration into Koshkonong from Norway in the last ten to twelve years has as good as come to a standstill. Newcomers remain here with friends or relatives for a few years, but only to gain a little money and experience, after which they go west to purchase land, where it can be obtained cheaper . . . So when a person goes to settlements in Iowa and Minnesota, he almost

everywhere comes in contact with individuals who for a longer or shorter time have lived in Koshkonong.[26]

As later immigrants used established settlements as footholds, a string of settlements based on kinship and Old World neighborhood ties matured in the west. One group from Stavanger, for example, moved to the Fox River settlement in Illinois. Since no land at low prices remained, they decided to move again toward land in Iowa or Minnesota. After arriving at a suitable area in Iowa in 1854, they took their claim; the settlement became known, appropriately enough, as Stavanger Prairie.[27] As settlement continued in the sixties and seventies, eastern Minnesota communities came to play a similar role for those moving to western Minnesota or the Dakotas. One sizable migration from Goodhue County, Minnesota, to counties farther west began in the 1870s, "since no more land was available in Goodhue." A Goodhue Norwegian noted that "a large number went to Lac qui Parle County, Minnesota, so that this county so to speak became a daughter of Goodhue, and anyone who travels around in these two counties, as I have done, finds the same names in both places."[28]

It is important to note that ties among those of similar regional Norwegian backgrounds were often maintained even during this secondary migration. One settlement in Goodhue County was peopled largely by immigrants from the region of Valdres. According to a settler, however, "most of them remained there only a short while, for each year smaller or larger groups of Goodhue County people left for farming districts lying farther to the west where the land lay open to settlement, and one may find in the west several large Valdres settlements formed mainly by people who moved from Goodhue County."[29] Likewise, a caravan that arrived in 1867 in Houston County, Minnesota, consisted mainly of people from around Trondheim, Norway. The group decided the land there was too heavily populated, so they moved again in 1873 to South Dakota.[30] And so the migration continued. As settlement moved farther west, stopping-off places followed the movement. Yet for significant elements of the immigrant population, a moving community based in large part on Old World affinities tied colonies together throughout the Upper Middle West.

Balestrand settlement patterns in the United States

The broad outlines of settlement patterns among Norwegian immigrants throughout the Upper Middle West can be more intensively analyzed through an examination of the behavior of the Balestrand

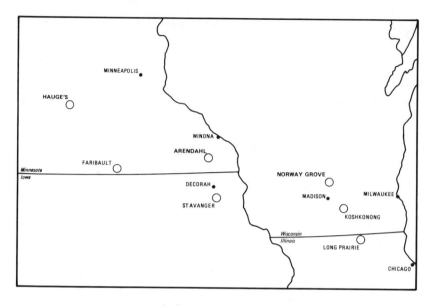

Fig. 6. Settlements in the Upper Middle West peopled by Balestrand immigrants

immigrants. Like most other regional groups, the early Balestrand immigrants gravitated toward settlement areas peopled largely by those from their home valleys. When most of the land had been purchased in these settlements, segments of the Balestrand community migrated to land farther west to improve their well-being. For those who "became infected with the prevailing restlessness," to borrow Hansen's phrase, group migration first to the United States and later within the Upper Middle West served as a strategy to reduce uncertainties and risks in coping with differences in the new environment. Certainly, as some became acclimated, such ties became less binding, and individuals or families gravitated less often toward the moving community. Yet a chain of settlements ranging from central Wisconsin westward manifests the importance of group settlement through most of the Balestrand emigration (see Figure 6).

The Balestrand colonies, of course, were not created full-blown by their settlers but had to be built over time through land transactions. The earliest migrants from Balestrand and Sogn moved to established Norwegian settlements in Illinois and Wisconsin. Per Iversen Unde, the first emigrant from Sogn, lived in Chicago for two years before settling in the Muskego settlement in Wisconsin.[31] Other early Sogning emigrants who left Norway in 1844 settled on Long Prairie, in north-central Illinois.[32] The Koshkonong settlement in Dane County, Wisconsin, eventually took precedence among the earliest Sogning immigrants. The first Balestrand immigrants in 1844, like those from neighboring Leikanger, moved to Koshkonong. The influx was so extensive that by 1846 Sogn-born immigrants exceeded those from Voss and Numedal, early Koshkonong groups, and were equal to about half of those from Telemark.[33]

By the mid-forties, however, the major Balestrand colony in Wisconsin was already in the process of settlement. Although the first Norwegian settler who moved to what would become the Spring Prairie and Norway Grove settlements in 1845 was born in Flatdal, Øvre Telemark, he was deluged by Sogning immigrants the following year.[34] Germans, Irish, Scots, Yankees, and Yorkers, in addition to Norwegians, peopled the environs of Norway Grove and Spring Prairie in this area of northern Dane County (see Figure 7). Yet the Norwegians, as well as the other nationality groups, maintained distinct enclaves in the townships of Vienna, Windsor, and Bristol in Dane County. The ethnic colonies enlarged or decreased as settlement progressed. Many of the early American-born settlers, for example, began to leave in 1847 when Norwegians moved in and purchased their claims.[35] These early Norwegian settlers were overwhelmingly of Sogning background.[36] The many letters home from the initial Sogning settlers, encouraging emigration to America and, more specifically, to Norway Grove, apparently were quite convincing. In the three years following 1848, according to a local historian, "so many immigrants came from Sogn and located in Norway Grove that the settlement came to be called 'Sogn.'"[37] By 1861, when the first plat map was published, most of the Sognings in Spring Prairie and Norway Grove settlements were immigrants from Balestrand and Leikanger (see Figure 8).

Not only were many Norwegians in Norway Grove and Spring Prairie from Balestrand, but most immigrants from Balestrand were moving to Norway Grove and Spring Prairie (see Plate 12). Using the emigrant lists in the Balestrand church books and the church records of Norway Grove and Spring Prairie, I determined the degree to which Balestrand immigrants moved to Norway Grove. Some immigrants who moved to the settlement were lost, since they became what the early high-church pastors disparagingly called "Norwegian indians" and did not join a church. Still, between 1844 and 1853, the first decade of immigration, at least 223 out of 345 (64.6%) of Balestrand's immigrants moved to the Norway Grove

146

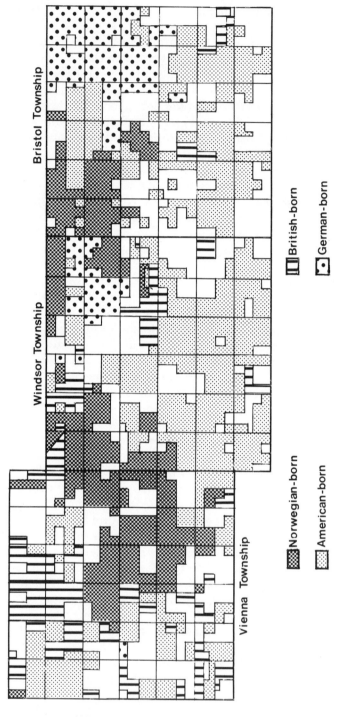

Fig. 7. Nation of birth of landholders in Norway Grove–Spring Prairie region, 1861. *Sources*: Data from published 1861 plat map, Dane County; U.S. manuscript population census, Vienna, Windsor, and Bristol townships, 1860

Bristol Township

Windsor Township

Vienna Township

Norwegian-born

American-born

British-born

German-born

(Blank spaces are unowned land.)

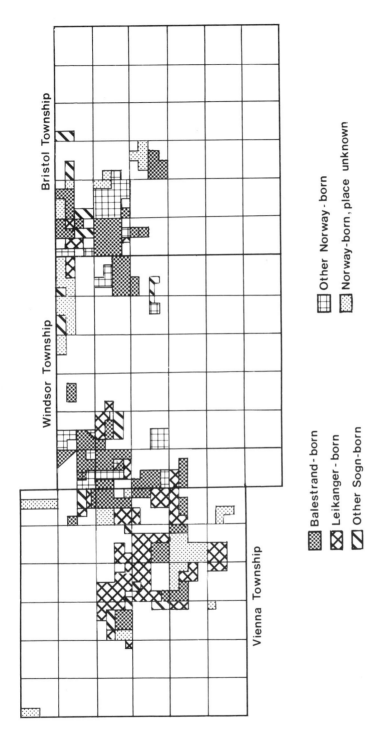

Fig. 8. Place of birth of Norwegian landholders in Norway Grove–Spring Prairie region, 1861. *Sources:* Data from published 1861 plat map; Norway Grove and Spring Prairie church books, which identified the parish of confirmation among the Norwegians

147

Plate 12. One of the many Balestrand households to build a farm in Norway Grove was the Hans Sværen family, shown here in the mid-1870s in front of its house, barn, and outbuildings. *Source*: State Historical Society of Wisconsin; photograph by Andrew Dahl

settlement. In the next decade (1854–63), only 30.6% joined the Norway Grove or Spring Prairie churches, as settlements farther west had become more alluring and the Norwegian settlement had largely moved accordingly.[38] In the Norway Grove–Spring Prairie area, these Balestranders settled together in pockets in eastern Vienna, western Bristol, and western Windsor township, whereas the Leikanger people dominated in central Vienna township (see Figures 8 and 9).[39]

Sognings, of course, could not monopolize the rich prairie lands around Norway Grove and Spring Prairie, for other nationalities and other Norwegian groups also moved to the region. A group of immigrants from Voss, for example, immigrated to Koshkonong in 1845 and found that the best land had already been claimed. They decided to look further and were led by one Ole Himle, a good judge of land. They had heard talk of outstanding land that lay about twenty-five miles to the northwest, and there they found Spring Prairie and Norway Grove already peopled by Sognings.[40]

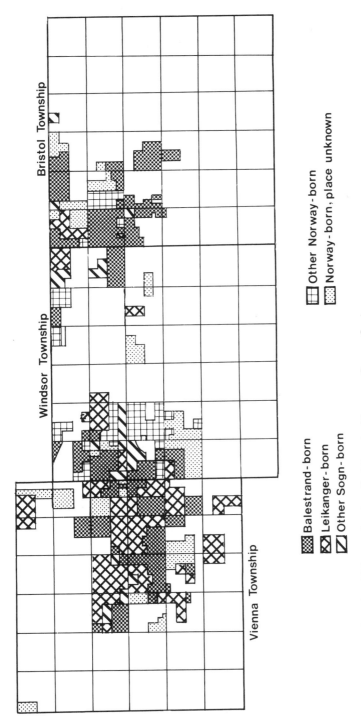

Fig. 9. Place of birth of Norwegian landholders in Norway Grove–Spring
Prairie region, 1874. *Sources*: Data from Norway Grove and Spring Prairie
church books; published 1874 plat map

Bristol Township

Windsor Township

Vienna Township

Balestrand-born
Leikanger-born
Other Sogn-born

Other Norway-born
Norway-born, place unknown

The Vossings, who had probably been informed about the land by these very Sognings, who had left the Koshkonong settlement the year before, settled in Spring Prairie and formed a distinct subcommunity among the Sogning throng.

As the area was settled, immigrants separated into different church communities, based both on local spatial organization and on place of origin in Norway.[41] Johannes W. C. Dietrickson, pastor in the Koshkonong settlement, who visited the region in 1847, already perceived the presence of distinct colonies. "This Norwegian settlement," he wrote, "is really composed of three smaller settlements, Spring Prairie, Bonnet Prairie to the north of it, and Norway Grove to the west." Three congregations, based on the "smaller settlements," were organized in 1847, but two years later one church was formed to serve the three units. In 1851 Herman Preus, the first permanent pastor of the settlement, held his first service in the Spring Prairie–Norway Grove congregation at the home of a Leikanger immigrant. Presumably only a portion of the communities attended, since the total congregations already consisted of 442 members, 259 of whom took communion.[42]

Although the congregations had the same pastor and at times worshiped together, they remained distinct from one another and eventually formed separate churches. This distinctiveness was due in part to the spatial divisions within the community noted by Dietrickson. Beyond this, however, the congregations consisted of people of various Norwegian origins (see Table 23). Whereas Norway Grove was dominated by immigrants from Balestrand and Leikanger, as well as other Sogning communities, Bonnet Prairie to the north in Columbia County (not mapped in plats here) was peopled by emigrants from Telemark, specifically from Seljord and Sande. The Spring Prairie church was largely Sogning, but a large group of Vossings, originating from the move from Koshkonong, was also present.

The degree to which regional ties were maintained in everyday life is difficult to measure. Certain indicators, however, imply that the ties reinforced by regional dialects and customs were a salient influence on community activity. The heavy dialect of Sogn, for example, was the butt of many jokes. A Norwegian admitted, "We made fun of the Sognings," and thus "they became Americans before we did because they were ashamed." A Sogning from Norway Grove concurred with this assessment of dialect differences. "When I have to talk with a man [whom I don't know]," he said, "I don't like to talk crude Sogning."[43] Patterns of intermarriage seem to con-

Table 23. *County of birth in Norway for Spring Prairie, Norway Grove, and Bonnet Prairie church members, 1845–96*

	N	%
Spring Prairie church		
Balestrand	158	20.7
Leikanger	57	7.5
Other Sogn	223	29.2
Lærdal	(72)	(9.4)
Lyster	(46)	(6.0)
Voss	214	28.0
Haug	59	7.7
Other Norway	52	6.8
Total	763	99.9
Norway Grove church		
Balestrand	178	28.7
Leikanger	232	37.4
Other Sogn	147	23.7
Vik	(48)	(7.7)
Lyster	(40)	(6.5)
Other Norway	63	10.2
Total	620	100.0
Bonnet Prairie church		
Balestrand	7	1.2
Leikanger	15	2.7
Other Sogn	137	24.4
Aurland	(101)	(18.0)
Sande	257	45.8
Bø	31	5.5
Other Norway	114	20.3
Total	561	99.9

Note: Listings are for counties contributing more than 5% of the congregations.
Source: Spring Prairie, Norway Grove, and Bonnet Prairie Lutheran Church records.

firm the presence and maintenance of regional differences (see Table 24). Seventy-three weddings, nearly three-fifths of all those in which Balestrand or Leikanger immigrants took part between 1850 and 1874, married a couple from Balestrand or Leikanger. Nearly three times as many immigrants from Balestrand and Leikanger, therefore, took spouses from their home county as from other areas.[44]

Table 24. *Birthplaces of marriage partners of Balestrand- and Leikanger-born: Norway Grove, Spring Prairie, Lodi, and Bonnet Prairie, 1850–74*

	Bale–Leik/ Bale–Leik		Bale–Leik/ other Sogn		Bale–Leik/ other Norway	
	N	%	N	%	N	%
1850–54	11	73.3	4	26.7	0	.0
1855–59	18	60.0	9	30.0	3	10.0
1860–64	18	54.5	12	36.4	3	9.1
1865–69	12	52.2	8	34.8	3	13.0
1870–74	14	63.6	4	18.2	4	18.2
Total	73	59.3	37	30.1	13	10.6

Note: Balestrand and Leikanger have had to be combined here since the two counties were in one administrative district until 1847 and many of the Balestrand immigrants were listed as born in Leikanger by the American clergy early in the settlement period.
Source: Spring Prairie, Norway Grove, and Bonnet Prairie Lutheran Church records.

Although regional ties remained important in the formation and maintenance of kinship structures, factors such as geographical proximity and ideological conformity also influenced community interaction. Christian doctrinal differences that soon evolved in the area created strong ideological cleavages among the immigrants. Dietrickson's Kirkebog No. 1, written beginning in 1857, declared that Elling Eielsen, the leader of an intensely pietistic group, "had gotten special influence in Spring Prairie" before Dietrickson arrived. Dietrickson found the peoples' demeanor in Norway Grove and Bonnet Prairie more agreeable than in Spring Prairie, where many in the congregation were Eielsen followers.[45] An immigrant whom we have been following in past chapters, Arne E. Boyum, gave a sympathetic internal view of the revival. Through proselytization, a movement that Boyum called a "spiritual awakening," with meetings on Sunday and in the middle of the week, began in the fall of 1853. The awakening continued until twelve to sixteen families joined the movement, and "if one was working in the fields he could at times hear prayers, at other times humming of hymns."[46] Communities based on regional backgrounds, growing kinship networks, and evolving theological proclivities not only influenced interaction in this complex of settlements in northern Dane County; the migrations to the west, as we shall see, were frequently based on these same ties.

The process of community growth and development faced increasing constraints as the land was rapidly claimed. As late as 1861 some open land did still exist in the Spring Prairie–Norway Grove area, and Norwegian settlement did enlarge in the thirteen succeeding years in spite of the smaller tracts of open land (compare Figures 8 and 9). Yet although land clearing and estate division could permit a larger population, open land to the west had become a more viable option for some members of the community as early as the mid-1850s. A chain migration evolved as households that had lived in Norway Grove and Spring Prairie for a time moved in groups to newly opened western lands. Once a foothold had been gained, other families followed, either leaving settlements farther east or moving directly from Norway. This pattern of migration created a glaring break from the household strategies followed in Balestrand. When population increased in Balestrand, people intensified their use of land; in the United States migration opportunities encouraged a pattern of extensification.

Norway Grove became the source of several chains of settlements to the west based on Balestrand origins. Even though open land in Norway Grove was scarce, the area remained a place where newly arrived immigrants could settle for short periods before moving west to more land-rich settlements.[47] One secondary migration, for example, began in the spring of 1857 to a region in Faribault County, Minnesota. The household heads involved all had been born in Sogn, about a third of them in Balestrand. The three Balestranders were aged thirty-one or thirty-two, and only one was married. The following years saw continued migration from Balestrand, Aardal, and Hafslo until the Faribault settlement was called a "main settlement area of Sognings" by an early chronicler.[48] Another settlement, ultimately more significant in the Sogning secondary migration, had been founded three years earlier when a group of Balestrand and Sogning immigrants moved from Norway Grove to an area in northeast Fillmore County in Minnesota, centered in Arendahl township. In addition to similar Norwegian backgrounds, early Arendahl settlers also had bonds with the pietistic movement in Spring Prairie.[49]

Though routes from Norway Grove to southeastern Minnesota varied, they remained well-trodden paths, as early Arendahl settlers continued to rely on the mother settlement. The migrants usually traveled west on the Green Bay–Prairie du Chien military road, crossed the Mississippi River to McGregor, Iowa, and then proceeded to Decorah, Iowa, already a large Norwegian settlement, before moving into Fillmore County.[50] Early Arendahl settlers normally claimed land in the embryonic settlement and then returned to the safer confines of Norway Grove or Spring Prairie to continue work before moving back in the spring. A. E. Boyum, for example, secured land for his parents and two younger brothers in the small Arendahl settlement in 1857. He could not use draft animals for his return to Wisconsin in February of 1857 because of the deep snow, so he skied for three days over seventy miles to the Stavanger settlement in Ossian, Iowa. Since he was a lay preacher, Boyum held devotional meetings before skiing into Wisconsin. He took a train on the next leg of his journey, to Madison, and then walked the final seventeen miles in rain, slush, and poor footing to his relatives in Norway Grove. By mid-June the Boyum family and friends were ready to move west to Fillmore County. Equipped with a yoke of oxen and a wagon, the group arrived in two weeks, whereupon the clearing and building began.[51]

The Boyums were by no means the first colonists in the Arendahl settlement. Nearly one hundred Norwegian immigrants, many of them Sognings from Norway Grove, had arrived by 1856. The first Sognings moved to Arendahl in 1854 after living for a time in Koshkonong and Norway Grove. By 1855 Balestranders from Norway Grove, who undoubtedly had been advised of opportunities by their predecessors, began to arrive.[52]

Household composition indicates that these Sogning immigrants moved to exploit the more ample land opportunities in Minnesota. Of the settlers by 1854 that can be traced to the 1860 manuscript census, the men were young married adults ranging in age from 25 to 36, with a median age of 34. Their families were small, the median being one child. The pioneers in the following two years of settlement were of similar age, 27 to 38 years old, with a median age of 33. They were responsible for larger flocks of offspring, however, averaging about four children per household. Anders Olsen Ulvestad, for example, moved to Arendahl with his wife and infant son from Norway Grove. He had immigrated with his parents and siblings from Balestrand in 1850 and lived in Wisconsin for five years. But marriage and a fledgling family had encouraged movement to an environment more conducive to landed security. Until the beginning of the Civil War, Norway Grove continued to be the initial place of residence for Balestrand settlers who later moved to Arendahl. Of the thirty-nine Arendahl settlers who had been born in Balestrand and had emigrated between 1844 and 1854, 76.9% had lived for a time in the Norway Grove settlement. Only 13.5% of the emigrants who arrived in the following decade and none who came in the five years following the end of the Civil War could be traced to Norway Grove. By the later 1860s immigrants moved directly to Arendahl, and soon Arendahl became a mother settlement for yet other colonies to the west.[53]

When F. A. Husher, editor of the Norwegian-language newspaper *Budstikken*, visited Fillmore County in 1874, a score of years after initial settlement, he was especially impressed by the density of Norwegian settlement and by the fact that everyone in the region spoke Norwegian.[54] Like Norway Grove, however, this settlement was in fact even more culturally distinct than it first appeared. The Arendahl settlement retained its Sogning flavor. The first plat of the county, published in 1896, when mapped according to cultural background of landholder reveals that Balestrander and Sogning settlers remained a prominent element of the township more than four decades after initial settlement. Furthermore, Arendahl township was part of a region in Fillmore County considered one of the largest Sogning communities in the United States, numbering around three thousand near the turn of the century (see Figure 10).[55]

Many Arendahl settlement households were closely tied not only by similar regional background but by theological proclivities as well. The settlement was centered around a pietistic church affiliated with the Eielsen Synod, and later with the Haugean, both representing low-church activity among Norwegian-Americans. Some households that settled early in Arendahl township were neither of Sogning background nor from the Norway Grove settlement; yet they moved in Haugean circles and probably heard of settlement opportunities through these connections. Boyum, the lay preacher, in addition to working in the fields also pursued an itinerant course of teaching and visited Jefferson Prairie, Yorkville, Skoponong, and Koshkonong settlements in Wisconsin, as well as Long Prairie in Illinois.[56] Ideological inclinations thus influenced migration patterns and community formation in secondary settlements much as ties of region and kinship did.

Owing to different sectarian bonds among early settlers, the Lutheran church in Arendahl remained important not only in reinforcing affinities but in creating discord. The first religious service in Arendahl settlement was performed by Boyum in the home of Ole Petersen Mundalsskreen, a fellow native of Balestrand. A church building for the Arendahl Lutheran Church was completed by 1860, four years after the congregation had been organized. This "crude" structure, which measured only eighteen by thirty-four feet and was built of logs hewn on two sides, was replaced in 1863 when the

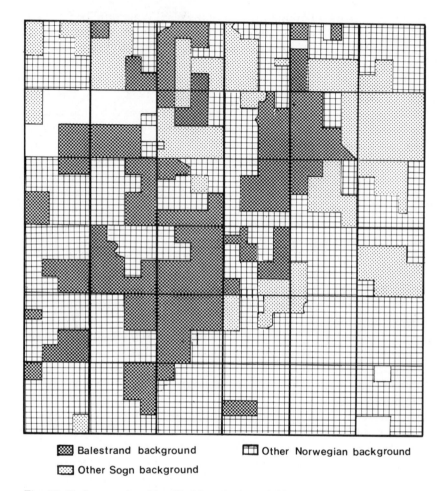

Balestrand background   Other Norwegian background

Other Sogn background

Fig. 10. Backgrounds of landholders in Arendahl township, 1896. *Sources*: Data from local histories, owing to incomplete church records for Arendahl; some Balestrand landowners probably missed

church membership (numbering 424) had become too large.[57] Meanwhile, another church with differing theological views was formed. The North Prairie Lutheran Church was organized in 1858 in Arendahl township, two years after first services were performed by U. V. Koren. Although a pastor was called in 1858, church services were held in homes for five years before a church building was constructed. Significantly, the North Prairie church in 1861 joined the Norwegian Synod, the "high-church" body.[58]

Although both churches were peopled by Norwegians, the lines of conflict were drawn. The Arendahl church, based on pietistic theological leanings and a Sogning past, was distinct from the high-church North Prairie organization, not so strongly associated with Sogn. These Norwegian groups maintained their distance for decades. As late as 1892, nearly forty years after initial settlement, the pastor of the North Prairie church resigned. The congregation thereupon voted to confer with the Arendahl congregation about joining together to form a call to one pastor. "Records show that representatives of Arendahl congregation were present at the meeting," noted the church historian. "But for reasons that may be hard to explain the two congregations are no nearer together today [1936], after several attempts, than they were at the time."[59]

While the propinquitous groups centered around the Arendahl and North Prairie churches fraternized less than one might expect, the Arendahl and Faribault settlements were part of a network of communities that sustained contact in spite of geographical distance. Marriages, on occasion, linked youths from different settlements. One early settler of Arendahl, after corresponding with a young woman in Balestrand and later in Norway Grove, returned to Wisconsin to propose. They were married in 1859 at the home of his brother-in-law and sister in Norway Grove, before beginning their "honeymoon" journey to Minnesota the same evening. A group visiting Arendahl from Dane County – all originally from Balestrand – joined to celebrate another wedding. This time the couple was married in Arendahl and returned to Norway Grove to set up a home.[60]

Other linkages based on theological concerns were fostered. Boyum made trips four to six times yearly to the Stavanger settlement, walking sixty miles each way. He also visited the Faribault settlement before 1861 and undoubtedly became reacquainted with people he had known in Balestrand who would later form a Haugean church. He served as temporary minister for eight other congregations in Wisconsin, Minnesota, and Iowa. Ideological similarities influenced settlement in Arendahl and its ties to other communities, and these doctrinal proclivities would continue to affect later Balestrand settlements to the west.

Like Norway Grove, Arendahl township offered fewer opportunities to become landed as settlement progressed. Accordingly, another major Balestrand settlement springing from the Arendahl and, to a lesser extent, Norway Grove areas again advanced toward the west-northwest. A settlement began near the Minnesota River in the central part of the state in the mid-1860s and was eventually centered around a Haugean church in Camp and Bandon townships of Renville County. Rapid colonization discouraged the area's becoming as regionally homogeneous as Norway Grove or even Arendahl. Membership in different churches, all with ties of nationality and many with regional bonds, created a patchwork impression on the tenure of land. By 1888 the Hauge's Lutheran Church membership was widely scattered, as were Balestrand-born members within the church (see Figure 11).[61]

Theological ties remained a salient feature of settlement around what became the Hauge's church. Indeed, the earliest settlers were not from Sogn but were mainly Haugean households arriving from Goodhue and Houston Counties, Minnesota, areas near Arendahl. Though a Sogning family did move to the region in 1866, not until 1867, two years after initial settlement, did the first Balestrander from Arendahl arrive.[62] The early households, as in Arendahl, consisted of young adults with small families. Peter Nilsen Rødbotten and his wife, Mari Hermundsdatter, the first Balestrand settlers in Camp township, were rather old at ages thirty-nine and forty-two, respectively, but they had lived in the Arendahl settlement for eleven years. More typical were Hans and Brita Boyum, who emigrated to Arendahl in 1867, when both were twenty-seven, before moving to Camp township a year later.[63]

After the Nilsen family arrived, the Balestrand contingent in the Hauge's church community swelled. According to the church books, nearly two-fifths of the foreign-born members had been baptized in Balestrand. An additional one-tenth were born in other areas of Sogn and were usually closely related through kin ties.[64] The relationship that existed between the mother settlement of Norway Grove and its offspring in Arendahl was replicated by that between Arendahl and the Hauge's church. Every child of the Balestrand-born who had been baptized in places other than Norway or Renville County had been christened in Fillmore County. Conversely, the children of those Norwegians who did not originate in Balestrand were born in other Minnesota areas. Repeatedly, households or individuals who had emigrated from Norway were fostered by kin and neighbors in Arendahl before they again moved west. This aid, moreover, did not necessarily end after settlement in Camp township. When the grasshoppers infested the community in the 1870s, for example, men in Camp used their old ties in the east and walked back to Arendahl to find work.[65] Certainly people in the mother settlement who hired the migrants were not acting totally out of benevolence: Labor was a commodity that the more easterly

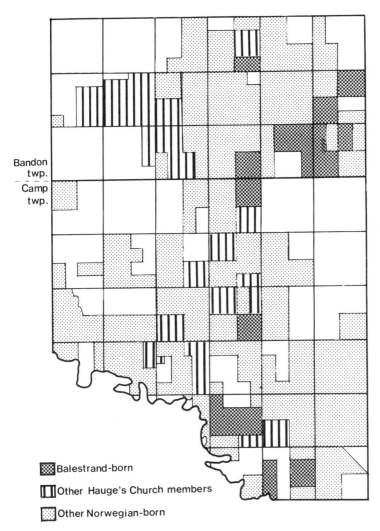

Fig. 11. Background of landholders in Camp and southern Bandon townships, 1888. *Sources*: Data from published 1888 plat map, Renville County; Minnesota manuscript population census, Camp and Bandon townships, 1885; Hauge's Lutheran Church records

farmers could easily have exploited. Still, the sustenance and safeguards provided by the mother community throughout the settlement process were a valuable source of protection for the new immigrants.

Migration from community to community was often an indication of a life-stage change. The son's leaving one settlement for another farther west often signified adulthood, marriage, a new household. Usually, therefore, only two of the three Balestrand communities in this string of settlements played a role in the transfer. The remarkable example of Turi Larsdatter Mæl, however, illustrates the ties of kinship through all three communities. Born in 1808, she moved in 1850 with her husband, Truls, a farm owner in Tjugum parish, and her family to the Spring Prairie community in Wisconsin. After her husband died, she moved with three sons and two daughters to Arendahl in 1858; one son and his wife remained in Wisconsin. Fifteen years later Turi again relocated: She took her three youngest sons to Camp township, where a niece already was living, and again left a part of her family behind. In Camp she lived out her life, one that had seen three moves which spaced her progeny as landed farmers and farmers' wives in Sogning settlements throughout the Upper Middle West.[66]

The string of settlements based on a combination of bonds of kinship, cultural affinities, and theological identification continued into the Dakotas. Yet another settlement was formed around the familiar Haugean church in Deuel County, South Dakota, by later Balestrand immigrants who had lived for a time in Arendahl and Camp.[67] Other Balestrand immigrants moved outside this network of communities stretching from central Wisconsin into the Dakotas, but unfamiliarity with many of America's customs and hunger for its resources encouraged a considerable proportion of the Balestrand immigrants to use the chain of settlements from Norway Grove westward as a means to both wealth and security.

Migration, whether it occurred within the network of informal insurance guaranteed by group migration or not, was based on the opportunity to acquire land and was concentrated among younger segments of the immigrant community. Though many youths did not move, the problem of an inheritance that would preclude a landed future was often solved by migration.[68] Yet in spite of the advantages of migration for some, other segments of the society enjoyed benefits by staying put. Those who secured land or stood to inherit it not only realized increasing values of their landed wealth but also utilized advantages of membership in a tightly knit community. Accordingly, the Balestrand settlements remained geographically stable and expanded at times, when land became available for purchase (compare Figures 8 and 9). In addition, advantages of community membership were also reflected in a greater population stability than was the norm for all settlers in the region.

Of the three Balestrand communities, one would expect the Camp and Bandon township settlement to have been the least stable. Settled later with a smaller Balestrand contingent than Norway Grove or Arendahl, the Hauge's church area presumably had the least tight community bonds. Hence this settlement has been chosen for extensive examination, on the presumption that if community interaction was strong and population was stable here, these factors characterized other Balestrand settlements to the east. Since other immigrant households of varying nationalities were parts of different church communities, the analysis covers a three-township region between 1885 and 1905 to set the Balestrand community into context.

The townships of Camp, Bandon, and Palmyra in Renville County were colonized mainly by Norwegian, Swedish, Irish, and Finnish settlers who lived in ethnically defined enclaves. Like the Hauge's church, the five other Norwegian churches were also based on Old World ties in addition to the usual theological inclinations. Some Norwegian settlers, however, chose not to belong to any church, partly because they lacked the regional ties that were so important in congregation formation. Because they rejected church membership and the bonds that developed within the community, these people were excluded from the benefits derived from membership.

As was typical in nineteenth-century America, migrations to and from the region were commonplace. Between 1885 and 1895, 35.4% of the men and 32.3% of the women in the three-township area left. As unpurchased land became scarcer and less desirable and as work opportunities became fewer in the next decade, outmigration increased to 43.1% of the men and 47.0% of the women. As one would expect, age-specific migration rates indicate that young people predominated (see Table 25). Over half of both men and women between ages ten and twenty-nine were leaving the region between 1895 and 1905. Moreover, those who were wealthiest were most likely to remain (see Table 26). Nearly nine-tenths of the wealthiest quartile of property holders stayed, compared to just under 70% of the poorest quartile, in the first decade. The gap was even larger in the following ten years, when nearly 80% of the upper quartile and just over half of the lowest quartile remained.[69]

Membership in a church community, however, also profoundly influenced migration tendencies, independently of age and wealth. Of the ten church communities in the region, members consistently were less prone than non–church members of the same nationality

Table 25. *Age-specific migration rates: Bandon, Camp, and Palmyra townships, 1885–95 and 1895–1905 (per 1,000)*

| | 1885–95 | | 1895–1905 | |
Age	Males	Females	Males	Females
0–9	241	277	333	344
10–19	445	570	528	588
20–29	407	333	591	493
30–39	358	300	341	400
40–49	269	211	329	299
50–59	143	306	205	406
60–69	350	200	413	257
70–79	500	286	800	769
Total	354	323	431	470

Source: Jon Gjerde, "The Effect of Community on Migration: Three Minnesota Townships, 1885–1905," *Journal of Historical Geography,* 5 (1979):415.

Table 26. *Migration according to wealth: Bandon, Camp, and Palmyra townships, 1885–95 and 1895–1905*

| | 1885–95 | | 1895–1905 | |
Property holders	Stable residents	Outmigrants	Stable residents	Outmigrants
Fourth quartile (wealthiest)				
N	40	5	76	20
%	88.9	11.1	79.2	20.8
Third quartile				
N	39	6	74	22
%	86.7	13.3	77.1	22.9
Second quartile				
N	34	11	59	37
%	76.1	23.9	61.5	38.5
First quartile (poorest)				
N	31	14	50	46
%	69.8	30.2	52.1	47.9

Source: Gjerde, "Effect of Community on Migration," p. 416.

Table 27. *Residential stability according to wealth and church membership: Bandon, Camp, and Palmyra townships, 1885–95 and 1895–1905*

Property holders	Church (1885–95)		Non church (1885–95)		Church 1895–1905		Non church 1895–1905	
	%	N	%	N	%	N	%	N
Fourth quartile (wealthiest)	97.7	43	63.6	11	76.2	42	52.2	23
Third quartile	90.5	42	53.8	13	76.6	47	72.2	18
Second quartile	77.5	40	64.3	14	80.9	42	24.0	25
First quartile (poorest)	67.7	31	30.4	23	71.4	42	26.1	23

Source: Gjerde, "Effect of Community on Migration," p. 420.

group. Since this difference could have been due to a correlation between wealth and community membership, the relationship between belonging to a church community and migration was considered according to categories of wealth. Propertied males aged twenty to forty-nine were divided into quartiles of wealth. The age group provides an indication of the passage from farm laborer to young farmer and from young farmer to the stage before retirement, two important steps in wealth transition (see Table 27). Church members as a group were wealthier than nonmembers, so their greater residential stability might have been due partially to greater wealth. When the church and nonchurch property holders of similar wealth were compared, however, the former had a considerably lower mobility rate. Church community members migrated less often in every wealth category; the difference was particularly strong in the lower quartiles, where nonchurchgoers were very restless whereas those in church communities were quite stable – more so, in fact, than in the wealthiest quartile of the non–church members.[70]

Of the ten church communities in the region that could be adequately examined, Hauge's church, with its strong Balestrand and Sogning constituency, possessed the most specific regional ties to Europe. Not surprisingly, Hauge's church members were quite sta-

Table 28. *Age-standardized migration rates (SMRs) according to nationality, church, and sex (ages 5–59): Bandon, Camp, and Palmyra townships, 1885–95 and 1895–1905*

	1885–95		1895–1905	
	SMR	N	SMR	N
Church males	20.9	585	35.9	718
Church females	34.7	564	42.9	620
Nonchurch males	78.2	241	62.9	403
Nonchurch females	42.3	180	54.6	312
Norwegian church males	15.9	353	34.8	422
Norwegian church females	29.1	351	42.1	387
Norwegian nonchurch males	80.1	126	58.1	146
Norwegian nonchurch females	30.6	86	44.9	106
Hauge's males	5.1	91	25.9	121
Hauge's females	18.1	82	39.1	97

Source: Gjerde, "Effect of Community on Migration,," p. 417.

ble in comparison with the other church communities (see Table 28). This stability was stronger still among the Balestrand- and other Sogn-born members. Usually the scale on this level was too small to determine mobility rates safely. An adequate sample of Sogn-born men within Hauge's church between 1895 and 1905, however, revealed that only 15.5% moved in that decade, compared to 25.9% for the church's males as a whole.[71]

Why were Balestranders less transient than others in the region? What did they gain by remaining? Activities among church members, which created both economic and social advantages, provide some explanation for this pattern. Social activities were dominated by church-related functions, ranging from the formal Sunday church service and parochial schools to informal "home parties," gatherings that invariably consisted of church community members. Stronger kinship bonds often resulted from intrachurch interaction, as youths tended to marry within their own churches. In Hauge's church and two others for which data were available, eleven of twenty-six males (42%) married women of their own churches even though there was in each case only a handful of possible marriage partners within the church.[72] Likewise, elderly church community members tended to board in the homes of other church members. Of the sixteen boarders who were church members between 1885 and 1905, twelve (75%) lived with people who belonged to their churches.

Economic gains were also facilitated by the church, which provided a source for a labor pool and a forum for potential transactions. That church members knew that another church member was selling land before the larger population was one advantage. Church members in the region did indeed sell land to one another proportionately more often than to others. Of the 214 transactions over a twenty-year period, Hauge's church members were involved in only 35. In 8 of these cases (22.8%) both buyer and seller were members of the Hauge's church. If the father-to-son or -daughter transfers had been included, the rates obviously would have been higher.[73] Likewise, farm laborers in the church worked for other church members. Since the occupation of farm laborer was a mobile one, most were not church members unless they were working for their parents. But the trend of intrachurch community ties was again apparent: twelve of twenty farm laborer church members (60%) were employed by people from their own churches.

The bonds of economic and social interaction among members of the church communities were themselves closely related to the life cycle of community families. Viewed in the abstract, the typical farm laborer worked for his parents or other community members before marrying a woman from his own church. Upon inheriting a farming operation, this couple might employ farm laborers because of the small labor source within the family, and again the church community was frequently a source for workers. As the farmer increased his operation, his need for more land was often satisfied by purchase from church members. When the farmer progressed toward retirement, he provided a market for land as he decreased his holdings, which were often either bought or inherited within the community. After retirement, the couple boarded within the community with children and frequently with other church members. The family tended to provide the functions of farm laborer, land giver and land taker, and board provider; but when it was unable to provide support, community members often took responsibility. Thus, as community ties grew closer and kinship ties became more complex, the benefits derived from these activities and interactions caused the personal costs of migration to another area to increase.

It is important to observe that a significant portion of immigrant communities based on Old World ties enjoyed both economic and social benefits. Informal networks that facilitated the transfer of land or the exchange of labor created economic benefits. But additional nonpecuniary utilities deriving from security of membership in the community were present as well. Social interaction among the membership and such old-age protection as boarding opportunities made stability within the community a more compelling option, especially for those less acclimated to American life. The tendency toward greater geographical stability within Balestrand settlements therefore was due not so much to Hansen's notion of "love of the soil" as to perceptions among community members that staying was in their interests. Thus the pecuniary and nonpecuniary utilities gained from remaining within a tightly bound immigrant community continued to override migration opportunities for large segments of the Balestrand group.

Conclusion

Although some Balestrand immigrants settled and migrated outside the networks of the Balestrand communities beginning in Norway Grove, a large share of immigrants and their children remained within the confines of the moving community. Many chose to stay in their home settlements to enjoy the utilities of community membership, especially if they expected landed futures. Although the Balestrand settlement areas were often augmented by additional land purchases, the customary impartible transfer of land encouraged many children and later immigrants to move. This migration, however, should not generally be perceived as rootless individualistic wanderings.[74] Later colonies to the west were frequently based on the Old World ties and ideological affinities developed in earlier Norwegian-American settlement areas. Later migrants often used the older communities to the east as footholds before setting out to find land farther west, and returned in the winter or in times of economic hardship in hopes of finding work. Contrary to Hansen's dichotomy of mobility and stability, therefore, the ties of kinship and regional background enabled geographical stability for some immigrants while they facilitated patterns of group migration for others. Stability and mobility were not contradictory strategies among the Balestrand households, but consistent attempts to permit landed futures amid kin within a string of compact settlements.

The Balestrand settlement patterns resulted in strongly defined communities centered on the church, a focal point of interaction. Kinship and friendship ties originating in Balestrand were maintained and, at times, accentuated by intermarriage within the community. Such continuing social patterns and relationships worked in many ways to recreate aspects of Balestrand society in America. Yet the distended settlement process – a compromise between the opportunities of American land and the desire for close-knit Norwegian colonies – worked to alter basic social patterns carried from Balestrand. Although farming operations in Balestrand were intensified when population increased, land opportunities to the west in the United States encouraged a more extensive, migration-prone farming pattern. The Balestrand farms could utilize the increased supplies of landless labor to make farm operations large and labor-intensive. Opportunities to move and acquire land in America, on the other hand, placed greater burdens on the exploitable labor supply – the nuclear family. Early migrants to the later Balestrand settlements characteristically were couples or small nuclear families attempting to become independent farmers. Migrating as nuclear families, the pioneers and their followers eventually would base their farm developments on the labor supplied by those same nuclear family units.

The opportunity to migrate that altered the land/labor ratio was one component of modified agricultural conditions faced by Balestrand immigrants to the United States. The striking contrasts between agriculture on the Norwegian mountainsides and on the American prairies encouraged even further changes within the Balestrand community. Crops in the United States were different, market structures were more complex, and implements were more widely available. As we will see in the next chapter, which examines the economic development of Norway Grove, Arendahl, and Camp, the Norwegian immigrants adapted rapidly to these new conditions. And just as patterns of family structure interacted with conditions of greater mobility, the dialectic between culture and environment created yet further adaptations. As Balestrand immigrants and their families began to enjoy the consequences of a booming wheat market and increasing wealth, cultural forms of family structure, divisions of labor, and marital fertility began to undergo widespread change.

8 *"Norwegians . . . must learn anew": economic development of the American communities*

The dramatic contrast between the fjords, mountains, and valleys of Norway, on the one hand, and the rolling prairies and woodlands of the Norwegian settlements in the American Middle West, on the other, was a frequent subject of comment among the immigrants. The differing landscapes favored such dissimilar agriculture methods that one immigrant wrote, "I can truthfully say that the only things that seem to be the same are the fleas, for their bite is as sharp and penetrating here as elsewhere."[1] The new agriculture implied modified use of labor and capital, which in turn encouraged further changes in Norwegian social patterns in the United States. One Norwegian, for example, "had come from a land where men plowed and harvested three, five, ten acres . . . There the life fortunes of individual cabbage, or a single stalk of tobacco growing under the hot house glass, were subject for discussion . . . Here, where Einar brought him to the endless rows, stretching like box hedges into the horizon, he was speechless."[2] Another immigrant remembered that "even the farm work was new to me – something quite different from the work at home on the croft. Here were enormous plains that seemed much too huge to harvest. And then those labor saving machines. Good heavens, such machines! I had to learn everything over again, greenhorn that I was."[3]

The agricultural adaptations made by the Balestrand immigrants provide yet further examples of reconciling traditional practices with a new environment. From earliest settlement, the immigrants were forced to adjust to unfamiliar agricultural conditions. Most immediately, the land on which they settled varied remarkably from the mountainsides of western Norway. Dominant crop types in the United States differed. Corn, for instance, was not grown in Norway, and wheat, which became the principal market crop in the developing Middle West, was of little importance. As immigrants learned how to choose good land and became acquainted with the new crops, they were obliged to make other fundamental changes in shaping their farms. Available hired laborers were rare in the rural

American settlements, a situation quite unlike that in Balestrand. Moreover, markets took on a greater importance after initial settlement, becoming much more essential to the farm operation in America than in Norway. The astonishing differences between Norway and the United States led one immigrant to write home in 1852 with a clear message. "It is not true that Norwegians or other national groups retain their old ways," he observed, "believing they are the best. He who hangs on to old ways when they do not pay will lose out. He must learn anew."[4]

The Balestrand immigrants did indeed learn anew. They rapidly acquired knowledge of new methods and quickly adapted to the cash grain farming of the Upper Middle West. However, cultural differences that cannot be totally related to variations in wealth evolved between the immigrants and their neighbors. Though the broad outlines of their crop patterns were similar, Balestrand immigrants showed distinctive inclinations based both on practices carried from Norway and on peculiar immigrant tendencies, such as fondness for large wheat acreages. And although work on the immigrant farm was performed mainly by the nuclear family, sexual divisions of labor carried to the United States stood in striking contrast to dominant American practices.

Yet though the Balestrand communities varied some farming patterns, they by and large experienced lines of development similar to those in the settlements about them. Immigrant households enjoyed a wheat boom period that created an opportunity for large accumulations of wealth. If they survived the decline of wheat and could diversify their farming operations, they could enjoy a material security quite unlike that in Balestrand. The choice of crop mixes and farming patterns permitted greater wealth, which in turn produced anomalies in the traditional division of labor between the sexes. Women saw their customary work roles in farm production decrease, and so they tended to concentrate on other traditional roles in the home. Just as migration patterns and labor needs increased the importance of the nuclear family in early settlement, so did changing cropping patterns and increasing wealth later alter relationships and work roles within the family.

Initial adaptation to the American environment

During initial settlement Balestrand immigrants were compelled to adjust to the new conditions, choose land, and learn about different crops. Often called the "dog years," this early period forced the immigrants to face a new environment in addition to occasional homesickness and frequent poverty. Some Norwegians, according to an early historian, were

> almost entirely without resources when they reached Wisconsin. They frequently worked out by the day or month for pitifully small wages in order to get the first fifty dollars to pay for a forty. Very often the only house they had was a "dugout" made by digging a cave in the side of a bluff and covering it with brush and hay.

It was "credit and courage," he added, that "carried them through."[5]

Work for "pitifully small wages," however, fulfilled a function other than acquisition of capital. Doing farm labor for Yankees permitted "greenhorns" to become acquainted with American farming techniques.[6] Even landed settlers often worked for pay, since their cleared land did not demand all their time. As settlement progressed to the west, men often planted small wheat fields and then returned to older Norwegian settlements to find work, only to return home for their harvest.[7] Thus whereas Yankees taught the earliest immigrants, later arrivals often worked for and were instructed by established Norwegians.[8] Although letters home at times expressed complaints about the difficulty of the work, the adjustment to labor in American fields "seems to have been a rapid one."[9]

Among the more glaring differences between rural Wisconsin and Balestrand were the land forms. Immigrants were unfamiliar with prairies, and "it took some time," according to an early historian, "before the newcomers realized that the prairies are not only easier to put under cultivation but are also usually more fertile than the forested regions." But "later emigrants knew how to profit by the mistakes of the first arrivals and it was not long before our countrymen began to settle in regions where nature generously offers the impecunious stranger the good fortune which he seeks."[10] Fredrika Bremer by 1853 argued that Norwegians in Koshkonong "wisely built their houses generally by some little river or brook, and understand how to select a good soil. They came here as old and accustomed agriculturists and know how to make use of the earth."[11]

Settlement patterns indicate that the earliest immigrants to Norway Grove and Arendahl already understood the advantages of the prairie. The first Balestrand immigrants moving from Koshkonong chose land on prairie clearings in northern Dane County. Land in what would become the Norway Grove–Spring Prairie settlement consisted of a large prairie region interspersed with oak groves.

Norwegian settlers on the first plat map of 1861 were living on the prairies while later arrivals, most notably the Germans in Windsor township, were nestled in oak openings. Apparently the early settlers, the Norwegians among them, were able to monopolize good land, which included the prairies.

We can observe the land taking in Arendahl township with greater clarity. Since the Norwegians were among the earliest claimants of land, we can compare their preferences with those of the old Americans, whose names do not appear on later censuses and who were probably land speculators. Although all the earliest settlers could have claimed a whole section of prairie land, Norwegians instead chose homes on the borders of prairie and woodland while the Yankee speculators took the prairie (see Figure 12). Because the speculators did not build farms on this land, they had no need for fires or buildings. Instead, they could wait for buyers to take the land as it increased in value. The first actual settlers, who happened to be Norwegians, had to face these very real challenges and chose the borders – land that supplied heat and shelter in addition to cropland. When the pioneering difficulties were over, some of the earliest Norwegian settlers bought greater portions of prairie land or even moved within the township to prairie land, after selling their original land to later Norwegian immigrants.[12]

Just as the immigrants quickly learned to claim land dissimilar in appearance from what they were used to in Norway, they began to grow crops strange to Norway soon after settlement commenced. In 1849, only five years after initial settlement, 9.0% of the crop output among Norwegians in Norway Grove consisted of corn, compared to 11.2% for non-Norwegians.[13] Wheat, sown in Balestrand in extremely small quantities, had become a primary crop in Norway Grove by 1849; Norwegians in Vienna township harvested 168.6 bushels per farm unit, 30.9% of all their crops. Yet the wheat harvest, like the corn harvest, made up a greater percentage of total agricultural output for non-Norwegians than for Norwegians (see Table 29). Still, if Norwegians did not plant as much corn and wheat as their neighbors, they were at least familiar with both grains.

Land and capital constraints and market availabilities

Acquiring familiarity with new soils and crops was a relatively simple learning process for the Balestrand immigrants. They rapidly became acquainted with prairie farming and its use of grains. Adapting to constraints of labor and capital was a more complicated,

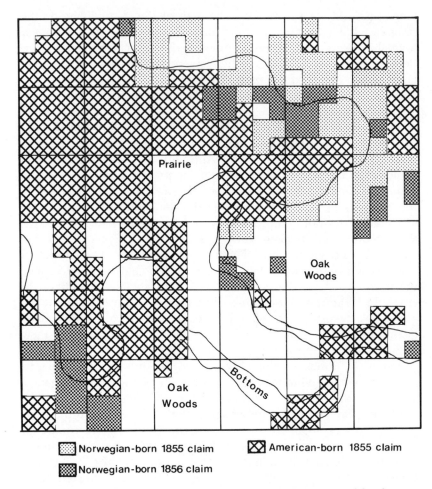

Fig. 12. Land alienation according to ethnocultural group and land type: Arendahl township. *Sources*: Data from land alienation records, Fillmore County Courthouse; surveyor maps available from the Minnesota secretary of state

but no less profound, adjustment. Just as these constraints influenced their crop and animal mixes, so did market demands for their products. Immigrants thus had to discover a production mix that could be grown on their farm units and could be sold in town. The result of both the constraints and the market demands encouraged Norwegians to develop farm operations that were different from those in Balestrand not only in crop mix but in farm organization as

Table 29. *Production of corn and wheat among Norwegians and non-Norwegians: Vienna township, 1849*

	Ave. improved acreage	Ave. total bushelage	% corn	% wheat
Norwegians (N = 19)	33.5	544.9	9.0	30.9
Non-Norwegians (N = 104)	44.1	589.8	11.2	40.5

Sources: U.S. manuscript agricultural census, northern Dane county, 1849; U.S. manuscript population census, northern Dane County, 1850.

well. If migration patterns tended to accentuate the nuclear family, so did labor on the farm.

With ample opportunities to own land or migrate, hired labor was scarce in the early settlement period. In addition to being rare, it was usually expensive and unreliable as well. Letters home often commented on high wage rates, especially early.[14] Laborers were often uncertain workers, too, since they were "waiting for a better opportunity elsewhere and took little interest in their present job." A farmer who increased his acreage knowing that a laborer might leave was taking on additional risks.[15] Though Norwegian farmers in succeeding stages of development would employ many hired laborers, the early settlers in Norway Grove, Arendahl, and Camp hired few. Less than two-thirds of the farms in Vienna township had farm laborers, and workers in Arendahl and Camp were even more scarce. In an important distinction from the situation in Balestrand, female hired laborers were uncommon from the very beginnings of settlement (see Table 30).[16]

The source of labor within the nuclear family thus became a major factor in determining the amount of land the immigrant farmer could put under cultivation, whereas in Balestrand servant labor had been of great importance (see Plate 13).[17] This unfamiliar situation was stressed by a letter writer who in 1844 advised his friends that "a person must either have labor power within his family corresponding to its size, or enough money [to hire it]. I pity those who arrive lacking both these factors." He added, "If a person has enough money to buy cultivated land, the size of the area [needed] will, of course, depend on the size of the family. They say here that a small family can get along on forty acres and a very large one on 160."[18]

Table 30. *Hired farm labor in Norwegian households, 1860, 1880, 1900*

	No. of farm households	No. of farm laborers		% of farms with laborers	
		Men	Women	Men	Women
Vienna twp.					
1860	33	20	5	60.6	15.1
1880	60	39	9	65.0	15.0
Arendahl twp.					
1860	33	5	2	15.1	6.1
1880	153	44	9	28.8	5.9
1900	140	35	0	25.0	0
Camp twp.					
1880	66	6	0	9.1	0
1900	65	15	1	23.1	1.5

Sources: U.S. manuscript population censuses, Vienna township, 1860, 1880; Arendahl township, 1860, 1880, 1900; Camp township, 1880, 1900.

Labor from outside the family often was acquired through mutual aid, similar to the dugnad in Norway, especially in the production of grain crops that had to be put out and harvested rapidly. Bremer noted that the Koshkonong Norwegians helped one another in their labor.[19] One frontier farmer illustrated in a letter home how he farmed with a neighbor and split the yield of wheat, barley, and oats.[20]

Like limited supplies of labor, capital scarcity also played a large role in early farm development. Immigrants who arrived in Wisconsin with limited resources after financing their passage to America and buying their land emphasized operations that required little initial capital. Small grains were the primary product of early farmers, since they were relatively cheap to grow. Only a breaking plow, a team of oxen, a harrow, and grain seed were needed in order to produce a crop. Moreover, returns were rapid: The crop, harvested only months after planting, could be used at home or as a commodity for sale. Animals required a greater initial investment for shelter, feed, and the animals themselves; and an intermediate stage of raising the animals delayed profits. Those few animals kept early in the settlement period therefore were mainly for home use.[21]

Small grains, particularly wheat, had a further advantage because

Plate 13. This austere Norwegian household in Norway Grove of the 1870s contained twelve children and one male laborer. Note the physical distance between the laborer and the family, a style repeated often in Dahl's photographs. Note also that the men and women are segregated in the photograph, a style that undergoes change. *Source*: State Historical Society of Wisconsin; photograph by Andrew Dahl

they were a marketable cash crop. An early observer of Norwegian immigrant life wrote in 1844 that although the settlers began with little capital, they "wish to become economically independent as soon as possible." To do that, they concentrated their "entire attention upon producing those commodities that demand the least care, preparation, and cash outlay – but at the same time provide [the farmers] a livelihood and find a regular market, even if at a low price." The commodity that was given such "attention" was mainly wheat, which was so profitable that a regular system of rotation was seldom used and the earth was burdened "year after year until the original fertility at last disappears."[22]

Farming patterns among Balestrand immigrants in Norway Grove

As noted, the need for a production mix manageable by the nuclear family was a radical change from the situation in Balestrand. Faced with the exigencies of pioneer farming, however, the immigrant farmers adapted quickly to the dominant patterns of the Upper Middle West. In the initial decades of settlement immigrant farming

Table 31. *Crop production among Norwegians and non-Norwegians: Vienna township, 1849*

	Ave. improved acreage	Wheat	Corn	Oats	Barley	Potato	Total
Norwegians (N = 19)	33.5						
Ave. bushelage		168.6	48.9	258.9	24.2	44.3	544.9
% of crop		30.9	9.0	47.5	4.4	8.1	99.9
Other (N = 104)	44.1						
Ave. bushelage		238.9	65.8	192.9	10.1	82.1	589.8
% of crop		40.5	11.2	32.7	1.7	13.9	100.0

Sources: U.S. manuscript agricultural census, northern Dane County, 1849; U.S. manuscript population census, northern Dane County, 1850.

households, smaller than those in Balestrand, increasingly relied more on grains than on animals, so that their operations were quite similar to those about them in crop mix and labor use. Yet although the Balestrand immigrants did adopt the general crop and animal patterns of the area, they also retained certain farming traits, probably carried over from Norway, that distinguished them from other farmers. Moreover, their behavior indicates an occasional lack of familiarity with market conditions that further set them apart from American farmers.

During the early periods of settlement, farmers tended to plant crops with which they were familiar. Since this was an era of semi-subsistence agriculture before transportation facilities had significantly reduced marketing costs, the crop mix was more broadly based than it would be in later stages. Farmers "discovered what variety of crops [they] should plant," according to a Norwegian observer in 1844, "to avoid the failure of one of them causing a disaster."[23] They also kept a variety of animals whose products were used at home. Despite the wide array of grains, potatoes, and animals, however, the Norwegian immigrants tended to grow crops that had been dominant in Balestrand. Though they produced corn and wheat, it was barley and oats – the principal cereals in Balestrand – that were most significant in the Vienna Norwegians' 1849 crop mix (see Table 31).

Even as the market for wheat developed, crops and animals that were used at home remained an area in which "people could afford to express their cultural preferences."[24] Grains other than wheat

Table 32. *Nonwheat grains and potatoes produced by Norwegian-born and New England-born farmers: Vienna township, 1859 and 1869*

	Corn (%)	Oats (%)	Barley (%)	Potatoes (%)	N
Norwegian-born					
1859	12.3	73.7	5.7	8.2	32
1869	12.9	72.2	8.9	6.0	45
New England-born					
1859	27.0	57.9	4.6	10.5	34
1869	22.3	62.1	8.9	6.7	52

Sources: U.S. manuscript agricultural censuses, Vienna township, 1859, 1869; U.S. manuscript population censuses, Vienna township, 1860, 1870.

were used primarily at home as a feed for animals. In these cases the market did not so completely prescribe production, and favorite crops could be grown. In both the 1859 and the 1869 censuses, when wheat had become the principal grain crop, the Norwegians retained their preference for oats, whereas the New England–born favored corn. In 1859, 73.7% of Norwegians' nonwheat crop production was oats, compared to 57.9% for the Yankees. On the other hand, 27.0% of the Yankees' nonwheat crop output was corn, much above the 12.3% grown by the Norwegians (see Table 32). Although the gap narrowed ten years later, the patterns remained consistent.[25]

Early Balestrand immigrant farmers, as already observed, also owned a wide array of animals whose products were used at home. Instead of relying on old animal types, however, the Balestrand immigrants chose a new mixture in their early Wisconsin settlements. Each Norwegian farm in 1849 in Vienna township owned about two cows for milk products and many kept sheep for their wool, although they owned fewer sheep than did non-Norwegians in Vienna (see Table 33).[26] Instead of cows and sheep, which had dominated in Balestrand, Norwegians raised swine, an animal preferred by the average farmer in the township.

As the settlement developed, milk and beef cattle holdings were augmented by the Norwegian farmers in Vienna township, while swine holdings decreased. By 1859 and 1869, when wheat production occupied much of the farmers' attentions, Norwegians had been able to increase their cattle herds even though the typical farmer in the township had not. Hogs had served well when acreages

Table 33. *Animals held per farm unit by Norwegian-born and all farmers: Vienna township, 1849, 1859, and 1869*

	Horses	Milk cows	Oxen	Other cattle	Sheep	Swine	N
Norwegian-born							
1849	0.7	2.2	1.8	2.5	2.3	5.1	19
1859	2.7	3.7	1.6	3.2	2.6	3.2	32
1869	5.4	3.9	0.1	3.5	10.2	3.4	45
All							
1849	1.2	2.7	1.6	4.4	4.3	4.7	123
1859	2.4	3.2	1.4	3.4	2.6	3.0	106
1869	4.5	3.0	0.1	3.0	9.9	3.1	159

Sources: U.S. manuscript agricultural censuses, northern Dane County, 1849, Vienna township, 1859, 1869; U.S. manuscript population censuses, northern Dane County, 1850, Vienna township, 1860, 1870.

were smaller and feed grains were less abundant. After years of settlement, with fields and meadows producing adequate feed, cattle – particularly milk cows – came to play a greater role.

The preference for dairy cattle seems to have been based on a fondness for dairy foods rather than a transplantation of the høstingsbruk system. Early immigrants wrote home that outbuildings for animals were rare. On most farms the animals were kept outside all winter, a stark contrast to the use of dark cowbarns in Balestrand.[27] The Balestrand system of transhumance was replaced by a more geographically stable system of husbandry – obviously, no støls were found on the Wisconsin prairies. But because American cows produced three to four times as much milk as those in Norway, dairy products could be consumed in great quantities and in traditional ways. Johan Reiersen argued that already established Americans, unlike Norwegians, valued milk very little because of their chosen diet. They did not eat clabbered milk but instead fed it to the cattle and pigs.[28] Yet even among Norwegians wheat was the major market commodity during this period, so that the animal herds reached neither the size nor the importance they had attained in Balestrand, while the wheat fields in the settlement broadened.

As transportation networks developed and demand for wheat increased, farmers in the Upper Middle West, including the Norwegian immigrants, adjusted their crop mixes accordingly. Wheat was particularly advantageous on frontier soil where harvests were

Plate 14. This large, flat Norway Grove field of grain, probably wheat, contrasts strikingly with the grain fields of Balestrand. Note that the field has been planted by machine. *Source*: State Historical Society of Wisconsin; photograph by Andrew Dahl

bountiful; according to Hamlin Garland, "We were all worshippers of wheat in those days."[29] "This was not just ordinary soil fit for barley, and oats, and potatoes, and hay," thinks Per Hansa in *Giants in the Earth*. "It was the soil for *wheat*, the king of all grains! Such soil had been especially created by the good Lord to bear this noble seed" (see Plate 14).[30] Farmers enjoyed immense wheat harvests that averaged 24.5 bushels per acre in Wisconsin in 1860, about a bushel more than Dane County's average of 23.1.[31] Wheat was also an excellent crop to market. It kept well, needed little refinement, demanded high prices, and was not too bulky. Corn, on the other hand, yielded about twice as much per acre but was bulky and commanded a lower price, so that it would not repay transportation costs and was thus relegated to home use, often as animal feed.[32]

As noted, Balestrand immigrant farmers in Vienna township did not concentrate as heavily on wheat as was the norm for the region during the early settlement period. Whether they were unfamiliar with marketing conditions or skeptical of large wheat acreages, the Norwegians harvested a smaller percentage of wheat than their neighbors in 1849. Ten years later, however, the Norwegians in Vienna township had entered the wheat market with great resolution. Although the market encouraged all farmers to increase wheat

Table 34. *Wheat production according to ethnocultural group: Vienna township, 1859 and 1869*

	Ave. improved acreage	Wheat as a % of crop output	N
Norwegian-born			
1859	60.4	66.2	32
1869	107.3	62.6	45
British-born			
1859	66.8	52.3	33
1869	105.9	50.1	39
American-born			
1859	70.6	49.6	34
1869	107.5	56.2	52

Sources: U.S. manuscript agricultural censuses, Vienna township, 1859, 1869; U.S. manuscript population censuses, Vienna township, 1860, 1870.

output, Norwegians now produced a larger percentage of wheat than their American- or British-born neighbors. Around one-half of the harvest of the latter two groups was wheat in 1859, whereas Norwegians reaped nearly twice as much wheat as all other crops combined. The Norwegians retained their preference for large wheat acreages in the next decade, although they harvested a slightly lower percentage in 1869 (see Table 34).[33]

The Norwegians' reliance on wheat can be partly explained by the nature of wheat production, the steady returns from wheat, and the peculiar economic situation of immigrants shortly after arrival. Wheat, as we have seen, was a good crop upon which to reap rich monetary rewards. The U.S. Commission of Agriculture, for example, determined in the mid-1860s that if a man bought and settled a quarter section in Wisconsin with housing and fencing and broke 40 acres, he could pay for the entire capital outlay in one year if he harvested 1,000 bushels of wheat (or 25 bushels an acre), not an extraordinary yield, and was paid 73 ½ cents a bushel, a price that was at times half the going rate.[34] Wheat prices in Madison, for example, peaked in 1855, one year after the railroad reached the state capitol. Owing to the Crimean War in Europe, prices leaped from 31 cents a bushel in May, 1854, to $1.70 a bushel a year later. In 1866 prices in Madison were quoted from $1.56 to $1.90 a bushel.[35] Through wheat, the pioneer farmer could obtain a necessary object: Immediate returns with small inputs of labor and capital.

Table 35. *Crop mix according to farm size: Vienna township, 1859*

	Arable acres	Wheat	Oats	Corn	Barley	Potatoes	Total
50 acres or fewer (N = 50)	37.3						
Ave. bushelage per unit		422.8	173.1	83.6	6.4	41.7	727.6
% of total crop		58.1	23.8	11.5	0.9	5.7	100.0
50 acres or more (N = 56)	91.8						
Ave. bushelage per unit		813.2	473.3	183.9	39.5	60.3	1,570.2
% of total crop		51.8	30.1	11.7	2.5	3.8	99.9

Sources: U.S. manuscript agricultural census, Vienna township, 1859; U.S. manuscript population census, Vienna township, 1860.

Poorer farmers were thus encouraged to risk planting proportionately large acreages of wheat, even if they were in debt, in hope of reaping rich profits. Those with smaller holdings consistently devoted a greater proportion of their land to wheat. In Vienna township, for example, although farmers holding over fifty acres of improved land harvested nearly twice as much wheat as those with fifty acres or less, the poorer farmers took in a larger percentage of wheat (see Table 35). Yet wealth was not the only factor. Norwegians, whether they owned more or less than fifty acres, remained more enamored with wheat production than their New England–born neighbors (see Table 36). That is, though poor New Englanders tended to risk fewer acres on wheat, poor Norwegians harvested even greater percentages of wheat than their richer countrymen. If the Norwegians were less aware of market demands than American-born settlers in the early periods, they were also less cognizant of the decline of wheat markets and soil fertility that had occurred previously in the eastern United States.

Wheat could become a lucrative gamble. A Norwegian writer in 1869 stressed that "the high price of wheat in recent years has particularly contributed to [the Wisconsin Norwegians'] economic progress. Many farmers who began with small plots of land have been able to buy more."[36] Those with large holdings could invest in implements that permitted larger wheat acreages. Even though soil fertility had declined, one Norwegian argued in 1869, "Implements

Table 36. *Crop mix according to farm size and place of birth: Vienna township, 1859*

	Arable acres	Wheat	Oats	Corn	Barley	Potatoes	Total
Norwegians with 50 acres or fewer (N = 18)	41.2						
Ave. bushelage per unit		437.8	158.8	20.8	7.5	21.7	646.6
% of total crop		67.7	24.6	3.2	1.2	3.3	100.0
Norwegians with 50 acres or more (N = 14)	81.6						
Ave. bushelage per unit		854.4	307.8	57.6	29.6	31.5	1,280.9
% of total crop		66.7	24.0	4.5	2.3	2.4	99.9
New Englanders with 50 acres or fewer (N = 18)	34.4						
Ave. bushelage per unit		327.7	214.4	104.2	9.3	49.7	705.3
% of total crop		46.5	30.4	14.8	1.3	7.0	100.0
New Englanders with 50 acres or more (N = 15)	112.3						
Ave. bushelage per unit		953.2	487.3	228.7	37.3	53.7	1,760.2
% of total crop		54.1	27.7	13.0	2.1	3.0	99.9

Sources: U.S. manuscript agricultural census, Vienna township, 1859; U.S. manuscript population census, Vienna township, 1860.

have improved so much that farming pays better now than it did when the farmers harvested 25 to 30 bushels an acre."[37] Wheat, however, was a fickle crop. Not only did it produce fewer bushels per acre than other grains, but it was more likely to fail; those who planted large acreages of wheat risked disaster as well as economic success. Animals, fed on corn and oats, were a less uncertain venture.

Though the Balestranders' fondness for wheat may have been

based on unfamiliarity with American conditions, their ability to maintain relatively large animal herds in addition to large wheat acreages was probably a transplantation of a Norwegian practice. Norwegian farmers on the average had a larger number of animal units and a higher value of livestock than the norm in Vienna township in both 1859 and 1869.[38]

Moreover, in the decade of great wheat production, between 1859 and 1869, Norwegians increased their holdings 68.5% in dollar value and 27.9% in animal units, compared to 57.3% and 15.7% for the township as a whole. Large wheat acreages and larger animal herds were possible simultaneously through an exploitation of nongrain feeds. Although Norwegians harvested relatively fewer feed grains, especially in 1859, they exploited grasses, including wild grasses, much as they had done in Norway. A Norwegian in 1844 wrote that immigrant farmers did not consider raising clover or timothy "so long as the wild prairie grass produces abundant hay."[39] The average Norwegian farmer in Vienna township harvested 19.2 tons of hay in 1859, compared to 10.4 tons for the next most hay-dependent ethnocultural group, the New Englanders, and 9.5 tons for non-Norwegians as a whole. The gap narrowed by 1869, when Norwegians averaged 15.9 tons, 3.1 tons more than British-born farmers and 4.7 tons more than all non-Norwegian farmers (see Table 37). The Balestrand and Leikanger immigrants continued to cut a significantly greater amount of hay in relation to feed grains than others in the township. Willingness to feed animals a large quantity of hay during the summer apparently worked to the advantage of the Norwegian farmer: He could both enjoy a large harvest of wheat and own a goodly stock of animals in spite of the constraints of labor and capital.

The magic of wheat began to fade in certain respects nearly as soon as it appeared. As early as 1851 John Y. Smith noted that although wheat yielded well in the early years, "in the last four years, it has proved almost an entire failure." He was therefore of the opinion "that Wisconsin farmers cannot depend upon the culture of wheat to balance their trade with other states."[40] Many farmers had overspeculated, however, so that, according to an observer, "no farmer was able to quit his attempt to raise wheat because he had absolutely no money with which to start other branches of farming."[41] An agricultural journal reiterated the complaint. "For several years," it noted, "wheat in every stage has been doomed to double risk, labor and expense, while the market has generally been at a low point in consequence of the almost illimita-

Table 37. *Hay production according to ethnocultural group: Vienna township,*
1859 and 1869

	Tons of hay per farm unit	Bushels of feed grains per ton of hay
Norwegians		
1859	19.2	14.9
1869	15.9	33.3
Non-Norwegians		
1859	9.5	59.2
1869	11.2	57.4

Sources: U.S. manuscript agricultural censuses, Vienna township, 1859,
1869; U.S. manuscript population censuses, Vienna township, 1860, 1870.

ble amount produced and the inferior quality of a large share, and
yet here it is all wheat, wheat, wheat."[42] Despite these foreshadow-
ing complaints, however, wheat not only remained a primary crop
but increased in significance when output improved and prices rose.

Good crops and high prices led to greater dependence on the
wheat market, and farmers felt little need to rotate crops. The wheat
farmer "knows there is danger of reducing the productive value of
his land through overcropping," wrote a government official, "but
its original cost was an insignificant fraction of its intrinsic value,
which is more than repaid by the net proceeds of a single crop."[43]
Better tillage with the use of manure and other fertilizers did not
sufficiently add to the yield to pay the cost of applying them. Ironically, poor farming became profitable farming and thus became
good farming, at least in the short term. Moreover, with abundant
harvests, farmers could speculate on continued success by taking
out loans, expanding their operations, planting yet more wheat, and
hoping to pay off their debts with yet another bumper crop.

When the halcyon days of large wheat harvests came to an end,
those who were dependent on wheat faced economic distress. The
lack of regular crop rotation led to declining yields, so that the
average wheat yield per acre in Wisconsin dropped from 24.5
bushels in 1860 to 12.8 by 1879. Dane County saw an even more
precipitous decline from 23.1 bushels per acre to 9.8, and Vienna
township was less fortunate still, with an average of only 5.4 bushels per acre in 1879.[44] Not only did soil depletion plague wheat
farmers, but pests such as the dreaded chinch bug reached Dane

County around 1861 and did considerable crop damage by 1864, when the fields were "swept clean."[45] High prices one year, which encouraged greater wheat acreages, were often followed by over-production and decreased prices the next. The alternations be-tween good year and bad year, high prices and low prices, caused the wheat farmer to be indeed in a "bad way," since they occurred in "such a way as to induce him to keep in the game and pay his forfeits in the hope of winning once again." Wheat growing suf-fered its first serious decline in Wisconsin in the 1870s and con-tinued to decline the following decade, so that by 1889 "wheat was no longer the staple. The dairy product was supreme."[46] Farmers who were able to invest in new operations began to diversify their farms with increased production of animal products, such as wool or beef cattle for the market, in addition to dairying. Others who were overextended in the wheat gamble were forced to reduce their holdings or, worse yet, sell out.

Just as Norwegians began planting large wheat acreages later than the norm in Vienna township, they were slower to respond to de-creasing wheat returns. The Balestrand and Leikanger immigrants in Vienna township reaped 8,013 bushels of wheat (12.1% of their total crops) in 1879, when only 9.9% of the remaining farmers' har-vests was wheat. Likewise, Norwegians devoted 44.6% of their ara-ble acreage to wheat, considerably more than the 38.5% so used by others.[47] Whether Norwegian immigrants were less familiar with the deteriorating conditions of wheat production than the American or did not possess the capital to diversify their operations, agri-cultural historians have argued that immigrants suffered more than others from the decline of wheat harvests and markets.

"The Scandinavian elements in Dane County acquired the habit of wheat growing to such an extent," wrote John Giffin Thompson, "that upon [its] failure in that county in 1870, many sold off their farms and like the native stock moved on toward the frontier."[48] It remains impossible to determine from the agricultural censuses if Norwegians in Vienna township were actually forced out of farming by overconcentration on the wheat market. Some clear patterns, however, indicate that greater dependence on wheat than on ani-mals by 1869 led to less residential stability in the area in the next decade. By comparing the agricultural output in 1869 of those farm-ers who remained until 1879 with that of those who left, we find that the movers owned less land. On their cropland they had produced a greater percentage of wheat, and they were much more reliant on crops in general than on animals (see Table 38). Whereas those who

Table 38. *Variations between Norwegian farmers who remained in Vienna township after 1869 and those who left*

	Farmers remaining in Vienna, 1869–79	Farmers leaving Vienna after 1869
Improved land ave. (acres)	120.6	87.4
Unimproved land ave. (acres)	52.7	40.3
Animal units (ave.)	30.8	6.4
Bushel output (ave.)	1,631.9	1,338.7
% wheat	61.6	64.5
Bushel output per acre	13.5	15.3
Bushels per animal unit	52.9	209.2
N	27	18

Sources: U.S. manuscript agricultural censuses, Vienna township, 1869, 1879; U.S. manuscript population censuses, Vienna township, 1870, 1880.

stayed owned an average of 30.8 animal units that were fed with feed grains and especially hay, those who left held only about one-fifth as many animals. Whether the migrants sold their land at a profit after succeeding in wheat speculation or were forced off their land cannot be determined. It seems safe to argue, however, that those who held more animals in 1869 were more resilient when the wheat market reversed in the following decade. Perhaps, as Thompson noted, more Norwegians were unable to weather the decline of wheat because they continued to rely on it for cash. Yet most Norwegian farmers endured and entered a more secure period of diversified farming in the later nineteenth century.

Farmers who could make the adjustment to diversified farming enjoyed benefits that reduced risk and more fully utilized resources and labor. As early as 1844 Reiersen observed that forcing "the greatest production from the soil more swiftly and easily" was the primary concern of the farmer when he was beginning to build his holdings. But "once this independence was assured," he noted, "the farmer usually begins to consider other products and the methods most advantageous in the long run, and how he can exploit the benefits that his property offers with the greatest profit and the least physical labor."[49] Diversified farming became "advantageous" because it was less risky than wheat farming, which was based entirely on an increasingly capricious harvest. Moreover, crop rotation and more thorough use of resources, such as the hay that was wasted in the early days of settlement, when animals were too expensive, permitted a fuller utilization of the land. Finally, with diversification, laborers worked not only in sowing and reaping grains but in stock raising or dairying, which provided a more even work load throughout the year. Accordingly, more year-round laborers were hired in the households of Vienna, Arendahl, and Camp as diversified farming developed (see Table 43, later in this chapter).

As wheat declined in Vienna township in the 1870s, feed grains such as oats and corn assumed greater importance. Wheat output was reduced over 80% by Norwegians between 1869 and 1879, while their harvest of oats increased 137%, that of barley 418%, and that of corn 690%. Since the lure of large wheat harvests was gone and Norwegian farmers were planting feed grains, their dependence on hay was reduced. With increasing stock, hay harvests remained stable, so that by 1879 few differences remained between Norwegians and the township as a whole. Grain patterns reflected a shift from crops as a market commodity to crops as feed, a shift that created a market commodity through animal production. Norwegians who remained in Vienna township from 1869 through 1879 increased their average number of animal units by 38.0%, concentrating on nondairy cattle (up 197%), sheep (up 210%), and swine (up 657%) (see Table 39).

The greater security of diversification was hailed by contemporaries. "As our herds increase," wrote the Wisconsin State Agricultural Society in 1879–80,

> our acres of grass multiply and a better system of farming is being pursued in Wisconsin. Sections [i.e., 640 acres] of wheat are a thing of the past. Mixed husbandry is universal and our people are wiser, happier, and richer therefore . . . It may safely be said that Wisconsin has passed that period of speculation, heavy loans, and exorbitant interest, incident to the settlement of a new state and has now entered upon a career of stability and solid permanent growth.[50]

According to some historians and geographers, this period of contentment was also a time of "cultural rebound" when ethnocultural groups regained lost practices they had discarded during the difficult initial pioneer years.[51] The preference for dairy cattle in 1859 among Norwegians, whose diet was dependent on milk products but who had held many swine in 1849, indicates some validity in the hypothesis. A cultural rebound did not occur, however, in market animal products during the period of diversification. Owing to the great reliance on sheep and cattle in Balestrand, one might have expected the Balestrand immigrants to have reintroduced similar

Table 39. *Growth in livestock holdings among groups remaining in Vienna township from 1869 to 1879*

	Norwegians				Non-Norwegians			
	1869 mean	1869 stand. dev.	1879 mean	1879 stand. dev.	1869 mean	1869 stand. dev.	1879 mean	1879 stand. dev.
Horses	8.2	5.5	6.5	2.5	5.4	3.2	5.2	3.5
Mules/asses	0.1	0.4	0.1	0.5	0.1	0.4	0.1	0.5
Milk cows	5.2	2.7	6.4	3.9	3.5	3.3	5.4	4.2
Working oxen	0.1	0.5	0	0	0.1	0.4	0	0
Other cattle	5.6	5.9	11.1	6.8	4.7	8.1	14.8	21.4
Sheep	12.9	10.4	25.9	28.6	12.1	29.8	48.1	113.4
Swine	4.6	3.6	30.4	17.0	4.4	4.1	28.2	24.1

Sources: U.S. manuscript agricultural censuses, Vienna township, 1869, 1879; U.S. manuscript population censuses, Vienna township, 1870, 1880.

farming practices. Instead they specialized in swine. And although cattle holdings increased in the 1870s among Norwegians, the growth was based more on beef cattle than on dairy cows. Conversely, it was the non-Norwegians who specialized in sheep, the large standard of deviation indicating that some farms had large commercial holdings while others owned few sheep, if any (see Table 39).

Farming patterns among Balestrand immigrants in Arendahl and Camp

The patterns of farming in the Balestrand settlements of Arendahl and Camp to the west indicated weaker carry-overs from Norway than in Norway Grove. Though certain traditional crop preferences were retained, others were less noticable. The immigrants in both settlements, however, again preferred large wheat acreages. The combination of new economic influences and the greater acclimation to American market activities therefore set the western settlements apart from Norway Grove.

Norwegian farmers in Arendahl and Camp not only planted much wheat but began to rely on it earlier than the Norway Grove settlers. The first agricultural census for Arendahl as for Norway Grove, was taken in 1859, five years after initial settlement of Arendahl and eight years before the railroad reached a nearby market. Yet the thirty-two Norwegian farmers, who averaged thirty-two im-

Table 40. *Wheat as a percentage of crop yield: Arendahl and Camp townships and environs, 1859, 1869, and 1879.*

	Wheat as a % of total crop	Number of farm units
Arendahl Norwegians		
1859	40.1	80
1869	60.5	131
Fremont Township		
1859	32.9	86
1869	53.3	150
Fillmore County		
1859	31.2	*a*
1869	51.9	*a*
Camp Norwegians		
1869	65.1	36
1879	45.7	65
Renville County		
1869	45.2	*a*
1879	41.6	*a*

*a*Figures for the counties are based on total crop output and hence are not comparable.
Sources: U.S. manuscript agricultural censuses, Arendahl township, 1859, 1869, Fremont township, 1859, 1869, Camp township, 1869, 1879; U.S. manuscript population censuses, Arendahl township, 1860, 1870, Fremont township, 1860, 1870, Camp township, 1870, 1880; *Agriculture of the United States in 1860 Compiled from the Original Returns of the Eighth Census* (Washington, D.C., 1864), 2:80–81; *The Statistics of the Wealth and Industry of the United States*, Ninth Census (Washington, D.C., 1872), 3:180–81; *Report on the Productions of Agriculture as Returned at the Tenth Census* (Washington, D.C., 1883), 3:194.

proved acres, devoted 37.1% of their crop production to wheat, more than Norwegian farmers in Vienna township ten years before. Norwegian preferences for wheat also continued: Arendahl Norwegians averaged a larger percentage of wheat than either their American-born neighbors in Fremont township to the north or the farmers of Fillmore County as a whole (see Table 40).[52]

Ten years later, with its successes and failures, the wheat boom reached Arendahl. Large harvests in Minnesota in 1860 and 1865, averaging over twenty-two bushels an acre, were tempered in 1867 by partial failures. The Norwegians in Arendahl continued to rely on wheat in 1869; it constituted 60.5% of their harvests, again considerably higher than Fremont township and the whole of Fillmore County. In Arendahl as in Wisconsin, the 1870s were a period of diversification, although the decline of wheat was not so precipitous in Arendahl. Fillmore County farmers devoted a little over one-third of their crop production to wheat in 1879, again less than the Arendahl Norwegians. A year before, however, the State Dairymen's Association had been organized at the inauguration of an industry that was, according to spokesmen, "more certainly remunerative than wheat growing because it is not so liable to injury by grasshopper depredations, unpropitious seasons, hail storms, etc., nor does it occasion duplication of the productive elements of the soil."[53]

Camp township Norwegians specialized in wheat even earlier in their farm development. In 1869, a few years after initial settlement, 65.1% of their crop output on an average 12.9 improved acres per unit was wheat, considerably higher than the 45.2% for Renville County as a whole. Camp township bordered the Minnesota River and was settled earlier than most of Renville County, a difference that partly explains the large variance in wheat production. In 1879 Camp Norwegians continued to average slightly more wheat than the whole of Renville County, an indication that the Norwegian preference for wheat continued to operate (see Table 40).[54]

Norwegian immigrants in Arendahl and Camp townships also retained the preference for small-grain, nonmarket crops discovered in Norway Grove. In spite of large acreages of corn during earliest settlement, Arendahl Norwegians later planted more oats and barley than the norm (see Table 41). By 1879 over four-fifths of their nonmarket crop harvest consisted of oats and barley, compared to less than three-fifths for Fillmore as a whole. Corn, on the other hand, which remained important in Fillmore County, declined in use among Norwegians after the pioneering years, a process consistent with the cultural rebound hypothesis. Though Arendahl Norwegians relied on oats less than Vienna township's Norwegians, they remained more partial to the traditional crops than the Camp Norwegians in central Minnesota. In Camp township Norwegians grew a corn, oats, and barley mix similar to that prevailing throughout Renville County (see Table 42).

Though traditional Norwegian crop preferences were retained in Arendahl, the importance of hay as a fodder declined rapidly. Arendahl Norwegians held on the average 4.1 fewer animal units than Vienna Norwegians in 1859 and 9.6 fewer in 1869. Yet in both censuses the Arendahl farmers harvested on the average more bushels of feed grains – oats, corn, and barley – than the Vienna Nor-

Table 41. *Nonmarket crops as percentages of total harvests: Arendahl Norwegians and Fillmore County farm units, 1859, 1869 and 1879*

	Corn	Oats	Barley	Potatoes	N
Arendahl					
1859	46.3	39.2	2.4	12.1	32
1869	15.7	64.3	15.7	4.3	80
1879	14.7	65.8	15.2	4.2	131
Fillmore Co.					
1859	50.4	34.3	1.9	13.4	[a]
1869	24.9	62.4	6.9	5.8	[a]
1879	35.9	50.8	6.6	6.7	[a]

[a]These figures are based on total crop output and hence are not comparable. *Sources:* U.S. manuscript agricultural censuses, Arendahl township, 1859, 1869, 1879; U.S. manuscript population censuses, Arendahl township, 1860, 1870, 1880; *Agriculture of the United States in 1860*, 2:80–81; *Statistics of the Wealth and Industry*, 3:180–81; *Report on the Productions of Agriculture*, 3:194.

wegians (nearly 50% more in 1869). In spite of extensive pastures, farmers in Arendahl, who averaged 79.7 acres of unimproved land, cut only 7.7 tons of hay in 1869, considerably less than the 15.9 tons averaged by the Vienna Norwegians.

Farmers from Balestrand who moved to Norway Grove and later to Arendahl and Camp thus sustained some farming preferences carried from Norway. Certainly the immigrants did not intend to reestablish a høstingsbruk system in the Upper Middle West, but

Table 42. *Nonmarket crops as percentages of total harvests: Camp Norwegians and Renville County farm units, 1869 and 1879*

	Corn	Oats	Barley	Potatoes	N
Camp					
1869	21.5	23.8	2.3	52.4	36
1879	30.8	60.7	1.8	6.6	65
Renville Co.					
1869	12.4	52.6	6.9	28.1	[a]
1879	27.4	59.3	3.9	9.3	[a]

[a]These figures are based on total crop output and hence are not comparable. *Sources:* U.S. manuscript agricultural censuses, Camp township, 1869, 1879; U.S. manuscript population censuses, Camp township, 1870, 1880; *Statistics of the Wealth and Industry*, 3:180–81; *Report on the Productions of Agriculture*, 3:194.

where the market did not dictate production, cultural background apparently influenced crop and animal choices. The attraction of the market, however, captured the attention of the Balestrand immigrants. Although they were slow in adjusting their operations to the wheat market, the Norwegians soon emphasized this grain to the point at which many apparently suffered when the profits and harvests decreased.

Even if the Balestrand immigrants retained old farming preferences, however, the adaptation to the wheat market was an event of great consequence to the Norwegian farmers. Some farmers who relied too heavily on the wheat market felt that they faced a greater likelihood of economic failure than they had in Norway. One Swede complained, "As poor as before on my croft now I stand / With greying hair and a trembling hand."[55] The majority, however, profited from the wheat boom, weathered the decline of the wheat market, and enjoyed the later period of diversified farming. A Norwegian journalist marveled in 1869 at the development of the Norwegian settlements. "If a person had last seen this region three decades ago," he wrote, speaking about the Koshkonong colony,

> everything would assuredly strike him now as a grand illusion, like stories in Oriental fairy tales. The forests have been cleared, the wild prairies have been plowed and transformed into billowing fields of grain, the Indian trails have vanished, the prairie grass has been replaced by cultivated species, luxuriant orchards surround the homes of prosperous farmers, good roads have been laid out, well-equipped schools provide education and refinement, factories have been founded, churches with their lofty spires testify to the peoples' respect for religion . . . In sum, the progress is phenomenal, the transformations are like a dream.

He added that less than thirty years before, "poor toilers came to this region; now they are well off and some of them even rich."[56] Successful farmers in the Balestrand communities thus not only adapted to new crops and agricultural systems but enjoyed the benefits of increasing wealth.

Labor organization among Balestrand immigrant households

Just as they carried their own crop preferences to the United States, Balestrand immigrants also brought a traditional division of labor among household members. This tradition influenced the work responsibilities in the settlements, but the new farming conditions also induced alterations, both directly and indirectly. The lack of available cheap hired labor, as we have seen, increased the importance of workers within the nuclear family. Farm patterns resulting from fewer laborers, moreover, emphasized grains and encouraged greater use of implements that altered labor within the family. And although immigrant children usually worked for their parents longer than their counterparts in Balestrand, wheat farming dramatically altered the sexual division of labor in America.

With few available wage laborers, large households of children were a blessing, especially in relation to former conditions in Norway. "In America," wrote Reiersen in 1844, "children may be counted as an asset rather than a burden for the poor father." Not only did children work at home, but they could earn wages from others. "And the children," Reiersen continued,

> even quite small ones, can earn something to help support the family by picking berries. Boys of twelve and thirteen earn seventy-five cents or a dollar a week plus their food by chopping firewood and doing other light chores. And I know of a Norwegian girl of eleven who earns half a dollar a week plus board taking care of chickens and gathering eggs."[57]

As the settlements developed, children remained essential labor sources. In 1869 one J. A. Johnson Skipnæs noted that labor was expensive, and "therefore it is often said here that a numerous flock of children make the man rich."[58] A Vossing who grew up near Norway Grove in Sun Prairie remembered working on the hay harvest each year. He "wasn't a very big fellow" when he "had to take up the scythe," so by age thirteen, after years of practice, he could cut hay as well as his father. Years later still, in the 1890s, a Norwegian from Wisconsin began to drive teams in the field at age six.[59] With greater mechanization and wealth, children's labor roles changed. Yet they continued to labor on their family's farms and remained a ready source of cheap labor for their fathers.

The division of labor according to sex, even among children, was modified dramatically as the Norwegian-American farmstead developed. Women's labor in Balestrand, it will be remembered, was of primary importance to farm production (see Chapter 3). Animal care and production was the woman's domain, whereas men were primarily concerned with grain production. Animal products were of such extreme importance, both for home use and for sale, that large herds and flocks were owned. The prominence of animals accordingly led to a larger proportion of women than of men in servant roles. Farm production on Norwegian-American farms obviously disrupted these patterns of labor. Animal products remained part of the farm output, but traditional male work expanded as capital and labor constraints and market demands encouraged grain production. Clearly, traditional work patterns faced modification either in the sexual definition of work roles or in the proportions of farm work performed by the two sexes.

In spite of the new agricultural conditions, immigrant women did not begin to perform traditional male work duties.[60] They concentrated instead on their customary duties in the home and on the farm. The maintenance of traditional female farm labor, however, did distinguish the Norwegians from their American-born neighbors early in the settlement period.[61] One Norwegian wrote, "The Americans never use female help out of doors, not even to milk and care for the cows. So they get no help from their wives and daughters in the operation of the farms." He added, significantly, that the Norwegian pattern was advantageous to the immigrant man because the labor he received from women saved him from having to pay hired hands.[62] Another writer, commenting on the heavy work demands on women in early settlements, also reiterated the traditional Norwegian labor division. "It was of course the woman who should care for both the pigs and the cows," he wrote.

> She should be the first up in the morning, make the fire, go out to the barn to feed the animals, milk the cows, and let the calves drink; then in to make breakfast and dress the children. The men weren't used to milking cows in the Old Country; because it was the woman who did all such, and then everybody thought it was only proper that she do it here too. She also had to take part in haying in the summertime. She should stack the hay, help with getting it in . . . and when evening came her program was: to milk, care for the calves and pigs, prepare supper for herself and family and then get the children to bed. Finally, when it was about eleven o'clock, she was finished with her day's work if the children did not screech or scream too much in the nighttime. But if she had a lot to do, she got paid for it. Usually she got one or two calico dresses a year, a pair of shoes that cost $1.75; and a hat that cost $1.50 every third year.[63]

The woman worked extremely hard in much the same fashion as she had in Norway, and she easily "earned her keep at various jobs such as washing, ironing, sewing, and the like."[64]

Increased dependence on wheat strained this Norwegian sexual division of farm labor. Women continued animal work and haying, both traditional roles, but concentration on cash grains brought the division of labor into greater disequilibrium. Not only was wheat production traditionally men's work, but its increasing mechanization forced it even further into the male domain. As Ester Boserup has argued in her work on Third World countries, cash crops that are cultivated by modern methods tend to become men's work as farming systems with permanently plowed fields are introduced in lieu of shifting cultivation and as implements increase in importance. Ironically, as agriculture becomes less dependent upon manpower and the difference in labor productivity might be expected to narrow, men predominate to an even greater degree in using the new types of equipment. Boserup adds significantly that "the adoption of a farming system when the main farming equipment is operated only by men entails a tremendous change in the economic and social relationship between the sexes."[65] A similar shift occurred in the nineteenth-century Balestrand-American settlement, and because wheat prices encouraged use of more implements, grain farming remained firmly the work of men.

These changing labor patterns resulted in different mixes of family and hired labor in the household. Household women continued to work in traditional areas, which by and large became nonmarket activities, with little hired female help. Care of the cows and pigs, work in the kitchen garden, and housekeeping – in short, tasks necessary to sustain the family – were performed by women. In Norway Grove women continued in their role as caretakers of the blood and entrails during the slaughter through the 1860s.[66] Additionally, some activities that brought income to the family, such as butter making, also remained in the woman's domain.[67] With fewer female servants the work load for women remained large. Although one pioneer Norwegian woman had heard claims that women in America had ample leisure time, she wrote that she met no woman who agreed: In America "the mistress of the house must do all the work that the cook, the maid, and the housekeeper would do in an upperclass family at home."[68]

Accordingly, the traditional sex ratio of farm laborers was reversed in the American rural settlements (see Table 43). Although early letters noted that labor for young women was available – often more available than labor for men – it was principally domestic work. Other letters praised the working conditions for servant women in American homes. One, written in 1841, noted the abundance of work for women in Chicago, where wages were high "and because of the high regard in which women are held in this country, they are exempt from all kinds of outdoor work and so are far less exposed to disease."[69] Ole Rynning simply stated that "women are

Table 43. *Sex ratio of servants: Balestrand and Balestrand settlements, 1860–1900*

	No. of men	No. of women	Ratio
Balestrand			
1865	210	312	67.3
Vienna twp.			
1860	20	5	400.0
1880	39	9	433.3
Arendahl twp.			
1860	5	2	250.0
1880	44	9	488.9
1900	35	0	—
Camp twp.			
1880	6	0	—
1900	15	1	1500.0

Sources: Balestrand manuscript population census, 1865; U.S. manuscript population censuses, Vienna township, 1860, 1880, Arendahl township, 1860, 1880, 1900, Camp township, 1880, 1900.

respected and honored far more than is the case among common people in Norway."[70]

Because women servants became concentrated in domestic work, they often moved to cities. One resident of Carver County, Minnesota, wrote in 1859 that "out here in the country there are not many jobs for servant girls, since all people here are settlers that have to get along as well as they can with their own hands. But in the cities jobs are available."[71] In Norway Grove, Arendahl, and Camp, therefore, male farm laborers who were not part of the nuclear family became an increasingly large occupational group, whereas the number of female "domestics" remained insignificant. Moreover, youths at home through age nineteen were predominantly boys, an indication that daughters were more likely to leave home to find work (see Table 44). Migration did not necessarily mean that young women left the power of the family.[72] But it did reveal a declining importance of female labor in farm production: Though the traditional role of the *innjente* (domestic) survived the emigration, the budeie was not replicated in American settlements.

Not only did the occupation of milkmaid vanish, but traditional duties of animal care were abandoned by women as housework and child care proved to be a heavy work burden. As early as 1835 an

Table 44. *Sex ratio of children aged 0–19 in households: Balestrand and Balestrand settlements, 1860–1900*

	No. of boys	No. of girls	Ratio
Balestrand			
1865	483	500	96.6
Vienna twp.			
1860	69	53	130.2
1880	84	76	110.5
Arendahl twp.			
1860	94	71	132.4
1880	281	250	112.2
1900	215	175	122.9
Camp twp.			
1880	100	94	106.4
1900	99	90	110.0

Sources: Balestrand manuscript population census, 1865; U.S. manuscript population censuses, Vienna township, 1860, 1880, Arendahl township, 1860, 1880, 1900, Camp township 1880, 1900.

immigrant wrote home noting that women servants got high wages and worked only in the house, with no heavy outdoor work (*"intet tungt eller Ude-Arbeide"*).[73] A prominent emigrant guide book written in 1838 said that women servants "had no outside work except to milk cows."[74] And whether they liked it or not, male servants soon did the milking. Reiersen wrote that "hands hired for the sort of work women do in Europe – hoeing, weeding, winnowing grain, yes, even milking – earn from 50 to 75 cents a day."[75] A letter from the Koshkonong settlement written to family in Luster, Sogn, in 1849 reported that "wages for women servants are naturally not as large as for men here, but then they do not perform any kind of work outside the house."[76]

Some observed the shift with humor, others with chagrin. An 1857 letter maintained that "everything is the wrong way here in America . . . in many families the men milk the cows.[77] A Swedish immigrant three years later noted that "the women never work in the fields – not even milking cows. We men must do that. When I first began to milk, some of it went into my coat sleeves, but that didn't bother me: I emptied them when they became full."[78] Changing responsibilities were even acknowledged in Rølvaag's semi-autobiographical account of his early life in late nineteenth-century

Plate 15. Three men and one boy milking a relatively large herd of cows in the Norway Grove vicinity, 1873–79. *Source*: State Historical Society of Wisconsin; photograph by Andrew Dahl

America. In his first letter home he wrote, "To think that a *grown man* should sit down and pull at a cow udder! A man as a milkmaid – as a *barn boy!*" Three letters later, when he had accommodated himself more fully to his new work role, he remarked, "Yes, indeed, I have to clean the stalls and do the milking and care for the pigs, too." But he added, reflecting a yet incomplete adjustment, "This you certainly don't need to repeat so the young people back home hear about it. They don't know anything about how things are here, and that I *have* to do it" (see Plate 15).[79]

Changing crop and animal patterns thus influenced the sexual division of labor both directly and indirectly. As grains were produced in increasing quantities, men and women continued to work in traditional roles that extended the male farm work responsibilities. Yet as the wheat boom produced greater wealth, a different propriety developed, indirectly encouraging women to forsake farm tasks that had once been their domain. Women, for example, could have regained their heavy work responsibilities when animals became increasingly important in the diversified farming stage that followed the wheat boom. Instead, the reverse occurred. Increasing wealth, greater reliance on implements, and more use of hired help encouraged the continuance of the new work patterns. As Boserup noted, the presence of landless families working for wages freed landed women from agricultural work, a situation that seems to

Plate 16. Though some daughters still might have to spin yarn under the direction of a stern mother, . . .

have occurred in Norwegian settlements.[80] Letters continued to observe that women were released from all the heavy outdoor work they had performed in Norway (see Plates 16 and 17). One woman reported that although she was busy all the time, she had no duties outside the house. She did not have to take care of the cattle. Washing was done in the kitchen, and "we do not beat the clothes as we did in Norway. We rub them on a board. We even pity ourselves," she concluded, "when we have to go outside to hang up clothes in wintertime."[81]

Indeed, as work became less strenuous, leisure was more plentiful. Writers who had early stressed the heavy work demands commented on the differences after the "dog years." "Farm wives who had regularly hurried through housework in the early years to get out into the fields were later pictured only in the kitchen or nursery, or at most weeding a garden!" Eventually younger wives were pictured as having no more to do than feeding the chickens.[82] At the turn of the century, when "scientific" farming brought in higher incomes,

> the farm wives wore silk dresses and in the winter fur coats . . .
> Now the men had to milk the cows, feed the pigs, hens and

Plate 17. Others could sew quilts with newfangled sewing machines (Norway Grove vicinity, 1873–79). *Source* (for Plates 16 and 17): State Historical Society of Wisconsin; photographs by Andrew Dahl

calves, and build the fire in the morning, chop wood, and even carry it in. Now the wife could stay in a comfortable room, play the piano, have a dressmaker to fit and sew stylish dresses and instead of a $1.50 hat every third year, nowadays she gets a five dollar hat – one in the spring and one in the fall.[83]

The traditional sexual division of labor thus changed in important ways in the Balestrand settlements. It was altered, however, not to equalize farm labor between the sexes but ultimately to separate farm labor – particularly farm work in market activities – which was associated with men, from domestic work, a woman's sphere. In part, the separation was based on the increasing female domestic duties that occupied much of the farm wife's time. Bearing and raising large households of children was a time-consuming occupation, especially without servants. Yet as greater wealth was acquired, farm households could emulate patterns of behavior observed among richer groups in Norway and the United States. Balestrand immigrants had noticed that wealthy women in the official classes at home did not work in the fields, and Norwegian-American magazines urged that this pattern be observed. "It is best for the farmer," wrote Svein Nilsson in an 1869 *Billed-Magazin*, "to tend the cattle himself. We Norwegians help the women too little with work like this which, following our old country ideas, falls to their lot."[84] American middle-class women in market centers, many of whom were served by immigrant women, offered yet another example of domestic, bourgeois propriety.

Just as greater internal migration and fewer available laborers increased the importance of the nuclear family in Norwegian-American farm structures, new economic patterns altered roles within the family. As Balestrand farmers made the rapid transitions necessary in the swiftly developing Upper Middle West, they also adjusted to a new wealth that permitted them to imitate bourgeois patterns they had previously only observed. As we will see in the next chapter, social standards that developed in the Balestrand settlements also resulted from the interaction of new conditions and old behavioral patterns. The bourgeois customs that were observed, exemplified in modifications of "moral behavior," were consonant with norms carried from Norway but were made possible only by the new well-being in the Balestrand settlements.

9 "There is good moral fiber in the sons of the mountains": social development of the American communities

O. E. Rølvaag's epic trilogy about Norwegian immigrants in the Upper Middle West portrayed many of the transitions to American life experienced by a developing community from earliest settlement to the turn of the century. One of Rølvaag's keen observations was his perception of changing social mores among the settlers. In Norway the protagonist of the trilogy, Beret, "had been gotten with child . . . out of wedlock; nevertheless, no one had compelled her to marry."[1] Yet as the community in America flourished, new perceptions about illegitimacy and proper behavior led to an incident that "set the tongues awagging." A young woman allegedly bore an illegitimate child that was stillborn or left to die. The circumstances that came to light were not clear, but the girl agreed to confess her sins before her entire church congregation, an ordeal so wrenching that she later committed suicide.[2] Puritanical propriety had become so strict that one member suggested she be led outside the city gates and stoned as the Law of Moses instructed – a punishment certainly not considered when Beret bore her first child.

Immigrants from Balestrand experienced a similar, although not so melodramatic, transition. Moving from an area with extremely high rates of illegitimacy (see Chapter 5), the immigrants lived in settlements that by the turn of the century rarely saw either illegitimate or prenuptially conceived births. The transition, however, did not occur overnight. In fact, customs of courtship and marriage prevalent in Balestrand at the time of emigration were sustained during the earliest periods of settlement. Shifts in social attitudes, like changes in economic patterns, developed as traditional patterns interacted with a different environment. If crop types and scarcity of hired labor expanded the role of men in agricultural production, other social and economic impetuses encouraged women to work in domestic tasks. Livelihoods upon which to base household formations were more abundant in the American settlements, so that lower marriage ages became possible. And since children were a ready source of labor, whereas women's farm work was declining, wives were inclined to bear more children.

Like work roles, propriety during courtship was modified. Night courting continued for a time in the Balestrand settlements, but since couples had a greater accessibility to livelihoods than in Balestrand, marriage usually occurred before an illegitimate child was born. In a sense, the pattern of marriage after conception but before the birth of the first child, which had been common in early nineteenth-century Balestrand, was reestablished. With increasing wealth and changing work roles, however, conduct during courtship became yet more strict. Night courting was condemned by community leaders, most noticeably the pastors of the rural churches; and even prenuptially conceived children became increasingly uncommon.

Changing courtship behavior is one graphic illustration of a morality profoundly different from Balestrand's that evolved in the American settlements. As in other instances of cultural change, the altered behavior was the result of new situations in the United States influencing cultural patterns carried from Norway. Modified social and economic patterns, such as the increasing importance of the nuclear family in farm organization and new work responsibilities according to gender, provided a base for the transition. The interaction between religious and cultural influences carried from Norway, on the one hand, and different American conditions, on the other, was an essential factor in generating social change. The leaven of pietistic thought that originated in Balestrand permeated segments of the American communities so that Haugean churches were formed in the chain of settlements. The increasing wealth in the Norwegian communities, moreover, provided the setting for behavior that can best be termed bourgeois. Conduct that had been observed in Norwegian towns and advocated by the Norwegian clergy became the norm among Balestrand immigrants in the United States.

Patterns of marriage and fertility in Balestrand-American settlements
Traditional marriage customs operating in the new American environment worked to lower age at marriage and increase the proportion of people ever married. Since marriages continued to be based on livelihoods, the availability of land and work in the American settlements permitted younger ages at first marriage. Norway Grove is the community examined here.[3] Marriage age for both sexes remained relatively high in Norway Grove during the earliest years of settlement (see Table 45). The median age for men in the 1850s, ranging from 26 to 28 years, was quite similar to the median in Mundal parish in the same decade (27 years for farmers and 28 for

Table 45. *Age at first marriage: Norway Grove, Spring Prairie, and Bonnet Prairie, 1851–96*

	Men		Women		
	Median	Mean	Median	Mean	N
1851–53	28	28.9	25	25.6	24
1854–56	26	27.4	25	25.7	108
1857–59	27	28.2	22	22.7	29[a]
1860–62	26	26.4	23	25.1	14[a]
1863–65	26	26.8	21	20.6	5[a]
1866–68	25	25.9	22	22.7	55
1869–71	25	26.7	23	23.1	79
1872–74	26	26.6	23	24.1	52
1875–77	26	27.0	22	23.4	38[a]
1878–80	24	25.1	21	21.7	16[a]
1881–83	26	26.2	24	24.1	14[a]
1884–86	27	27.5	24	25.0	44
1887–89	28	29.7	25	24.6	28
1890–92	27	27.1	23	24.6	29
1893–96	28	27.9	23	24.0	51

[a]Ages missing from the records for some marriages.
Source: Spring Prairie, Norway Grove, and Bonnet Prairie Lutheran Church records.

cotters). Women in Norway Grove between 1851 and 1856 married at a median age of 25, the same as the median for farmers' wives and a year younger than that for cotters' wives in the 1850s in Mundal. After that time, however, age at first marriage in Norway Grove declined. Men, as a rule, married around age 25 or 26 between 1860 and 1880, and the marriage age for women dropped even more. By 1858 women were marrying at a median age of 22, within a range from 21 to 23, a pattern that would last through 1880. Marriage age for women in Mundal parish fell in the 1870s as well, but the American Balestranders were wed about four years younger than their friends and relatives who remained in Norway.[4]

That age at marriage dropped more precipitously for women than for men was partly due to a scarcity of marriageable women in the pioneer settlements. In Vienna township in 1860, for example, there were 179.3 Norwegian men for every 100 Norwegian women between the ages of 15 and 44. Similar conditions existed in Camp in 1880, where the male/female ratio for those aged 15 to 44 was 130.9, and in Arendahl in 1860, where it was a less skewed 118.9. Since

Table 46. *Age differences between partners in first marriages: Norway Grove and Spring Prairie, 1851–96*

	Husband older				Wife older			
	9+ yrs. (%)	3–8 yrs. (%)	1–2 yrs. (%)	Same age (%)	1–2 yrs. (%)	3–8 yrs. (%)	9+ yrs. (%)	N
1851–59	15.3	38.3	14.9	4.5	11.7	11.3	4.0	222
1860–69	12.0	46.0	17.0	7.0	8.0	8.0	2.0	100
1870–79	7.6	49.1	14.6	10.2	7.6	6.0	3.8	157
1880–89	15.9	44.3	12.5	6.8	6.8	11.4	2.3	88
1890–96	17.5	37.5	15.0	8.7	10.0	11.2	0	80

Note: Only marriages with Balestrand-born partners are included.
Source: Spring Prairie and Norway Grove Lutheran Church records.

women were scarcer, they were likely to be courted by older men who had not found brides in their own age groups. Ironically, the proportion of wives older than their husbands grew during the early years of settlement when sex ratios were most skewed. In the 1850s, while just under 70% of the grooms in Norway Grove were older than their spouses, 27% of the brides were older (4% were nine or more years older). Beginning in the 1860s, however, the proportion of older brides fell to around one-fifth, a pattern that continued for the remainder of the century (see Table 46).

Greater availability of livelihoods led not only to lowered marriage ages but to lessened lifelong bachelorhood and spinsterhood as well. Women, since they were in the minority, were married in larger proportions than in Balestrand, especially in the early years of settlement. Whereas only about one-tenth of Balestrand women aged 20 to 24 were married in 1865, for example, nearly half of Vienna Norwegians of the same age group had entered matrimony in 1860. Although no women aged 20 to 24 lived in Arendahl in 1860, by 1880 just over two-fifths in that age group were married. The greater frequency of marriage continued up the age scale, so that all women over age 30 were married or widowed in both Vienna and Arendahl townships in 1860 (see Table 47). Men were marrying earlier than in Balestrand as well, a circumstance indicating a greater abundance of livelihoods in the United States. Among those aged 20 to 24, one-quarter of Vienna's Norwegian-born men in 1860 and one-fifth of the Arendahl Norwegians in 1880 were married, compared to just over 6% in Balestrand in 1865.

Table 47. *Percentage ever married at given ages: Balestrand and Balestrand settlements, 1860–1900*

Age	Balestrand, 1865		Vienna twp., 1860		Vienna twp., 1880	
	Men	Women	Men	Women	Men	Women
15–19	1.0	0	0	0	0	4.8
20–24	6.2	10.1	25.0	42.9	12.1	45.5
25–29	30.9	49.3	44.4	75.0	45.5	50.0
30–34	73.9	69.4	57.1	100.0	80.0	72.7
35–39	87.7	77.0	75.0	100.0	71.4	50.0
40–44	98.2	81.7	100.0	100.0	66.7	100.0
45–49	90.5	87.9	87.5	100.0	90.0	100.0
50–54	85.7	75.0	100.0	100.0	100.0	100.0
55–59	87.5	84.1	100.0	100.0	100.0	100.0
60–64	97.4	90.9	—	—	100.0	100.0
65+	96.4	90.6	100.0	100.0	100.0	100.0

Age	Arendahl twp., 1860		Arendahl twp., 1880		Arendahl twp., 1900	
	Men	Women	Men	Women	Men	Women
15–19	0	0	0	5.3	0	5.0
20–24	0	—	20.5	40.5	7.7	33.3
25–29	—	100.0	51.5	72.0	34.3	58.1
30–34	100.0	100.0	87.0	86.7	72.4	70.8
35–39	100.0	100.0	83.3	95.6	63.6	68.2
40–44	93.7	100.0	92.3	100.0	94.7	84.2
45–49	—	—	90.0	95.8	78.6	100.0
50–54	—	—	90.5	94.4	91.7	100.0
55–59	—	100.0	84.6	100.0	88.9	100.0
60–64	100.0	—	100.0	66.7	90.1	100.0
65+	—	—	100.0	100.0	90.5	92.8

Age	Camp twp., 1880		Camp twp., 1900	
	Men	Women	Men	Women
15–19	0	14.3	0	0
20–24	16.7	33.3	4.3	22.7
25–29	50.0	84.6	22.2	37.0
30–34	83.3	100.0	63.6	88.9
35–39	83.3	100.0	54.5	66.7
40–44	100.0	90.9	80.0	100.0

Table 47. (*cont.*)

Age	Camp twp., 1880		Camp twp., 1900	
	Men	Women	Men	Women
45–49	85.7	100.0	87.5	90.9
50–54	100.0	100.0	100.0	100.0
55–59	83.3	100.0	88.9	100.0
60–64	100.0	100.0	100.0	100.0
65+	100.0	100.0	—	100.0

*a*Dashes indicate no members of the age group in question.
Sources: Balestrand manuscript population census, 1865; U.S. manuscript population censuses, Vienna township, 1860, 1880, Arendahl township, 1860, 1880, 1900, Camp township, 1880, 1900.

Although a greater proportion of people married, and generally at younger ages than in Norway, couples retained the traditional marriage and wedding practices in the Balestrand settlements in Norway Grove and Arendahl. Marriage celebrations during early Arendahl settlement, for example, were much like those in Norway. An honored man journeyed from farm to farm to invite guests personally. After the ceremony, the wedding party went to the home of the bride or groom for a celebration, at which homemade beer, as well as brandy and wine, was served. The church historian wrote that drink at a wedding night might "shock some readers." But to have omitted it at "any important social event would have been highly unconventional, a violation of tradition of long standing in Norway." After dinner, people danced and drank in some households, but among the "austere Haugeans" in Arendahl "such activity was taboo."[5]

The season of marriage, moreover, followed a pattern similar to that in Balestrand. In Norway Grove 40.2% of the 127 marriages that included Balestranders between 1851 and 1889 were celebrated in May, June, and July, and another 36.2% occurred in October, November, and December. As in Balestrand, furthermore, women who married in the winter months were more likely to be pregnant than their summer counterparts. Well over half of the winter brides (56.5%) were with child, a marked contrast to the 29.4% pregnant at marriage in the preferred summer months. Not only was the custom of concentrating marriages either in winter or in early summer thus transferred to Norway Grove, but the function of the winter mar-

Plate 18. This Norway Grove extended family, engaged in various pursuits ranging from reading to spinning, also reveals its "children in abundance." *Source:* State Historical Society of Wisconsin; photograph by Andrew Dahl

riage was also transplanted: Those who had become pregnant during the summer married late in the year to avoid birth of the first child out of wedlock before the more attractive traditional marriage period around June (see Chapter 5).

One of the consequences of earlier marriage and larger segments ever married was increased fertility. A Norwegian immigrant writing home in 1850 noted new fertility patterns in America. Her brothers and sisters, who lived in her settlement, were "happy and content," since all had acquired land. "We all have cattle, driving oxen, and wagons," she continued. "We also have children in abundance."[6] A Norwegian journalist writing about Dane County two decades later noted, "'The Scandinavians in this county distinguish themselves by great fertility,' say the Yankees, and a comparison between birth rates in Norwegian and American families undeniably serves to corroborate this statement" (see Plate 18).[7] The high levels of fertility are underscored in the age structures of Norwegians in Vienna, Arendahl, and Camp townships, each with large segments of young people. In Vienna township in 1860, 45.5% of the population was aged 0 to 14. Children under 15 composed 64.2% of the population of Arendahl in 1860 and 42.4% in 1880. Camp township Norwegians were little different, with 46.9% of the population consisting of children in the same age group.[8] Simple fertility measures also indicate high rates of birth in the American

Table 48. *Child/woman ratios: Balestrand and Balestrand settlements,*
1845–1900

	No. of children aged 0–14	No. of women aged 15–49	Ratio
Balestrand			
1845	663	599	1.11[a]
1855	750	543	1.38
1865	787	550	1.43
Vienna twp.			
1860	119	50	2.38
1880	118	81	1.46
Arendahl twp.			
1860	150	36	4.17
1880	405	199	2.04
1900	300	181	1.66
Camp twp.			
1880	101	60	1.68
1900	149	93	1.60

[a]Here the ratio is children aged 0–9/women aged 20–49.
Sources: Balestrand manuscript population censuses, 1845, 1855, 1865; U.S. manuscript population censuses, Vienna township, 1860, 1880, Arendahl township, 1860, 1880, 1900, Camp township, 1880, 1900.

settlements. The child/woman ratio that stood at about 1.4 in Balestrand during the period of heavy emigration was as high as 4.2 in Arendahl in 1860 and remained well above the Balestrand figure throughout the century in all settlements (see Table 48).

The differences between child/married woman ratios in the American settlements and in Balestrand were pronounced (see Table 49). Although these ratios were higher in the American settlements in every instance but one, the variation in all cases was less than with the child/woman ratios. Similar findings have led Hans Norman to argue that marital fertility did not increase in a Swedish-American settlement, since larger child/woman ratios were due simply to a greater frequency of marriage in the United States.[9] The consistent child/married woman ratios, according to Norman, indicated that although more women were marrying, their fertility did not increase within marriage.

Yet earlier wedlock did work to increase the average number of fertile years for married women in the Balestrand-American settlements, and mothers bore children more frequently in all age groups.

Table 49. *Child/married woman ratios: Balestrand and Balestrand settlements, 1845–1900*

	No. of children aged 0–14	No. of married women aged 15–49	Ratio
Balestrand			
1845	663	235	2.82[a]
1855	750	247	3.04
1865	787	246	3.20
Vienna twp.			
1860	119	35	3.40
1880	118	38	3.11
Arendahl twp.			
1860	150	31	4.84
1880	405	110	3.68
1900	300	84	3.57
Camp twp.			
1880	101	44	2.30
1900	149	43	3.46

[a]Here the ratio is children aged 0–9/women aged 20–49.
Sources: Balestrand manuscript population censuses, 1845, 1855, 1865; U.S. manuscript population censuses, Vienna township, 1860, 1880, Arendahl township, 1860, 1880, 1900, Camp township, 1880, 1900.

Children, an essential source of labor, were born "in abundance" in the pioneer settlements. By standardizing children aged 0 to 4 in relation to married women aged 20 to 49, we can see that each Vienna township Norwegian woman averaged 1.57 children under age five in 1860, compared to 1.51 children in 1880 Arendahl and 1.55 in 1880 Camp (see Table 50).[10] All the figures for Balestrand-American communities during early settlement were considerably above the 1.03 children under age 5 for every married woman in Balestrand. Higher standardized child/woman ratios in the early periods of American settlement, moreover, were not due solely to earlier marriage. Women under age 25 residing in the United States bore more living children than their counterparts in Balestrand, but so did those in their late twenties and thirties. Norwegian-American married women in Balestrand settlements who were in their thirties at the time of the 1860 census, for example, averaged a little over 2 living children. Married women of the same age in Balestrand bore only 1.16 children on the average over the five years ending in 1865

Table 50. *Age-standardized marital fertility: Balestrand and Balestrand settlements, 1860–1900*

	No. of children aged 0–4 per 1,000 married women aged 20–49
Balestrand	
1865	1,027.0
Vienna twp.	
1860	1,566.1
1880	943.9
Arendahl twp.	
1860	1,416.7
1880	1,505.0
1900	1,149.2
Camp twp.	
1880	1,551.5
1900	1,199.8

Sources: Balestrand manuscript population censuses, 1865; U.S. manuscript population censuses, Vienna township, 1860, 1880, Arendahl township, 1860, 1880, 1900, Camp township, 1880, 1900.

(see Figure 13). Norwegian-American standardized marital fertility ratios declined after 1860. Yet the falling ratios for Balestrand-American settlements continued to exceed those for Balestrand throughout the nineteenth century.

The younger age at marriage for women, which prolonged their length of marital fertility, undoubtedly worked, in combination with more frequent childbearing throughout most of married life, to increase women's domestic work loads. Although Norwegian-American women in their forties seemed to experience levels of marital fertility similar to those of their counterparts in Balestrand, in all other cases more children were born to increasingly large families. Such household strategies were logical, as labor performed by children waxed in importance while mothers' farm work duties were declining. Accordingly, domestic work, largely related to raising more children, became a principal duty for women, whether they were mothers, daughters, or hired female help. If conditions in the United States worked to transform basic patterns of marriage and fertility, however, these new patterns in conjunction with the different conditions also profoundly influenced courtship behavior in the American settlements.

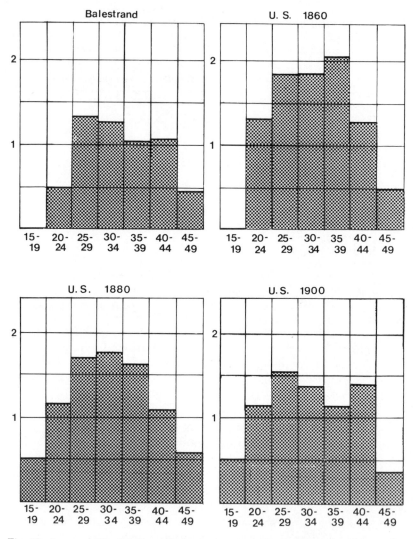

Fig. 13. Age-specific child/married woman ratios: Balestrand and Balestrand settlements, 1860–1900. *Sources:* Data from U.S. manuscript population censuses, Vienna township, 1860, 1880, Arendahl township, 1860, 1880, 1900, Camp township, 1880, 1900; Balestrand manuscript population census, 1865

Patterns of courtship in the Balestrand-American settlements

Just as marriages were based on livelihoods and were timed according to customary marriage seasons, the practice of night courting in Norwegian settlements was transplanted as well. Night courting among the Norwegian immigrants often attracted notice, much to the chagrin of Americans, who regarded such behavior with disdain. A missionary who in 1850 visited a Norwegian settlement in Dane County and found pervasive drunkenness in addition to night courting wrote, "Such gross immorality I have never witnessed before – it was offensive to come within the sphere poisoned by their breath."[11] Fredrika Bremer, on her visits to settlements in the same area, agreed, noting that "it is said to be difficult to give one part of these Norwegian people any sense of religious or civil order. They are spoken of as obstinate and unmanageable. But they are able tillers of the soil," she added prophetically, "and they prepare the way for a better race."[12]

Norwegian journalists reiterated American concerns, urging the immigrants to discontinue such unfortunate customs as night courting. In 1852 *Emigranten,* a newspaper based in central Wisconsin, observed the persistence of night courting in Norwegian-American settlements and strongly urged an end to its practice. "This abominable social abuse [*vederstyggelig uskikk*] unfortunately has been transferred here to the strange land," it lamented, "and in many places has brought about questions and bloody disorders [*optøier*]." The editor felt compelled in the interest of Norwegian immigrants to advise them against participation in this "unlawful and licentious [*ryggeløse*] custom." These comments came at a time when Eilert Sundt was studying the background and effects of night courting, illegitimacy, and "morality" in Norway, and *Emigranten*'s editors urged the adoption of measures to end night courting similar to those proposed by Sundt. Like their Norwegian counterparts, American fathers and farmers were held responsible for recognizing the evil of night courting and taking steps against it.[13]

Because night courting continued, the possibility of conceiving children out of wedlock remained great.[14] However, the abundance of livelihoods, by expanding marriage opportunities, worked to reduce the incidence of prenuptial births: When a woman became pregnant, it was usually possible to find a livelihood upon which to base a marriage before the child was born. Balestrand sustained an illegitimacy rate of 13.4% between 1850 and 1854 and one of 16.3% in the next five years, but only 1.5% and 2.2% of the children in the

Norway Grove settlement were born prenuptially during the same periods (see Table 51). Whereas 73 and 89 children were born prenuptially for every 100 marriages in these two five-year spans in Balestrand, only 4 and 9 per 100, respectively, were born prenuptially in Norway Grove during the same two periods. After the percentage of illegitimate births peaked in Norway Grove at 2.9% between 1865 and 1869, it fell gradually so that only 0.2% of the children born in the 1890s were illegitimate. The relationship between illegitimate births and marriages revealed a similar trend: Only 1 prenuptially born child occurred for every 100 marriages by the 1890s.

Members of the more pietistic Arendahl settlement were even less prone to prenuptial births. Indeed, between the first church records in 1858 and 1865, not a single illegitimate child was baptized. Thereafter, the rates hovered around 1.0%, peaking between 1891 and 1895 at 2.7%. Though one might argue that the lower illegitimacy rates were due to different practices in record keeping, this seems not to be the case. Baptism of a child, whether legitimate or not, was a spiritual duty of the parents within the Lutheran faith. Parents of illegitimate children, even if they did not belong to the church congregation, brought their infants to the rural church to baptize and therefore wash away original sin, and that sacrament was assiduously recorded in the church book.

If prenuptial births were rare in the American settlements, it was even more uncommon for an illegitimate child to be legitimized by marriage. In Norway Grove only 4 of the couples in the 140 marriages involving Balestrand immigrants or their offspring had had a child before marriage; none of the 34 couples in the Arendahl settlement had born a child before nuptials (see Table 52). Obviously, greater work opportunities in the United States permitted younger ages at marriage and thus tempered the frequency of illegitimate births, in spite of continued night courting.

As prenuptial births became a rarity, community pressure to discourage them became more stringent, and ostracism of the mother was not unknown. The baptism records themselves provide a key to the changing behavior within the community. In the Norway Grove church, illegitimacy early in the settlement period, though rare, was noted in the church book much as it had been in Norway: The mother and father were entered as parents, and the mother and godparents all took part in the baptismal ceremony. Moreover, women who bore illegitimate children during this period were more likely to marry within the congregation than were their later coun-

Table 51. *Illegitimate births according to year baptized: Norway Grove, Spring Prairie, Bonnet Prairie, and Arendahl, 1851–1900*

	Norway Grove					Arendahl		
	Total births	Illegit. births	% illegit.	Total marriages	Illegit. births per 100 marriages	Total births	Illegit. births	% illegit.
1851–55	322	5	1.5	120	4.2	—[a]	—	—
1856–60	534	12	2.2	130	9.2	82	0	0
1861–65	561	8	1.4	122	6.6	212	0	0
1866–70	517	15	2.9	153	9.8	161	2	1.2
1871–75	494	7	1.4	118	5.9	168	2	1.2
1876–80	425	4	0.9	95	4.2	143	1	0.7
1881–85	328	6	1.8	74	8.1	145	1	0.7
1886–90	281	2	0.7	70	2.8	121	2	1.6
1891–96	387	1	0.2	79	1.3	111	3	2.7
1897–1900	—	—	—	—	—	103	0	0

[a]Dashes indicate no data.
Sources: Spring Prairie, Norway Grove, and Bonnet Prairie Lutheran Church records; Arendahl Lutheran Church records.

Table 52. *Conception of first child of marriage: Balestrand immigrants in Norway Grove, Spring Prairie, Bonnet Prairie, and Arendahl, 1850–96*

	Norway Grove				Arendahl			
Year of marriage	Legit. (%)	Prenup. con. (%)	Illegit. (%)	N	Legit. (%)	Prenup. con. (%)	Illegit. (%)	N
1850–54	54.5	45.5	0	11	—[a]	—	—	—
1855–59	59.1	40.9	0	22	—	—	—	—
1860–64	45.5	54.5	0	22	78.6	21.3	0	14
1865–69	56.2	37.6	6.2	16	66.6	33.3	0	12
1870–74	52.9	41.2	5.9	21	100.0	0	0	8
1875–79	57.9	31.6	10.5	19	—	—	—	—
1880–84	62.5	37.5	0	8	—	—	—	—
1885–89	70.0	30.0	0	10	—	—	—	—
1890–96	81.2	18.8	0	11	—	—	—	—

[a]Dashes indicate no data.
Sources: Spring Prairie, Norway Grove, and Bonnet Prairie Lutheran Church records; Arendahl Lutheran Church records.

terparts. Whereas four of seventeen unwed mothers married members of the congregation in Norway Grove before 1860, only one of the forty-one unwed mothers married after that time, according to the church records. Beginning in the 1860s the notations in the church book increasingly omitted the father's name; when he was recorded, it was only "according to the girl" who accused him. The church records cited one father as an "unknown Irishman" in 1861 and another as, "according to the girl," "Henry W———, a married man." In all seventeen illegitimate births in the Norway Grove church records through the 1850s, and in all but one in the 1860s, both mother and father were cited, but only for eleven of seventeen was complete parenthood information provided in the 1870s, a trend that continued throughout the century. The pattern in Arendahl was similar, in spite of the fewer illegitimacies and poorer records to document them. Clearly conditions in American settlements that limited illegitimacy worked to single out the few unwed mothers, whose behavior, tolerated in Balestrand, was increasingly viewed with condemnation in the United States.

As noted, even though availability of livelihoods led to fewer prenuptial births, the maintenance of night courting customs produced a continued incidence of prenuptially conceived children. Indeed, marriages in Norway Grove that included immigrants from Balestrand and Leikanger or their progeny were often celebrated when the bride was pregnant. In the 1850s nearly half of all marriages were followed by the birth of a prenuptially conceived children. The incidence of such marriages peaked in the following five years, when 54.5% of the brides of Balestrand and Leikanger descent were pregnant. Thereafter, an increasingly large proportion of the first births occurred at least nine months after the wedding (see Table 52). In Arendahl, possibly because of its pietistic Haugean inclinations, bridal pregnancy was more rare. Although the sample is small and the records in general are poor, the wife was pregnant in only a little more than one-fifth of Arendahl marriages over a fifteen-year span between 1861 and 1875, a percentage significantly lower than in Norway Grove. By the early 1870s no marriages in the Arendahl congregation occurred when a child was on the way. Since youths were marrying at earlier ages and the traditional courting customs that resulted in prenuptially conceived children continued, in Norway Grove, at least, there developed a pattern of sexual initiation at younger ages than in Balestrand. Women, who were married as early as age fifteen and at a median age of about

Table 53. *Background in Norway in relation to conception of first child of marriage: Norway Grove, Spring Prairie, and Bonnet Prairie, 1850–96*

	Men				Women			
	Illegit. (%)	Prenup. con. (%)	Legit. (%)	N	Illegit. (%)	Prenup. con. (%)	Legit. (%)	N
Cotters								
1850–69	0	57.1	42.9	7	0	66.7	33.3	3
1870–96	16.7	41.7	41.7	12	0	40.0	60.0	10
Farmers								
1850–69	0	33.3	66.7	9	0	47.1	52.9	17
1870–96	10.0	40.0	50.0	10	0	14.3	85.7	7

Source: Family-reconstitution forms, Spring Prairie, Norway Grove, and Bonnet Prairie Lutheran Church records.

twenty-two, still were pregnant in nearly half the Norway Grove marriages.[15]

Although night courting began at an earlier age, Balestrand class distinctions in courting patterns were replicated in Norway Grove. It will be remembered that the children of cotters were more likely to produce prenuptially born or conceived first births than farmers' children in Balestrand. Tracing couples married in the United States back to their parents' civil standing in Norway is difficult and leads to a small sample, but those of cotter background did consistently show a greater tendency toward prenuptial conception (see Table 53). Farmers' daughters in Norway Grove were consistently 20% more likely than cotters' daughters to give birth for the first time nine or more months after marriage, in spite of the decline of illegitimacies and prenuptial conceptions for both groups.[16]

American-born parents of all class backgrounds were more likely to bear legitimate first children than Norwegian-born (see Table 54). Prenuptially conceived or born children were declining for all groups, but the first child of couples both of whose members were born in the United States was legitimate four-fifths of the time; among couples both of whom were of Norwegian birth, the first child was legitimate in only one-third of the cases. Class distinctions carried from Norway and place of birth must in part have been related to wealth, which could have influenced the incidence of prenuptial births or conceptions. Those of cotter background, for example, had fewer resources with which to begin farm operations

Table 54. *Conception of first child of marriage according to place of parents'
birth: Norway Grove, Spring Prairie, and Bonnet Prairie, 1870–96*

	Illegitimate		Prenup-tially conceived		Legitimate	
	%	N	%	N	%	N
Both American-born						
1870–79	0	0	23.1	3	76.9	10
1880–96	0	0	14.3	2	85.7	12
One American- and one Norwegian-born						
1870–79	0	0	36.4	4	63.6	7
1880–96	0	0	20.0	2	80.0	8
Both Norwegian-born						
1870–79	21.4	3	50.0	7	28.6	4
1880–96	0	0	50.0	2	50.0	2

Source: Family-reconstitution forms, Spring Prairie, Norway Grove, and
Bonnet Prairie Lutheran Church records.

in the United States. Likewise, American-born children who married in the 1870s and 1880s were likely the sons and daughters of
earlier immigrants who had had the opportunity to expand their
operations and accrue greater wealth. Clearly, however, these two
examples illustrate both behavioral carryovers from Balestrand and
the influences of American conditions. Conduct according to class
background was reestablished even as adjustments to a new environment were occurring.

The core Balestrand courting and marriage patterns thus were
transplanted early in the American settlement. In some respects
behavior in Norway Grove and, to a lesser extent, in the more puritanical Arendahl settlement replicated that in Balestrand before the
great population growth, when night courting was the norm but
when illegitimacy was not yet so prevalent as it would later be. As
illegitimate births occurred less often in American settlements, they
were condemned by society, whereas the incidence of prenuptially
conceived births apparently remained acceptable. Yet in spite of the
transplantation of customs of marriage ceremony and timing, the
initial retention of high marriage ages, and the maintenance of night
courting, American influences played a significant role. Not only
did the conjunction of greater opportunities and traditional patterns

of courtship reduce the frequency of prenuptial births and lower the age of premarital sex and marriage, but soon conditions in the American settlements provided for an attack on the old courtship practice.

Fewer illegitimate births can be related safely to greater occupational opportunities in America, but increasingly infrequent prenuptial conceptions must be associated with a decline in traditional customs of courtship. Moral condemnation of night courting, a practice that more and more was considered improper behavior, apparently was increasingly successful. Certainly new housing arrangements and intervention of parents might have precluded the opportunities for night courting – a change urged earlier by *Emigranten*. But even these steps were related to the development of strong moral constraints against premarital sex. In a close parallel to Rølvaag's fictional account, both Norway Grove and Spring Prairie churches began to censure "immoral" activities. Pastors who detected sinful conduct could summon members before the congregation "to be shown their error or sin that they might be brought to repentance and seek forgiveness." Among the sins, in addition to adultery, were drunkenness, slander, dancing, and misconduct at weddings. If people were found guilty, they were denied communion until they acknowledged their guilt, asked forgiveness, and promised to change their ways.[17] Obviously, such pressure was strong both from the pastor, moral leader of the community, who could dispense or withhold the sacraments, and from the community itself.[18]

Similar behavioral trends occurred not only in Norway Grove and Arendahl but in Norwegian settlements throughout the Middle West. Svein Nilsson, who visited and reported on Wisconsin Norwegian settlements for *Billed-Magazin* in the late 1860s, perceived both a decline in illegitimate births and an improvement in "moral conditions" that included less night courting and less alcoholism. According to one settler in the Muskego community, for example, theft was unheard of and no Norwegians had been charged with violating the law for twenty-five years. "And only one illegitimate child has been born," he added, "to a woman seduced by an American." Moral conditions were "exemplary" in the Yorkville and Racine settlements as well. "The cholera took all the drunkards," one settler explained with tongue in cheek, "so now only sober people remain, night courting would not be tolerated, and only one illegitimate child has been born since the Norwegians arrived."[19] At Jefferson Prairie, according to Nilsson, "addiction to strong drink has almost died out; night courting is a thing of the past; and only two illegitimate children have been born in the settlement."[20] Conditions in the Koshkonong settlement were also praised, since illegitimate births were rare and night courting "has ceased almost entirely."[21] The Rock Prairie settlement, for one reason or another, was judged less commendable. Nilsson believed that moral conditions were good there "in comparison with the way things are in many communities in the Old Country, but much is still to be wished for in this respect." Illegitimate births still occurred, "the dancing craze" among young people was increasing, and night courting was "by no means eradicated."[22]

A more rigorous inquiry undertaken three decades later discovered similar tendencies. The survey considered changing attitudes toward night courting in twenty-five Norwegian-American congregations: Thirteen in Wisconsin, seven in Minnesota, and five in South Dakota. These investigators, like Nilsson, related changes in courtship to other shifts in propriety. The churches surveyed noted that night courting still occurred quite frequently around 1870 but that it had already been "worked against" by that time; by 1900 it did not occur at all.[23] Common sleeping rooms for boys and girls or sleeping rooms in the outhouses, though still found in Norway, were also unknown in the American settlements. One respondent wrote, "I don't think they exist or could be regarded as other than a scandal that would be intolerable."[24]

The result of these changes was an illegitimacy rate ranging from 0% to 2.12% in the twenty-five congregations, with an average rate of 0.8%. (The report was quick to note that Norway's rate at the same time was 7.43%.) Moreover, frequency of prenuptially conceived children was also low in the United States.[25] One congregation reported that children were born shortly after marriage about 15% of the time, but added that these quick births were less frequent than they had been twenty years before. In two other churches that gave concrete figures, the rates ranged from 7 out of 104, or 6.7% (between 1892 and 1902), to 3 out of 70, or 4.3%.[26]

Moral strictures had also decreased the frequency of other activities regarded as sinful in turn-of-the-century Norwegian settlement areas. Unchaperoned dances with "immoderate drink and other debauchery" were rare. One congregation noted that dances were frequent, but seldom with drink. Another wrote that although drinking dances were held, "folk who allow or take part in debauchery of this type become branded [brændemærket] by the common opinion even among the youth." In short, there was general agreement that "moral" conditions were better than in Norway or than earlier in the settlement period. In coming to the United States – a new environment where they were forced to think about entrenched customs – the settlers had encouraged processes of change that helped to break the old patterns.[27]

Nilsson and the later surveyors both stressed the relationships between a decline in night courting and improved "moral conditions" in other aspects of life. Broad modifications in what was considered proper might be attributed to the success of the church in transferring pietistic principles to American settlements. But though the pietism that thrived in the Balestrand communities probably worked to generate a stricter propriety, an improved material welfare was an essential factor in its success. Nilsson quoted an early immigrant to the Yorkville settlement who stressed the internal changes among Norwegians in his community. Before emigrating, he had believed that Norway was experiencing a moral decline. Under better economic conditions in the United States, however, he felt reassured that "there is good moral fiber [Malm] in the sons of the mountains."[28] Greater wealth in the Balestrand communities influenced changes in other aspects of social interaction in addition to propriety in courtship. As the immigrants became more affluent, conduct was a reflection not solely of pietism but of bourgeois behavior that had been observed in both Norway and the United States.

Bourgeois patterns in the Balestrand settlements

Increasing wealth permitted landed Balestrand immigrant households to fashion even greater changes in their patterns of life. Photographs from Norway Grove in the 1870s reveal not only that the girls had traded in their homespun woolens for breezy muslins, that men had indeed taken on traditional female work roles, and that large white frame houses were now the sleeping quarters of youths, but also that leisure activities ranging from croquet to stereoscope viewing had become increasingly important (see Plates 19, 20, and 21). Svein Nilsson, after visiting Jefferson Prairie in the late 1860s, concurred: "Nine pianos and melodeons are to be found among Norwegians in the settlement. This last remark may seem unimportant, but it acquires a certain significance by suggesting that the taste for nobler things in life begins to develop among our countrymen when their spirits are released from the ever-gnawing anxiety about making a living."[29] Increasing leisure was accompanied by addi-

Plate 19. Two examples of increasing leisure, the melodeon and the newspaper, are arrayed in front of this Norwegian household in the 1870s.
Source: State Historical Society of Wisconsin; photograph by Andrew Dahl

tional modifications in family behavior – such as fertility decline or
alterations in naming patterns – that were consistent with changing
courtship styles. Innovations in conduct were in part, as noted,
imitations of bourgeois behavior observed by the immigrants in
Norwegian and American cities. Yet although certain attitudes were
learned elsewhere, changes in behavior developed in ways consistent with community membership and according to the community's norms and institutions.

Women in the Balestrand settlement experienced a fertility decline as the settlements aged. Child/woman ratios that had stood as
high as 4.2 in Arendahl in 1860 dropped to 1.7 there by the turn of
the century. Standardized child/married woman ratios in the American settlements showed a secular decline: 1,000 women in the Balestrand settlements in 1900 averaged 1,187.3 children under five
years of age, compared to 1,553.3 such children forty years before
(see Table 48 and Figure 13). Increasing marriage ages were reflecting fewer open positions in the rural societies, but the decline in
fertility was based not so much in the early age groups as among

Plate 20. Croquet is played by male and female, young and old, on this 1870s Norway Grove farmstead. *Source:* State Historical Society of Wisconsin; photograph by Andrew Dahl

women over age thirty-five. Clearly, after the rigors of pioneering, the wives in the succeeding decades were practicing some type of birth control.[30] Yet while the number of children declined, a consecration of child raising evolved. Aphorisms such as "The mother's heart is the child's school," printed in a Norwegian immigrant magazine in 1869, painted a bourgeois picture quite unlike what would have been expected in premigration Balestrand.[31]

It was not only a strict pietism that worked to alter courtship under these conditions. Though increasingly important child-rearing responsibilities remained within the domain of wives augmenting their power, sexual restraint before marriage enhanced the marketability of unmarried young women. The changing courtship patterns reflect Tocqueville's emphasis on the free marriage market as an additional check on premarital sex. "No girl," he wrote, "believes that she cannot become the wife of the man who loves her, and this renders all breaches of morality before marriage very uncommon."[32] As wealth increased, a family structure was created wherein affective relationships between husband and wife and parents and children were quite unlike those that had existed in peasant Balestrand.

Plate 21. This rare photograph of an interior displays symbols of wealth – a library and clock – as well as handicrafts probably crocheted or needle-pointed by the women of the household. *Source:* State Historical Society of Wisconsin; photograph by Andrew Dahl

The shift toward a bourgeois-like behavior in the Balestrand settlements was undoubtedly in part an imitation of the more American, more urban subcultures about them. As marketing of goods continued, as rural–urban interaction increased, as young women took service and lived within the homes of American families, and as increasing wealth on the Balestrand farms permitted greater luxury, Norwegian settlers had more opportunities to view and inculcate American behavior. The changing naming patterns practiced by the Balestrand immigrants and their children are a case in point.

It will be remembered that according to Balestrand custom, the first boy born to a couple in a first marriage was named after his father's father and the second after his mother's father. The rule was reversed when the farm on which the family lived had descended through the wife.[33] From the 1820s through the 1870s, the first male in Balestrand first marriages was named after his mother's or father's father about nine out of ten times. Only rarely did the firstborn receive the name of a great-grandfather on either side, his father's name, or some name not traceable from the immediate family.[34]

Naming customs for firstborn boys were initially transferred to the Balestrand settlements in the United States. In the 1850s, for example, more than four-fifths of the time, the first boy of a Norway Grove first marriage was named after his father's father or, to a lesser degree, his mother's father.[35] Thereafter, however, the custom was observed increasingly less often. By the 1880s only half of the firstborn, and a decade later none of a small sample, were named after their grandfathers. The practice was modified in Norway Grove beginning in the 1870s as resistance to Norwegian names developed. Instead of adhering exactly to the old custom, people in Norway Grove developed what Einar Haugen calls "symbolic alliterative repetition" naming. As a man from another settlement observed, "They were going to call me Rasmus after my grandfather; but the name was so weird and old-fashioned that they decided to trim it up and called me Robert instead."[36] In Norway Grove only two of the sixteen patronyms after 1870 were not either symbolic alliterative repetition or another variation, principally the patronym followed by a "middle" name. Furthermore, all of the names of unknown origin after 1865 were obviously American. For example, when the first boy of Anders Olsen Husebø and his wife, Gunhilde Pedersdatter Engesæther, was born in 1880, he was named not Ole or Peder but, improbably enough, Gifford Melvin (see Table 55).[37]

Nonetheless, it would be a mistake to attribute changing conduct in the Balestrand settlements solely to imitations of American customs. For one thing, perceptible cultural differences remained between Norwegians and their American neighbors. Both cultural groups repeatedly observed that whereas Americans were less likely than Norwegians to produce prenuptial births or conceptions, they

Table 55. *Naming patterns for firstborn boys of first marriages: Balestrand and Norway Grove, Spring Prairie, and Bonnet Prairie, 1820–99*

	% named after one parent's father	N
Balestrand		
1820–29	90.4	32
1830–39	94.0	33
1840–49	88.6	53
1850–59	82.5	40
1860–69	92.9	37
1870–79	92.3	26
Norway Grove, Spring Prairie, and Bonnet Prairie[a]		
1850–59	81.2	16
1860–69	53.8	13
1870–79	60.0	20
1880–89	50.0	8
1890–99	0	4

[a]Names involving symbolic alliterative repetition are included.
Sources: Family-reconstitution forms, Balestrand; family-reconstitution forms, Spring Prairie, Norway Grove, and Bonnet Prairie Lutheran Church records.

were much more prone to divorce, a practice quite rare among Norwegians.[38] Even as increasing wealth encouraged the immigrants to alter their behavior, powerful ethnic institutions like the church were often the arbiters of cultural change. And the roots of these institutions' principles were found not in American market centers so much as in a rapidly changing Norwegian society.

As Balestrand immigrants were fashioning changes consonant with the conditions they found in America, but based largely on attitudes carried from Norway, the cultural adaptations created ironies in the interplay between tradition and change. Women increasingly maintained domestic roles, for instance, but their behavior simultaneously remained traditional and underwent great modification. On the one hand, their domestic inclination in a sense insulated them from American life. Women's duties kept them closely tied to the farm and the Norwegian social group, so that they were less likely to learn English than men. Whereas 3.2% of men could not speak English as late as 1900 in Arendahl township, nearly twice as many women (6.3%) were monolingual.[39] When Americans came to Norwegian homes, the women on occasion would hide rather than face the ordeal of speaking English. Accordingly, English loan words were more prevalent in spheres of activity dominated by men. A study of Norwegian immigrants in western Wisconsin indicated that English words constituted 72.7% of the terms related to machinery, 53.2% of those concerning farming, and 50.3% of those involved with business and trade. In contrast, terms dealing with the female concerns of housekeeping, social relations, and home and family were only 32.0%, 21.1%, and 4.9% English, respectively.[40]

Women's activities in the home, on the other hand, reflected a transition to a more "modern" behavior in both work and leisure. Upon arriving in America, Norwegians were quick to notice conduct among native women. A Norwegian woman traveling between Toronto and Chicago in 1862 viewed what she called the "vainest women I've ever seen." She continued, "They were loaded down with golden trinkets. No moderation, no taste. They seemed to be interested only in themselves and their finery. Such vulgar looking women!"[41] Yet other immigrants had remarked even before this on similar changes occurring among Norwegian women. A pastor's wife wrote in 1857, "Everything is the wrong way here in America" since "the wife sits in her rocking chair with the children and reads or usually just drones."[42]

Another complainer was more long-winded. "Women dress in bad taste, since all they are interested in is to have expensive looking clothes," Frithjof Meidell wrote in 1854.

> Besides they are unforgivably lazy, truly pampered creatures. All day they sit quietly in a rocking chair and rock themselves, and then they sew a little once in a while by way of change. You ought to see our Norwegian peasant girls and servant girls here. Big-heeled, round-shouldered, plump, good-natured cooks who at home [in Norway] waddled about in all their primitiveness in front of the kitchen fire between brooms and garbage cans here trip about with a peculiar, affected twisting of parasols and fans and with their pretty heads completely covered with veils. Aase, Birthe, and Siri at an incredible speed become changed to Aline, Betsey, and Sarah and these ladies like to have a little "Miss" in front of their names.[43]

Over fifty years later a Swedish immigrant agreed. "Here in this country," he said,

> I don't have such high thoughts about the girls as I had at home, for the girls here in this country have another kind of upbringing, demand an awful lot of fuss and attention, and I don't respect

that. So if I find a girl here who is different from the others, I respect her, for there are not many of them . . . There are girls who doll themselves up enough to frighten you. They would be better as scarecrows than anything else, so if you need any of those I can send you a boatload.[44]

In spite of their misogynist stamp, these comments reiterate the presence of domesticity, which in these cases resulted not from a maintenance of Norwegian folkways so much as from the development of a new bourgeois conduct.

Similarly, the juxtaposition of tradition and change set the church in a position at once of conservatism and of progressivism in the community. The church remained the keeper of the tradition, the keeper of the faith. Services using the Norwegian language and the Lutheran liturgy were obvious links to a European past. Even small changes in church ceremonies could meet with stiff resistance. When the practice of having the congregation rise while the pastor read the Scripture during the service was introduced in the Arendahl church, some members refused to comply. Many members strongly disapproved of the purchase of an organ for Arendahl around 1886. It was not the cost of the instrument that was the question but the belief among a handful that the Devil was in the organ, a belief that prompted one member to declare that he would not come to church as long as it was played. He finally appeared on Christmas, commenting that he did not think the congregation would have the audacity to play the organ on such a solemn occasion.[45]

Yet the keeper of the tradition could also facilitate change. The pastor and the congregation used a powerful peer pressure to work against night courting and the use of alcohol through public confession before the congregation. In a sense, however, attempts to end night courting were a tradition that had begun in Balestrand. The efforts of Balestrand's pastor and his anti–night courting associations, as well as organizations begun by women's groups in other Norwegian areas, were all mildly successful ventures to decrease illegitimacy (see Chapter 5). Although the church was the center of the community, then, the keeper of the tradition, of the language, and of the faith, the use of its influence to facilitate change in traditions such as night courting was not inconsistent. The pressure to alter behavior had also developed in Balestrand, but communities in the American Middle West simply found change easier in a different, richer environment where their "good moral fiber" could become more apparent.

If both women and the church manifested ironies of tradition and change, the Ladies Aid (*Kvindeforening*) within the church provides a graphic example of the new female role in society. The Kvindeforening for Arendahl church, for example, was organized in 1881. Women met periodically for entire working days to sew and knit articles sold to farmers and hired men in the area. Though this work was not unlike the evening work performed on peasant farms in Balestrand, the efforts of the Kvindeforening played an entirely different role, since profits were used to provide for foreign missions, most notably that in China. Although the organization was disparagingly called *Kaffeforeningen* (the Coffee Society) or *Sladreforeningen* (the Gossip Society) by some cynics, it was an example of a group organized and run by women that exploited leisure time to work for causes it felt were worthy. Established within the Norwegian church, speaking Norwegian at meetings, and performing traditional women's work, the Kvindeforening in the Arendahl church fulfilled obligations quite unlike those that had existed in Balestrand.[46]

When the glaring differences between Balestrand and its immigrant settlements are considered, then, we can go far beyond the incongruous landscapes of mountains and prairies. The large white Victorian frame houses with pianos and parlors, the fine carriages driven throughout the settlements, the well-dressed families attending the white-spired rural Lutheran churches – all illustrated conditions in America that worked to modify behavior and attitudes.

As we have seen in the past three chapters, changed conditions induced changes in the Norwegian settlements. As internal migration continued, the nuclear family took on greater significance. Likewise, farm organization and operations magnified the importance of labor within the nuclear family while it encouraged shifts in work responsibilities. Women took on increasing domestic tasks of child raising and housekeeping, and men steadily assumed greater responsibilities in farm production. The changes for women were not necessarily unwelcome. One immigrant, writing his "honest opinion about emigration," felt "very glad about it all" and regarded himself as "freed." He did not want anybody to "think that we have escaped all worry by having come here. Still, there is a big difference, especially for women."[47] Clearly Hansen was incorrect, at least for the Norwegian immigrants, when he wrote, "The notion that 'women's place is in the home' fitted in with every ideal that the peasant had brought with him from Europe."[48]

Modifications in attitude paralleled and were interconnected with changes in behavior. As increasing wealth was realized, Balestrand immigrants began to practice customs of which they were aware but which they had not previously observed. Traditional conduct during courtship gave way to a new propriety, alcoholism apparently declined, and opportunities for greater leisure even permitted piano or melodeon playing. Such changes in behavior and attitude, which I have termed bourgeois, diffused throughout the immigrant settlements and set them radically apart from the peasant Balestrand they had left.

The acceptance of bourgeois conduct, however, was not the immediate result of the new environment but the consequence of a dialectic between premigration Norwegian culture and new American conditions. While Balestrand farmers were adjusting patterns of farm production, labor, and marriage and fertility to their needs in American settlements, they were also adopting these new attitudes within the parameters of movements such as a maturing pietism carried from Norway.

Behavior among the immigrants was thus the result of innumerable individual decisions within the settlements that together created a climate for a new propriety. Although the vast tracts of fertile land and the great demand for wheat and later for beef and butter created the basis for this new climate, the immigrants who attained greater wealth and altered their behavior were acting partly according to cultural values and norms that originated in Balestrand.

10 *Conclusion*

When H. A. Foss's *Husmandsgutten* (*The Cotter's Son*) appeared in
serial form in *Decorah-posten* in 1884 and 1885, it so captured the
Norwegian-American readership that the Iowa newspaper was res-
cued from financial difficulty by attracting six thousand new readers.[1] Certainly artistic quality did not explain the serial's success; it
read like a Norwegian Horatio Alger story. The cotter's son won the
love of a farmer's daughter, his childhood sweetheart, in his Norwegian home and moved to America when the social division between the two prohibited marriage. After making his fortune in the
New World, he returned home toting two six-shooters and bought
out his loved one's father, who through drink and other debauchery
had brought his family to financial ruin. The young couple married
and were living happily ever after as the story ended.[2]

If the novel was not good fiction, *Husmandsgutten* struck a chord
among Norwegian-Americans and reflected their conceptions about
America and Norway. The United States was perceived as a land of
wealth, of social justice, and of moral propriety. Foss certainly
would not malign the Fatherland, but he did point out features of
nineteenth-century peasant life that had besmirched Norwegian
communities. Drunkenness, illicit sexual relations, and extreme parental control over children's destinies created situations that undermined proper lives. The young couple ultimately settled in Norway,
but it was only through emigration that the cotter's son could marry
his sweetheart and the young bride could escape hardships caused
by her profligate father. The story line thus contained elements that
would capture Norwegian immigrants' interest. Although Foss in
the end romanticized the bucolic Norwegian peasant life, he also
approved in no uncertain terms the moral propriety that was encouraged in the United States. Throughout *Husmandsgutten*, probably the most popular Norwegian-American fiction ever written, Foss
promoted bourgeois conceptions of upward mobility and "proper"
moral behavior.

As we have seen in the preceding three chapters, Norwegians

who emigrated to the United States, reacting to environmental influences, behaved very differently from those who remained in Norway. Yet Balestrand immigrants who remained in compact settlements also retained influential patterns of language and culture. Norwegian-born writer and editor Waldemar Ager contended that in some respects immigrants in the United States, particularly early immigrants nestled in rural communities, represented a more peasant-like culture than Norway. "In some ways," he wrote, "we are more Norwegian here [in the United States] than they are in Norway . . . The mass of Norwegian immigrants were almost exclusively made up of peasants." "Speaking in a literary sense," Ager continued, "we belong to the age of Hans Nielsen Hauge [the early nineteenth-century pietist leader for whom the Haugean Synod is named] . . . Much is being read especially by the farmers, but they read newspapers, devotional or religious tracts about predestination before they choose Bjørnson, Ibsen, and Hamsun."[3]

People in the settlements of Norway Grove, Arendahl, and Camp, who read *Husmandsgutten* when it appeared in a newspaper in the late nineteenth century, reflected these seemingly incongruous patterns of tradition and change. A deep-seated conservative Haugean pietism coexisted with novel adaptations in work and leisure. Whereas the American environment encouraged, and on occasion heightened, the maintenance of certain peasant practices, it promoted change in others. Yet the forging of the new behavior did not result from a direct conversion from a peasant lifestyle to a more modern one.

Patterns of emigration, particularly those of the early immigrants, were powerfully directed by ties of kin and friendship. A sizable portion of Balestrand's immigrants settled in contiguous areas, quickly forming a church around which the community interacted. The continued migration from Balestrand to the United States created settlements dominated by single culture groups that could retain patterns of speech and culture fairly easily. Because a community stability among church members resulted, they were likely to remain in the original settlement to enjoy the benefits of community membership.

As most of the property was claimed in the early settlements, land opportunities in the west, which facilitated the formation of further compact communities, encouraged migration of other immigrants to land-rich areas. This mobility itself was often based on traditional practices that demanded livelihoods in order to marry and form ·households. The movement to realize a livelihood, originally initiated in the emigration from Balestrand, carried over to American settlements, where youths tended to be mobile. Yet migration re- sulted in the creation of new settlements tied through kin and friendship to older communities to the east and ultimately to Bal- estrand. The outcome of the tension between availability of land and the benefits of community membership was a widely distended pat- tern of settlement beginning in Norway and stretching across the Upper Middle West.

The abundance of land also worked to change traditional eco- nomic patterns. Ample land opportunities for settlers increased the costs of labor while they reduced the prices of land in comparison with Balestrand patterns. Different land/labor ratios forced immi- grant farmers to alter emphases in farm production. Grains, which were easy to produce with household labor, predominated during periods of early settlement in America, whereas animals were kept only for home use. Market demand for wheat reinforced the useful- ness of grain production, so that Balestrand immigrants, who had been husbandmen in Norway, were encouraged to become cereal farmers. Census manuscripts indicate that the Norwegian immi- grants did indeed produce a crop mix similar to that of the aggregate of farmers in the region in which they lived. Ironically, census data suggest that although Balestrand farmers may have been inclined to emphasize for home use crops with which they were familiar, they entered the wheat market more enthusiastically than more accultu- rated ethnic groups, encountering economic difficulties in many cases when wheat prices and harvests declined. In spite of cultural nuances, however, most Balestrand farm operations weathered the stages of development and basically resembled those of other cultur- al groups operating under similar economic constraints.

Social patterns similar to those in Balestrand were faithfully repli- cated in early stages of settlement and thus set the Norwegian immi- grants apart from others about them. The Balestrand sexual division of labor continued as women and men performed traditional tasks. Women helped in the hay harvest and considered work with the animals to be their domain, whereas men concentrated on grain production. Traditional patterns of courtship and marriage were also transplanted. Night courting, a method of courtship that often involved premarital sex, continued, much to the chagrin of Ameri- can observers. Marriage remained dependent on attainment of a livelihood upon which a household could be based, although a greater abundance of opportunities permitted earlier marriages. Many of the young wives were pregnant at their weddings, a circumstance consistent with night courting and the norms of Balestrand at the time of emigration.

Although certain cultural patterns persisted in the homogeneous communities, their maintenance in conjunction with the American environment often encouraged change. Farm units in the Balestrand communities differed radically from those in the Norway the immigrants had left. Rather than comprising the head family, multiple servants, and cotters with their families, the American farm was based on a nuclear family upon which it depended for labor. With large tracts of land and constrained quantities of labor, Norwegian-American families concentrated on land-intensive crops while attempting to enlarge their labor supplies. Both changes altered the traditional sexual division of labor. On the one hand, such land-intensive crops as grains, traditionally man's work, increased in importance while the more labor-intensive woman-produced goods, such as animal products, declined. On the other hand, the labor needs, supplied within the family, increased the economic utility of children and thereby encouraged greater marital fertility. As their reproductive roles grew and their productive roles declined, women were compelled to move further into domestic roles, which included care for large households of children. Men continued to specialize in farm work as grain fields were enlarged with the help of bigger families and greater mechanization.

With the nuclear family remaining the principal household structure and with labor needs encouraging changes in sex roles, demand for wheat created a wealth heretofore unknown by the immigrant farmers. Those who did not overspeculate on wheat were able to realize secure futures from diversified farm production as the century progressed. As wealth increased, the course of change away from traditional roles quickened. Women remained in the domestic workplace of the nuclear family even as fertility declined. Men continued as farm producers even when animals took on greater importance; hired men, rather than women in the household, cared for the cattle, sheep, and hogs. Courtship patterns changed as women sought to protect their virtue by refusing the frequent premarital sex that had once been the norm. Bourgeois behavior came to dominate the Balestrand immigrant communities.

In adjusting to environmental circumstances such as cheap land and expensive labor, the Balestrand immigrants changed their behavioral patterns and were in a sense "simplified overseas."[4] The adaptation of Balestrand immigrants, however, was not a simple acquiescence to American environmental patterns but, rather, the result of the tension and interaction between old cultural norms and new environmental configurations.[5] Traditional work roles according to gender, for instance, were not immediately altered in the new environment. Yet when women did accept increased domestic duties, the modern work roles were the result of compromises between the new production demands and old divisions of labor. The roles of men as grain laborers and of women as domestic producers remained strictly defined. The interaction between environment and culture also produced varying rates of cultural change. In the economic sphere, where environmental demands were great, change was rapid. Yet in the realm of religion and speech, cultural retention was quite strong. Different rates of change themselves led to new cultural configurations, so that compactly settled Balestrand immigrants, while retaining patterns of speech and religion, exhibited social and economic behavior not unlike that of the various ethnocultural settlements about them.[6]

Likewise, the increasingly bourgeois behavior that was also the result of the dialectic between the immigrants' cultural patterns and their new environment should not be attributed simply to "Americanization." One might argue, for example, that the photographs taken in and about Norway Grove in the 1870s by Andrew Dahl revealed few Norwegian artifacts and instead showcased American acquisitions and therefore Americanization. Yet a more realistic appraisal of the immigrants' rationale for displaying their American-made material possessions is that they wanted to prove to viewers of the photographs not so much their Americanness as their entrance into spheres of greater wealth (see Plate 22). The immigrants had been aware of the lifestyles of gentlefolk in Norway and had been urged by the official classes to choose patterns similar to those lifestyles. And while they were able to enjoy a more opulent existence in the United States, they also altered their social behavior to admit modifications that had been requested even before they emigrated. The clergyman in Balestrand was trying to encourage an end to night courting at a time when many of his flock were leaving for America. Arguing that night courting was being abandoned by those landed families who had some familiarity with city folk and their values, Sundt claimed that the custom would decline in general as changing behavior percolated down from the top among the "better farmer families" to the servant class.[7]

Religious divisions within the peasant society itself reflected growing concern about moral propriety among segments of Balestrand society. The pietistic movements that flourished in Norway

Plate 22. This large Norway Grove household, no longer divided by sex, displays its immense white Victorian home and its fine carriage, a graphic evidence of its material success (taken about 1873–79). *Source:* State Historical Society of Wisconsin; photograph by Andrew Dahl

were faithfully replicated in the Balestrand-American settlements. Arguments against night courting met with success even in Norway: Rates of illegitimacy and prenuptial conception declined in later nineteenth-century Balestrand, a trend that continued through much of Europe into the twentieth century.[8] Although the rates clearly remained higher in Balestrand than in the Balestrand settlements in the United States, courtship behavior was altered in both places (see Chapter 5).

Research throughout Scandinavia has demonstrated a transition to other bourgeois household behavior similar to, yet later than, that which occurred in Balestrand communities in the United States. Diaries and account books from the late nineteenth century reveal that some peasant farmers began to purchase urban-style clothing, furniture, and wallpaper for their private rooms, in addition to ready-made bread, cakes, beer, and cigars. Household utensils of copper or silver or tin, sofas, armchairs, wall clocks, and china adorned the interiors of rural folk's homes. By the 1880s "still more typically bourgeois furniture," according to one historian, was introduced in Swedish farmhouses, including bookcases, upholstered chairs, mirrors, chests of drawers, glassware, and buggies. "The competition between farm wives" in a rural Danish community around 1890 "was no longer over who could produce the most and best wool and flax, homespun and linen, but rather over who could display the shiniest waxed floors, polished and upholstered furniture (needing daily dusting), white curtains (requiring washing) and flowers in the window."[9] As in Norway Grove and Arendahl, the altered domestic activities, which included piano playing, crocheting, and fine sewing, were the result of a further sexual division of labor expressed in increased differentiation between a female inner sphere based on consumption and family well-being and a male outer sphere revolving around production.[10]

The transition to a more modern behavior in Balestrand settlements in the United States was in large part due to cultural ideals carried from Norway that could be operationalized within a new ecological structure. Though the rural Balestrand immigrants may have been imitating urban folk in Madison or Minneapolis, they may also have been emulating patterns of urban behavior observed in Bergen or even among the better-off administrators who resided in Balestrand. Yet the pietistic influences carried from Balestrand profoundly colored the development of attitudes in Norwegian settlements and resulted in distinct behavior. By sympathizing with the characters in Foss's novel, Norwegian-Americans were reflecting what might be termed bourgeois, but not necessarily American, behavior.

The migration from Balestrand to the United States in the nineteeth century was a saga of a relatively few families and individuals carrying a cultural tradition from an area that practiced a transhumance type of agriculture to one well suited for production in the world grain market. The interaction between the patterns of their past and the exigencies of their present worked to create new and different cultural patterns. On a larger scale, however, the immigrants from Balestrand exemplified the obstacles faced by the millions of rural immigrants to the United States. Balestrand throughout the early nineteenth century was a dynamic, preindustrial society incompatible with the static stereotypes often attributed to the peasant world. In the face of a great population growth, households worked to alter the agricultural structure so as to enlarge the harvests. Production of more food, however, not only demanded more rigorous work schedules but altered the prospects for future generations, which might not be able to realize relative prosperity in an increasingly landless society. The alternative of emigration, when information about the United States drifted into the community, was an opportunity to avoid increased work loads and potentially less secure future prospects.

Emigration provided a chance to exploit what the emigrants perceived as the advantages of life in the United States. They certainly could have remained in Balestrand had emigration opportunities not appeared. Indeed, life in the increasingly stratified society at home remained more desirable than migration to the Norwegian coasts. By moving abroad, however, the emigrants could retain the essential social fabric of their community in a rural environment that was much more conducive to economic growth than Balestrand.[11] Thus, as Ingrid Semmingsen has written, emigration, particularly among those who left early from the mountain regions that practiced høstingsbruk, had at heart an irony, a radical attempt to conserve. By breaking out and moving across the sea, they could reestablish the essential features of home in the New World.

Yet whereas the new environment did permit the retention of certain central elements of the social fabric that might have been lost had emigration not occurred, it also encouraged widespread change. The immigrants became active participants in an interplay between their culture and the new environment. As some cultural components were maintained quite fully and as others were changed, the evolution that occurred impelled the immigrants toward new cultural forms. But the forms were not incompatible with the core beliefs of the community and actually reflected the immigrants' ability to express their world view in new ways.[12]

The white Victorian frame houses that were scattered throughout the Norwegian settlements represented a community literally and figuratively a world apart from the roughhewn wood dwellings in Balestrand. They also constituted an entrance into the middle class, which encouraged social patterns unlike those they had left. The immigrants who left Balestrand in order to preserve their social fabric were successful in doing so. The creation of a more certain existence, for example, provided for ample inheritances for their children. Ironically, they also encountered glaring environmental differences that encouraged rapid cultural change. The households in Balestrand and those in the Balestrand immigrant communities underwent processes of cultural modification throughout the nineteenth century that in some ways were parallel. Yet the impact of new ecological structures promoted a course of development in the Balestrand settlements that not only influenced the timing and sequence of the change but led to new cultural patterns as well.

Notes

Chapter 1. Introduction

1 Frank Thistlethwaite, "Migration from Europe Overseas in the Nineteenth and Twentieth Centuries," in *XIe Congres International des Sciences Historiques*, Rapport V (Uppsala, 1960), pp. 32–60; Birgitta Odèn, "Emigrationen från Norden till Nordamerika under 1800-talet: Aktualla Forskningsuppgifter," *Historisk Tidsskrift* (Stockholm), 83 (1963):276.

2 Notable exceptions are Hans Norman, *Från Bergslagen till Nordamerika: Studier i Migrationsmönster, Social Rörlighet och Demografisk Stuktur med Utgångspunkt från Örebro län 1851–1915* (Uppsala, 1974); Robert C. Ostergren, "Rättvik to Isanti: A Community Transplanted" (Ph.D. diss., University of Minnesota, 1976); and Walter D. Kamphoefner, "Transplanted Westfalians: Persistence and Transformation of Socioeconomic and Cultural Patterns in the Northwest German Migration to Missouri" (Ph.D. diss., University of Missouri, Columbia, 1978). Moreover, Virginia Yans-McLaughlin, *Family and Community, Italian Immigrants in Buffalo, 1880–1930* (Ithaca, N.Y., 1971); John W. Briggs, *An Italian Passage: Immigrants to Three American Cities, 1890–1930* (New Haven, Conn., 1978); Josef Barton, *Peasants and Strangers: Italians, Rumanians, and Slovaks in an American City, 1890–1950* (Cambridge, Mass., 1975); and John E. Bodnar, *Immigration and Industrialization: Ethnicity in an American Mill Town, 1870–1940* (Pittsburgh, 1977), have considered European sending areas.

3 A useful survey of recent Norwegian history is T. K. Derry, *A History of Modern Norway, 1814–1972* (Oxford, 1973).

4 See Andreas Holmsen, "The Old Norwegian Peasant Community: General Survey and Historical Introduction," *Scandinavian Economic History Review*, 4 (1956):25–29, for a description of the oral history; and Michael Drake, *Population and Society in Norway, 1735–1865* (Cambridge, 1969), pp. 6–7, 19–41, for a short biography of Sundt.

5 Ingrid Semmingsen, *Veien Mot Vest: Utvandringen fra Norge til Amerika, 1825–1865* (Oslo, 1941), 1:234.

6 A. N. Kiær, *Oversigt over de Vigtigste Resultater af de Statistiske Tabeller Vedkommende Folkemængdens Bevegelse, 1866–1885* (Christiania, 1890), pp. 10–11.

7 *United States Census*, 1910, *Population*, 2:991.

8   Norman, *Från Bergslagen till Nordamerika*, and Ostergren, "Rättvik to Isanti," provide notable exceptions.

9   Kathleen Neils Conzen, "Historical Approaches to the Study of Rural Ethnic Communities," in Frederick C. Luebke, ed., *Ethnicity on the Great Plains* (Lincoln, Nebr., 1980), pp. 1–14. In her essay Conzen cites neglect of immigrant studies in rural areas.

10 T. A. Hoverstad, *The Norwegian Farmers in the United States* (Fargo, N.D., 1915), pp. 11–12.

11 Nicholay A. Grevstad, "The Norwegians in America," in Martin Ulvestad, ed., *Norsk-Amerikaneren Vikingesaga samt Pioneerhistorie, Statistik og Biografiske Oplysninger om Nordmænd i Amerika* (Seattle, 1928), p. 215.

12 Arnfinn Engen, "Utvandringa i Historiebøkene," in Engen, ed., *Utvandringa – Det Store Oppbrotet* (Oslo, 1978), p. 173.

13 Semmingsen, *Veien Mot Vest*, 1:221. Swedish research resulted in similar findings. See Gustaf Utterström, "Some Population Problems in Pre-Industrial Sweden," *Scandinavian Economic History Review*, 2 (1954):103–65.

14 See Andres A. Svalestuen, *Tinns Emigrasjons Historie, 1837–1907: En Undersøkelse med Særlig Vekt på den Demografiske, Økonomiske og Sosiale Bakgrunn for Amerikafarten, og en Statistik Analyse av Selve Utvandringen* (Oslo, 1972), pp. 38–39; and Einar Hovdhaugen, *Husmannstida* (Oslo, 1975), p. 91.

15 Andreas Holmsen, "Økonomisk og Administrativ Historie," in Hans Aall, ed., *Norske Bygder: Sogn* (Bergen, 1937), p. 88.

16 Rasmus Sunde, "Ei Undersøking av Utvandringa til Amerika frå Vik i Sogn, 1839–1915" (major thesis, Universitetet i Trondheim, 1974), p. 36.

17 See Svalestuen, *Tinns Emigrasjons Historie*, p. 55; Sunde, "Ei Undersøking," pp. 36, 44–46; and Rasmus Sunde, "Utvandringa frå Sogn," (unpublished paper, Sogn of Fjordane Distrikthøgskole, n.d.), p. 4. See also Stein Tveite, " 'Overbefolkning,' 'Befolkningspress,' og Vandring," in Sivert Langholm and Francis Sejerstad, eds., *Vandringer: Festskrift til Ingrid Semmingsen på 70-årsdagen 29. Mars 1980* (Oslo, 1980), p. 43; Kjell Haarstad, "Utvandrerne fra Bygdene – Presset eller Lokket?" in Engen, *Utvandringa*, p. 55; and Dorothy Burton Skårdal, *The Divided Heart: Scandinavian Immigrant Experience through Literary Sources* (Lincoln, Nebr., 1974), p. 58.

18 See Fartein Valen-Sendstad, *Norske Landbruksredskaper 1800–1850 Årene* (Lillehammer, 1964), pp. 8–9.

19 See, for example, *Beretning om Koneriget Norges Økonomiske Tilstand i Aarene 1840–1845 med Tilhørende Tabeller* (Christiania, 1847), p. 138.

20 Anders Ohnstad, "Folketal og Utflytting," in Hans Lavik, ed., *Pacific Coast Sognalag 50 Year Jubilee, 1912–1962* (Tacoma, Wash., 1962), p. 51; S. Skappel, "Høstingsbruk og Dyrkingsbruk: Streiftog Gjennom 600 År av Vår Landbrukshistorie," *Historisk Tidsskrift*, 31 (1937–40):146; Derry, *History of Modern Norway*, p. 99.

21 Haarstad, "Utvandrerne fra Bygdene," p. 40. Valen-Sendstad, *Norske Landbruksredskaper*, pp. 8–9, argues that the theory of a stagnant agriculture through 1850 has been the dominant school of thought among Norwegian scholars.

22 Edgar Hovland et al., "Poteta og Folkeveksten i Noreg etter 1815: Fire Debattinnlegg," *Historisk Tidsskrift*, 57 (1978):261, 265; Edgar Hovland, "Åkerbruket i Norge i Begynnelsen av 1800-tallet," *Historisk Tidsskrift*, 57 (1978):331–46; Ståle Dyrvik et al., *Norsk Økonomisk Historie, 1500–1970*, vol. 1, *1500–1850* (Bergen, 1979), pp. 143, 144–46.

23 Dyrvik et al., *Norsk Økonomisk Historie*, 1:147.

24 See Julian L. Simon, *The Economics of Population Growth* (Princeton, N.J., 1977), p. 150; and Ester Boserup, *The Conditions of Agricultural Growth: The Economics of Agrarian Change under Population Pressure* (Chicago, 1965).

25 See Robert C. Ostergren, "Kinship Network Dispersion and Migration: A Nineteenth Century Swedish Example" (paper presented to the Social Science History Association, 1981), pp. 20–21.

26 Yans-McLaughlin, *Family and Community*. The classic example of the former argument is Oscar Handlin, *The Uprooted: The Epic Story of the Great Migrations That Made the American People* (Boston, 1951).

Chapter 2. "The worlds we have lost"

1 Quoted in Einar Haugen, *The Norwegian Language in America: A Study in Bilingual Behavior* (Philadelphia, 1953), 1:9.

2 Quoted in Theodore C. Blegen, *Norwegian Migration to America, vol. 1, 1825–1860* (Northfield, Minn., 1931), p. 199.

3 A. N. Kiær, *Oversigt over de Vigtigste Resultater af de Statistiske Tabeller Vedkommende Folkmængdens Bevegelse, 1866–1885* (Christiania, 1890), p. 117.

4 See Sølvi Sogner, *Folkevekst og Flytting: En Historisk-Demografisk Studie i 1700-Årenes Øst-Norge* (Oslo, 1979), for an excellent overview of demographic variations in eastern Norway.

5 David Gaunt, "Pre-Industrial Economy and Population Structure," *Scandinavian Journal of History*, 2 (1977):208. Gaunt is referring, of course, to Peter Laslett's seminal work, *The World We Have Lost* (London, 1965).

6 Sogner, *Folkevekst og Flytting*, p. 133.

7 Arnfinn Engen, "Fattigdom og Utferd," in Ingrid Semmingsen, ed., *Norges Kulturhistorie*, vol. 4, *Den Gjenfødte Norge* (Oslo, 1980), p. 75.

8 Engen, "Fattigdom og Utferd," p. 75; Einar Hovdhaugen, *Husmannstida* (Oslo, 1975), p. 105; Ingrid Semmingsen, *Veien Mot Vest: Utvandringen fra Norge til Amerika, 1825–1865* (Oslo, 1941), 1:240; Ståle Dyrvik et al., *Norsk Økonomisk Historie, 1500–1970*, vol. 1, *1500–1850* (Bergen, 1979), p. 131. The author Knut Hamsun's parents were a part of this movement in 1862.

9 See Arnfinn Engen, "Nordland – Småkårsfolks Amerika? Trekk ved Befolkningsutvikling og Migrasjon i Nordlandsamt, 1801–1865," in Sivert Langholm and Francis Sejerstad, eds., *Vandringer: Festskrift til Ingrid Semmingsen på 70-årsdagen 29. Mars 1980* (Oslo, 1980), pp. 53–72.

10 Sogner, *Folkevekst og Flytting;* Sølvi Sogner, "De Barnrike Familier," in Semmingsen, *Det Gjenfødte Norge*, p. 38.

11 Dyrvik et al., *Norsk Økonomisk Historie*, 1:130.

12 Semmingsen, *Veien Mot Vest*, p. 242; Dyrvik et al., *Norsk Økonomisk Historie*, 1:131.

13 Kiær, *Oversigt over de Vigtigste Resultater*, pp. 28–29, 32.

14 Dyrvik et al., *Norsk Økonomisk Historie*, 1:201–02.

15 Kiær, *Oversigt over de Vigtigste Resultater*, p. 32.

16 Engen, "Fattigdom og Utferd," pp. 76, 78–79.

17 Semmingsen, *Veien Mot Vest*, p. 270.

18 Jon Laberg, *Balestrand, Bygd og Ætter* (Bergen, 1934), p. 20; Hjalmar Aarskog, "Gard og Grannesamfunn: Balestrand" (unpublished paper, Institutt for Samanliknande Kulturforskning, 1956), p. 113. Workers in search of seasonal work were also common in the eastern part of Norway. See Engen, "Fattigdom og Utferd," p. 79. International migration was of minor importance before the great American emigration began. Before 1800 most outmigrants moved largely to Denmark and Holland. From the turn of the century until 1845, when journeys to America began in earnest, there was a weak net immigration of about ten thousand people, many of them Swedes searching for work in Norway. The migration continued; between 1866 and 1875 there was a yearly Swedish immigration of about sixteen hundred. Dyrvik et al., *Norsk Økonomisk Historie*, 1:130; Kiær, *Oversigt over de Vigtigste Resultater*, pp. 110–11; Hans Try, *To Kulturer, En Stat, 1851–1884* (Oslo, 1979), p. 65.

19 Dyrvik et al., *Norsk Økonomisk Historie*, 1:9.

20 Stein Tveite, *Jord og Gjerning – Trekk av Norsk Landbruk i 150 År* (Christiansand, 1959), pp. 33–34, 37, 72.

21 Johannes Brynjulf Thue, "Gardproduksjon, Handel, og Sjøtransport i Jord- og Skogbruksbygdene i Sogn, 1830–1900: Det Økonomiske Systemet i Nokre Lokalsamfunn på Vestlandet" (major thesis, Universitetet i Bergen, 1971), p. 43.

22 Luke M. Peterson, "Nineteenth Century Social Change in Lesja, Norway" (unpublished undergraduate paper, University of Minnesota, 1980), p. 7.

23 Dyrvik et al., *Norsk Økonomisk Historie*, 1:182.

24 Thue, "Gardproduksjon, Handel, og Sjøtransport," pp. 3, 36–38, 62–63, 71.

25 Ibid., pp. 45–46; Oskar Nesse, "Handel med Husdyr frå Sogn og Austover i Eldre Tider," *Tidsskrift Utgjeve av Historielaget for Sogn*, 27 (1981):51–60.

26 Thue, "Gardproduksjon, Handel, og Sjøtransport," pp. 1–2; Tveite, *Jord og Gjerning.*

27 Eilert Sundt, *Om Sædeligheds-Tilstanden i Norge* (Christiania, 1857; reprint, Oslo, 1976).
28 A basic work in English on Norwegian folk art is Janice S. Stewart, *The Folk Arts of Norway* (New York, 1953).
29 Arne Berg, *Norske Gardstun* (Oslo, 1968), p. 8. The many other regional differences are too voluminous to cite here, ranging from the incidence of leprosy to the utilization of various tool and implement types. See, for example, Fartein Valen-Sendstad, *Norske Landbruksredskaper 1800–1850 Årene* (Lillehammer, 1964).
30 See Orvar Löfgren, "Family and Household among Scandinavian Peasants: An Exploratory Essay," *Ethnologica Scandinavica*, 1974, pp. 17–52, for a basic discussion of these issues in the Scandinavian context.
31 Andreas Holmsen, "The Old Norwegian Peasant Community: General Survey and Historical Introduction, *Scandinavian Economic History Review*, 4 (1956):21.
32 Gunnar Urtegaard, "Jordbruksdrift og Sosial Lagdeling i Balestrand frå 1500 til 1865" (major thesis, Universitetet i Bergen, 1980), pp. 2–4, 167.
33 Sundt, *Om Sædeligheds-Tilstanden i Norge*, p. 448.
34 Semmingsen, *Veien Mot Vest*, pp. 240–43; Andres A. Svalestuen, "Om den Regionale Spreiinga av Norsk Utvandring før 1865," in Arnfinn Engen, ed., *Utvandringa – Det Store Oppbrotet* (Oslo, 1978), p. 76; Kjell Erik Skaaren, "Utvandring fra Helgeland," in ibid., pp. 122–28.
35 Svalestuen, "Om den Regionale Spreiinga," p. 78; Skaaren, "Utvandring fra Helgeland," pp. 122–28.
36 Sverre Ordahl, "Utvandring frå Agder til Amerika, 1890–1915," in Engen, *Utvandringa*, pp. 137–39.
37 Elisabeth Koren and Arnfinn Engen, "Masseutvandringa frå Austlandet etter 1865," in Engen, *Utvandringa*, pp. 86–89.
38 Andres A. Svalestuen, *Tinns Emigrasjons Historie, 1837–1907: En Undersøkelse med Særlig Vekt på den Demografiske, Økonomiske og Sosiale Bakgrunn for Amerikafarten, og en Statistik Analyse av Selve Utvandringen* (Oslo, 1972), pp. 60, 92; Semmingsen, *Veien Mot Vest*, 1:244. See Ingrid Semmingsen, *Norway to America: A History of the Migration*, trans. Einar Haugen (Minneapolis, 1978), for maps (facing p. 88) showing regional intensity of migration from Norden.
39 Svalestuen, "Om den Regionale Spreiinga," pp. 67, 68.
40 Andreas Holmsen, "Økonomisk og Administrativ Historie," in Hans Aall, ed., *Norske Bygder: Sogn* (Bergen, 1937), p. 90; Svalestuen, "Om den Regionale Spreiinga," pp. 76–77.
41 Emigration figures were derived from Balestrand church records, and population from the 1845 and 1855 Folketelling. See also Hjalmar Aarskog, "Frå Dagliglivet i Bygdene Våre, om lag 1850 og Fram Mot Vår Tid," *Balestrand Gard og Grend*, 1 (1973):34; and Amund Helland, *Norges Land og Folk: Topografisk-Statistisk Beskrevet*, vol. 14, *Topografisk-Statistisk Beskrivelse over Nordre Bergenhus Amt* (Christiania, 1901), p. 214.

Chapter 3. "The grass so fat it glistened"

1 Paul B. duChaillu, *The Land of the Midnight Sun* (London, 1881), p. 235, reported the bridge. See also Pastor A. E. Boyum's autobiography in Ernest M. Maland, *Remember the Days of Old: The Centennial Saga of Arendahl Evangelical Lutheran Congregation, 1856–1956* (Decorah, Iowa, 1956). Boyum's family was forced to move often, as snow slides nearly enveloped their home. Eventually, the family emigrated.

2 Gunnar Urtegaard, "Jordbruksdrift og Sosial Lagdeling i Balestrand frå 1500 til 1865" (major thesis, Universitetet i Bergen, 1980), pp. 19, 21, 25, 43. Urtegaard's early population information is based on tax lists taken in 1522, 1563, 1567, and 1603; a tithe list from 1627; a tax census in 1647; and the tax register of 1667.

3 Ibid., pp. 28–34, 36, 41. See also Knut Kolsrud, "The Settlement Process: A Norwegian Example," *Ethnologica Scandinavica*, 1980, pp. 83–101, for a further examination of diffusion of settlement on an unspecified Norwegian fjord.

4 See A. V. Chayanov, *The Theory of Peasant Economy*, ed. Daniel Thorner, Basile Kerbley, and R. E. F. Smith (Homewood, Ill., 1966), for a classic statement on the peasant economy.

5 Ibid., p. 6.

6 Much of the material comes from an extensive oral history project carried out by the Institutt for Samanliknande Kulturforskning. Unfortunately, these sources are not dated, but their reliability has been confirmed reaching far back in the past. One informant could account for traditions dating to the middle of the eighteenth century. He usually confirmed his tales by noting "The old man said so and he got it from grandma." See Andreas Holmsen, "The Old Norwegian Peasant Community: General Survey and Historical Introduction," *Scandinavian Economic History Review*, 4 (1956):25–29; and Halvard Bjørkvik, "The Old Norwegian Peasant Community: The Farm Territories," ibid., 4 (1956):33–35. The latter explains the development of this valuable project and indicates its reliability.

7 Peter A. Munch, "Gard, the Norwegian Farm," *Rural Sociology*, 12 (1947):357, 358.

8 Bjørkvik, "Old Norwegian Peasant Community," pp. 44, 50, 52.

9 Kristofer Visted and Hilmar Stigum, *Vår Gamle Bondekultur* (Oslo, 1951), pp. 54–55. In one southern area of Norway, large-scale division of gards occurred in the 1800s. According to custom and law, all parcels of land were partitioned when a gard was divided, so that fields varied in shape and size. One small crop field, for example, measured two by nine meters, whereas others were extremely narrow; there were fields with dimensions of one by eighty-four and two by seventy-two meters. See Hans Try, *Gardsskipnad og Bondenæring: Sørlandsk Jordbruk på 1800-talet* (Bergen, 1969), p. 85.

10 Bjørkvik, "Old Norwegian Peasant Community," p. 58. This belief, carried over to the United States, was reflected fictionally in O. E. Rølvaag's *Giants in the Earth* (New York, 1927), p. 124.

11 Try, *Gardsskipnad og Bondenæring*, p. 92; Visted and Stigum, *Vår Gamle Bondekultur*, p. 54.

12 For a regional distribution of tun types, see Arne Berg, *Norske Gardstun* (Oslo, 1968), p. 8.

13 Bjørkvik, "Old Norwegian Peasant Community," p. 42.

14 Visted and Stigum, *Vår Gamle Bondekultur*, pp. 63–127.

15 Einar Hovdhaugen, *Husmannstida* (Oslo, 1975), pp. 71, 75.

16 Urtegaard, "Jordbruksdrift og Sosial Lagdeling," p. 139.

17 Basic rules for utmark use were well developed through custom. Generally, one could set out only so many animals as one could feed through the winter. When a farmer in a southern Norwegian parish allowed too many out in 1825, conflict occurred. See Try, *Gardsskipnad og Bondenæring*, p. 88. Balestrand, because of its large units of production, however, rarely faced such discord.

18 Hjalmar Aarskog, "Gard og Grannesamfunn: Balestrand" (unpublished paper, Institutt for Samanliknande Kulturforskning, 1956), p. I33. See also Hjalmar Aarskog, "Frå Dagliglivet i Bygdene Våre, om lag 1850 og Fram Mot Vå Tid," *Balestrand Gard og Grend*, 1 (1973):31; and Hjalmar Aarskog, "Noko om den Gamle Arbeidsdagen," ibid., 2 (1974):39.

19 Regional variations in animal holdings caused two basic systems of crop production. Since Balestrand had plenty of manure, grain could be sown year after year in the same field. In areas without the manure supplies, particularly in the flatter east, crops were rotated. See Visted and Stigum, *Vår Gamle Bondekultur*, pp. 146–47.

20 Ibid., p. 143

21 Hjalmar Aarskog, "Noko om Kornavl frå Midten av Fyrre Hundreår og i dei Første Ti-åri av Dette (Hundreåret)," *Balestrand Gard og Grend*, 1 (1973):77; Andreas Holmsen, "Økonomisk og Administrativ Historie," in Hans Aall, ed., *Norske Bygder: Sogn* (Bergen, 1937), p. 86. On multiple bruker the arable land was painstakingly divided into strips, as it often was in other Norwegian areas.

22 Visted and Stigum, *Vår Gamle Bondekutur*, p. 155.

23 Aarskog, "Noko om Kornavl," p. 79; Visted and Stigum, *Vår Gamle Bondekultur*, pp. 155–56.

24 Aarskog, "Nolo om Kornavl," p. 77. Visted and Stigum, in *Vår Gamle Bondekultur*, pp. 155–56, detail the carrying of manure in Leikanger, a county neighboring Balestrand.

25 Aarskog, "Noko om Kornavl," p. 77; Jens Kraft, *Topographisk-Statistisk Beskrivelse over Kongeriget Norge* (Christiania, 1830), p. 739; Fartein Valen-Sendstad, *Norske Landbruksredskaper 1800–1850 Årene* (Lillehammer, 1964). Valen-Sendstad divided Norway into four agricultural regions according to implement type. Balestrand was part of the Sunnmøre and

west Norwegian ploughing culture, more advanced than the Jæren spade culture, but less advanced than the Gudbrandsdal plough and the Aker farm machinery cultures to the east, both of which enjoyed higher outputs per man. See ibid., pp. 28–74.

26 Valen-Sendstad, *Norske Landbruksredskaper*, p. 46; Aarskog, "Noko om Kornavl," p. 79.

27 Kraft, *Topographisk-Statistisk Beskrivelse*, p. 735.

28 Visted and Stigum, *Vår Gamle Bondekultur*, p. 155.

29 Aarskog, "Noko om Kornavl," p. 79; Jon Laberg, *Balestrand, Bygd og Ætter* (Bergen, 1934), p. 101.

30 If a woman sowed, a situation that rarely occurred, she wore a white kerchief. Aarskog, "Noko om Kornavl," p. 78; Visted and Stigum, *Vår Gamle Bondekultur*, p. 161.

31 Aarskog, "Noko om Kornavl," pp. 77–8; Kraft, *Topographisk-Statistisk Beskrivelse*, p. 735; *Beretning om Kongeriget Norges Økonomiske Tilstand i Aarene 1836–1840* (Christiania, 1843), p. 169.

32 Visted and Stigum, *Vår Gamle Bondekultur*, p. 161; Kraft, *Topographisk-Statistisk Beskrivelse*, p. 735.

33 Rasmus Sunde, "Ei Undersøking av Utvandringa til Amerika frå Vik i Sogn, 1839–1915" (major thesis, Universitetet i Trondheim, 1974), pp. 56–59; Johannes Brynjulf Thue, "Gardproduksjon, Handel, og Sjøtransport i Jord- og Skogbruksbygdene i Sogn, 1830–1900: Det Økonomiske Systemet i Nokre Lokalsamfunn på Vestlandet" (major thesis, Universitetet i Bergen, 1971), p. 14; *Beretning . . . 1836–1840*, p. 169; *Beretning om Kongeriget Norges Økonomiske Tilstand i Aarene 1840–1845 med Tilhørende Tabeller* (Christiania, 1847), p. 139.

34 Kraft, *Topographisk-Statistisk Beskrivelse*, p. 739.

35 Laberg, *Balestrand*, p. 101.

36 Aarskog, "Noko om Kornavl," p. 79; Visted and Stigum, *Vår Gamle Bondekultur*, pp. 182–83.

37 Visted and Stigum, *Vår Gamle Bondekultur*, p. 186; Aarskog, "Noko om Kornavl," p. 81.

38 Aarskog, "Noko om Kornavl," p. 81.

39 Ibid., p. 82; Visted and Stigum, *Vår Gamle Bondekultur*, p. 189.

40 Aarskog, "Noko om Kornavl," p. 82.

41 In addition to entreaties to the Almighty during sowing, rites continued as the plants grew. On Midsummer Eve farmers recited the Lord's Prayer and went to the fields appealing for good harvests. See Visted and Stigum, *Vår Gamle Bondekultur*, p. 182. Other examples of old beliefs can be seen in the notion that when oats were sowed in certain fields, they were transformed into barley, since the soil was too good for oats. See Aarskog, "Noko om Kornavl," p. 77.

42 Sunde, "El Undersøking," p. 56.

43 See Chayanov, *Theory of Peasant Economy;* and Stein Tveite, *Jord og Gjerning – Trekk av Norsk Landsbruk i 150 År* (Christiansand, 1959).

44 Cited in S. Skappel, "Høstingsbruk og Dyrkingsbruk: Streiftog Gjen-

nom 600 År av Vår Landbrukshistorie," *Historisk Tidsskrift*, 31 (1937–40):170–71.

45 Høstingsbruk is distinguished from *dyrkingsbruk* (arable land farming): The former permitted the harvesting (*høster*) of forage such as hay, leaves, and twigs without a previous investment in land clearing, fertilizing, and planting.

46 *Beretning om Kongeriget Norges Økonomiske Tilstand: Aarene 1851–1855 med Tilhørende Tabeller* (Christiania, 1858), p. O3.

47 Aarskog, "Gard og Grannesamfunn"; Johannes B. Thue, "Husmannskår," *Balestrand Gard og Grend*, 2 (1974):66.

48 Aarskog, "Noko om den Gamle Arbeidsdagen," p. 31.

49 G. F. Heiberg, "Seterbruket i Norge: Herraderne Jostedalen, Luster, Hafslo, Årdal, Borgund, Lærdal, Aurland, Sogndal, Leikanger, Balestrand og Vik" (unpublished paper, Institutt for Samanliknande Kulturforskning, 1969).

50 Urtegaard, "Jordbruksdrift og Sosial Lagdeling," pp. 173–74.

51 Heiberg, "Seterbruket i Norge," pp. 4, 58–60.

52 Ibid., pp. 61, 63.

53 Ibid., pp. 5, 58–59, 61–65, 70, 74.

54 Aarskog, "Noko om den Gamle Arbeidsdagen," pp. 23–24, 26, 29, 31.

55 Andres A. Svalestuen, *Tinns Emigrasjons Historie, 1837–1907: En Undersøkelse med Særlig Vekt på den Demografiske, Økonomiske og Sosiale Bakgrunn for Amerikafarten, og en Statistik Analyse av Selve Utvandringen* (Oslo, 1972), p. 258.

56 Aarskog, "Noko om den Gamle Arbeidsdagen," pp. 24, 30.

57 Visted and Stigum, *Vår Gamle Bondekultur*, p. 249. Although the dialect of this quotation probably originates from Østerdalen, the thoughts in Balestrand were undoubtedly similar.

58 Hjalmar Aarskog, "Verdsetjing av Markafor, Hamnegang og Husdyr i 1860-Åri," *Balestrand Gard og Grend*, 1 (1973):48–49.

59 Visted and Stigum, *Vår Gamle Bondekultur*, pp. 205, 210, 228; Kraft, *Topographisk-Statistisk Beskrivelse*, p. 747; Hjalmar Aarskog, "Høying i Utmarki," *Balestrand Gard og Grend*, 1 (1973):42; Urtegaard, "Jordbruksdrift og Sosial Lagdeling," p. 140; Hjalmar Aarskog, "Markateigar og Andre Slåtteteigar i Eldre Tid," *Balestrand Gard og Grend*, 1 (1973):57.

60 The use of the utmark is an interesting example of utilization of resources. A wild area, it provided not only forage but other "luxuries" as well. Caraway and other spices found there had a variety of uses, including bread baking and as tobacco substitutes. Mosses were also collected for yellow and red dyes. See Hjalmar Aarskog, "Omkring Utmarki som Arbeidsplass," *Balestrand Gard og Grend*, 1 (1973):37; Urtegaard, "Jordbruksdrift og Sosial Lagdeling," p. 173; and Skappel, "Hostingsbruk og Dyrkingsbruk," p. 154.

61 Aarskog, "Høying i Utmarki," pp. 140–41.

62 Heiberg, "Seterbruket i Norge," pp. 70–72; Urtegaard, "Jordbruksdrift og Sosial Lagdeling," pp. 173–74.

63 Aarskog, "Markateigar," p. 57; Aarskog, "Gard og Grannesamfunn,"
    p. I33.
64 Aarskog, "Markateigar," p. 55.
65 Aarskog, "Høying i Utmarki," p. 45; Visted and Stigum, *Vår Gamle
    Bondekultur*, p. 219.
66 Aarskog, "Markateigar," p. 53; Aarskog, "Gard og Grannesamfunn,"
    p. I33. More will be said about this matter in the following chapter.
67 Aarskog, "Høying i Utmarki," pp. 44–45. See Heiberg, "Seterbruket i
    Norge," p. 72, for a detailed explanation of the haying tools and their
    transportation to the støl.
68 Aarskog, "Høying i Utmarki," p. 43.
69 Visted and Stigum, *Vår Gamle Bondekultur*, p. 221; Aarskog, "Høying i
    Utmarki," p. 42.
70 Urtegaard, "Jordbruksdrift og Sosial Lagdeling," p. 140; Aarskog,
    "Høying i Utmarki," p. 45; Visted and Stigum, *Vår Gamle Bondekultur*,
    p. 225.
71 Heiberg, "Seterbruket i Norge," pp. 73–74; Urtegaard, "Jordbruksdrift
    og Sosial Lagdeling," p. 140; Visted and Stigum, *Vår Gamle Bondekultur*,
    p. 225; Aarskog, "Høying i Utmarki," p. 45.
72 Urtegaard, "Jordbruksdrift og Sosial Lagdeling," p. 174.
73 Hjalmar Aarskog, "Ris, Beit, og Skav," *Balestrand Gard og Grend*, 1
    (1973):72; Aarskog, "Noko om den Gamle Arbeidsdagen," p. 23;
    Chayanov, *Theory of Peasant Economy*; Visted and Stigum, *Vår Gamle
    Bondekultur*, p. 202; Svalestuen, *Tinns Emigrasjons Historie*, pp. 69–76.
    See also *Beretning . . . 1836–1840*, pp. 169–70.
74 Tveite, *Jord og Gjerning*, pp. 23–26; Visted and Stigum, *Vår Gamle Bond-
    ekultur*, p. 238.
75 Tveite, *Jord og Gjerning*, pp. 23–26; Visted and Stigum, *Vår Gamle Bond-
    ekultur*, p. 238.
76 Laberg, *Balestrand*, p. 137. See also Aarskog, "Ris, Beit, og Skav," pp.
    67–68.
77 Aarskog, "Ris, Beit, og Skav," pp. 67–68.
78 Quoted in ibid., p. 67.
79 Hjalmar Aarskog, "Om Lauving Slik den Vart Bruke i Desse Bygdene
    ved Hundreårsskiftet," *Balestrand Gard og Grend*, 1 (1973):62.
80 Aarskog, "Gard og Grannesamfunn," p. I33; Aarskog, "Om Lauving,"
    p. 62. For a regional comparison of the leaving responsibilities in Nor-
    way, see Visted and Stigum, *Vår Gamle Bondekultur*, p. 239.
81 Visted and Stigum, *Vår Gamle Bondekultur*, p. 241.
82 Aarskog, "Gard og Grannesamfunn," p. I33; Visted and Stigum, *Vår
    Gamle Bondekultur*, p. 244.
83 Aarskog, "Noko om den Gamle Arbeidsdagen," p. 24.
84 Aarskog, "Om Lauving," pp. 63–64; Visted and Stigum, *Vår Gamle
    Bondekultur*, p. 243.
85 Aarskog, "Om Lauving," p. 62. It was determined that twenty-five to
    thirty lambs could be kept alive through the winter with two thousand
    to three thousand bundles of leaves.

86   Cited in Tveite, *Jord og Gjerning*, pp. 23–25.
87   Aarskog, "Ris, Beit, og Skav," p. 71; Urtegaard, "Jordbruksdrift og Sosial Lagdeling," p. 140; Visted and Stigum, *Vår Gamle Bondekultur*, p. 249. See Aarskog, "Gard og Grannesamfunn," p. I33, for a different formula concerning collection patterns.
88   Aarskog, "Ris, Beit, og Skav," p. 70. As late as the 1920s one man reported that they collected twigs two days a week from the time they set in the animals in the fall until they were let out in the spring.
89   Aarskog, "Om Lauving," p. 63; Aarskog, "Ris, Beit, og Skav," p. 70; Aarskog, "Gard og Grannesamfunn," p. I33.
90   Aarskog, "Ris, Beit, og Skav," p. 72; Urtegaard, "Jordbruksdrift og Sosial Lagdeling," p. 140.
91   Heiberg, "Seterbruket i Norge," p. 73.
92   Aarskog, "Gard og Grannesamfunn," p. I16.
93   Aarskog, "Noko om den Gamle Arbeidsdagen," pp. 35–38.
94   Ibid., pp. 35–38; Urtegaard, "Jordbruksdrift og Sosial Lagdeling," p. 68.
95   Aarskog, "Omkring Utmarki som Arbeidsplass," pp. 38–39; Visted and Stigum, *Vår Gamle Bondekultur*, p. 182.
96   Thue, "Gardproduksion, Handel, og Sjøtransport," p. 62.
97   Randi Bjørkvik, "Gardfolk og Plassfolk," in Ingrid Semmingsen, ed., *Norges Kulturhistorie, vol. 4, Det Gjenfødte Norge* (Oslo, 1980), p. 47.
98   Munch, "Gard," pp. 360–63; Aarskog, "Gard og Grannesamfunn," pp. I53, I55.
99   Aarskog, "Gard og Grannesamfunn," p. I54.
100 Ståle Dyrvik, in Dyrvik et al., *Norsk Økonomisk Historie, 1500–1970*, vol. 1, *1500–1850* (Bergen 1979), pp. 191–92; Rigmor Frimannslund, "The Old Norwegian Peasant Community: Farm Community and Neighborhood Community," *Scandinavian Economic History Review*, 4 (1956):65; Aarskog, "Gard og Grannesamfunn," p. I33. Divisions of labor varied depending on the ecological structures of the area. In fishing districts, for example, men were absent during sowing, so that it became women's work. See Frimannslund, "Old Norwegian Peasant Community," p. 65. Since it was within this farm group that most social and economic activities were enacted, it has been argued that the role of the household on the farm was more important than kinship. Accordingly, people conceived of kin as a matter of people on the farm rather than of blood relationships. See Orvar Löfgren, "Family and Household among Scandinavian Peasants: An Exploratory Essay," *Ethnologica Scandinavica*, 1974, p. 23.
101 Data from family-reconstitution forms for Mundal Parish derived from Balestrand church records. See Chapter 9 for further discussion of naming patterns in Balestrand and the United States.
102 Laberg, *Balestrand*, pp. 146–47; Visted and Stigum, *Vår Gamle Bondekultur*, p. 318; Forrest Brown, "Norwegian-American Family History: Tracing the Family within Norway," *Minnesota Geneologist*, 10

(1979):53–73. The practical result of this naming practice in the area of primogeniture was that every other farmer in the line would have the same name. Hermund Olson would be followed by Ole Hermundson, who would in turn be followed by Hermund Olson.

103 Ståle Dyrvik, "Om Giftermål og Sosiale Normer: Ein Studie av Etne, 1715–1801," *Tidsskrift for Samfunnsforskning*, 11 (1970):297–98.

104 Those who did not inherit the farm had three options apart from leaving. They could stay on the farm, where they worked for themselves. The man could cut wood, strip bark; the woman could do handwork, weaving, and so on. If they wished to form a household, they could become cotters on already settled places or they could clear their own. According to one source, as cotters they did not have work obligations to the farmer and could be reckoned just as good as farmers, but cotterhood was still a sign of downward mobility. See Aarskog, "Gard og Grannesamfunn," pp. I59, I64.

105 Aarskog, "Gard og Grannesamfunn," p. I70; Dyrvik, "Om Giftermål," pp. 297–98; Frimannslund, "Old Norwegian Peasant Community," pp. 66–69; Kjeld Helland-Hansen, "Kårskipnaden," *Heimen*, 13 (1964–66):182–95. The German equivalent was the altenteil; see H. W. Spiegel, "The Altenteil: German Farmers' Old Age Security," *Rural Sociology*, 4 (1939):203–18.

106 Aarskog, "Gard og Grannesamfunn," p. I71.

107 Ibid. A random sample of kårkontrakter showed that the yearly amount of grain and potatoes increased from 847 pounds around 1830 to 902 between 1860 and 1865. Thue, "Garproduksjon, Handel, og Sjøtransport," pp. 16–17.

108 Try, *Gardsskipnad og Bordenæring*, p. 73; Aarskog, "Gard og Grannesamfunn," p. I70. This discrepancy between legal stipulations and the actual interworkings of the kår make it a difficult aspect of study in the Norwegian social past.

109 Aarskog, "Gard og Grannesamfunn," p. I71; Löfgren, "Family and Household," pp. 40–44; Bjørkvik, "Old Norwegian Peasant Community," p. 54. The kår could be especially burdensome in instances when a buyer took over responsibility for a kår couple and later retired himself, leaving his heir two couples to feed.

110 Aarskog, "Gard og Grannesamfunn," p. I59. Very rarely did the heir refuse the right to take the farm, but he might do so if his prospects were better in other places. See Ibid., p. I56.

111 Ibid., pp. I54, I59.

112 Ibid., p. II5. People also used the terms *nabokona* (neighbor wife), *nabogjenta* (neighbor girl), and *nabogutt* (neighbor boy), although *naboson* was not used. In general, there was little friction between granne members, and no informants remembered anyone being driven from the granne circle. Ibid., p. II6. See also ibid., p. II4; and Hjalmar Aarskog, "Samkomer og Samarbeid i Grendi," *Balestrand Gard og Grend*, 2 (1974):8–9.

113 Aarskog, "Gard og Grannesamfunn," p. II33; Aarskog, "Samkomen og Samarbeid i Grendi," pp. 12–13.
114 Aarskog, "Gard og Grannesamfunn," p. II3.
115 Ibid., pp. II3–4; Aarskog, "Samkomen og Samarbeid i Grendi," pp. 8–11 (containing a geographical delineation of the grend boundaries in Balestrand); Frimannslund, "Old Norwegian Peasant Community," pp. 70–72.
116 Aarskog, "Gard og Grannesamfunn," p. II13; Aarskog, "Samkomen og Samarbeid i Grendi," p. 11.
117 Aarskog, "Gard og Grannesamfunn," p. II20.
118 Ibid., p. II21; Frimannslund, "Old Norwegian Peasant Community," pp. 70–72.
119 Aarskog, "Gard og Grannesamfunn," p. II51; Helge Norddølum, "The 'Dugnad' in the Pre-Industrial Peasant Community: An Attempt at an Explanation," Ethnologica Scandinavica, 1980, pp. 102–12; Frimannslund, "Old Norwegian Peasant Community," p. 72; Holmsen, "Old Norwegian Peasant Community," p. 25. Although grend divisions were firm, farms that lay on the borders between two grends asked for help from neighbor farms. Aarskog, "Gard og Grannesamfunn," p. II16.
120 Laberg, Balestrand, pp. 85, 87.
121 Ibid., p. 80.
122 Ibid., pp. 80–81; Aarskog, "Gard og Grannesamfunn," p. II21; Visted and Stigum, Vår Gamle Bondekultur, p. 338.
123 Dyrvik, "Om Giftermål," pp. 298–99. Dyrvik's analysis also gives an excellent description of the timing of marriage and the constraints on engagement and marriage.
124 For hygienic conditions, see Aarskog, "Frå Dagliglivet," p. 30; Laberg, Balestrand, p. 92; and Visted and Stigum, Vår Gamle Bondekultur, p. 315. See Anne Helene Bolstad Skjelbred, Uren og Hedning: Barselkvinnen i Norsk Folketradisjon (Bergen, 1972), for a study of childbirth and its Christian customs in Norwegian peasant society.
125 Sølvi Sogner, "De Barnrike Familier," in Semmingsen, Den Gjenfødte Norge, p. 30, borrowed from Pierre Goubert.
126 Visted and Stigum, Vår Gamle Bondekultur, pp. 357–58.
127 Sogner, "De Barnrike Familier," p. 30; Dyrvik et al., Norsk Økonomisk Historie, 1:127.
128 More precisely, 0.93% between 1801 and 1845 and 1.16% between 1845 and 1855. Dyrvik et al., Norsk Økonomisk Historie, 1:125.
129 The average growth for Europe between 1815 and 1855, excluding Turkey and the other Balkan states, was 0.75% yearly, compared with Norway's 1.23%. In Scandinavia, Norway grew faster between 1770 and 1885 than Sweden or Denmark, although not as rapidly as Finland.
130 Laberg, Balestrand, p. 20. See also Jan Oldervoll, "Kva Hadde Befolkningsveksten Å Seie for Utvandringa," in Arnfinn Engen, ed.,

Utvandringa – Det Store Oppbrotet (Oslo, 1978), p. 21; and A. N. Kiær, *Oversigt over de Vigtigste Resultater af de Statistiske Tabeller Vedkommende Folkemængdens Bevegelse, 1866–1885* (Christiania, 1890), pp. 1–11.

Chapter 4. "It will be man's fortune to see business extended"

1 Anders Ohnstad, "Folketal og Utflytting," in Hans Lavik, ed., *Pacific Coast Sognalag 50 Year Jubilee, 1912–1962* (Tacoma, Wash., 1962), p. 51.

2 Andreas Holmsen, "Økonomisk og Administrativ Historie," in Hans Aall, ed., *Norske Bygder: Sogn* (Bergen, 1937), pp. 88–89.

3 Eilert Sundt, *On Marriage in Norway*, trans. Michael Drake (Cambridge, 1980), pp. 98–99, from the Norwegian, *Om Giftermål i Norge* (Christiania, 1855; reprint, Oslo, 1975).

4 See A. V. Chayanov, *The Theory of Peasant Economy*, ed. Daniel Thorner, Basile Kerbley, and R. E. F. Smith (Homewood, Ill., 1966); Ester Boserup, *The Conditions of Agricultural Growth: The Economics of Agrarian Change under Population Pressure* (Chicago, 1965); Ester Boserup, *Population and Technology* (Chicago, 1981); Julian L. Simon, *The Economics of Population Growth* (Princeton, N.J., 1977); Richard G. Wilkinson, *Poverty and Progress* (London, 1973); Colin Clark and Margaret Haswell, *The Economics of Subsistence Agriculture* (New York, 1967); and D. E. Dumond, "Population Growth and Cultural Change," *Southwestern Journal of Anthropology*, 21 (1965):302–24. See also Kjell Haarstad, "Sult, Sykdom, Død: Et Teoretiske Problem Belyst med Empirisk Materiale," *Historisk Tidsskrift*, 59 (1980):1–25, for a critical examination of the Boserup school in Norwegian historiography.

5 Simon, *Economics of Population Growth*, p. 10.

6 Ibid., p. 160; Boserup, *Conditions of Agricultural Growth;* Chayanov, *Theory of Peasant Economy*, p. 68.

7 Simon, *Economics of Population Growth*, pp. 3, 11.

8 See Christer Winberg, *Folkökning och Proletarisering: Kring den Sociala Strukturomvandlingen på Sveriges Landsbygd under den Agrara Revolutionen* (Göteborg, 1975); Christer Winberg, "Population Growth and Proletarianization," in Sune Åkerman, Hans Christian Johansen, and David Gaunt, *Chance and Change: Social and Economic Studies in Historical Demography in the Baltic Area* (Odense, Denmark, 1978), pp. 170–84; and Orvar Löfgren, "The Potato People: Household Economy and Family Patterns among the Rural Proletariat in Nineteenth Century Sweden," in ibid., pp. 95–106.

9 Boserup, *Conditions of Agricultural Growth;* Edward J. Nell, in Julius Rubin et al., "Symposium: A Review of Ester Boserup, *Conditions of Agricultural Growth: The Economics of Agrarian Change under Population Pressure,*" *Peasant Studies Newsletter*, 1 (1972):39.

10 Rudolf Braun, "Early Industrialization and Demographic Change in the Canton of Zürich," in Charles Tilly, ed., *Historical Studies of Changing Fertility* (Princeton, N.J., 1978), p. 311.

11 For the most notable examples of this school of thought see Franklin F. Mendels, "Proto-industrialization: The First Phase of the Industrialization Process," *Journal of Economic History*, 32 (1972):241–61; Braun, "Early Industrialization," pp. 289–334; Hans Medick, "The Proto-Industrial Family Economy: The Structural Function of Household and Family during the Transition from Peasant Society to Industrial Capitalism," *Social History*, 3 (1976):291–315; David Levine, *Family Formation in an Age of Nascent Capitalism* (New York, 1977); and E. L. Jones, "Agricultural Origins of Industry," *Past and Present*, 11 (1968):58–71.

12 Ståle Dyrvik et al., *Norsk Økonomisk Historie, 1500–1970*, vol. 1, *1500–1850* (Bergen, 1979), pp. 154, 156.

13 Stein Tveite, *Jord og Gjerning – Trekk av Norsk Landbruk i 150 År* (Christiansand, 1959), pp. 14–15.

14 Johannes Brynjulf Thue, "Gardproduksjon, Handel, og Sjøtransport i Jord- og Skogbruksbygdene i Sogn, 1830–1900: Det Økonomiske Systemet i Nokre Lokalsamfunn på Vestlandet" (major thesis, Universitetet i Bergen, 1971), p. 12. See Jan de Vries, in Rubin et al., "Symposium," who argues that the market must be integrated into Boserup's model.

15 See Hans Try, *Gardsskipnad og Bondenæring: Sørlandsk Jordbruk på 1800-talet* (Bergen, 1969), pp. 51, 59, 85; and Halvard Bjørkvik, "The Old Norwegian Peasant Community: The Farm Territories," *Scandinavian Economic History Review*, 4 (1956):52, 53.

16 Gunnar Urtegaard, "Jordbruksdrift og Sosial Lagdeling i Balestrand frå 1500 til 1865" (major thesis, Universitetet i Bergen, 1980), pp. 30, 67; *Beretning om Kongeriget Norges Økonomiske Tilstand: Aarene 1851–1855 med Tilhørende Tabeller* (Christiania, 1858), p. O6; *Beretning om Amternes Økonomiske Tilstand i Aarene 1866–1870* (Christiania, 1873), p. O6; *Beretning om Kongeriget Norges Økonomiske Tilstand i Aarene 1856–1860 med Tilhørende Tabeller* (Christiania, 1863), p. O5. Sources indicate that new occupations were opening up in handwork and the transport of wares to district markets throughout the nineteenth century. Craft shops did not exist in Balestrand until the late nineteenth century, and in 1840 only six "factories" were based in all of Sogn: two tile kilns, one knitting machine, one dye house, one stamping mill, and one tannery. Many were not successful; five years later one of the tile kilns and the knitting machine had been closed. By 1860 sixteen factories were in operation, but the number of employees still remained insignificant. *Beretning om Kongeriget Norges Økonomiske Tilstand i Aarene 1836–1840* (Christiania, 1843), p. 172; *Beretning om Kongeriget Norges Økonomiske Tilstand i Aarene 1840–1845 med Tilhørende Tabeller* (Christiania, 1847), p. 141; *Beretning om Kongeriget Norges Økonomiske Tilstand i Aarene 1846–1850 med Tilhørende Tabeller* (Christiania, 1853), p. O4; *Beretning . . . 1851–1855*, p. O6; *Beretning . . . 1855–1860*, p. O5; *Beretning . . . 1866–1870*, p. O5; *Beretning om Amterne Økonomiske Tilstand i Aarene 1871–1875* (Christiania, 1879), p. XIV14. See also Edgar Hovland, Helge W. Nordvik, and Stein Tveite, "Proto-Industrialisation in

Norway, 1750–1850: Fact or Fiction?" *Scandinavian Economic History Review*, 30 (1982):45–56.

17 Urtegaard, "Jordbruksdrift og Sosial Lagdeling," pp. 168–71; Thue, "Gardproduksjon, Handel, og Sjøtransport," p. 102.

18 Hjalmar Aarskog, "Gard og Grannesamfunn: Balestrand" (unpublished paper, Institutt for Samanliknande Kulturforskning, 1956), p. 18; Thue, "Gardproduksjon, Handel, og Sjøtransport," pp. 105–106; Johannes Brynjulv Thue, "Utkant og Sentrum i Balestrand, 1860–1900," *Balestrand Gard og Grend*, 1 (1973):10–13. See also Stephen Hyman and Stephen Resnick, "A Model of an Agrarian Economy with Non-agricultural Activities." *American Economic Review*, 59 (1969):493–506, which argues that farmers *could* change their agrarian production system to fit nonagricultural economic activities.

19 Thue, "Gardproduksjon, Handel, og Sjøtransport," pp. 99, 100.

20 Urtegaard, "Jordbruksdrift og Sosial Lagdeling," pp. 168–71; Thue, "Gardproduksjon, Handel, og Sjøtransport," pp. 108, 109; Jon Laberg, *Balestrand, Bygd og Ætter* (Bergen, 1934), pp. 48, 661–708.

21 Urtegaard, "Jordbruksdrift og Sosial Lagdeling," pp. 2–4, 167. See Winberg, "Population Growth and Proletarianization," p. 171. Winberg argues that all heirs benefited from the value of a farm not subdivided, since those who did not inherit the farm were compensated by the new farm owner and therefore also had an indirect interest in the economy of scale derived from the large unit of production.

22 Thue, "Gardproduksjon, Handel, og Sjøtransport," pp. 108, 109.

23 See Hyman and Resnick, "Model of an Agrarian Economy," which emphasizes the importance of "Z" goods, that is, nonagricultural goods, in the agrarian society.

24 Urtegaard, "Jordbruksdrift og Sosial Lagdeling," pp. 48, 53, 55; Aarskog, "Gard og Grannesamfunn," p. 111. See Sølvi Sogner, "Freeholder and Cotter," *Scandinavian Journal of History*, 1 (1976):181–99; and Andreas Holmsen, "The Transition from Tenancy to Freehold Peasant Ownership in Norway," *Scandinavian Economic History Review*, 9 (1961):152–64.

25 Urtegaard, "Jordbruksdrift og Sosial Lagdeling," p. 67; Hyman and Resnick, "Model of an Agrarian Economy"; Löfgren, "The Potato People," p. 96.

26 Chayanov, *Theory of Peasant Economy*, p. 6; Boserup, *Conditions of Agricultural Growth*.

27 Rubin, in Rubin et al., "Symposium," p. 370.

28 Urtegaard, "Jordbruksdrift og Sosial Lagdeling," pp. 140–41, 159. When farmers relied more on butter and cheese production than on meat, the labor demand grew even greater. See Holmsen, "Økonomisk og Administrativ Historie," p. 86.

29 Hjalmar Aarskog, "Noko om Kornavl frå Midten av Fyrre Hundreår og i dei Første Ti-åri av Dette (Hundreåret)," *Balestrand Gard og Grend*, 1 (1973):77.

30 Urtegaard, "Jordbruksdrift og Sosial Lagdeling," p. 136; Aarskog,

"Gard og Grannesamfunn," p. I16; Kristofer Visted and Hilmar Stig-um, *Vår Gamle Bondekultur* (Oslo, 1951), pp. 148–53. See Winberg, "Population Growth and Proletarianization," p. 172.

31 Urtegaard, "Jordbruksdrift og Sosial Lagdeling," p. 6. The earliest farms cleared after the Black Death were flatland farms; only as settlement continued were shoreline farms taken, a pattern which clearly indicates that earlier farmers valued the flatland more highly. Ibid., p. 19.

32 Aarskog, "Gard og Grannesamfunn."

33 Utegaard, "Jordbruksdrift og Sosial Lagdeling," pp. 146, 147, 153.

34 Responsibilities were sometimes set out in verbal agreements, but since the cotter was at the mercy of the farmer for his livelihood, it was to his advantage to have all the conditions written in the contract. The farmers' general philosophy, on the other hand, was "Write the least possible." One cotter complained that the conditions were not followed when the farmer's son took over the farm: The cotter was supposed to fence a part of the farm and was told that he would find finished stakes in the tun; but when asked where they were, the farmer said that he would have to find the stakes himself. Aarskog, "Gard og Grannesamfunn," p. I18. Cotters' contracts in Balestrand are difficult to find. Although they were legal documents, few were recorded in the *panteregister* (list of mortgages).

35 Aarskog, "Gard og Grannesamfunn," Festeseddel; Urtegaard, "Jordbruksdrift og Sosial Lagdeling," p. 157.

36 Aarskog, "Gard og Grannesamfunn," p. I17. Work methods also differed from place to place. In one contract one husmann was to cut while another raked – possibly a more efficient operation. In others the cotter was responsible for his individual piece.

37 Ibid., pp. I16, I17, I33; Hjalmar Aarskog, "Markateigar og Andre Slåtteteigar i Eldre Tid," *Balestrand Gard og Grend*, 1 (1973):53–54.

38 Aarskog, "Gard og Grannesamfunn," p. I17; Hjalmar Aarskog, "Ris, Beit, og Skav," *Balestrand Gard og Grend*, 1 (1973):71.

39 Urtegaard, "Jordbruksdrift og Sosial Lagdeling," p. 159. See Aarskog, "Gard og Grannesamfunn," p. I17, for a typical husmann's contract; see Johannes B. Thue, "Husmannskår," *Balestrand Gard og Grend*, 2 (1974):65, for a description of the benefits given the husmann for his work.

40 Jan Oldervoll, "Det Store Oppbrotet," in Sivert Langholm and Francis Sejerstad, eds., *Vandringer: Festskrift til Ingrid Semmingsen på 70-Årsdagen 29. Mars 1980* (Oslo, 1980), p. 100; 1801 and 1865 census for Balestrand.

41 This tendency is surmised from the censuses' age structure for servants. The drop in women servants over thirty years of age between 1801 and 1865 was from 34.8% in 1801 to 19.7% in 1865 in Mundal and from 40.5% to 31.9% in Tjugum.

42 From the beginning of emigration, when the amount of labor available was decreasing, until the 1880s, around two hundred servants came to

Balestrand, the most from Hafslo. Aarskog, "Gard og Grannesamfunn," p. I13, II44; Laberg, *Balestrand*, p. 20.

43 See Sundt, *On Marriage in Norway*, p. 145; Joan W. Scott and Louise A. Tilly, "Women's Work and the Family in Nineteenth Century Europe," *Comparative Studies in Society and History*, 17 (1975):36–64; and Ragnar Pedersen, "Die Arbeitsteilung Zwischen Frauen und Männern in einem Marginalen Ackerbaugebeit – Das Beispiel Norwegen," *Ethnologica Scandinavica*," 1975, pp. 37–48.

44 Urtegaard, "Jordbruksdrift og Sosial Lagdeling," pp. 139, 144. The distinction in Mundal was not as great – a 46% increase for men, compared to a 50% gain for women. The figures are derived from the 1801 and 1865 censuses for Balestrand.

45 Urtegaard, "Jordbruksdrift og Sosial Lagdeling," pp. 141–42.

46 Many examples attest to the strict division of labor. When women aided in the cutting of hay, the women raked and put the hay on drying racks while the men cut; it was thought shameful for men to do women's work. Hjalmar Aarskog, "Høying i Utmarki," *Balestrand Gard og Grend*, 1 (1973):45; Urtegaard, "Jordbruksdrift og Sosial Lagdeling," p. 141; Visted and Stigum, *Vår Gamle Bondekultur*, p. 219. Taboos prohibited crossing the division of labor. In Norwegian society, it was said that if a woman even moved a man's implements, it would ruin his luck with his work. This restriction concerned especially work, such as hunting and fishing, that was strongly controlled by sex roles. If a boy balled yarn, he would be expected to have bad luck if he went to sea and to be incompetent in fights. See Ann Helene Bolstad Skjelbred, *Uren og Hedning: Barselkvinnen i Norsk Folketradisjon* (Bergen, 1972), pp. 20, 81.

47 Aarskog, "Gard og Grannesamfunn," pp. I33, I48; G. F. Heiberg, "Seterbruket i Norge: Herrederne Jostedalen, Luster, Hafslo, Årdal, Borgund, Lærdal, Aurland, Sogndal, Leikanger, Balestrand og Vik," (unpublished paper, Institutt for Samanliknande Kulturforskning, 1969), p. 61; Hjalmar Aarskog, "Noko om den Gamle Arbeidsdagen," *Balestrand Gard og Grend*, 2 (1974):24, 28, 35–38.

48 Aarskog, "Gard og Grannesamfunn," p. I17; Aarskog, "Noko om Kornavl," pp. 79, 81.

49 Aarskog, "Gard og Grannesamfunn," p. I33; Hjalmar Aarskog, "Frå Dagliglivet i Bydgene Våre, om lag 1850 og Fram Mot Vår Tid," *Balestrand Gard og Grend*, 1 (1973):32.

50 Given these cries of labor scarcity, it is difficult to argue that Balestrand was no longer providing labor opportunities and that this lack created the need to emigrate. See Tveite, *Jord og Gjerning*, pp. 91–92; and Rasmus Sunde, "Ei Undersøking av Utvandringa til Amerika frå Vik i Sogn, 1839–1915" (major thesis, history, Universitetet i Trondheim, 1974), p. 50.

51 A valuable way of considering the use of land in agriculture is to conceive of land as "man-made," just as are the other inputs to farm production. See Simon, *Economics of Population Growth*, p. 238.

52 Boserup, *Conditions of Agricultural Growth.*
53 Edgar Hovland, in Dyrvik et al., *Norsk Økonomisk Historie*, 1:142.
54 Tveite, *Jord og Gjerning*, pp. 91–92. Official records from 1835 to 1870, moreover, continually report the clearing of land in Sogn. See *Beretning . . . 1836–1840*, p. 168; *Beretning . . . 1840–1845*, p. 138; *Beretning . . . 1846–1850*, p. O2; *Beretning . . . 1856–1860*, p. O2; *Beretning . . . 1866–1870*, p. O2; and *Lensmannsberetning, Leikanger, 1861–1865.* The clearing of land accelerated between 1840 and 1865: Between 1840 and 1845 about 90 acres of land were cleared in Sogn; twenty years later the total was 940 for the five-year span.
55 Census of Balestrand, 1801, 1845, 1855, 1865.
56 *Beskrivelse over de Matrikulerede Eiendomme og Forslag til Ny Skatteskyld for Herredet iflg. Lov. av 6 Juni 1863. No. 260, Balestrand* (Christiania, 1863).
57 Urtegaard, "Jordbruksdrift og Sosial Lagdeling," pp. 89–92.
58 The *extensive* nature of agricultural expansion in Norway has led some historians to contest Boserup's view that the population push encouraged land *intensification.* See Dyrvik et al., *Norsk Økonomisk Historie,* 1:11–14.
59 Heiberg, "Seterbruket i Norge," p. 6.
60 Ibid., p. 63; Try, *Gardsskipnad og Bondenæring*, p. 88; Urtegaard, "Jordbruksdrift og Sosial Lagdeling," pp. 173–78.
61 Urtegaard, "Jordbruksdrift og Sosial Lagdeling," pp. 174–75.
62 Aarskog, "Gard og Grannesamfunn," p. I16.
63 Aarskog, "Noko om Kornavl," p. 82; Fartein Valen-Sendstad, *Norske Landbruksredskaper 1800–1850 Årene* (Lillehammer, 1964), p. 85.
64 Aarskog, "Noko om Kornavl," pp. 77–79; Valen-Sendstad, *Norske Landbruksredskaper*, p. 46.
65 *Beretning . . . 1851–1855*, p. O1.
66 *Beretning om Rigets Oeconomiske Tilstrand i Aarene 1861–1865* (Christiania, 1867), p. O1.
67 Valen-Sendstad, *Norske Landbruksredskaper*, pp. 8, 122–23, 270, 272; George T. Flom, *A History of Norwegian Immigration to the United States* (Iowa City, Iowa, 1909), pp. 223–25.
68 Laberg, *Balestrand*, p. 228.
69 *Beretning . . . 1856–1860*, p. O9.
70 See Andres A. Svalestuen, *Tinns Emigrasjons Historie, 1837–1907: En Undersøkelse med Særlig Vekt på den Demografiske, Økonomiske og Sosiale Bakgrunn for Amerikafarten, og en Statisktik Analyse av Selve Utvandringen* (Oslo, 1972), p. 64. In 1845, for example, the official reports said that a farm with a harvest of seventy to eighty tønder of grain had an average of two horses, ten to twelve cows, and thirty sheep or goats. Five years later, with the same number of animals, the output was thirty to thirty-five tønder of grain and seventy to eighty tønder of potatoes. *Beretning . . . 1840–1845*, p. 139; *Beretning . . . 1846–1850*, p. O2.
71 Sogn had more animals in relation to crops than neighboring districts of

Sunnfjord and Nordfjord because of the greater use of høstingsbruk, which in turn was related to the more abundant utmark resources. Sogn and Fjordane, for example, had more of their cattle on støls than Hardanger in 1890; in 1907 Sogn and Fjordane sent greater percentages of their milk cows to støls than any other region in Norway. The enormous reliance on the utmark is further reflected by the fact that 53% of all farm units in Sogn had two or more støls, as compared to only 17% and 16% of Hardanger and Nordfjord farms. Finally, the pressure for støls that often caused stress for available land in other areas was not felt in Sogn despite this extended use of grazing land. *Beretning . . . 1846–1850*, p. O3; Urtegaard, "Jordbruksdrift og Sosial Lagdeling," p. 176.

72 Urtegaard, "Jordbruksdrift og Sosial Lagdeling," pp. 148–52; Tveite, *Jord og Gjerning*, p. 72; Rubin, in Rubin et al., "Symposium," p. 37.

73 Urtegaard, "Jordbruksdrift og Sosial Lagdeling," pp. 96–98. The end period of 1865 in these figures is somewhat unfortunate, since emigration had already commenced. But the censuses of 1801 and 1865, with complete agrigultural figures, are the only two sources of data on harvest size according to farmer or cotter status in the first two-thirds of the nineteenth century. Data on farms alone from 1845 and 1855, in addition to the two more complete censuses, indicate that grain and potato production and animal holdings per individual were increasing from 1801 to 1845 and 1855 in both Tjugum and Mundal parishes. Grain harvests, moreover, actually reached their peak per individual in 1855, before declining in the following decades. See ibid., p. 89.

74 The trade also clouds the use of calorie output as an index for well-being. Balestrand farmers, for example, sold animal products with low calorie content at a high price and bought food grains with high calorie content at a low price. The output that exceeded three thousand calories per day therefore was actually probably higher still. Calorie estimates are Urtegaard's and are based on Kåre Lunden's formula in "Potetdrykinga og den Raskare Folketalsvoksteren: Noreg frå 1815," *Historisk Tidsskrift*, 54 (1975):275–315.

75 The boat traffic that set Vangsnes apart from the remainder of Balestrand was an important carrier of the trade that developed. By 1869 there were 102 "larger" sailing boats in Sogn, and the trade continued until larger steamboats captured much of the local trade. One of the causes of the decline of Lærdal's market was the falling away of the barter economy by 1875, whereas the district boats with regular routes to Bergen knit the communities of Sogn ever more closely to Bergen. Thue, "Gardproduksjon, Handel, og Sjøtransport," pp. 3, 94.

76 Johannes B. Thue, in "Gardproduksjon, Handel, og Sjøtransport," p. 25, argues that the *amtmenn* (officials) always placed importation too low; using consumption estimates, he figures that 21,614 tønder of grain was imported in 1835 and 25,392 in 1865; Thue believes that

imports actually increased throughout the century. Even if he is correct, the increasing production of goods for export discussed in the text certainly offset increasing grain importation.

77 Ibid., p. 28; Holmsen, "Økonomisk og Administrativ Historie," p. 86; Aarskog, "Gard og Grannesamfunn," p. I23.
78 *Lensmannsberetning, Leikanger, 1861–1865*.
79 Thue, "Gardproduksjon, Handel, og Sjøtransport," p. 38; *Beretning . . . 1861–1865*, pp. O4–O5; *Beretning . . . 1856–1860*, pp. O3–O4; *Beretning . . . 1871–1875*, pp. XIV8–11.
80 Tveite, *Jord og Gjerning*, pp. 182–84.
81 *Beretning . . . 1851–1855*, pp. O4, O13.
82 Tveite, *Jord og Gjerning*, p. 184.
83 Thue, "Husmannskår," pp. 65, 67.
84 Aarskog, "Gard og Grannesamfunn," p. I16.
85 Einar Hovdhaugen, *Husmannstida* (Oslo, 1975), p. 50.
86 Bjørkvik, "Old Norwegian Peasant Community," p. 74.
87 Thue, "Husmannskår," p. 68; Thue, "Gardproduksjon, Handel, og Sjøtransport," pp. 30–31.
88 Urtegaard, "Jordbruksdrift og Sosial Lagdeling," p. 101; Aarskog, "Gard og Grannesamfunn," p. I16.
89 Thue, "Gardproduksjon, Handel, og Sjøtransport," p. 17.
90 Urtegaard, "Jordbruksdrift og Sosial Lagdeling," pp. 101–01, 103, 120.
91 Ibid., p. 129.
92 Aarskog, "Gard og Grannesamfunn," p. I15, I17.
93 Hovdhaugen, *Husmannstida*, p. 116; Daniel Dypevig, "Husmannsvesenet i Numedal," *Norsk Geografisk Tidsskrift*, 14 (1954):378.
94 Aarskog, "Gard og Grannesamfunn," pp. I15, I16, I18.
95 *Beretninger . . . 1840–1845*; Stein Tveite, " 'Overbefolkning,' 'Befolkningspress,' og Vandring," in *Vandringer*, p. 46.
96 *Lensmannsberetning, Leikanger, 1861–1865*. Both the lensmannsberetning and Aarskog, "Gard og Grannesamfunn," p. I11, noted, however, that wages in Balestrand and Leikanger were somewhat lower than for the whole of Sogn. In 1840 the day laborer in Balestrand got twelve skillings per day. In any case, wages were rising *before* the great emigration.
97 *Beretninger . . . 1846–1850*, p. O7; Laberg, Balestrand, p. 20.
98 Urtegaard, "Jordbruksdrift og Sosial Lagdeling," p. 72.
99 See Aarskog, "Gard og Grannesamfunn," p. I45; Rigmor Frimannslund, "The Old Norwegian Peasant Community: Farm Community and Neighborhood Community," *Scandinavian Economic History Review*, 4 (1956):64; and Hovdhaugen, *Husmannstida*, p. 67, for examinations of the conditions for servants.
100 In addition to wages, servants sometimes were provided their own fields in which to sow a little grain or some potatoes. One farm in Tjugum had fields that were jokingly called *brennvinsaokkradn*, small areas where men could dig up enough land to sow grain for malt in order to brew liquor (*brennvin*). Some farms even allowed servants to

have their own sheep. Aarskog, "Gard og Grannesamfunn," p. I11.
101 Larger units that created specialized work kept laborers more fully
    employed than the smaller farms in places such as Voss, which experi-
    enced overmanning at some times in the year. See Urtegaard,
    "Jordbruksdrift og Sosial Lagdeling," pp. 176, 182.
102 Sunde, "Ei Undersøking," p. 75; *Beretning . . . 1846–1850*, pp. O3,
    O6; *Beretning . . . 1856–1860*, p. O2; *Beretning . . . 1861–1865*, p. O7;
    Lensmannsberetning, Leikanger, 1861–1865.
103 The sale prices of smaller farms in a southern area of Norway were
    higher per taxable unit than those of larger farms, since farm buildings
    existed on both large and small farms. This might have been the case
    in Balestrand as well, but the results are probably not distorted. In
    southern Norway the value was also rising. See Try, *Gardsskipnad og
    Bondenæring*. See also Tveite, " 'Overbefolkning,' " p. 46.
104 Aarskog, "Gard og Grannesamfunn," p. I71.
105 Luke M. Peterson's "Nineteenth Century Social Change in Lesja, Nor-
    way" (unpublished undergraduate paper, University of Minnesota,
    1980) illustrates overspeculation in Lesja.
106 *Billed-Magazin*, October 3, 1868.

Chapter 5. Inheritance, marriage, fertility, and economic growth

1 Kjeld Helland-Hansen, "Kårskipnaden," *Heimen*, 13 (1964–66):185.
2 Ibid., p. 191. See also Kingsley Davis and Judith Blake, "Social Structure and Fertility: An Analytic Framework," *Economic Development and
  Cultural Change*, 4 (1956):215–18, which notes the difference between
  joint household or clan organization and independent nuclear households in age at marriage and transfer of estates. In the former inheritance is not a problem, since the clan owns the property, marriage is
  arranged by the elders, and the power of the elder is not diminished
  but enhanced after his sons wed. In nuclear family structure, as in
  Balestrand, on the other hand, the son who inherited his father's land
  took on the prestige, while the father experienced a decline in status.
  Elders in this latter case attempted to keep control longer and thereby
  encouraged higher marriage ages.
3 Davis and Blake, "Social Structure and Fertility," p. 217.
4 Ibid. The Norwegian term *levebrød* (literally, "living bread") was used
  to indicate a livelihood.
5 See, for example, Rudolf Braun, "Early Industrialization and Demographic Change in the Canton of Zürich," in Charles Tilly, ed., *Historical Studies of Changing Fertility* (Princeton, N.J., 1978), p. 290, which
  discusses the interrelationships. See also J. Hajnal, "European Marriage Patterns in Perspective," in D. V. Glass and D. E. C. Eversley,
  eds., *Population in History: Essays in Historical Demography* (London,
  1965), pp. 101–43.

6   Although there is evidence that farmers and cotters stayed in their positions longer as the nineteenth century wore on, nevertheless the kår was used increasingly after the middle of the eighteenth century as life expectancy lengthened. See Randi Bjørkvik, "Gardfolk og Plassfolk," in Ingrid Semmingsen, ed., Norges Kulturhistorie, vol. 4, Det Gjenfødte Norge (Oslo, 1980), p. 52.

7   Quoted in Orvar Löfgren, "Family and Household among Scandinavian Peasants: An Exploratory Essay," Ethnologica Scandinavica, 1974, p. 31.

8   Quoted in Michael Drake, Population and Society in Norway, 1735–1865 (Cambridge, 1969), p. 145.

9   See Edward Shorter, "Illegitimacy, Sexual Revolution, and Social Change in Modern Europe," in Theodore K. Rabb and Robert I. Rotberg, eds., The Family in History: Interdisciplinary Essays (New York, 1971), pp. 48–84; and Lofgren, "Family and Household," p. 32. Whereas bundling seemed indecent to town folk in Norway, Eilert Sundt, in On Marriage in Norway (trans. Michael Drake [Cambridge, 1980], p. 162, from the Norwegian, Om Giftermål i Norge [Christiania, 1855; reprint, Oslo, 1975]), reported that a kiss in public between engaged or married people seemed indecent to people from the country.

10 Kristofer Visted and Hilmar Stigum, Vår Gamle Bondekultur (Oslo, 1951), pp. 326, 328, 330; Löfgren, "Family and Household," p. 32.

11 Sundt, On Marriage in Norway, pp. 158–59.

12 Eilert Sundt, Om Sædeligheds-Tilstanden i Norge (Christiania, 1857; reprint, Oslo, 1976), p. 62. See also Drake, Population and Society, p. 144; Visted and Stigum, Vår Gamle Bondekultur, p. 326.

13 Jan Oldervoll, "Det Store Oppbrotet," in Sivert Langholm and Francis Sejerstad, eds., Vandringer: Festskrift til Ingrid Semmingsen på 70-Årsdagen 29. Mars 1980 (Oslo, 1980), p. 106.

14 Eilert Sundt, Om Sædeligheds-Tilstanden i Norge, Tredie Beretning (Christiania, 1866; reprint, Oslo, 1976), p. 448.

15 Jon Laberg, Balestrand, Bygd og Ætter (Bergen, 1934), pp. 152, 153.

16 Visted and Stigum, Vår Gamle Bondekultur, p. 126; Hjalmar Aarskog, "Gard og Grannesamfunn: Balestrand" (unpublished paper, Institutt for Samanliknande Kulturforskning, 1956), p. I38. See Sundt, Om Sædeligheds-Tilstanden (1857), pp. 25–34, for an examination of housing in Norway in relation to night courting.

17 Hjalmar Aarskog, "Noko om den Gamle Arbeidsdagen," Balestrand Gard og Grend, 2 (1974):32. For a specific example of concern about a young servant girl without supervision on the Bjåstad farm, see Aarskog, "Gard og Grannesamfunn," p. I38.

18 G. F. Heiberg, "Seterbruket i Norge: Herrederne Josterdalen, Luster, Hafslo, Årdal, Borgund, Lærdal, Aurland, Sogndal, Leikanger, Balestrand, og Vik" (unpublished paper, Institutt for Samanliknande Kulturforskning, 1969), pp. 71–72.

19 Sundt, Om Sædeligheds-Tilstanden (1857), p. 36.

20 Laberg, *Balestrand*, pp. 79–80.
21 Visted and Stigum, *Vår Gamle Bondekultur*, pp. 325, 335.
22 Between 1715 and 1794, in the parish of Etne, for example, no truloving
    was broken except by death of one of the partners. See Ståle Dyrvik,
    "Om Giftermål og Sosiale Normer: Ein Studie av Etne, 1715–1801,"
    Tidsskrift for Samfunnsforskning, 11 (1970):290.
23 See ibid. for an excellent account of peasant marriage patterns in Nor-
    way. See also Lizzie Carlsson, *"Jag Giver Dig Min Dotter"*: *Trolovning och
    Äktenskap i den Svenska Kvinnans Äldre Historia* (Stockholm, 1965), for a
    Swedish description of similar patterns.
24 Löfgren, "Family and Household," pp. 32–33, noted that in Sweden,
    for example, wealthy Scånian peasants preferred premarital conception
    because it made the marriage more certain.
25 The sexual debut was often made under institutionalized forms: In
    Gotland, Sweden, for example, it was customary to bed down the
    engaged couple in the same bed at the bride-to-be's home after the
    suitor had been accepted as son-in-law. See Jonas Frykman, "Sexual
    Intercourse and Social Norms: A Study of Illegitimate Births in Sweden,
    1831–1933," *Ethnologica Scandinavica*, 1975, pp. 144–45.
26 Dyrvik, "Om Giftermål," p. 289.
27 Frykman, "Sexual Intercourse and Social Norms," p. 146; Dyrvik,
    "Om Giftermål." See also Sølvi Sogner and Jan Oldervoll, "Illegiti-
    mate Fertility and the Matrimonial Market in Norway circa 1800–1850"
    (unpublished paper, Universitetet i Oslo og Bergen, n.d.), pp. 10–12;
    and Sølvi Sogner and Jan Oldervoll, "Illegitimate Fertility and the
    Marriage Market in Norway, 1800–1850: Regional Variations," in J.
    Dupâquier et al., eds., *Marriage and Remarriage in Populations of the Past*
    (London, 1981), pp. 495–510. The latter considers the regional varia-
    tions of illegitimacy in Norway. According to the argument, lower il-
    legitimacy rates can be grossly correlated with poorer regions having
    restricted fertility patterns, whereas greater frequency of illegitimacy
    occurred in wealthier regions with higher percentages of persons ever
    married.
28 Dyrvik, "Om Giftermål," p. 286; Visted and Stigum, *Vår Gamle Bonde-
    kultur*, p. 338.
29 Local studies indicate that in the older peasant communities before
    1800, between one-half and two-thirds of the brides were pregnant. Sølvi
    Sogner, "De Barnrike Familier," in Semmingsen, *Det Gjenfødte
    Norge*, p. 37. In Sweden the picture was similar. Ann-Sofie Kälvemark
    found 30.6% of all brides pregnant at marriage in Sörmland in the
    mid-1800s; the figure was 44% among farmers' daughters in Östra
    Blekinge at the same time. Frykman, "Sexual Intercourse and Social
    Norms," pp. 137–38.
30 Dyrvik, "Om Giftermål," p. 288.
31 Timing of marriage varied according to the ecological structure of the
    region. The majority of marriages in the parish of Ibestad, for example,

occurred between September and December because of the different patterns of the fishing work year. Likewise, temporal changes have caused a greater emphasis on April and, more recently still, Christmas weddings (see the table in Sundt, *Om Sædeligheds-Tilstanden* [1857], p. 108). See also Julie E. Backer, *Ekteskap, Fødsler og Vandringer i Norge, 1856–1960* (Oslo, 1965).

32   Dyrvik, "Om Giftermål," pp. 291–92. In Etne, 72% of November marriages' first children were illegitimate or prenuptially conceived, compared to only 56% of the children of June and July marriages. See Table 9, which shows a higher percentage of illegitimate and prenuptially conceived first births in October–November marriages in Balestrand.

33   Sundt, *On Marriage in Norway*, pp. 157–58. See also David Levine, *Family Formation in an Age of Nascent Capitalism* (New York, 1977), p. 108, which notes that men in England similarly chose older brides in response to deteriorating conditions.

34   Dyrvik, "Om Giftermål," p. 296; Drake, *Population and Society*, p. 124. The Balestrand figures were taken from church records. Likewise, Sundt, in *On Marriage in Norway*, pp. 143–45, found that farmers' wives were just under one year younger than cotters' wives in the mid-nineteenth century for Christiania and Christiansand dioceses.

35   Dyrvik, "Om Giftermål," p. 299.

36   Jan Oldervoll, in "Kva Hadde Befolkningsveksten Å Seie for Utvandringa," in Arnfinn Engen, ed., *Utvandringa – Det Store Oppbrotet* (Oslo, 1978), p. 26, determined cohort sizes of marriageable-age youth in relation to the number of livelihoods. In the 1700s about two thousand new livelihoods were needed each year, about two for each parish in Norway. By the first half of the 1800s the number had increased to sixty-five hundred.

37   Kingsley Davis, "The Theory of Change and Response in Modern Demographic History," *Population Index*, 29 (1963):362.

38   Sundt, *Om Sædeligheds-Tilstanden* (1866), pp. 480, 486.

39   Ibid., pp. 471, 473, 475, 484–85.

40   Ibid., p. 453. See also Drake, *Population and Society*, p. 137, and Visted and Stigum, *Vår Gamle Bondekultur*, p. 324, for descriptions of the same procedure. Also common was *heimdabytepenge*, which occurred when a man married a woman from another farm and paid his sister money that she could use as a dowry.

41   Sundt, *Om Sædeligheds-Tilstanden* (1866), pp. 478, 480.

42   Ibid., pp. 451, 467–68. One observer in Sunnfjord in 1785 noted that "love and natural inclinations" were usually the least of the reasons why people chose one another as marriage partners. More often it was family connections. Widows remarried quickly; "few widows who possess land bury their husbands before the suitors have again appeared." Ibid., p. 451.

43   Ibid., p. 485.

44   Ibid., pp. 447–48; Eilert Sundt, *Fortsatte Bidrag Angaaende Sædeligheds-Tilstanden i Norge* (Christiania, 1864; reprint, Oslo, 1976), p. 343.
45   1855 published census for Norway; stillborn babies included.
46   Gunnar Urtegaard, "Jordbruksdrift og Sosial Lagdeling i Balestrand frå 1500 til 1865" (major thesis, Universitetet i Bergen, 1980), p. 164. See also Hèctor Pèrez Brignoli, "Deux Siècles D'Illègitimitè au Costa Rica, 1770–1974," in Dupâquier et al., *Marriage and Remarriage*, pp. 481–89, which describes the regional variation in illegitimacy between a coffee-producing family farm area and a large-scale livestock-raising region, with the latter exhibiting the higher illegitimacy ratio.
47   In a large sample of kårkontrakts, transfer of farms to a son was by far the most common practice from the Middle Ages onward. After 1800, 74.9% of all transfers were between fathers and sons, an increase from 51.7% before 1750. Helland-Hansen, "Kårskipnaden," p. 193. The *odelsrett* and *åsætesrett* laws of 1821, moreover, gave males and the oldest highest priority in written law. Bjørkvik, "Gardfolk og Plass-folk," p. 47.
48   Aarskog, "Gard og Grannesamfunn," p. I18.
49   Ibid., p. I58.
50   Sundt, *Om Sædeligheds-Tilstanden* (1857), pp. 51–54.
51   Aarskog, "Gard og Grannesamfunn," p. I8. This tendency was not new. Bachelors often married widows only for property, a matter that caused complaints from Sundt as well as others; a priest in the 1700s said, "Young bachelors take old widows primarily to get a piece of land." See Sundt, *On Marriage in Norway*, p. 118.
52   See, for example, Arne Boyum's autobiography in Ernest M. Maland, *Remember the Days of Old: The Centennial Saga of Arendahl Evangelical Lutheran Congregation, 1856–1956* (Decorah, Iowa, 1956), p. 90. In Etne, moreover, between 1701 and 1815, 48% of cotters' wives had been farmers' daughters. Dyrvik, "Om Giftermål," p. 294.
53   There are examples of children of cotters taking kår, but this step was quite rare. Aarskog, "Gard og Grannesamfunn," p. I18.
54   Marriage ages throughout Norway showed similar patterns. In Christiania and Christiansand dioceses Sundt found that farmers married one-and-one-half years later than cotters or other laborers by the mid-nineteenth century. In Etne the ages at marriage of farmers and cotters were nearly identical on the average between 1755 and 1794. Marriage age on the whole had been falling in Etne throughout the eighteenth century as well. Men's average age dropped from 30.4 between 1715 and 1734 to 28.3 between 1775 and 1794, and the figure for women saw a similar drop (from 29.8 to 26.9) in the same time periods. In general, however, most European countries still had lower marriage ages than Norway. In 1865, for example, only 8.7% of men aged 20–25 and 19.6% of women of the same age group were married in Norway, compared tc the average of 15.3% and 33.8% for all European lands, a circumstance

that was replicated around the end of the nineteenth century. Sundt, *On Marriage in Norway*, pp. 143–45; Dyrvik, "Om Giftermål," pp. 294, 296; A. N. Kiær, *Oversigt over de Vigtigste Resultater af de Statistiske Tabeller Vedkommende Folkemængdens Bevegelse, 1866–1885* (Christiania, 1890), pp. 51–52; Backer, *Ekteskap, Fødsler, og Vandringer*, pp. 78–79.

55 Such patterns were not unique to Balestrand or even to Norway. In the canton of Zürich, Switzerland, a member of the upper class noted that youths in protoindustrial areas "carelessly . . . married without consideration, if they can manage to support wife and children"; another complained that "these people, who have two spinning wheels but no bed, contract early marriage fairly often." In protoindustrialized areas of England, the patterns were similar. As in Balestrand, traditional sanctions against early marriage were weakened by fewer prospects of inheritance while expanding economic opportunities offered openings for employment. Braun, "Early Industrialization," pp. 313, 314; see also Levine, *Family Formation*, p. 11.

56 *Beretning om Kongeriget Norges Økonomiske Tilstand i Aarene 1840–1845 med Tilhørende Tabeller* (Christiania, 1847), p. 143.

57 It might be argued that anticipated opportunities in America, rather than increasing livelihoods in Balestrand, were the reason for lowered marriage ages. The increased household sizes in Balestrand, however, indicate that youths were marrying earlier and creating larger households even when they remained at home.

58 Cited in Laberg, *Balestrand*, pp. 152, 157, 158–59.

59 See Sølvi Sogner, "Illegitimacy in Old Rural Society: Some Reflections on the Problem Arising from Two Norwegian Family-Reconstitution Studies," in Sune Åkerman, Hans Christian Johansen, and David Gaunt, eds., *Chance and Change: Social and Economic Studies in Historical Demography in the Baltic Area* (Odense, Denmark, 1978), pp. 61–68.

60 Elisabeth Haavet, "Illegitime Fødsler i Leikanger Prestegjeld" (unpublished paper, Universitetet i Bergen, 1980), p. 2.

61 Increasing illegitimacy was common throughout nineteenth-century Norway. Two Norwegian districts (Akershus and Bergen stifter) experienced a continual rise between 1736 and 1885. Whereas there were 3.86 living illegitimate children for every 100 living births between 1736 and 1745, the figure had reached 8.77 by 1846–55. General figures for all of Norway saw a rise from 2.5% in 1760 to around 6% in 1800 to around 10% by 1850. Some regions within Norway, including Sogn, rated higher than the norm. In one area investigated by Sundt, for example, the years between 1848 and 1853 saw only two exceptions to marriages where the bride had had an illegitimate child or was pregnant at the time of marriage: One couple was over fifty years old at the time of marriage; the other remained childless throughout their marriage. Sogn and particularly Inner Sogn remained in this pattern well into the nineteenth century. In proportion of illegitimate children, Inner Sogn ranked third out of fifty-three districts between 1831 and 1840, fourth

between 1841 and 1850, and first between 1851 and 1860. Illegitimacy was increasing throughout much of Europe at the time. Sweden, for example, had a pattern of illegitimacy strikingly similar to that of Norway, peaking in the early 1850s. Norway's figure remained above the rate for all Europe, which stood at a little over 6% in the mid-nineteenth century (Norway's was approximately 8.5%) and was considerably higher than those for countries such as Greece, Serbia, and Russia (around 1% to 3%). Kiær, *Oversigt over de Vigtigste Resultater*, pp. 84, 87; Ståle Dyrvik et al., *Norsk Økonomisk Historie, 1500–1970*, vol. 1, 1500–1850 (Bergen, 1979), p. 129; Sundt, *Om Sædeligheds-Tilstanden* (1857), pp. 19–20, 109; Sundt, *Om Sædeligheds-Tilstanden* (1866), pp. 282, 396–97.

62   The data collected by Sundt, although not as striking as those for Balestrand, indicated a similar tendency toward more illegitimate children in the "working class" than in the "owner class." See Sundt, *Om Sædeligheds-Tilstanden* (1866), pp. 330, 332.

63   Such is Levine's argument; see *Family Formation*, pp. 127, 128. See also Sogner, "Illegitimacy in Old Rural Society," pp. 62–63.

64   Aarskog, "Gard og Grannesamfunn," p. I14.

65   Haavet, "Illegitime Fødsler," pp. 10–14.

66   Peter Laslett, *Family Life and Illicit Love in Earlier Generations* (Cambridge, 1977), p. 107. Furthermore, Scandinavian microstudies dealing with Ramdala, Blekinge, Sweden, and with Lesja, Gudbrandsdalen, Norway, have noted similar tendencies. Frykman, "Sexual Intercourse and Social Norms," p. 140; Luke M. Peterson, "Nineteenth Century Social Change in Lesja, Norway" (unpublished undergraduate paper, University of Minnesota, 1980), p. 80.

67   Sundt, *Om Sædeligheds-Tilstanden* (1857), pp. 196, 132.

68   Single-parent families existed in English protoindustrial areas because women played such a large role economically; they were uncommon in agricultural areas. Sundt noted that Sunnfjord was basically a fishing district where men played the major economic role, whereas Sogn used both men and women in important tasks. Others have argued that a breaking down of the sexual division of labor allowed women greater latitude in social, sexual, and economic intercourse. Levine, *Family Formation*, p. 143; Sundt *Om Sædeligheds-Tilstanden* (1866), pp. 485–86; Hans Medick, "The Proto-industrial Family Economy: The Structural Function of Household and Family during the Transition from Peasant Society to Industrial Capitalism," *Social History*, 3 (1976):311–14.

69   See Sundt, *Om Sædeligheds-Tilstanden (1857)*, pp. 9–12, 54–60, which describes the miseries of illegitimate children living with their unmarried mothers. Shorter has argued, in "Illegitimacy, Sexual Revolution, and Social Change," pp. 53–59, that the increase in illegitimacy was due to a change in consciousness, that peasants were moving from a manipulative sexuality to an expressive one. Though this is an engaging theory, it remains impossible to evaluate the collective con-

sciousness of the nineteenth-century European peasantry. The fact that propertylessness changed the relationships between youths and their parents and the strategies for marriage, however, can be empirically verified by the changing patterns of illegitimacy.

70 Sogner, "Illegitimacy in Old Rural Society," p. 63.
71 "Prestsberetning, Balestrand, 1861–1865" (official report).
72 Beretning om Rigets Oeconomiske Tilstand i Aarene 1861–1865 (Christiania, 1867), p. O9.
73 Laberg, Balestrand, p. 153.
74 Beretning . . . 1861–1865, p. 90. Reinhard Sieder has suggested that peasants did little to prevent the increasing incidence of illegitimate births in Austria because they needed more laborers to maintain their rapid agricultural expansion. See Michael Mitterauer and Reinhard Sieder, The European Family (Chicago, 1982), pp. 125–26.
75 Laberg, Balestrand, p. 159.
76 Boyum's autobiography in Maland, Remember the Days of Old, pp. 93, 95.
77 Laberg, Balestrand, p. 82; Visted and Stigum, Vår Gamle Bondekultur, p. 342. It was in areas like Sunnfjord, where the strictures against illegitimacy were quite uncompromising, that such public exhibitions were most visible. In Swedish society, for example, although some argue that there was no difference between weddings of pregnant and nonpregnant women (see Frykman, "Sexual Intercourse and Social Norms," p. 145), various regions, such as Götaland, developed strong controls against premarital intercourse. Women who mothered illegitimate children were considered whores who supposedly had the ability to evoke rickets (horeskäver) supernaturally. With such a belief, the society created a barrier between these women and larger society that worked as an expression of society's control over sexual behavior. The most spectacular expression of public punishment was the gåsagång. Married women had the authority of the community to inspect the breasts of unmarried girls annually. If a girl had breast milk – a sign of immoral conduct – her hair was immediately covered with a scarf. The supernatural dangers to children and animals were alleviated by this public noting of the girl's status as a whore, but more powerful was the public notice of any private immoral behavior. See Jonas Frykman, Horan i Bondesamhället (Lund, 1977), pp. 106–17.
78 Aarskog, "Gard og Grannesamfunn," p. I58.
79 Ibid., pp. I44, I48, I49. See also Einar Hovdhaugen, Husmannstida (Oslo, 1975), p. 94; and Rigmor Frimannslund, "The Old Norwegian Peasant Community: Farm Community and Neighborhood Community," Scandinavian Economic History Review, 4 (1956):64. For a discussion of mechanisms that maintained egalitarianism in the peasant society, see Dyrvik, "Om Giftermål," p. 294.
80 Urtegaard, "Jordbruksdrift og Sosial Lagdeling," p. 118; Hjalmar Aarskog, "Frå Dagliglivet i Bygdene Våre, om lag 1850 og Fram Mot

Vår Tid," *Balestrand Gard og Grend*, 1 (1973):31–32. A growing division between servants and cotters, on the one hand, and their "betters," on the other, was more graphically illustrated in regions where social differentiation had been great even before the large population growth, such as eastern Norway. In the east, where cotters had been landless for generations, the social gap had created more established traditions; servants began to have their own social activities, which isolated the classes from each other especially among the young. See Hovdhaugen, *Husmannstida*, pp. 9, 99; Bjørkvik, "Gardfolk og Plassvolk," p. 64; and Andres A. Svalestuen, *Tinns Emigrasjons Historie, 1837–1907: En Undersøkelse med Særlig Vekt på den Demografiske, Økonomiske og Sosiale Bakgrunn for Amerikafarten, og en Statisktik Analyse av Selve Utvandringen* (Oslo, 1972), pp. 55–56.

Similar divisions occurred in other places in Scandinavia. With growing population, the relationships between servants and the family changed in Sweden in the nineteenth century. Farmers talked more and more of "unruly servants," and in southern Sweden in 1885 a report stated that "the time has long passed since the servant was considered a member of the family." This widening social gap was manifested in everyday patterns of behavior. Farmhands, for example, began to eat separately, and in some cases the notion of "farm people" as an integrated unit was no longer considered. In Denmark the distance between the farmer and his servants also increased. A middle room (*mellomrom*) where only the farmer's family could eat became common, while the farmer took on a more paternalistic attitude toward cotters. Löfgren, "Family and Household," pp. 24–27; Palle Ove Christiansen, "Peasant Adaptation to Bourgeois Culture? Class Formation and Cultural Redefinition in the Danish Countryside," *Ethnologica Scandinavica*, 1978, pp. 132, 136–38.

81 Sundt, *Om Sædeligheds-Tilstanden* (1857), pp. 64–66.
82 Ibid. (1866), pp. 501–03; "Prestsberetning. Balestrand, 1861–65"; *Beretning om Kongeriget Norges Økonomiske Tilstand i Aarene 1856–1860 med Tilhørende Tabeller* (Christiania, 1863), p. O10. Night courting was a major issue that could openly divide communities; Sundt reported that a club of young women formed to combat night courting within the community of Surendalen, Nordmøre, caused great conflict within the community over the organization itself. He also noted a minister from Urskoug who read the number of illegitimate children each New Year's Day: "The people thus learned that this was something that should not be . . . and all who had any thoughts wished that it must become better with the thing in the community." Sundt, *Om Sædeligheds-Tilstanden* (1857), p. 122; ibid. (1866), pp. 506–08.
83 Boyum's autobiography in Maland, *Remember the Days of Old*, pp. 93, 95.
84 Aarskog, "Gard og Grannesamfunn," pp. I48, I50, I51.
85 Aarskog, "Frå Dagliglivet," p. 33.

86   Hans Try, in *Gardsskipnad og Bondenæring: Sørlandsk Jordbruk på 1800-talet*
     (Bergen, 1969), p. 205, perceives a parallel between growing volun-
     teerism in religious and political life. The community-wide church ser-
     vice was being replaced by the voluntary meeting.
87   Aarskog, "Gard og Grannesamfunn," p. I50; Laberg, *Balestrand*, pp.
     239–40. Others in the reader movement in Balestrand included Ola
     Ness, a carpenter who was converted by Mundal; Botolf A. Hove, a
     farmer who became a carpenter after conversion; and Iver Ven-
     jumshola. See Ola Rudvin, *Indremisjons – Selskapets Historie*, vol. 1, *Det
     Norske Lutherstiftelse, 1868–1891* (Oslo, 1967), pp. 468, 471–72.
88   Aarkog, "Frå Dagliglivet," p. 34.
89   Hjalmar Aarskog, "Samkomer og Samarbeid i Grendi," *Balestrand Gard
     og Grend*, 2 (1974):13.
90   Boyum's autobiography, in Maland, *Remember the Days of Old*, pp. 92–
     95.
91   Ibid.
92   Sundt, *On Marriage in Norway*, p. 93.
93   Sogner, "Illegitimacy in Old Rural Society," p. 63.

Chapter 6. The children of Askeladden

1   Svein Nilsson, *A Chronicler of Immigrant Life: Svein Nilsson's Articles in
    Billed-Magazin, 1868–1870*, trans. C. A. Clausen (Northfield, Minn.,
    1982), pp. 10–11. (I have often, though not always, followed Clausen's
    translation of this important oral history of early Norwegian-American
    settlements.)
2   Quoted by Nilsson, in *Billed-Magazin*, January 9, 1869.
3   Quoted by Carlson C. Qualey, *Norwegian Settlement in the United States*
    (Northfield, Minn., 1938), p. 42.
4   Andres A. Svalestuen, "Om den Regionale Spreiinga av Norsk Utvan-
    dring før 1865," in Arnfinn Engen, ed., *Utvandringa – Det Store Opp-
    brotet* (Oslo, 1978), p. 63. See also Ingrid Semmingsen, *Veien Mot Vest:
    Utvandringen fra Norge til Amerika, 1825–1865* (Oslo, 1941), 1:86.
5   K. A. Rene, *Historie om Utvandringen fra Voss og Vossingene i Amerika,
    med Beskrivelse og Historie af Voss, Karter og Billeder* (Madison, Wis.,
    1930), p. 185.
6   See ibid., pp. 236–38 for one of Unde's letters.
7   Svalestuen, "Om den Regionale Spreiinga," p. 68; Semmingsen, *Veien
    Mot Vest*, 1:86; Rasmus Sunde, "Ei Undersøking av Utvandringa til
    Amerika frå Vik i Sogn, 1839–1915" (major thesis, Universitetet i
    Trondheim, 1974), pp. 36, 44–46.
8   *Beretning om Koneriget Norges Økonomiske Tilstand i Aarene 1840–1845 med
    Tilhørende Tabeller* (Christiania, 1847), p. 143.
9   *Beretning om Kongeriget Norges Økonomiske Tilstand i Aarene 1846–1850
    med Tilhørende Tabeller* (Christiania, 1853), p. O10; *Beretning om
    Kongeriget Norges Økonomiske Tilstand i Aarene 1856–1860 med Tilhørende
    Tabeller* (Christiania, 1863), p. O8.

10 Svalestuen, "Om den Regionale Spreiinga," pp. 68, 76.

11 Figures for Sogn were taken from *Beretninger;* figures for Balestrand were derived from the church books through 1873 and from the immigrant protocol for Bergen, a listing of emigrants from ports of departure, for later dates. (Just as the church books became less reliable, the emigrant protocol, which forced all emigrants to register, was instituted). A few of the Balestrand emigrants may have been omitted, if they left from a port other than Bergen, but since Bergen was the obvious place of departure, most are accounted for. The immigrant protocol has been put on computer at the University of Bergen, and so the particular immigrants from various parishes can be identified.

12 *Beretning om Kongeriget Norges Økonomiske Tilstand: Aarene 1851–1855 med Tilhørende Tabeller* (Christiania, 1858); Anders Ohnstad, "Folketal og Utflytting," in Hans Lavik, ed., *Pacific Coast Sognalag 50 Year Jubilee, 1912–1962* (Tacoma, Wash., 1962), p. 59.

13 See *Beretning . . . 1846–1850,* p. O7, and *Beretning . . . 1856–1860,* p. O8, which show similar trends for Sogn as a whole.

14 In the 1855 census for Balestrand, farm family members constituted 44.7% of the population; 55.3% of the people were landless folk. These figures omit servants, since their backgrounds cannot be adequately determined. Because most servants were cotters' children, however, it seems safe to say that up to 1879, farm members were more likely to emigrate than their landless counterparts.

15 Sunde, "Ei Undersøking," p. 132. See also Stein Tveite, *Jord og Gjerning – Trekk av Norsk Landbruk i 150 År* (Christiansand, 1959), p. 45.

16 Daniel Dypevig, "Husmannsvesenet i Numedal," *Norsk Geografisk Tidsskrift,* 14 (1954):394.

17 Andres A. Svalestuen, *Tinns Emigrasjons Historie, 1837–1907: En Undersøkelse med Særlig Vekt på den Demografiske, Økonomiske og Sosiale Bakgrunn for Amerikafarten, og en Statistik Analyse av Selve Utvandringen* (Oslo, 1972), pp. 183–87.

18 Ibid., p. 211; Semmingsen, *Veien Mot Vest,* 1:260–61. Currency values were taken from George T. Flom, *A History of Norwegian Immigration to the United States* (Iowa City, Iowa, 1909), pp. 223–25. See also Svalestuen, "Om den Regionale Spreiinga," p. 82. This pattern was not limited to Norway. For Swedish examples see Hans Norman, *Från Bergslagen till Nordamerika: Studier i Migrationsmöster, Social Rörlighet och Demografisk Struktur med Utgångspunkt från Örebro län 1851–1915* (Uppsala, 1974), pp. 83–84; Robert C. Ostergren, "Rättvik to Isanti: A Community Transplanted" (Ph.D. diss., University of Minnesota, 1976), p. 51; and John G. Rice and Robert C. Ostergren, "The Decision to Emigrate: A Study in Diffusion," *Geografiska Annaler,* 60 (1978):9.

19 Hjalmar Aarskog, "Gard og Grannesamfunn: Balestrand" (unpublished paper, Institutt for Samanliknande Kulturforskning, 1956), p. I8.

20 Svalestuen, *Tinns Emigrasjons Historie,* p. 211.

21 See also Tveite, *Jord og Gjerning,* p. 194. Just as in Balestrand, farmers'

children from Ullensaker in the eastern portion of Norway predominated in the migration. Largely unmarried and young, they moved because they had no prospect of taking over land. Elisabeth Koren and Arnfinn Engen, "Masseutvandringa frå Austlandet etter 1865," in Engen, *Utvandringa*, p. 105.

22 Johan Reinart Reiersen, *Pathfinder for Norwegian Emigrants*, trans. Frank G. Nelson (Northfield, Minn., 1981), p. 60, from the Norwegian, *Veiviser for Norske Emigranter* (Christiania, 1844).

23 *Beretning . . . 1851–1855*, pp. O11–O12.

24 Svalestuen, *Tinns Emigrasjons Historie*, p. 128.

25 Arnfinn Engen, "Slektinger, Yankees og Prepaid Tickets: Medverkande Årsaker til og Forhold Omkring Utvandringer," in Engen, *Utvandringa*, p. 170.

26 Semmingsen, *Veien Mot Vest*, 1:421. See also Svalestuen, *Tinns Emigrasjons Historie*, p. 205, which likewise notes how often letter writers used the argument of the better future for youth and children, an argument that was weighty for many.

27 Quoted from *Morgenbladet*, May 25, 1866, in Theodore C. Blegen, *Norwegian Migration to America*, vol. 1, *1825–1860* (Northfield, Minn., 1931), p. 174.

28 *Billed-Magazin*, June 26, January 2, 1869.

29 Theodore C. Blegen, *Land of Their Choice: The Immigrants Write Home* (Minneapolis, 1955), pp. 195–96. See also Jan Oldervoll, "Kva Hadde Befolkningveksten Å Seie for Utvandringa," in Engen, *Utvandringa*, which argues that the livelihood problem was the main consideration for migration.

30 *Beretning . . . 1846–1850*, p. O7.

31 *Beretning om Rigets Oeconomiske Tilstand i Aarene 1861–1865*, (Christiania, 1867), p. O8–O9; See also *Beretning . . . 1856–1860*, p. O8.

32 "Prestsberetning, Balestrand, 1861–1865 (official report).

33 Ibid.

34 Reiersen, *Veiviser for Norske Emigranter*, p. 61.

35 Blegen, *Land of Their Choice*, pp. 78, 268.

36 Svalestuen, *Tinns Emigrasjons Historie*, p. 180.

37 Ingrid Semmingsen, "Amerikaferd," in Engen, *Utvandringa*, p. 17.

38 Blegen, *Land of Their Choice*, p. 424.

39 Arnfinn Engen, "Fattigdom og Utferd," in Ingrid Semmingsen, ed., *Norges Kulturhistorie*, vol. 4, *Det Gjenjødte Norge* (Oslo, 1980), p. 86. A study of letters from immigrants from the region of Dovre shows that the greater availability of land in America and the greater access to, and higher wages for, labor were the primary reasons for emigration – in short, better conditions. Engen, "Slektninger, Yankees og Prepaid Tickets," p. 108.

40 Reiersen, *Pathfinder for Norwegian Emigrants*, pp. 70, 71, 72, 107; *Beretning om Kongeriget Norges Økonomiske Tilstand i Aarene 1836–1840* (Christiania, 1843); *Beretning . . . 1856–1860*; Rene, *Historie om Utvandringen*,

pp. 153, 193; and Blegen, *Land of Their Choice*, pp. 23, 26, 69, 76, 86, 181, 182, 262, 263, 410, 411, 423, 424, 425. The unit of comparison was the Norwegian skilling, commonly equated in letters to the U.S. cent, though the skilling was actually worth slightly less. Annual wages are based on hundreds of skillings in relation to dollars, i.e., hundreds of cents. All are averages of the ranges reported for wages. See Flom, *History of Norwegian Immigration*, pp. 223–25. Note that men received even greater pay than women in the United States, a reflection of the value of male labor in America (to be discussed in Chapter 8).

41 J. A. Johnson Skipnæs, in *Billed-Magazin*, January 30, 1869.
42 Blegen, *Land of Their Choice*, p. 195; Reiersen, *Pathfinder for Norwegian Emigrants*, p. 71.
43 Reiersen, *Pathfinder for Norwegian Emigrants*, pp. 115–19.
44 *Beskrivelse over de Matrikulerede Eiendomme og Forslag til Ny Skatteskyld for Herredet iflg. Lov. ar 6 Juni 1863, No. 260, Balestrand* (Christiania, 1863).
45 See Rice and Ostergren, "The Decision to Emigrate," p. 9.
46 See Kjell Haarstad, "Utvandrerne fra Bygdene – Presset eller Lokket?" in Engen, *Utvandringa*, which argues that emigration led to mechaniza-tion rather than the reverse.
47 *Beretning . . . 1856–1860*, p. O8; Sunde, "Ei Undersøking," p. 50; Tveite, *Jord og Gjerning*, p. 196. The same complaints were common in other regions as well (Telemark, for instance), and Svalestuen argues that the whole system of høstingsbruk collapsed around 1875 because of depletion of labor sources from emigration. See *Tinns Emigrasjons Historie*, pp. 85–86, 258.
48 Aarskog, "Gard og Grannesamfunn," p. I18.
49 Ole O. Mølmen's diary, quoted in Luke M. Peterson, "Nineteenth Century Social Change in Lesja, Norway" (unpublished undergraduate paper, University of Minnesota, 1980), pp. 29–30.
50 *Beretning . . . 1856–1860*, p. O8; Aarskog, "Gard og Grannesamfunn," p. I25; Jon Laberg, *Balestrand, Bygd og Ætter* (Bergen, 1934), p. 20. See Table 19, which documents increasing migration to Balestrand.
51 Engen, "Slektinger, Yankees og Prepaid Tickets," p. 111; Sunde, "Ei Undersøking," p. 148.
52 See Arnfinn Engen, "Utvandringshistorie og Amerikabrev," in Engen, *Utvandringa*, pp. 158–70.
53 *Beretning . . . 1846–1850*, p. O7; *Beretning . . . 1851–1855*, pp. O8–O9; *Beretning . . . 1856–1860*, p. O8; "Prestsberetning, Balestrand, 1861–1865."
54 Cited in Svalestuen, "Om den Regionale Spreiinga," p. 63.
55 The official of Tinn's district reported by 1855 that emigrants were moving to relatives in America. See Svalestuen, *Tinns Emigrasjons Histo-rie*, p. 198. Likewise, the amtmann from Stavanger thought emigration was increasingly the result of kinship, as family ties across the sea became more widespread. See Semmingsen, *Veien Mot Vest*, 1:421.

56 Hjalmar Aarskog, "Frå Dagliglivet i Bygdene Våre, om lag 1850 og Fram Mot Vår Tid," *Balestrand Gard og Grend*, 1 (1973):34.
57 See Svalestuen, *Tinns Emigrasjons Historie*, p. 205; *Beretning . . . 1851– 1855*, p. O12.
58 Emigrant protocol from Bergen, 1874–1900; data for earlier times are difficult to find, but prepaid tickets undoubtedly played a role early in the emigration as well.
59 Sunde, "Ei Undersøking," p. 158; Svalestuen, *Tinns Emigrasjons Historie*, p. 208; Engen, "Slektninger, Yankees og Prepaid Tickets," p. 119.
60 Svalestuen, *Tinns Emigrasjons Historie*, p. 208. Tenant farmers were relatively rare in Balestrand, although in Tinn they and their families made up 13.5% of the population in 1835. Ibid., p. 40.
61 Earlier emigration throughout Norway was often based on family units (nuclear, extended, or husband–wife). In Tinn, for example, 55% of adult emigrants between 1837 and 1843 were married people, compared to only around 20% in the 1891–1907 period; likewise, about 75% was "family emigration" between 1837 and 1880, whereas only 50% could be characterized as such from 1881 to 1907. Svalestuen, *Tinns Emigrasjons Historie*, pp. 175–82; see also Koren and Engen, "Masseutvandringa," pp. 101–02; A. N. Kiær, *Oversigt over de Vigtigste Resultater af de Statistiske Tabeller Vedkommende Folkemængdens Bevegelse, 1866–1885* (Christiania, 1890), pp. 120–23; and especially Semmingsen, *Veien Mot Vest*, vols. 1–2. The Balestrand data are taken from church books.
62 The data are derived from family-reconstitution forms and church book emigration listings. Husbands often left wives and children behind in Norway while they accumulated capital in America to pay for passage. Research on families in Dovre who used this strategy indicates that men often left during periods of heavy emigration and were followed by their wives during the downswing of the peak period. The interval between the husband's emigration and his family's varied between one and twelve years, but most followed from one to three years later. Koren and Engen, "Masseutvandringa," pp. 92, 94, 99.
63 Church books for Balestrand; Arendahl Lutheran Church records; Ernest M. Maland, *Remember the Days of Old: The Centennial Saga of Arendahl Evangelical Lutheran Congregation, 1856–1956* (Decorah, Iowa, 1956), pp. 57–95.
64 Koren and Engen, "Masseutvandringa," p. 97. Near relatives were defined as spouse, child, parent, and sibling. See also Paul B. duChaillu, *The Land of the Midnight Sun* (London, 1881), p. 264, for a romantic illustration of the ties between kin in Norway and the Middle West.
65 Aarskog, "Gard og Grannesamfunn," p. I55; emigration records; Norway Grove Lutheran Church records. The whole group settled in the Norway Grove colony in Wisconsin; see the following chapters.
66 For definition of grends in Balestrand, see Aarskog, "Gard og Grannesamfunn," p. I14; and Hjalmar Aarskog, "Samkomer og Samarbeid i Grendi," *Balestrand Gard og Gard*, 2 (1974):9–11.

67 See Chapter 4 for a discussion of the difference between flatland and shoreline farms.

68 Although no letters from these areas have survived, Anders Ulvestad, who emigrated in 1850 from Vetlefjord, was regionally famous for his letters advocating emigration. See Hjalmar R. Holand, *De Norske Settlementers Historie: En Oversigt over den Norske Invↄ`dring til og Bebyggelse af Amerikas Nordvesten fra Amerikas Opdagelse til Indiankrigen in Noraʋesten med Bygde- og Navneregister* (Ephraim, Wis., 1909), p. 371.

69 See Aarskog, "Samkomer og Samarbeid i Grendi," p. 11, which emphasizes the importance of grend in social structure and interaction. Orvar Löfgren, in "Family and Household among Scandinavian Peasants: An Exploratory Essay," *Ethnologica Scandinavica*, (1974):46, has argued that the importance of kinship links should not be taken for granted, that in small villages the links between neighbors and within the farm household were equally important. Although links of kinship seem to have been more important in influencing emigration, the neighborhood was still a notable unit for providing information about American opportunities.

70 Not only in Balestrand did the farmer class predominate early in the emigration and then become less important in the later stages. See Svalestuen, "Om den Regionale Spreiinga," p. 82; Koren and Engen, "Masseutvandringa," p. 105; Dypevig, "Husmannsvesenet i Numedal," pp. 394, 409; Sunde, "Ei Undersøking," p. 129; Svalestuen, *Tinns Emigrasjons Historie*, pp. 183–87; and Tore Pryser, in Einar Haugen, Jørn Sandres, and Tore Pryser, "I Søkelyset: Det Norske Amerika," *Heimen*, 17 (1976–78):467.

71 Semmingsen, "Amerikaferd," pp. 13–16; Semmingsen, *Veien Mot Vest*, 1:255.

72 Tveite, *Jord og Gjerning*, p. 195.

73 See Svalestuen, *Tinns Emigrasjons Historie*, pp. 107–08, 234; see also Haarstad, "Utvandrerne fra Bygdene," p. 55.

74 duChaillu, *Midnight Sun*, pp. 232–33. Swedish research has argued that a "rural–industrial barrier" developed, so that few migrated from farming areas to nearby industrial places with work opportunities. Bjørn Rondahl contends that the barrier was a social-psychological predisposition among farm folk against industry, its work rhythms, its housing patterns, and so on. For critical examinations of this theory see Ingrid Semmingsen, "Nordisk Utvandringforskning," *Historisk Tidsskrift*, 56 (1977):152–53; Ingrid Semmingsen, "Nordic Research into Emigration," *Scandinavian Journal of History*, 3 (1978):115–17; and Sune Åkerman, "The Psychology of Migration," *American Studies in Scandinavia*, 8 (1972):49–51.

75 A similar pattern was noted in Tinn, Telemark, where most who left the region went to America. The internal migrants usually moved to neighboring communities and only a few went to the city. This finding has led Svalestuen to argue that areas in Norway with maximum emigra-

tion had relatively little internal migration, owing to a fear of the city and a preference for farming. See *Tinns Emigrasjons Historie*, pp. 60, 92.

76 While 77% of the emigrants from Mundal moved to America between 1889 and 1915, only 52% of those who left Vangsnes went to America. See Johannes Brynjulv Thue, "Utkant og Sentrum i Balestrand, 1860–1900," *Balestrand Gard og Grend*, 1 (1973):14–15.

77 Ingrid Semmingsen, *Norway to America: A History of the Migration* (Minneapolis, 1978), p. 40. Likewise, Mack Walker pointed out, in his study of German emigration (*Germany and the Emigration, 1816–1885* [Cambridge, Mass., 1964], p. 69), that emigrants were people who "went to America less to build something new than to regain and conserve something old." And John W. Briggs noted, in *An Italian Passage: Immigrants to Three American Cities, 1890–1930* (New Haven, Conn., 1978), p. 11, that "emigration constituted not so much a search for an alternative to the old order as a logical extension of it."

78 Government officials observed, for example, that drunkenness in Sogn was a contributing factor to emigration, since people wished to escape its deleterious effects and it created a dissatisfaction that "struck deep roots in Sogn." *Beretning . . . 1840–1845*, p. 143. See also *Beretning . . . 1846–1850*, p. O7. Those who took communion significantly more often than the average (i.e., those who took it eight times or more annually) were also more likely to move than those who did not take it at all. Of the frequent communicants, 8% left between 1860 and 1867, all but one from the cotter class, compared to only 2% of the noncommunicants. See Chapter 5.

79 R. Cole Harris, "The Simplification of Europe Overseas," *Annals of the AAG*, 67 (1977):469–83.

80 Quoted in Ohnstad, "Folketal og Utflytting," pp. 61–62.

Chapter 7. "They rushed from place to place"

1 *Amerika* (Chicago), July 29, 1885, quoted in Carlton C. Qualey, *Norwegian Settlement in the United States* (Northfield, Minn., 1938), pp. 12–13.

2 Waldemar Ager, "Norsk-Amerikansk Skjønliteratur," in Johannes B. Wist, ed., *Norsk-Amerikanernes Festskrift, 1914* (Decorah, Iowa, 1914), p. 292.

3 Gustav O. Sandro, *The Immigrants' Trek: A Detailed History of the Lake Hendricks Colony in Brookings County, South Dakota Territory, from 1873–1881* (Hendrick, Minn., 1929), pp. 7–8.

4 Lee letters, private collection.

5 See Kingsley Davis, "The Theory of Change and Response in Modern Demographic History," *Population Index*, 29 (1963):355.

6 Marcus Lee Hansen, *The Immigrant in American History*, ed. Arthur M. Schlesinger (Cambridge, Mass., 1940), pp. 60, 61.

7 Ibid., pp. 66, 76.

8   Ibid., pp. 71–72.
9   See Robert C. Ostergren, "Cultural Homogeneity and Population Sta-
     bility among Swedish Immigrants in Chisago County," *Minnesota Histo-*
     ry, 47 (1973):256.
10   For other examples of settlement based on nationality, see, for instance,
     ibid.; and John G. Rice, *Patterns of Ethnicity in a Minnesota County, 1880–*
     1905, University of Umeå, Department of Geography, Geographical
     Reports no. 4 (Umeå, Sweden, 1973).
11   *Hvad Jeg Har Oplevet,* p. 180, cited in Einar Haugen, *The Norwegian*
     Language in America: A Study in Bilingual Behavior (Philadelphia, 1953),
     1:39.
12   See Ingrid Semmingsen, *Veien Mot Vest: Utvandringen fra Norge til Amer-*
     ika, 1825–1865 (Oslo, 1941), 1:320–21; and Hansen, *The Immigrant in*
     American History, pp. 68, 71.
13   Haugen, *Norwegian Language,* 2:341; Semmingsen, *Veien Mot Vest,*
     1:269–70. See also Peter A. Munch, "Segregation and Assimilation of
     Norwegian Settlements in Wisconsin," *Norwegian-American Studies and*
     Records, 1954, pp. 102–40.
14   Swedish research has also emphasized these regional European com-
     munities in the rural settlement areas. Helge Nelson, in his extensive
     study of Swedish settlement in America (*The Swedes and the Swedish*
     Settlements in North America [Lund, 1943], p. 64), referred to such settle-
     ments as "kinsfolk colonies." See also Robert C. Ostergren, "Rättvik to
     Isanti: A Community Transplanted" (Ph.D. diss., University of Min-
     nesota, 1976), pp. 55, 59, which argues that ties of kinship were influen-
     tial in encouraging emigration from a Swedish parish. Of the sixteen
     emigrating households from the village of Övre Gärdsjo that followed
     the first between the advent of emigration in 1866 and 1883, all but two
     were associated with earlier migration through family or marriage ties.
     Moreover, 46.8% of the emigrants from the parish of Rättvik eventually
     settled in the community of countrymen in Isanti County, Minnesota.
     Similarly, three culture groups in the Dalesburg community of South
     Dakota originated from different areas of Sweden. Although they set-
     tled together, the groups lived in defined communities, and the divi-
     sions within the church to which they belonged reflected these dif-
     ferences. See Robert C. Ostergren, "Prairie Bound: Migration Patterns
     to a Swedish Settlement on the Dakota Frontier," in Frederick C.
     Luebke, ed., *Ethnicity on the Great Plains* (Lincoln, Nebr., 1980), pp. 73–
     91.
15   Haugen, *Norwegian Language,* 2:345. One man was even nicknamed
     Thomas Northman, probably because there were so few from Sogn in
     his community.
16   Ibid., pp. 348, 518.
17   Ibid., p. 539.
18   The amount of interaction among regional groups, of course, varied
     from area to area according to patterns of settlement. Areas that were

less densely peopled by Norwegians tended to have a higher degree of interaction. One force militating against such interaction, however, was language: Some dialect groups simply could not understand one another. A storekeeper from eastern Norway who lived in Spring Grove, Minnesota, had difficulty waiting on Sognings. Moreover, a common story in many settlement areas concerned the recent immigrant who, when he heard another dialect, did not realize it was Norwegian. See ibid., pp. 346, 347.

19 *Executive Documents of the State of Minnesota for the Year 1877* (Minneapolis, 1878), p. 533.

20 Svein Nilsson, in *Billed-Magazin*, January 29, 1870.

21 Quoted in Qualey, *Norwegian Settlement*, p. 98. Qualey argued that good land in the vicinity of the Norwegian settlements in Wisconsin was largely taken up by 1850.

22 *Daily Minnesotan*, June 17, 1854.

23 David T. Nelson, "Sognings in America," in Hans Lavik, ed., *Pacific Coast Sognalag 50 Year Jubilee, 1912–1962* (Tacoma, Wash., 1962), p. 73.

24 L. R. Moyer and O. G. Dale, eds., *History of Chippewa and Lac Qui Parle Counties, Minnesota: Their People, Industries, and Institutions* (Indianapolis, 1916), p. 175.

25 See Semmingsen, *Veien Mot Vest*, 1:263.

26 *Billed-Magazin*, August 7, 1869.

27 Hjalmar R. Holand, *De Norske Settlementers Historie: En Oversigt over den Norske Invandring til og Bebyggelse af Amerikas Nordvesten fra Amerikas Opdagelse til Indiankrigen i Nordvesten med Bygde- og Navneregister* (Ephraim, Wis., 1909), p. 372. Like later immigrants who arrived in settlements after most land was taken, earlier landed settlers also decided at times to join colonization groups, in order to acquire even larger tracts of land. A "lively migration" began in the 1850s, for example, from the Muskego, Wisconsin, settlement, once noted for its unhealthy climate. "Those who had gone on before sent back glowing reports of the wonderful prospects in the west," a resident noted. "'There one really finds America,' they said. As a consequence the migration fever grew strong. It looked for awhile as though everyone would sell out and go. It was not difficult to sell as the Germans had come into the neighborhood and were more than willing to buy and paid rather good prices." Theodore T. Nydahl, "The Early Norwegian Settlement of Goodhue County" (master's thesis, University of Minnesota, 1929), pp. 15, 29.

28 "Trondere i Goodhue County, Minnesota," *Trondelagets Aarbok* (1924):50.

29 *Valdris-Helsing*, 8 (1932):112.

30 Sandro, *The Immigrants' Trek*, pp. 5–6.

31 K. A. Rene, *Historie om Utvandringen fra Voss og Vossingene i Amerika, med Beskrivelse og Historie af Voss, Karter og Billeder* (Madison, Wis., 1930), p. 193; Nelson, "Sognings in America," p. 70.

32 Nelson, "Sognings in America," p. 71; Holand, *De Norske Settlementers Historie*, p. 124. Holand called Long Prairie the Sognings' "original home in America."

33 George T. Flom, *A History of Norwegian Immigration to the United States* (Iowa City, Iowa, 1909), p. 305. These early Sogning immigrants moved from the counties of Lærdal, Lyster, Hafslo, Leikanger, and Balestrand; later immigrations from Aurland (1845–46), Sogndal (1846), and Vik (1845) continued the Sogning influx.

34 Flom, *History of Norwegian Immigration*, p. 331; Holand, *De Norske Settlementers Historie*, p. 159. Eventually the lone Telemarking married a Sogning from Aardal.

35 *Madison, Dane County, and Surrounding Towns* (Madison, Wis., 1877), p. 253.

36 For descriptions of the early settlers in the Norway Grove–Spring Prairie settlement, see Flom, *History of Norwegian Immigration*, pp. 331–33, Holand, *De Norske Settlementers Historie*, pp. 160, 163, 662; *Madison, Dane County, and Surrounding Towns*, pp. 261, 383, 385, 564, 566, 567; *A History of Dane County, Wisconsin* (Chicago, 1880), pp. 1103–04, 1134, 1135; and *Biographical Review of Dane County, Wisconsin* (Chicago, 1893). See also Rasmus Sunde, "Ei Undersøking av Utvandring til Amerika frå Vik i Sogn, 1839–1915" (major thesis, Universitetet i Trondheim, 1974), p. 136; and Haugen, *Norwegian Language*, 2:608.

37 Flom, *History of Norwegian Immigration*, p. 333. See also Holand, *De Norske Settlementers Historie*, p. 159, which notes that Sjur Grinde and Erik Engesæther, both early immigrants from Leikanger, were prolific letter writers.

38 Similar behavior has been observed in other communities of different nationalities. Emigrants from Rättvik, Dalarna, Sweden, concentrated in Isanti County, Minnesota, so that 46.8% of all emigrants from Rättvik between 1864 and 1885 eventually settled there. Ostergren, "Rättvik to Isanti," p. 59.

39 Norway Grove church books; Spring Prairie church books; published plat maps, 1861, 1874.

40 Rene, *Historie om Utvandringen*, p. 304.

41 For similar arguments regarding the church as a central institution in the rural communities, see Rice, *Patterns of Ethnicity*, pp. 39–48; Ostergren, "Cultural Homogeneity and Population Stability"; and Jon Gjerde, "The Effect of Community on Migration: Three Minnesota Townships, 1885–1905," *Journal of Historical Geography*, 5 (1979):403–22.

42 *Spring Prairie Lutheran Church One Hundredth Anniversary, 1847–1947* (Madison, Wis., 1947); *En Kort Menihedshistorie Skrevet paa Opfording af Fest-Komiteen i Anledning af Norway Grove Menigheds Femtiaars-Fest* (n.p., 1899), p. 7.

43 Haugen, *Norwegian Language*, 2:348–49.

44 Taken from family-reconstitution forms derived from Norway Grove–Spring Prairie, Lodi, and Bonnet Prairie church books. The small sam-

ple of children born in the United States to Balestrand–Leikanger parents continued to conform to this pattern. Of seven such marriages concentrated in the 1870–74 period, four were among couples from Balestrand–Leikanger, one was to another Sogning, and two were to Norwegians of non-Sogning descent.

45 *En Kort Menihedshistorie . . . af Norway Grove*, p. 7. The Spring Prairie Hauge's church eventually was formed following these pietistic views.

46 A. E. Boyum's autobiography in Ernest M. Maland, *Remember the Days of Old: The Centennial Saga of Arendahl Evangelical Lutheran Congregation, 1856–1956* (Decorah, Iowa, 1956), pp. 99–101.

47 That Norway Grove remained the largest Balestrand–Leikanger settlement lends credence to Zelinsky's notion that ethnic homogeneity decreased with the westward spread of American settlement. Settlement in the Middle West was where "rural immigrant blocks seldom prevailed beyond the township scale, giving rise to intricately meshed mosaics." Wilber Zelinsky, *The Cultural Geography of the United States* (Englewood Cliffs, N.J., 1972), p. 26.

48 Holand, *De Norske Settlementers Historie*, pp. 446, 447. The earliest settlers (1847), in addition to the three Balestranders, were from Lærdal (two), Hafslo (two), and Lyster (one). H. O. Mosby, *Seventieth Anniversary of the Blue Earth Lutheran Church at Dell, Minn.* (n.p., 1931), pp. 6–7.

49 See Maland, *Remember the Days of Old*, p. 103.

50 Ibid., p. 10; Martin Ulvestad, *Nordmændene i Amerika, Deres Historie og Rekord* (Minneapolis, 1907), p. 80; Edward Van Dyke Robinson, *Early Economic Conditions and the Development of Agriculture in Minnesota* (Minneapolis, 1915), pp. 34–35. As the railroads reached the Mississippi at Prairie du Chien, Wisconsin, in 1857 and La Crosse, Wisconsin, in 1858, travel was facilitated.

51 Maland, *Remember the Days of Old*, pp. 12, 103–05.

52 Holand, *De Norske Settlementers Historie*, pp. 370–71; Maland, *Remember the Days of Old*, p. 7.

53 The poor church records of Arendahl place some constraints on analysis of the settlement.

54 Qualey, *Norwegian Settlement*, p. 115.

55 Holand, *De Norske Settlementers Historie*, p. 370.

56 See Maland, *Remember the Days of Old*, pp. 34–36, 102.

57 Ibid., pp. 8, 18, 19.

58 S. Theo Severtson, ed., *Eightieth Anniversary Year Book* [North Prairie Lutheran Church, Arendahl Township, Fillmore Co., Minn.] (Minneapolis, 1936), pp. 5–7.

59 Ibid., p. 10. Congregational conflict within Norwegian settlements was frequent. The completion of the very first Norwegian church building in the United States, characteristically enough, was delayed because of conflict within the congregation. See Semmingsen, *Veien Mot Vest*, 1:334.

60 Maland, *Remember the Days of Old*, p. 108.

61 Jon Gjerde, "The Development of Church Centered Communities

among European Immigrants: A Case Study of Three Minnesota Townships" (master's thesis, University of Minnesota, 1978).

62 Hauge's Norwegian Evangelical Lutheran Church records; Ulvestad,
Nordmændene i Amerika, p. 122.

63 Balestrand church books; Hauge's church books; Franklin Curtiss-
Wedge, *The History of Renville County, Minnesota* (Chicago, 1916), p. 362.

64 The records of Hauge's church, like those from Arendahl, are not as
complete as the Norway Grove records in specifying birthplace in Norway. Of the 118 foreign-born members, 19 Norwegian-born did not
have their location of birth specified. If any of these were Balestrand- or
Sogn-born, the percentages would have been higher.

65 Mrs. Anna S. Bossenecker correspondence, private collection.

66 Ibid.; Balestrand church books; Norway Grove church books; Arendahl
church books; Hauge's church books.

67 See Qualey, *Norwegian Settlement*, p. 146; Sandro, *The Immigrants' Trek*,
p. 24; and Maland, *Remember the Days of Old*, p. 36.

68 See David P. Gagen, "The Indivisibility of Land: A Microanalysis of the
System of Land Inheritance in Nineteenth Century Ontario," *Journal of
Economic History*, 36 (1976): 126–41. Gagen notes that estates were divided in what he calls the "Canadian system of inheritance" – the
division of estates, but not of land. This system was also practiced in
Balestrand and apparently in Balestrand-American communities as
well.

69 Gjerde, "Effect of Community on Migration," pp. 415–16.

70 Ibid., p. 417.

71 The same tendency was discovered in that the other churches for which
such comparisons could be made, those of Swedlanda in Palmyra
township. The standard migration rates standardize the age structures
so that intergroup comparisons are possible independent of age. The
method used was

$$Y = \frac{N_{0-9}X_{0-9} + N_{10-19}X_{10-19} + N_{20-29}X_{20-29} \cdots + N_{70-79}X_{70-79}}{N_{0-79}}$$

where Y is the standard migration rate for the subpopulation per 1,000,
N_{0-9} is the number of people in the total population aged 0 to 9, X_{0-9} is
the number of migrants per 1,000 in the subpopulation aged 0 to 9, and
so on, with N_{0-79} being the number of people in the total population.

72 Note that similar marriage patterns were also occurring among Balestranders in Norway Grove.

73 See also Ingolf Vogeler, "Ethnicity, Religion, and Farm Land Transfer
in Western Wisconsin," *Ecumene*, 7 (1975):6–13. Vogeler attempts to
show that land sales within community groups have been found to
exist from 1950 to the present in Wisconsin.

74 See A. Gordon Darroch, "Migrants in the Nineteenth Century:
Fugitives or Families in Motion?" *Journal of Family History*, 6 (1981):257–
77. See also Virginia Yans-McGlaughlin, *Family and Community: Italian
Immigrants in Buffalo, 1880–1930* (Ithaca, N.Y., 1971), pp. 78–80.

Chapter 8. "Norwegians . . . must learn anew"

1 Pauline Farseth and Theodore C. Blegen, trans. and ed., *Frontier Mother: The Letters of Gro Svendsen* (Northfield, Minn., 1950), p. 28.

2 Anthony Rud, *The Second Generation* (New York, 1928), p. 183.

3 Bernt Askevold, *Trang Vei* (Fergus Falls, Minn., 1899), p. 33.

4 Carlton C. Qualey, ed., "Seven American Letters to Valdres," *Norwegian American Studies,* 22 (1965):152.

5 Benjamin Horace Hibbard, *The History of Agriculture in Dane County, Wisconsin,* Economic and Political Science Series, vol. 1, no. 2 (Madison, Wis., 1904), p. 90.

6 Johan Reinart Reiersen, *Pathfinder for Norwegian Emigrants,* trans. Frank G. Nelson (Northfield, Minn., 1981), pp. 71–72, from the Norwegian, *Veiviser for Norske Emigranter* (Christiania, 1844); Ingrid Semmingsen, *Veien Mot Vest: Utvandringen fra Norge til Amerika, 1825–1865* (Oslo, 1941), 1:286.

7 Gustav O. Sandro, *The Immigrants' Trek: A Detailed History of the Lake Hendricks Colony in Brookings County, South Dakota Territory, from 1873 to 1881* (Hendricks, Minn., 1929), p. 28.

8 Einar Haugen, *The Norwegian Language in America: A Study in Bilingual Behavior* (Philadelphia, 1953), 1:40–45.

9 Allan G. Bogue, *From Prairie to Cornbelt: Farming on the Illinois and Iowa Prairies in the Nineteenth Century* (Chicago, 1963), p. 238. See also Andres A. Svalestuen, *Tinns Emigrasjons Historie, 1837–1907: En Undersøkelse med Særlig Vekt på den Demografiske, Økonomiske og Sosiale Bakgrunn for Amerikafarten, og en Statistik Analyse av Selve Utvandringen* (Oslo, 1972), p. 155; and Theodore C. Blegen, *Land of Their Choice: The Immigrants Write Home* (Minneapolis, 1955), p. 185.

10 Svein Nilsson, *A Chronicler of Immigrant Life: Svein Nilsson's Articles in Billed-Magazin, 1868–1870,* trans. C. A. Clausen (Northfield, Minn., 1982), p. 25.

11 Fredrika Bremer, *Hemmen i den Nya Verlden: En Dagbok i Bref, Skrifna under Tvenne Års Resor i Norra Amerika och på Cuba* (Stockholm, 1853), 2:273.

12 The Andreas Atlas of 1874, the first plat of Fillmore County, shows original settlers in places other than those of their original claims. Poor judgment of land is the basis of Curti's explanation for smaller accumulations of wealth among Norwegians in Trempeleau County, Wisconsin. See Merle Curti, *The Making of an American Community* (Stanford, Calif., 1959), pp. 176–221. The rapid diffusion of knowledge about the advantages of the prairies noted here casts some doubt on Curti's conclusion.

13 Vienna township is used as a case study for the Norway Grove–Spring Prairie settlements. It was chosen because of the large Norwegian population, but also because it had a concentration of immigrants from Balestrand and Leikanger. Conclusions from the 1849 agricultural cen-

sus are particularly difficult because northern Dane County was enumerated not by township but by numbered administrative units, so that residents of each township must be inferred from succeeding censuses. The Arendahl and Hauge's church communities are closely represented by Arendahl and Camp townships, so no sample township is needed.

14 See Blegen, *Land of Their Choice*, pp. 38, 58, 66, 181, and 182, for letters that cited "high wages" in the years 1837, 1842, and 1843.

15 Gavin Wright, *The Political Economy of the Cotton South: Households, Markets, and Wealth in the Nineteenth Century* (New York, 1978), pp. 45, 46, 55. See also Bogue, *From Prairie to Cornbelt*, which notes the possibility of laborers' leaving before the harvest. "The thought of harvest wages," he writes, "was always linked with the worry that it might be impossible to obtain helpers when the crop was ready for sickle" (p. 159).

16 These circumstances explain why early immigrants often worked for Americans, those who had a greater ability to pay wages. See Blegen, *Land of Their Choice*, p. 86.

17 See Wright, *Political Economy of the Cotton South;* and Reiersen, *Pathfinder for Norwegian Emigrants.* Written 134 years apart, the two accounts give similar assessments of the relationship between labor within the family and the farm. Reiersen wrote, "It is still difficult to estimate how much land a settler can manage to bring under cultivation with his own labor, because this depends in part upon his own ability and in part upon how much help he can get from his family" (p. 107). Wright reiterated Reiersen's claim that farms were primarily limited to family labor, so that "the size of farms was largely determined by the acreage which the family could cultivate" (p. 47).

18 C. A. Clausen, ed., "Three America Letters to Lesja," *Norwegian American Records*, 23 (1967):72.

19 Bremer, *Hemmen i den Nya Verlden*, 2:273.

20 Blegen, *Land of Their Choice*, pp. 424–25.

21 Bogue, *From Prairie to Cornbelt*, pp. 123–24; Elisha W. Keyes, *History of Dane County* (Madison, Wis., 1906), 1:275; Hibbard, *Agriculture in Dane County*, p. 123.

22 Reiersen, *Pathfinder for Norwegian Emigrants*, pp. 124, 105.

23 Ibid., p. 127. See also Semmingsen, *Veien Mot Vest*, 1:127.

24 See John G. Rice, "The Role of Culture and Community in Frontier Prairie Farming," *Journal of Historical Geography*, 3 (1977):165.

25 Of the principal ethnocultural groups not considered here, the British settlers resembled the New Englanders in preference for corn whereas the German reflected the Norwegians' pattern in oats.

26 See Semmingsen, *Veien Mot Vest*, 1:294. Reiersen, in *Pathfinder for Norwegian Emigrants*, p. 111, noted that Americans did not weave their own cloth at home, so sheep were kept only by those who raised sheep for wool and made it a main business.

27 See Semmingsen, *Veien Mot Vest*, 1:294.

28 Helene Munch and Peter A. Munch, eds., *The Strange American Ways: Letters of Caja Munch from Wiota, Wisconsin, 1855–1859, with "An American Adventure" by Johan Storm Munch* (Carbondale, Ill., 1970), p. 25; Reiersen, *Veiviser for Norske Emigranter*, p. 110.

29 Hamlin Garland, *A Son of the Middle Border* (New York, 1917), p. 147.

30 O. E. Rølvaag, *Giants in the Earth* (New York, 1927), p. 110.

31 John Giffin Thompson, *The Rise and Decline of the Wheat Growing Industry in Wisconsin*, Economic and Political Science Series (Madison, Wis., 1909), p. 198. See also Bogue, *From Prairie to Cornbelt*, pp. 123–24; Hibbard, *Agriculture in Dane County*, p. 123; Keyes, *History of Dane County*, 1:275; and *Madison, Dane County, and Surrounding Towns* (Madison, Wis., 1877), p. 567.

32 Bogue, *From Prairie to Cornbelt*, p. 130. See also Johan Heinrich von Thünen, *Von Thünen's Isolated State: An English Edition of "Der Isolierte Staat,"* trans. Carla M. Wartenbery (Oxford, 1966), for his theory of intensity of land use in relation to cost of transportation.

33 Agricultural censuses enumerated output rather than acreage until 1879, when both were included. Comparisons would be better if acreage could be considered. Yet since fewer bushels of wheat than of the more prolific crops such as corn, oats, and potatoes were usually harvested per acre, the Norwegian penchant for wheat is probably understated.

34 Thompson, *Rise and Decline of the Wheat Growing Industry*, pp. 127, 128; *Report of the Commissioner of Agriculture*, United States, 1868, p. 18.

35 See Edward Van Dyke Robinson, *Early Economic Conditions and the Development of Agriculture in Minnesota* (Minneapolis, 1915), p. 57; and Keyes, *History of Dane County*, 1:275. A letter from 1854 in Blegen, *Land of Their Choice*, p. 278, noted the high prices and rich harvests.

36 Nilsson, *Chronicler of Immigrant Life*, p. 75. The immigrant inclination to grow wheat was not peculiar to Vienna township; many other microstudies have noted the tendency of the more recently arrived to be more devoted to wheat. For Wisconsin as a whole, Keyes noted that the heavy yields in the 1840s convinced Norwegians and Germans that no other crop was better. In Kandiyohi County, Minnesota, while wheat growing was predominant in both 1870 and 1880, Swedes and Norwegians were growing a larger percentage of wheat (compared to oats) than either old Americans or Irish (an immigrant group that had resided in the United States much longer than the Scandinavians). Finally, in Bremer and Hamilton Counties, Iowa, though there was little difference between foreign- and native-born farmers in 1880, a notable exception was the immigrants' preference for wheat. See Keyes, *History of Dane County*, 1:275; Rice "Culture and Community in Frontier Prairie Farming," p. 165; and Bogue, *From Prairie to Cornbelt*, p. 211.

37 Nilsson, *Chronicler of Immigrant Life*, p. 75.

38 See Chapter 4 on the use of the animal unit measure.

39 Reiersen, *Veiviser for Norske Emigranter*, p. 106.

40 *Transactions of the Wisconsin State Agricultural Society,* 1 (1851):152–53, quoted in Michael P. Conzen, *Frontier Farming in an Urban Shadow: The Influence of Madison's Proximity on the Agricultural Development of Blooming Grove, Wisconsin* (Madison, Wis., 1971), p. 166.

41 Keyes, *History of Dane County,* pp. 275–76.

42 *Wisconsin and Iowa Farmer and Northwestern Cultivator,* 2 (1850):216, quoted in Thompson, *Rise and Decline of the Wheat Growing Industry,* p. 22.

43 *Report of the Commissioner of Agriculture,* United States, 1868, p. 18. See also Thompson, *Rise and Decline of the Wheat Growing Industry,* p. 128.

44 Thompson, *Rise and Decline of the Wheat Growing Industry,* p. 198; agricultural census, Vienna township, 1879.

45 Conzen, *Frontier Farming,* p. 166.

46 Thompson, *Rise and Decline of the Wheat Growing Industry,* pp. 59, 88.

47 U.S. manuscript agricultural census, Vienna township, 1879.

48 Thompson, *Rise and Decline of the Wheat Growing Industry,* pp. 29–30; Conzen, *Frontier Farming,* p. 87. Robert Hugh Downes, in "Economic and Social Development of Kenosha County," *Transactions of the Wisconsin Academy of Sciences, Arts, and Letters,* 13 (1901):561, argued that it was ethnic characteristics that led the immigrants from Germany, England, and Ireland to remain in wheat farming while the native-born moved rapidly into dairying in Kenosha County.

49 Reiersen, *Pathfinder for Norwegian Emigrants,* p. 124.

50 *Transactions of the State Agricultural Society,* 1879–80, cited in Thompson, *Rise and Decline of the Wheat Growing Industry,* p. 124.

51 Terry G. Jordan, *German Seed in Texas Soil: Immigrant Farmers in Nineteenth-Century Texas* (Austin, Tex., 1966), p. 199; Bradley H. Baltensperger, "Agricultural Change among Nebraska Immigrants, 1880–1900," in Frederick C. Luebke, ed., *Ethnicity on the Great Plains* (Lincoln, Nebr., 1980), pp. 170–89.

52 Since the residents of Arendahl township were almost totally Norwegian-born, Fremont township, similar in geographical attributes but dominated by the American-born, was chosen for purposes of comparison.

53 Robinson, *Early Economic Conditions,* pp. 60, 81.

54 The Minnesota settlements experienced a transition from wheat farming to diversification similar to that traced in Wisconsin. Microanalysis is not possible for Arendahl and Camp townships, however, since the 1889 agricultural census was destroyed by fire and the one taken in 1899 was discarded. Later censuses are not yet available.

55 Johan Enander, "Farmeren," *Svenska Journalen-Tribunen,* September 5, 1894, p. 2, quoted in Dorothy Burton Skårdal, *The Divided Heart: Scandinavian Immigrant Experience through Literary Sources* (Lincoln, Nebr., 1974).

56 Nilsson, *Chronicler of Immigrant Life,* p. 99.

57 Reiersen, *Pathfinder for Norwegian Emigrants,* pp. 120, 72.

58 *Billed-Magazin,* February 6, 1869.

59 Haugen, *Norwegian Language,* 2:494, 520.

60 A similar pattern occurred among the urban Italian immigrants in Buffalo. Although their traditional work duties differed from those of Norwegian women, the Italian women's patterns of work remained similar after emigration. They did not work outside the home, and thus men were able to retain their cultural power as breadwinners. See Virginia Yans-McLaughlin, *Family and Community: Italian Immigrants in Buffalo, 1880–1930* (Ithaca, N.Y., 1971), pp. 180–217.

61 Foreign-born settlers not only from Norway but from other parts of Scandinavia and Germany apparently impressed their neighbors in their willingness to allow their womanfolk to work beside them in the fields. See Bogue, *From Prairie to Cornbelt,* pp. 236–37.

62 Reiersen, *Pathfinder for Norwegian Emigrants,* p. 107. Another observer, however, argued that the needs of pioneer conditions caused people not to "pay much attention to what was women's work or men's work. The main thing was to get done what lay at hand." Kristian Østergaard, *Danby Folk* (Cedar Falls, Iowa, n.d.), p. 11, quoted in Skårdal, *The Divided Heart,* p. 242.

63 L. M. Bothum, *En Historie fra Nybyggerlivet* (Dalton, Minn., 1915), pp. 104–05. Whereas haying was a job that was traditionally women's work, ploughing was more firmly defined as male work. Some references of German immigrants, however, point to heavy field work done by women. One observer from Texas said in about 1870 that he had "actually seen a German woman holding the plow drawn by six pair of cattle while her little son, not more than nine or ten years old, drove the same"; he added, "It is a common thing among these people to behold women toiling in the fields." An Englishman, some years later, wrote that "the women have been afield, ploughing with the reins round their neck and the plough handles grasped in their strong hands." John Ise's biography of his German immigrant mother in western Kansas (*Sod and Stubble*) noted that she worked side by side with her husband; as the farm prospered, care of the kitchen garden and much of the care for cattle, pigs, and poultry remained in her hands. Likewise, pioneering women in a German settlement called Heartland worked all day in the fields before coming home to bake bread, even though the practice ran counter to the attitude in American agriculture at the time about appropriate women's work. See Jordan, *German Seed,* p. 185; Robert W. Smuts, *Women and Work in America* (New York, 1959), p. 7; and Sonya Salamon and Ann Mackey Keim, "Land Ownership and Women's Power in a Midwestern Farming Community," *Journal of Marriage and the Family,* 41 (1979):112.

64 Reierson, *Pathfinder for Norwegian Emigrants,* p. 107.

65 Ester Boserup, *Women's Role in Economic Development* (London, 1970), pp. 32, 33, 53, 56.

66 Gracia Grindal, "Linka's Sketchbook: A Personal View of the Nor-
    wegian Synod" (paper presented at the Scandinavian Immigration
    Conference, Decorah, Iowa, October 30, 1981).
67 Bogue, *From Prairie to Cornbelt*, pp. 253–56. Evidence that cows "re-
    mained the special province of women," as they had in Norway, is seen
    in the names given the cattle by women. See Haugen, *Norwegian Lan-
    guage*, 1:216.
68 H. Arnold Barton, "Scandinavian Immigrant Women's Encounter with
    America," *Swedish Pioneer Historical Quarterly*, 25 (1974):39. See also
    Smuts, *Women and Work*, p. 7.
69 Blegen, *Land of Their Choice*, pp. 69, 76, 424–25.
70 Ole Rynning, "Ole Rynning's True Account of America," trans. The-
    odore C. Blegen, *Minnesota History Bulletin*, 2 (1917):261, from the Nor-
    wegian, *Sandfærdig Beretning om Amerika til Oplysning og Nytte for Bonde
    og Menigmænd* (Christiania, 1838). See also Reiersen, *Pathfinder for Nor-
    wegian Emigrants*, p. 121: "For our females there is domestic service
    everywhere, especially with the native American families. This work is
    exclusively indoors; the men do all outdoor work, including milking
    and birthing calves. Because the American way of life calls for hot food
    three times a day . . . the women folk have enough to do with all the
    cooking, cleaning, washing, and scouring."
71 Blegen, *Land of Their Choice*, p. 423.
72 Willa Cather, in *My Ántonia* (Boston, 1918), p. 227, noted that the wages
    of Swedish and Bohemian servants in Nebraska towns went to aid their
    fathers' farms. Fathers born in Pennsylvania or Virginia, on the other
    hand, would not let their daughters go into service, a distinction that of
    course led to a greater prosperity among the immigrants. See also
    Smuts, *Women and Work*, p. 9; Joan W. Scott and Louise A. Tilly,
    "Women's Work and the Family in Nineteenth Century Europe," *Com-
    parative Studies in Society and History*, 17 (1975):55; and Bengt Ankarloo,
    "Agriculture and Women's Work: Directions of Change in the West,
    1700–1900," *Journal of Family History*, 4 (1979):111–20.
73 Blegen, *Land of Their Choice*, p. 26.
74 Rynning, "Ole Rynning's True Account of America," p. 254.
75 Reiersen, *Pathfinder for Norwegian Emigrants*, p. 107.
76 Gunnar Urtegaard, ed., " 'Og Huen Takes Ikke av Hovedet for Noget
    Menneske,' " *Tidsskrift Utgjeve af Historielaget for Sogn*, 27 (1981):73.
77 Munch and Munch, *The Strange American Way*, p. 73.
78 Quoted in Bogue, *From Prairie to Cornbelt*, p. 238.
79 O. E. Rølvaag, *Amerika-Breve* (Minneapolis, 1912), pp. 12–13, 42–43
    (Rølvaag's italics).
80 Boserup, *Women's Role in Economic Development*, p. 31.
81 Lee letters. Haugen, in *Norwegian Language*, 1:219, noted that a prime
    factor in the disappearance of Norwegian names for cows was the
    growth of industrial dairying. Men took over the barn chores and the

breeds became standarized; the cow was no longer in the immediate care of the woman and not in the same sense a member of the family.

82 Østergaard, *Danby Folk*, p. 11.

83 Bothum, *En Historie fra Nybyggerlivet*, pp. 104–05. For the changing work roles of German women immigrants see Oscar F. Hoffman, "Cultural Change in a Rural Wisconsin Ethnic Island," *Rural Sociology*, 14 (1949):47–48; and Salamon and Keim, "Land Ownership and Women's Power," p. 113.

84 *Chronicler of Immigrant Life*, p. 36.

Chapter 9. "There is good moral fiber in the sons of the mountains"

1 *Giants in the Earth* (New York, 1927), p. 224.

2 *Peder Victorious* (New York, 1929), pp. 20–48.

3 The church records for Norway Grove are more complete than those for the other Balestrand settlement areas and are the only ones that can be adequately examined for data concerning marriage age.

4 The marriage age for those born in the United States was lower than for the Norwegian-born people in Norway Grove. This difference, no doubt, was largely because the average U.S.-born person at risk was younger. In 1871, for example, the oldest American-born Norwegian could only be twenty-seven years old. Even at the end of the period examined, however, when marriage partners were predominantly born in the United States, the median age of marriage was older among those who had emigrated.

Age at first marriage of American-born in Norway Grove and Spring Prairie

	Men		Women		
	Median	Mean	Median	Mean	N
1869–71	22	22.2	20	20.3	6
1872–74	24	24.7	21	21.4	14
1875–77	25	25.9	22	21.7	19
1878–80	23	25.1	21	21.6	8
1881–83	25	25.9	25	24.4	12
1884–86	26	26.8	24	24.6	35
1887–89	28	28.2	25	23.8	22
1890–92	26	26.9	23	24.2	27
1893–96	27	27.4	23	23.2	42

5   Ernest M. Maland, *Remember the Days of Old: The Centennial Saga of Arendahl Evangelical Lutheran Congregation, 1856–1956* (Decorah, Iowa, 1956), p. 31. Einar Haugen, in *The Norwegian Language in America: A Study in Bilingual Behavior* (Philadelphia, 1953), 2:514, notes a similar pattern in Coon Valley, Wisconsin. Guests were invited orally to both weddings and funerals. "But one thing here in Coon Valley," the informant added, "was that I never heard of such big drinking parties after funerals as they had in some places."

6   Quoted in Theodore C. Blegen, *Land of Their Choice: The Immigrants Write Home* (Minneapolis, 1955), p. 268.

7   Svein Nilsson, *A Chronicler of Immigrant Life: Svein Nilsson's Articles in Billed-Magazin, 1868–1870*, trans. C. A. Clausen (Northfield, Minn., 1982), p. 155.

8   See Michael P. Conzen, *Frontier Farming in an Urban Shadow: The Influence of Madison's Proximity on the Agricultural Development of Blooming Grove, Wisconsin* (Madison, Wis., 1971), for a general overview of the demographic development of another township in Dane County that progressed similarly.

9   Hans Norman, *Från Bergslagen till Nordamerika: Studier i Migrationsmönster, Social Rörlighet och Demografisk Struktur med Utgångspunkt från Örebro län 1851–1915* (Uppsala, 1974), pp. 271–87. See also Harald Runblom and Hans Norman, eds., *From Sweden to America: A History of the Migration* (Uppsala, 1976), pp. 284–90, for an English summary of Norman's argument.

10   By using the standardized child/woman ratios it is possible to compare the different age structures in the United States and Norway. Using simple child/married woman ratios with different age structures could result in misleading measures, as has probably happened in Norman's work. The more mature Swedish population probably registered more children aged 0–4 than the younger Swedish settlements in the United States. See Tamara A. Hareven and Maris A. Vinovskis, "Patterns of Childbearing in Nineteenth Century America: The Determinants of Marital Fertility in Five Massachusetts Towns in 1880," in Hareven and Vinovskis, eds., *Family and Population in Nineteenth Century America* (Stanford, Calif., 1978), pp. 85–125, for a description of the procedure and use of standardized child/woman ratios.

11   *Home Missionary and American Pastor's Journal*, 23 (1850):120, cited in Marcus Lee Hansen, *The Immigrant in American History*, ed. Arthur M. Schlesinger (Cambridge, Mass., 1940), pp. 113–14.

12   Frederika Bremer, *Hemmen i den Nya Verlden: En Dagbok i Bref, Skrifna under Tvenne Års Resor i Norra Amerika och på Cuba* (Stockholm, 1853), 2:273. See also Helene Munch and Peter A. Munch, eds., *The Strange American Way: Letters of Caja Munch from Wiota, Wisconsin, 1855–1859, with "An American Adventure" by Johan Storm Munch* (Carbondale, Ill., 1970), which describes the trials and tribulations of a minister of the

state church of Norway who attempted to organize and maintain a frontier Norwegian church in Wisconsin.

13 *Emigranten,* September 25, 1852. See also Ingrid Semmingsen, *Veien Mot Vest: Utvandringen fra Norge til Amerika, 1825–1865* (Oslo, 1941), 1:321–22.

14 The Hauges church in Camp township did not have records adequate for comparisons. The figures following are therefore based on Arendahl and especially Norway Grove. The illegitimacy ratios, i.e., illegitimate births as a percentage of total births, when compared between populations, can be misleading. In a population with few unmarried women, such as Norwegian immigrant settlements in the United States, the illegitimacy ratio might be lower than in areas with many unmarried, such as Norway, even though the illegitimacy rates for women at risk are identical. Illegitimacy rates – the number of illegitimate births per thousand unmarried women of childbearing age standardized for the age distribution – are the best measure for comparison, but are unavailable from the existing data. A substitute used by Sundt is the relationship between marriages that were finalized and marriages that were not (represented in illegitimate births). Clearly, from comparing the data, illegitimacy rates were lower in the American settlements than in Norway. See Sølvi Sogner, "Illegitimacy in Old Rural Society: Some Reflections on the Problem Arising from Two Norwegian Family-Reconstitution Studies," in Sune Åkerman, Hans Christian Johansen, and David Gaunt, eds., *Chance and Change: Social and Economic Studies in Historial Demography in the Baltic Area* (Odense, Denmark, 1978), pp. 61–62; and Edward Shorter, John Knodel, and Etienne van de Walle, "The Decline of Non-Marital Fertility in Europe, 1880–1940," *Population Studies,* 25 (1971):379–83.

15 The incidence of prenuptially conceived first births was actually more common among young brides than among their older counterparts. From earliest settlement through the mid-1870s, for example, 42.7% of brides aged 15–19 ($N = 14$) and 48.1% of those aged 20–24 ($N = 27$) were with child at marriage, a clear indication of sexual experiences at an age much below that usual in Balestrand. One might expect the interval between birth of prenuptially conceived children and marriage to lessen as legitimate first births in marriage increased. No patterns of change occurred, however. The wife was within three months of delivery when the wedding took place in 17 of the 54 Norway Grove marriages. Yet the incidence of marriage when birth was imminent in Norway Grove varied from 9.1% to 17.9% to 7.7% and back to 16.7% in successive time periods (see table). The small sample in Arendahl precludes examination for any such pattern. Pastors in Norway Grove and Arendahl failed to list truloving (engagement) dates, which would have better illuminated the practices of premarital sexuality in relation to Balestrand.

Span of months between marriage and birth in Norway Grove

	0–3		3–6		6–8		8–9		9+	
	N	% of all mar- riages	N	% of all mar- riages	N	% of all mar- riages	N	% of all mar- riages	N	% of all mar- riages
1850–59	3	9.1	5	15.2	3	9.1	3	9.1	19	57.6
1860–69	7	17.9	5	12.8	2	5.1	4	10.2	20	51.3
1870–79	3	7.7	5	12.8	3	7.7	3	7.7	22	56.4
1880–89	3	16.7	1	5.5	1	5.5	1	5.5	12	66.7
1890–96	1	9.1	1	9.1	0	0	0	0	9	81.2

16 Note that the farmers, who were the earlier immigrants, saw their offspring married in the earlier stages of settlement. The cotters, on the other hand, dominated the later periods; this change explains the bulge in illegitimate births later in the settlement, when one would expect a decline.

17 *100th Anniversary – Norway Grove Lutheran Church, 1847–1947* (Madison, Wis., 1947), p. 15.

18 Community cleavage, similar to that which occurred in Norway, developed in Norway Grove and Spring Prairie. The church history noted that some did change their ways, but the pastor's pressure led others merely to hate him for it. *Spring Prairie Lutheran Church One Hundredth Anniversary, 1847–1947* (Madison, Wis., 1947).

19 Nilsson, *Chronicler of Immigrant Life*, p. 21.

20 Nilsson, in *Billed-Magazin*, March 6, 1869.

21 Ibid., November 27, 1869.

22 Nilsson, *Chronicler of Immigrant Life*, p. 76.

23 A. N. Kiær, *Sedelighedstilstander Blandt Vore Norske Landsmænd i Amerika* (Christiania, 1903), p. 5. This survey was taken by the Herværende Centralstyre for de Norske Sedilighedsforeninger in order to compare the differences between Norway and Norwegian-American settlements. Note that the dates given for the end of night courting are later than those I have cited elsewhere, perhaps because later settlements in Minnesota and South Dakota were studied in the survey.

24 Ibid.

25 The question asked was: Does it happen that married people have children shortly after marriage?

26 Kiær, *Sedelighedstilstander*, pp. 3, 4.

27 Ibid., pp. 5–6, 7.

28 Quoted by Nilsson, *Chronicler of Immigrant Life*, p. 64.

29 Nilsson, in *Billed-Magazin*, March 6, 1869.

30 For work on fertility decline in the Upper Middle West see George W. Hill and James D. Tarver, "Indigenous Fertility in the Farm Population of Wisconsin, 1848–1948," *Rural Sociology*, 16 (1951):359–62; Douglas G. Marshall, "The Decline in Farm Fertility and Its Relationship to Nationality and Religious Background," *Rural Sociology*, 15 (1950):42–49; Richard Easterlin, "Population Change and Farm Settlement in the Northern United States," *Journal of Economic History*, 36 (1976):45–83; and George W. Hill and Harald T. Christensen, "Some Factors in Family Fertility among Selected Wisconsin Farmers," *Sociological Review*, 7 (1942):498–504.

31 *Billed-Magazin*, January 9, 1869.

32 Quoted in Daniel Scott Smith and Michael S. Hindus, "Premarital Pregnancy in America, 1640–1971: An Overview and Interpretation," *Journal of Interdisciplinary History*, 4 (1975):552.

33 Jon Laberg, *Balestrand, Bygd og Ætter* (Bergen, 1934), p. 146. As mentioned earlier, second marriages saw the first children named after the deceased spouses.

34 Even in Balestrand, however, naming-pattern changes were occurring throughout the nineteenth century. For one thing, around 1830 girls began to get male names with the feminine suffix. Between 1821 and 1870, for example, fifty-two girls were named Hansine, Jensine, Oline, and so on. In Lesja, Gudbrandsdal, there was an increasing use of multiple names rather than the traditional single name followed by the patronym. Single male names that had been dominant from around 1770 through the mid-nineteenth century showed a drop in usage from 1860 onward. Significantly, however, names for firstborn males were the most resistant to change. Laberg, *Balestrand*, p. 149; Luke M. Peterson, "Nineteenth Century Social Change in Lesja, Norway" (unpublished undergraduate paper, University of Minnesota, 1980), pp. 62, 66.

35 These naming customs were used throughout much of Norway and were generally honored in other settlements as well by the first generation. Haugen, *Norwegian Language*, 1:209.

36 Ibid.

37 As in Balestrand, girls were increasingly given two names, another break from past experience. See ibid., p. 211. In addition to names of American origin, some children received names reflecting a concern about national events – such as John Brown Olson, born in Arendahl in 1859.

38 See ibid., 2:495; and Kiær, *Sedelighedstilstander*, pp. 6–7.

39 1900 manuscript population census, Arendahl township.

40 Haugen, *Norwegian Language*, 1:46, 94. See also ibid., pp. 40–45, 77–87, and 95, for further examination of loan words on the farm.

41 Blegen, *Land of Their Choice*, p. 392.

42 Munch and Munch, *The Strange American Way*, p. 73.

43 Blegen, *Land of Their Choice*, pp. 306–07.

44 H. Arnold Barton, ed., *Letters from the Promised Land: Swedes in America, 1840–1914* (Minneapolis, 1980), p. 324.

45 Maland, *Remember the Days of Old*, pp. 39–40.

46 Ibid., pp. 41–46.

47 A letter from 1860 quoted in Blegen, *Land of Their Choice*, p. 424. Letters written by women also clearly reiterated this preference for American work patterns. See Chapter 8.

48 Hansen, *The Immigrant in American History*, p. 92.

Chapter 10. Conclusion

1 Theodore C. Blegen, *Norwegian Migration to America*, vol. 2, *The American Transition* (Northfield, Minn., 1940), p. 590; Dorothy Burton Skårdal, *The Divided Heart: Scandinavian Immigrant Experience through Literary Sources* (Lincoln, Nebr., 1974), p. 30.

2 Hans Anderson Foss, *Husmandsgutten: En Fortælling fra Sigdal* (Decorah, Iowa, 1889).

3 Waldemar Ager, "Vor Kulturelle Muligheter,"reprinted in Ager, *Cultural Pluralism vs. Assimilation* (Northfield, Minn., 1981), pp. 47, 49.

4 See R. Cole Harris, "The Simplification of Europe Overseas," *Annals of the AAG*, 67 (1977):469–83.

5 See Virginia Yans-McLaughlin, *Family and Community: Italian Immigrants in Buffalo, 1880–1930* (Ithaca, N.Y., 1971), p. 22; Lloyd I. Rudolph and Susanne Hoeber Rudolph, *The Modernity of Tradition* (Chicago, 1967), pp. 1–14; and Joan W. Scott and Louise A. Tilly, "Women's Work and the Family in Nineteenth Century Europe," *Comparative Studies in Society and History*, 17 (1975):42.

6 See Peter A. Munch, "Segregation and Assimilation of Norwegian Settlements in Wisconsin," *Norwegian-American Studies and Records*, 1954, p. 105; and Robert C. Ostergren, "Rättvik to Isanti: A Community Transplanted" (Ph.D. diss., University of Minnesota, 1976), p. 140.

7 Eilert Sundt, *Om Sædeligheds-Tilstanden i Norge* (Christiania, 1857; reprint, Oslo, 1976), pp. 64, 66.

8 See A. N. Kiær, *Oversigt over de Vigtigste Resultater af de Statistiske Tabeller Vedkommende Folkemængdens Bevegelse, 1866–1885* (Christiania, 1890), p. 87, for European examples. See also Edward Shorter, John Knodel, and Etienne van de Walle, "The Decline of Non-Marital Fertility in Europe, 1880–1940," *Population Studies* 25 (1971):375–93.

9 Palle Ove Christiansen, "Peasant Adaptation to Bourgeois Culture? Class Formation and Cultural Redefinition to the Danish Countryside," *Ethnologica Scandinavica*, 1978, p. 133. See also Palle Ove Christiansen, "The Household in the Local Setting: A Study of Peasant Stratification," in Sune Åkerman, Hans Christian Johansen, and David Gaunt, eds., *Chance and Change: Social and Economic Studies in Historical Demography in the Baltic Area* (Odense, Denmark, 1978), p. 58; and Börje Hans-

sen, "The Oicological Approach," in Åkerman, Johansen, and Gaunt, *Chance and Change,* pp. 153–54.

10 Christiansen, "Peasant Adaptation to Bourgeois Culture?" p. 132.

11 For a Swedish example see Robert C. Ostergren, "Kinship Network Dispersion and Migration: A Nineteenth Century Swedish Example" (paper presented to the Social Science History Association, 1981), p. 20.

12 See Elaine M. Bjorklund, "Ideology and Culture Exemplified in Southwestern Michigan," *Annals of the AAG,* 54 (1964):227–41.

A note on secondary sources

The massive trans-Atlantic migration to America in the nineteenth and early twentieth centuries has been a subject of research and comment for over a century, and the shifting historiographical winds have created a diverse and frequently tendentious field of study. The earliest works in the United States, often undertaken by amateur authors representing their own ethnic groups, tended to be filiopietistic and characteristically celebrated the integration of each nationality into American life. European scholars initially ignored emigration, since it revealed a sign of national weakness; when they did study it, they often were more concerned with the faults of migration policy than with the emigrants themselves. As immigration increased in the early twentieth century, government commissions and professional scholars in the United States also examined the phenomenon. Though many academics were confident that the frontier or the city would create a melting pot in America, others perceived the immigrant as a threat. The forty-volume Dillingham Commission Report, for example, published in 1911 and replete with its own a priori judgments, concluded that the "new" immigrants from eastern and southern Europe were not as desirable as their earlier counterparts from northern and western Europe. Partly as a result of these findings and the concern they evoked, the open doors to America were largely closed to immigrants in the 1920s; thus an era of widespread immigration into the United States ended.

In spite of a long history of concern about immigration, a concern initially expressed primarily by sociologists and economists, the social history of the great migration across the Atlantic in the nineteenth and early twentieth centuries came relatively late to the field. While European researchers concentrated on the causes of the emigration and American policy makers were interested in the national results of immigration, very few investigations dealt with the migrants themselves. Accordingly, such topics as the relationship between cycles of business activity and migration have been investigated by economists and economic historians for nearly eighty years (Harry Jerome, *Migration and Business Cycles* [New York: National Bureau of Economic Research, 1926]; Dorothy Swaine Thomas, *Social and Economic Aspects of Swedish Population Movements, 1750–1933* [New York: Macmillan, 1941]; Brinley Thomas, *Migration and Economic Growth: A Study of Great Britain and the Atlantic Economy* [Cambridge: Cambridge University Press, 1954]).

Although social historians, sympathetic with the immigrant yet confident of his or her ultimate assimilation, did complete a number of significant monographs before World War II, they often concentrated on the institutions of immigrant life rather than its social development (Marcus Lee Hansen, *The Atlantic Migration, 1607–1860: A History of the Continuing Settlement of the United States*, ed. Arthur M. Schlesinger [Cambridge, Mass.: Harvard University Press, 1940]; Marcus Lee Hansen, *The Immigrant in American History*, ed. Arthur M. Schlesinger [Cambridge, Mass.: Harvard University Press, 1940]; Theodore C. Blegen, *Norwegian Migration to America*, vol. 1, *1825–1860*, vol. 2, *The American Transition* [Northfield, Minn.: Norwegian American Historical Association, 1931–40]; Ingrid Semmingsen, *Veien Mot Vest: Utvandringen fra Norge til Amerika, 1825–1865* [Oslo: Aschehoug, 1941]; George M. Stephenson, *The Religious Aspects of Swedish Immigrations: A Study of Immigrant Churches* [Minneapolis: University of Minnesota Press, 1932]; Carl Wittke, *We Who Build America: The Saga of the Immigrant* [Englewood Cliffs, N.J.: Prentice-Hall, 1939]; Oscar Handlin, *Boston's Immigrants: A Study of Acculturation* [Cambridge, Mass.: Harvard University Press, 1941]; Robert Ernst, *Immigrant Life in New York City, 1825–1863* [New York: King's Crown Press, 1949]).

Oscar Handlin's *The Uprooted,* published in 1951, served as a model for future social histories of immigration (*The Uprooted: The Epic Story of the Great Migrations That Made the American People* [Boston: Little, Brown]). Attempting to portray the effects of migration upon the migrants themselves, Handlin concluded that it was a "history of alienation." *The Uprooted*, in dramatic prose, recreated the pattern of an archetypal migration. Beginning his story in Europe, Handlin described the breakup of the peasant society and followed the immigrants through a frightful voyage to the strange land where they ultimately failed to escape alienation.

Despite the influence of Handlin's work, his conclusions soon faced harsh attacks. As an increasingly large group of social historians began to study the United States "from the bottom up" in the 1960s, they discovered a richness of life in the immigrant community. Transplanted Europeans did not appear alienated, nor did they necessarily seem to have been assimilated into American life as rapidly as previously had been assumed (Rudolph J. Vecoli, "Contadini in Chicago: A Critique of *The Uprooted*," *Journal of American History*, 51 [1964]:404–17; Virginia Yans-McLaughlin, *Family and Community: Italian Immigrants in Buffalo, 1880–1930* [Ithaca, N.Y.: Cornell University Press, 1971]). Other research in the past few decades, relying on traditional sources as well as novel uses of quantifiable material and an increasingly complex computer methodology, examined social mobility and varying ethnic strategies within immigrant communities (Josef Barton, *Peasants and Strangers: Italians, Rumanians, and Slovaks in an American City, 1890–1950* [Cambridge, Mass.: Harvard University Press, 1975]; John E. Bodnar, *Immigration and Industrialization: Ethnicity in an American Mill Town, 1870–1940* [Pittsburgh: University of Pittsburgh Press, 1977]; John W. Briggs, *An Italian Passage: Immigrants to Three American Cities, 1890–1930* [New Haven, Conn.: Yale University Press, 1978]; Kathleen Neils Conzen, *Immigrant Milwaukee, 1836–1860: Accommodation and Community in a Frontier City* [Cambridge, Mass.: Harvard University Press, 1976]; Stephan Thernstrom, *Poverty and Progress: Social Mobility in a Nineteenth Century City* [Cambridge, Mass.: Harvard University Press, 1964]).

As the social history of the trans-Atlantic migration was coming of age, yet another quantum leap was suggested in 1960 by Frank Thistlethwaite, who argued that the study of migration had to be expanded to include the background of the immigrants as well as their adaptation to the place of their arrival. Scholars, he contended, needed to introduce a new viewpoint "from neither the continent of origin nor from the principal country of reception . . . neither of emigrants nor immigrants, but of migrants, and to treat the process of migration as a complete sequence of experiences" ("Migration from Europe Overseas in the Nineteenth and Twentieth Centuries," in *XIe Congres International des Sciences Historiques*, Rapport V, [Uppsala, 1960]), pp. 32–60; see also Birgitta Odèn, "Emigrationen från Norden till Nordamerika under 1800-talet: Aktualla Forskningsuppgifter," *Historisk Tidsskrift* [Stockholm], 83 [1963]: 261–77).

Whereas Handlin's arguments elicited a broad range of comment and counterresearch, Thistlethwaite's new conceptions evoked praise but little substantive research along their lines. Those few scholars who have actually followed Thistlethwaite's suggestions have by and large studied regions in northern Europe and have examined primarily agricultural migrations to the United States (Dino Cinel, *From Italy to San Francisco: The Immigrant Experience* [Stanford, Calif.: Stanford University Press, 1982]; Robert C. Ostergren, "Rättvik to Isanti: A Community Transplanted" [Ph.D. diss., University of Minnesota, 1976]; Walter D. Kamphoefner, "Transplanted Westfalians: Persistence and Transformation of Socioeconomic and Cultural Patterns in the Northwest German Migration to Missouri" [Ph.D. diss., University of Missouri, Columbia, 1978]; Hans Norman, *Från Bergslagen till Nordamerika: Studier i Migrationsmönster, Social Rörlighet och Demografisk Struktur med Utgångspunkt från Örebro län 1851–1915* [Uppsala: Acta Universitatus Upsaliensis, 1974]); The Uppsala Project entitled "Sweden and America after 1860: Emigration, Remigration, Social and Political Debate" was a direct result of Thistlethwaite's challenge; it resulted in Harald Runblom and Hans Norman, eds. *From Sweden to America: A History of the Migration* (Minneapolis: University of Minnesota Press, 1976).

The Norwegian migration to the United States and the immigrants' adaptation to America have been rich areas of study on both sides of the Atlantic, but no study prior to this one has probed the migration process by following a circumscribed group of migrants from their point of departure to their new American home. Norwegian studies include Arnfinn Engen, ed., *Utvandringa – Det Store Oppbrotet* (Oslo: Det Norske Samlaget, 1978); Ingrid Semmingsen, *Norway to America: A History of the Migration*, trans. Einar Haugen (Minneapolis: University of Minnesota Press, 1978); Andres A. Svalestuen, *Tinns Emigrasjons Historie, 1837–1907: En Undersøkelse med Særlig Vekt på den Demografiske, Økonomiske og Sosiale Bakgrunn for Amerikafarten, og an Statistik Analyse av Selve Utvandringen* (Oslo: Universitetsforlaget, 1972); and Stein Tveite, "'Overbefolkning,' 'Befolkningspress,' og Vandring," in Sivert Langholm and Francis Sejerstad, eds., *Vandringer: Festskrift til Ingrid Semmingsen på 70-årsdagen 29. Mars 1980* (Oslo: Asckehoug, 1980), pp. 43–52.

American studies include Blegen's *Norwegian Migration to America*; Einar Haugen, *The Norwegian Language in America: A Study in Bilingual Behavior*, 2 vols. (Philadelphia: University of Pennsylvania Press, 1953); Carlton C. Qualey, *Norwegian Settlement in the United States* (Northfield, Minn.: Norwegian American Historical Association, 1938); Dorothy Burton Skårdal, *The Divided Heart: Scandinavian Immigrant Experience through Literary Sources* (Lincoln: University of Nebraska Press, 1974); and the periodic publications of the Norwegian-American Historical Association.

Given the quality of primary source materials in both Norway and the United States, such research has long been possible. But not until methods of historical demography and use of the computer were developed, and, perhaps more important, interest in the common European peasant or the ordinary American immigrant increased, were such monographs encouraged.

Recent research relying on similar methodologies, source materials, and concerns of social and economic development, moreover, though not directly concerned with the trans-Atlantic migration, has advanced the study of the European peasant or the American farmer. Theoretical work on economic change in Europe has been complemented by studies of specific historical incidences of protoindustrialization or other export-led growth (Ester Boserup, *The Conditions of Agricultural Growth: The Economics of Agrarian Change under Population Pressure* [Chicago: Aldine, 1965]; Ester Boserup, *Woman's Role in Economic Development* [London: Allen & Unwin, 1970]; Ester Boserup, *Population and Technology* [Chicago: University of Chicago Press, 1981]; A. V. Chayanov, *The Theory of Peasant Economy*, ed. Daniel Thorner, Basile Kerbley, and R. E. F. Smith [Homewood, Ill.: Irwin, 1966]; Colin Clark and Margaret Haswell, *The Economics of Subsistence Agriculture* [New York: St. Martin's Press, 1967]; Julian L. Simon, *The Economics of Population Growth* [Princeton, N.J.: Princeton University Press, 1977]; Rudolf Braun, "Early Industrialization and Demographic Change in the Canton of Zürich," in Charles Tilly, ed., *Historical Studies of Changing Fertility* [Princeton, N.J.: Princeton University Press, 1978], pp. 289–334; Edgar Hovland, Helge W. Nordvik, and Stein Tveite, "Proto-Industrialisation in Norway, 1750–1850: Fact or Fiction?" *Scandinavian Economic History Review*, 30 [1982]: 45–56; E. L. Jones, "Agricultural Origins of Industry," *Past and Present*, 11 [1968]: 58–71; David Levine, *Family Formation in an Age of Nascent Capitalism* [New York: Academic Press, 1977]; Peter Kriedte, Hans Medick, and Jürgen Schlumbohm, *Industrialization before Industrialization: Rural Industry in the Genesis of Capitalism*, trans. Beate Schempp [Cambridge: Cambridge University Press, 1981]; Hans Medick, "The Proto-Industrial Family Economy: The Structural Function of Household and Family during the Transition from Peasant Society to Industrial Capitalism," *Social History*, 3 [1976]: 291–315; Franklin F. Mendels, "Proto-industrialization: The First Phase of the Industrialization Process," *Journal of Economic History*, 32 [1972]: 241–61; Robert McC. Netting, *Balancing on an Alp: Ecological Change and Continuity in a Swiss Mountain Community* [Cambridge: Cambridge University

Press, 1981]; Eric R. Wolf and John W. Cole, *The Hidden Frontier: Ecology and Ethnicity in an Alpine Valley* [New York: Academic Press, 1974]).

Norwegian historians, influenced by an anti-Malthusian bias, have begun to question traditional arguments on the timing and nature of Norwegian agricultural growth in the late eighteenth and nineteenth centuries. While some have contended that agricultural productivity began to increase much earlier than was previously believed, others have argued that that growth was due not so much to the introduction of the potato as to grain or animal farming expansion. Counterresearch has in turn questioned both new interpretations (Ståle Dyrvik, Andreas Bjarne Fossen, Tore Grønlie, Edgar Hovland, Helge Nordvik, and Stein Tveite, *Norsk Økonomiske Historie, 1500–1970*, vol. 1, *1500–1850* [Bergen: Universitetsforlaget, 1979]; Kjell Haarstad, "Sult, Sykdom, Død: Et Teoretiske Problem Belyst med Empirisk Materiale," *Historisk Tidsskrift*, 59 [1980]: 1–25; John Herstad, "Folkevekst, Akerbruk og Kornimport i Norge Tidlig på 1800-tallet," ibid., 59 [1980]: 355–88; Edgar Hovland, "Åkerbruket i Norge i Begynnelsen av 1800-tallet," ibid., 57 [1978]: 331–46; Edgar Hovland, Ståle Dyrvik, Håvard Teigen, and Kåre Lunden, "Poteta og Folkeveksten i Noreg etter 1815: Fire Debattinlegg," ibid., 57 [1978]: 251–99; Kåre Lunden, "Potetdrykinga og den Raskare Folketalsvoksteren: Noreg frå 1815," ibid., 54 [1975]: 275–315; Kåre Lunden, "Poteter og Folketal," ibid., 56 [1977]: 207–20; Kåre Lunden, "Marknadsverdi i Forhold til Næringsverdi av Potater og Korn 1832–65," ibid., 59[1980]: 389–405; Håvard Teigen, "Poteta og Folkeveksten in Noreg, 1815–1865," ibid., 55 [1976]: 438–51; Hans Try, *Gardsskipnad og Bondenæring: Sørlandsk Jordbruk på 1800-talet* [Bergen: Universitetsforlaget, 1969]; Stein Tveite, *Jord og Gjerning – Trekk av Norsk Landbruk i 150 År* [Christiansand: Børdenes Forlag, 1959]; Fartein Valen-Sendstad, *Norske Landbruksredskaper 1800–1850 Årene* [Lillehammer: De Sandivske Samlinger, 1964]).

The question of economic development is inexorably tied to demographic change, and the population history of Norway has influenced and has been affected by new theories of changing agricultural productivity (Michael Drake, *Population and Society in Norway, 1735–1865* [Cambridge: Cambridge University Press, 1969]; Daniel Dypevig, "Husmannsvesenet i Numedal," *Norsk Geografisk Tidsskrift*, 14 [1954]: 369–463; Ståle Dyrvik, "Om Giftermål og Sosiale Normer: Ein Studie av Etne, 1715–1801," *Tidsskrift for Samfunnsforskning*, 11 [1970]: 285–300; Ståle Dyrvik, "Norway, 1660–1801: A Short Survey," *Scandinavian Economic History Review*, 20 [1972]:27–

44; Sølvi Sogner, *Folkevekst og Flytting: En Historisk-Demografisk Studie i 1700-Årenes Øst-Norge* [Oslo: Universitetsforlaget, 1979]; Gunnar Urtegaard, "Jordbruksdrift og Sosial Lagdeling i Balestrand frå 1500 til 1865" [major thesis, Universitetet i Bergen, 1980]).

Scandinavian ethnography has also become an increasingly fertile field on which immigration historians may draw. General studies include Halvard Bjørkvik, "The Old Norwegian Peasant Community: The Farm Territories," *Scandinavian Economic History Review*, 4 (1956): 33–61; Rigmor Frimannslund, "The Old Norwegian Peasant Community: Farm Community and Neighborhood Community," ibid., 4 (1956): 62–81; Andreas Holmsen, "The Old Norwegian Peasant Community: General Survey and Historical Introduction," ibid., 4 (1956): 17–32; Orvar Löfgren, "Historical Perspectives on Scandinavian Peasantries," *Annual Review of Anthropology*, 9 (1980): 187–215; Orvar Löfgren, "Family and Household among Scandinavian Peasants: An Exploratory Essay," *Ethnologica Scandinavica*, 1974, pp. 17–52; Kristofer Visted and Hilmar Stigum, *Vår Gamle Bondekultur* (Oslo: J. W. Cappelens Forlag, 1951); and Sune Åkerman, Hans Christian Johansen, and David Gaunt, eds., *Chance and Change: Social and Economic Studies in Historical Demography in the Baltic Area* (Odense, Denmark: Odense University Press, 1978).

Anthropologists and ethnologists interested in cultural change, have used the abundant and diverse source materials to flesh out conceptions of peasant life and provide a rich texture in pictures of the peasant community. Of particular interest is research on such varied fields as life within the different economic classes of Scandinavia (Palle Ove Christiansen, "Peasant Adaptation to Bourgeois Culture? Class Formation and Cultural Redefinition in the Danish Countryside," *Ethnologica Scandinavica*, 1978, pp. 98–152; Børje Hanssen, "Common Folk and Gentlefolk," ibid., 1973, pp. 67–100; Einar Hovdhaugen, *Husmannstida* [Oslo: Samlaget, 1975]; Christer Winberg, *Folkökning och Proletarisering: Kring den Sociala Strukturomvandlingen på Sveriges Landsbygd under den Agrara Revolutionen* [Göteborg: Universitet, Historiska Institutionen, 1975]); farm morphology (Arne Berg, *Norske Gardstun* [Oslo: Universitetsforlaget, 1968]; Knut Kolsrud, "The Settlement Process: A Norwegian Example," *Ethnologica Scandinavica*, 1980, pp. 83–101; Peter A. Munch, "Gard, the Norwegian Farm," *Rural Sociology*, 12 [1947]: 356–63]); courtship and marriage (Lizzie Carlsson, "Jag Giver Dig Min Dotter": *Trolovning och Äktenskap i den Svenska Kvinnans Äldre Historia* [Stockholm: Nordiska Bokhandeln, 1965]; Jonas Frykman, "Sexual Intercourse and Social Norms: A Study of Illegitimate Births in Sweden, 1831–1933," *Ethnologica Scandinavica*, 1975, pp. 110–50; Jonas Frykman, *Horan i Bondesamhället* [Lund: LiberLäromedel, 1977]; Knut Kolsrud, "'Om Sædeligheds-tilstanden i Norge' – Nokre Drag av Analysen," *Norveg*, 21 [1978]: 25–46; the place of women in society (Ragnar Pedersen, "Die Arbeitsteilung Zwischen Frauen und Männern in einem Marginalen Ackerbaugebiet – Das Beispiel Norwegen," *Ethnologica Scandinavica*, 1975, pp. 37–48; Anne Helene Bolstad Skjelbred, *Uren og Hedning: Barselkvinnen i Norsk Folketradisjon* [Bergen: Universitetsforlaget, 1972]); and inheritance (Kjeld Helland-Hansen, "Kårskipnaden," *Heimen*, 13 [1964–66]: 182–95; Einar Hovdhaugen, "Frå det Gamle Bondesamfunnet i Gudbrandsdalen: Det Gamle Føderådsskipnaden," *Norveg*, 9 [1962]: 1–78). Perhaps inspired by that great ethnologist of the last century Eilert Sundt, whose work still is worth reading today, Scandinavians remain interested in their peasant past, producing a rich array of secondary sources that contribute to a better understanding of their history.

European works on similar themes include Kingsley Davis, "The Theory of Change and Response in Modern Demographic History," *Population Index*, 29 (1963): 345–66; Kingsley Davis and Judith Blake, "Social Structure and Fertility: An Analytic Framework," *Economic Development and Cultural Change*, 4 (1956): 211–35; Edward Shorter, "Illegitimacy, Sexual Revolution, and Social Change in Modern Europe," in Theodore K. Rabb and Robert I. Rotberg, eds., *The Family in History: Interdisciplinary Essays* (New York: Harper & Row, 1971); Edward Shorter, John Knodel, and Etienne van de Walle, "The Decline of Non-Marital Fertility in Europe, 1880–1940," *Population Studies*, 25 (1971): 375–93; and H. W. Spiegel, "The Altenteil: German Farmers' Old Age Security," *Rural Sociology*, 4 (1939): 203–18.

The developing farming regions of the northern United States in the nineteenth century were a world apart from the Scandinavian peasant communities, but present-day American historians have delved into questions of social and economic development similar to those posed by their European counterparts. Whereas numerous works have depicted the agricultural development of the United States and its specific regions, other specific studies have focused on rural fertility, farm succession, and agricultural practices. General works include Clarence H. Danhof, *Change in Agriculture: The Northern United States, 1820–1870* (Cambridge, Mass.: Harvard University Press, 1969); and Paul W. Gates, *The Farmer's Age: Agriculture, 1815–1860* (New York: Holt, Rinehart & Winston, 1960). More specific studies include Allan G. Bogue, *From Prairie to Cornbelt: Farming on the Illinois and Iowa Prairies in the Nineteenth Century* (Chicago: University of Chicago Press, 1963); Michael P. Conzen, *Frontier Farming in an Urban Shadow: The Influence of Madison's Proximity on the Agricultural Development of Blooming Grove, Wisconsin* (Madison: State Historical Society of Wisconsin, 1971); Merle Curti, *The Making of an American Community* (Stanford, Calif.: Stanford University Press, 1959); Edward Van Dyke Robinson, *Early Economic Conditions and the Development of Agriculture in Minnesota* (Minneapolis: University of Minnesota, 1915); Joseph Schafer, *Wisconsin Domesday Book*, vol. 1, *A History of Agriculture in Wisconsin* (Madison: State Historical Society of Wisconsin, 1922); and John Giffin Thompson, *The Rise and Decline of the Wheat Growing Industry in Wisconsin*, Economic and Political Science Series (Madison: University of Wisconsin, 1909).

For works on fertility see Richard Easterlin, "Population Change and Farm Settlement in the Northern United States," *Journal of Economic History*, 36 (1976): 45–83; George W. Hill and James D. Tarver, "Indigenous Fertility in the Farm Population of Wisconsin, 1848–1948," *Rural Sociology*, 16 (1951): 359–62; and Douglas G. Marshall, "The Decline in Farm Fertility and Its Relationship to Nationality and Religious Background," ibid., 15 (1950): 42–49. On farm succession see David P. Gagen, "The Indivisibility of Land: A Microanalysis of the System of Land Inheritance in Nineteenth Century Ontario," *Journal of Economic History*, 36 (1976): 126–41; James D. Tarver, "Intra-Family Farm Succession Practices," *Rural Sociology*, 17 (1952): 266–71; and Sonya Salamon and Ann Mackey Keim, "Land Ownership and Women's Power in a Midwestern Farming Community," *Journal of Marriage and the Family*, 41 (1979): 109–19; and on agricultural practices see Hildegard Binder Johnson, "King Wheat in Southeastern Minnesota: A Case Study of Pioneer Agriculture," *Annals of the American Association of Geographers*, 47 (1957): 350–62.

Significant research has concentrated on similar questions in agricultural development specifically within immigrant settlements. Since immigrant farming communities were so large a part of the cultural mosaic of rural America, researchers have sought to determine and explain different behavior. Most studies have argued that given their opportunities and constraints, immigrant farmers behaved in crop mix and farming methods much as their American-born neighbors did. Yet other behavior, most notably inheritance patterns, has revealed striking variations that in turn dramatically affected community development. On immigrant farming practices see Bogue, *From Prairie to Cornbelt*; Robert Hugh Downes, "Economic and Social Development of Kenosha County," *Transactions of* the Wisconsin Academy of Sciences, Arts, and Letters, 13 (1901): 545–81; Eva M. Hamberg, Studier i Internationell Migration (Stockholm: Almqvist & Wiksell International, 1976); Benjamin Horace Hibbard, The History of Agriculture in Dane County, Wisconsin, vol. 1, no. 2 (Madison: University of Wisconsin, 1904); Terry G. Jordan, German Seed in Texas Soil: Immigrant Farmers in Nineteenth-Century Texas (Austin: University of Texas Press, 1966); John G. Rice, "The Role of Culture and Community in Frontier Prairie Farming," Journal of Historical Geography, 3 (1977): 155–75; and selections from Frederick C. Luebke, ed., Ethnicity on the Great Plains (Lincoln: University of Nebraska Press, 1980). On farm succession see Robert C. Ostergren, "Cultural Homogeneity and Population Stability among Swedish Immigrants in Chisago County," Minnesota History, 45 (1973): 255–69; and Sonya Salamon, "Ethnic Differences in Farm Family Land Transfers," Rural Sociology, 45 (1980): 290–308. On land ownership and cultural change see Marian Deininger and Douglas C. Marshall, "A Study of Land Ownership by Ethnic Groups from Frontier Times to the Present in a Marginal Farming Area in Minnesota," Land Economics, 31 (1955): 351–60; and Oscar F. Hoffman, "Cultural Change in a Rural Wisconsin Ethnic Island," Rural Sociology, 14 (1949): 39–50.

Social change within immigrant communities has also been examined. Studies of the spatial development of rural immigrant communities have revealed an ethnic segregation that dramatically affected social interaction ranging from intermarriage to "visiting" and, ultimately, to acculturation. Others have briefly examined the changing place of immigrant women in American society. On ethnic segregation in rural areas see Peter A. Munch, "Segregation and Assimilation of Norwegian Settlements in Wisconsin," Norwegian-American Studies and Records, 1954, pp. 102–40; Ostergren, "Rättvik to Isanti": John G. Rice, Patterns of Ethnicity in a Minnesota County, 1880–1905, Geographical Reports no. 4 (Umeå, Sweden: University of Umeå, Department of Geography, 1973); and John Useem and Ruth Hill Useem, "Minority-Group Patterns in Prairie Society," American Journal of Sociology, 51 (1945): 377–85. On the place of women in the new society see Bengt Ankarloo, "Agriculture and Women's Work: Directions of Change in the West, 1700–1900," Journal of Family History, 4 (1979): 111–20; and H. Arnold Barton, "Scandinavian Immigrant Women's Encounter with America," Swedish Pioneer Historical Quarterly, 25 (1974): 37–42.

After decades of study, the topics of emigration and immigration may one day be subsumed under the larger analysis of migration in the developing world economy. A social historian, in undertaking a study of trans-Atlantic migration, will have to examine the economic and social development of each side of the migration and attempt to understand their connecting threads. Given the conclusions of those few monographs dealing with the trans-Atlantic rural migration, new findings might well continue to reveal profound, kaleidoscopic change. Similar concerns in a world community of social historians, ethnologists, geographers, economists, and sociologists have created parallel research interests on both sides of the Atlantic that might work to facilitate that research. American scholars are interested in inheritance, the changing place of women and men in society, courtship and marriage, fertility, and spatial organization; but so are Europeans. Investigating behavior that often deviates strongly in different areas of study, researchers are still examining issues that in the human context are fundamentally similar. And the fact that similar questions are being investigated in spite of their different locations in the world economy can only aid the study of immigrant populations before and after their migration.

Index

Note: The word *immigrant* in this index refers to Norwegians who emigrated to the Upper Middle West of the United States in the 19th century.

agriculture, *see* farming
agriculture, transhumance, *see* farming, traditional patterns of
allodial right, *see* inheritance, patterns of
"America fever," 12, 22, 23, 116–17, 118, 119, 135, 137
animal husbandry and production, immigrant
  crop patterns, 185
  market for, 187,
  sexual division of labor, 193–4, 196–7, 287 n67
  strategies of, 10, 125–6, 174, 188t, 234, 235
animal husbandry and production, Norwegian
  cotters, 79–80
  crop patterns, 74, 75t, 76
  market for, 7, 16, 17, 46, 76
  naming of cows, 287 n67, 287–8 n81
  sexual division of labor, 65, 67–9
  strategies of, 10, 13, 19, 27–41 *passim*, 44–5, 49, 64, 82, 246 n17, n19, 258–9 n71, 259 n73
  see also forage, natural; hay; milkmaid
ard, *see* farm implements
Arendahl township, Minnesota, 160, 170, 173
  as colonizer, 158–9
  as colony, 153–7

farming patterns, 188–91
fertility patterns, 208–9, 210t, 212t, 223
land taking, 171, 172t
Lutheran churches of, 5, 155–6, 229, 230
marriage patterns, 204–5, 206t, 207, 208, 238
prenuptial and illegitimate births, 214, 215t, 216t, 217, 220, 290 n15
religious conflict, 155–7
Aurland, Sogn, 117, 119, 279 n33

Balestrand, Sogn
  described, 25, 46
  emigration-prone area, xii, 5–6, 21, 22–3, 117, 118–19, 120, 121, 122t, 123, 127–8, 134
  and immigrant settlements, 131, 134, 233–4, 279 n33
  internal migration vs. emigration, 19, 120t, 121t
  map, 60
  population, 25, 54, 61t
  regional differences, 59, 61–2
Bandon township, Minnesota, *see* Camp and Bandon townships, Minnesota
barley production, Norwegian vs. immigrant, 32, 176, 187, 190, 191t, 247 n41
Bergen, Norway, 17
  as emigration port, 271 n11
  illegitimacy rate, 266 n61

Bergen, Norway (*cont.*)
  internal migration to, 15, 121t
  as trade center, 17, 46, 76, 78,
    259 n75
births
  customs of, 53–4
  and inheritance patterns, 85–6
  prenuptially conceived, 10, 19,
    93t, 103–4, 213–14, 215t, 216t,
    217
  see also conceptions, pre-engage-
    ment; conceptions, prenup-
    tial; illegitimacy
boats, and trade, 17, 259 n75
Bonnet Prairie, Wisconsin, 150,
  151t
bourgeois behavior, *see* social
  patterns
Boyum, Arne Endresen, 110–11,
  152, 154, 155, 157, 245 n1
Bristol township, Wisconsin, 145,
  146t, 147t, 148
bundling, *see* night courting
burial, customs of, 52, 54, 289 n5

Camp and Bandon townships,
  Minnesota
  churches, 5, 158, 161, 163–4,
    164–5
  as colonies, 157–60
  farming patterns, 188–91
  fertility patterns, 208, 209t, 210t,
    212t
  landholding, 159t
  marriage patterns, 204, 206t,
    207t, 208
  and secondary migration, 161,
    162t, 163–5
capital, *see* farming, capital for
cattle, *see* animal husbandry and
  production
children, of cotters
  and immigrant illegitimate
    births, 218–19, 291 n16
  livelihoods for, 96, 97–8, 265
    n53
  marriage patterns, 98–100, 265–
    6 n54, 266 n55
  as servants, 66–7

children, of farmers
  as emigrants, 120, 121, 122t,
    123–4, 125, 271–2 n21
  as farm laborers, 64
  and landlessness, 96, 97, 265
    n52
  marriage and inheritance pat-
    terns, 96–7, 99t
children, of immigrants
  as labor force, 9, 193, 210, 235
  see also family, nuclear
    (immigrant)
churches, immigrant
  and community stability, 10,
    161, 163–5, 166, 233
  divisions within, 152, 277 n14
  and intrachurch marriages, 164,
    165, 281 n72
  and morality, 203, 213, 220, 221,
    227, 288–9 n12
  records of, 4, 145, 148
  and Norwegian traditions, 150,
    151t, 161, 229, 236
  see also Haugean church
churches, Norwegian, worship
    patterns in, 109–10, 270 n86
  see also communion celebration
    patterns; pietistic movement;
    reader movement
colonies, immigrant, 139–40, 278
    n27
  see also settlements, immigrant
communion celebration patterns,
    111, 112t, 113t
  and emigration, 276 n78
conceptions, pre-engagement, 92,
    264 n32
conceptions, prenuptial, 89–90,
    91, 92, 93t, 203, 207–8, 216t,
    217–19, 221, 234–5, 237, 263
    n24, n25, 264 n32
corn, American
  as immigrant crop, 9, 168, 176,
    179, 187, 190, 191t
  immigrant vs. American pro-
    duction, 171, 173t, 177, 282
    n25, 284 n33
cost of living, American vs. Nor-
    wegian, 78, 126

cotters
  age at marriage, 53, 98–9
  contracts with farmers, 34, 65–
    6, 72, 78, 256 n34
  defined, 25
  as emigrants, 8, 121, 122t, 131,
    276 n78
  family size, vs. farmers, 54–5,
    101
  household formation patterns,
    97–102, 104–5, 265 n54
  inheritance patterns, 86–7
  land clearing, 72–3
  numbers of, 26, 54, 79
  prenuptial births, 103–4, 105t
  productivity, 55, 65, 69, 74, 78–
    80, 80–1, 82
  social status, 251 n104, 268–9
    n80
  as wage workers, 62, 68–9, 72
  work responsibilities, 32, 39, 41,
    64, 65–6
  see also children, of cotters;
    landless
courtship, patterns of
  changes in, 94–5
  and land ownership, 95–6
  Norwegian vs. immigrant, 10,
    202–3, 213–14, 215–22, 224,
    232, 234, 235
  regional variations in, 19–20
  traditional, 8, 53, 87, 88–92, 262
    n9
  see also births, prenuptially con-
    ceived; conceptions, prenup-
    tial; engagement; night
    courting
craftsmen, landless as, 58–9, 62,
  74, 80–1, 97, 254 n16
crop production, immigrant, 168,
  187, 234, 235
  vs. American, 171, 173t
  see also barley production; corn;
    grain; hay; oat production;
    potato production; wheat,
    American
crop production, Norwegian
  and animal husbandry, 74, 75t,
    76

and arable land, 70–2
  traditional patterns of, 26, 28,
    30–3, 247 n41
  see also barley production; grain;
    hay; oat production; potato
    production
crop rotation, 32, 184, 186, 246
  n19
culture, immigrant
  adaptation of Norwegian tradi-
    tional, xii, xiv, 5, 10–11, 187,
    190, 233, 239
  as imitation of American
    culture, 223, 224–5
  see also social patterns,
    immigrant
culture, Norwegian, regional variations in, 18, 19–20, 26, 46–
    54, 87, 244 n29

Dahl, Andrew, 236
  photographs of, reproduced,
    148, 175, 179, 198, 200, 208,
    223, 224, 225, 237
dairy products, 7, 19, 36, 177, 178,
  185, 255 n28
  as trade item, 16, 17, 46, 76, 77t
death, see burial, customs of
Denmark, 2
  outmigration to, 243 n18
dialects, 141, 150
Dietrickson, Johannes W. C., 150,
  152
Dovre, county of Norway, emigration from, 123, 131, 132, 272
  n39, 274 n62
drunkenness, immigrant attitudes
  toward, 220–1, 229, 232, 276
  n78

economy, American, and immigrants, 20, 21, 114–15, 119,
  123-4, 125, 234, 272 n26
economy, Norwegian
  and emigration, 24, 56–7, 82,
    83, 115, 133, 134
  and household formation, 86–7
  and inheritance patterns, 24

economy, Norwegian (*cont.*)
  and marriage patterns, 100, 101,
    266 n55
  regional differences in, 18–19,
    20, 26, 133, 134
Eielsen, Elling, 152, 155
emigrants
  destinations of, 119, 130, 132,
    273 n55
  and kinship groups, 131, 132,
    274 n61, n62
  numbers of, 3, 12, 20, 21–3,
    118, 119, 120t, 129, 131, 132–
    3
  and prepaid tickets, 21, 131, 174
    n58
  protocol lists, 131, 271 n11, 174
    n58
  wealth and social status of, 117,
    119–21, 122t, 123, 128, 232
emigration
  and American wealth, 124–8,
    272 n39
  and land availability, 61, 121,
    123, 124, 126–7, 272 n39
  and improved livelihoods, 87,
    123–6, 272 n39
  local effect of, 6, 12, 81, 95, 128–
    9
  regional differences in, 12, 20–3
  theories regarding causes of,
    xiii, 6–7, 23–4, 54, 55, 56–7,
    82–4, 101–2, 114–15, 117, 119,
    128, 135, 238–9, 257 n50, 262
    n57, 276 n77
  see also migration, internal
    (Norway)
engagement, customs of, 53, 91,
    92, 263 n22
  see also courtship, patterns of
Etne, county of Norway, marriage
    patterns in, 92, 93, 263 n22,
    265 n54
exports, *see* trade

family, nuclear
  bourgeois behavior of, 224–31,
    235, 236–8
  as farm work force, 9, 167, 169,
    173, 193, 283 n17

and Norwegian cultural pat-
    terns, 6, 137, 138, 203
  American migration patterns of,
    138–54, 173
family, size of, 193
family, structure of
  and emigration, 131–2, 274 n61,
    n62
  and landlessness, 8
  single-parent, 106, 266 n68
  see also kinship groups
Faribault County, Minnesota, sec-
    ondary migration to, 153–4,
    157, 280 n48
farmers
  capital inputs, 73–4
  vs. city people, 134–5, 275 n74
  contracts of, with cotters, 34,
    65–6, 72, 78, 256 n34
  courtship patterns of, 107, 108
  as emigrants, 4–5, 8–9, 82, 83,
    120, 122t
  land inputs of, 69–72
  numbers of, 271 n14
  and poor crop years, 82–3
  and prenuptial births, 103–4
  tenant, 131, 274 n60
  and trade, 16, 17, 57, 59, 62
  as wage payers, 63–9
  see also children, of farmers
farmers, propertyless, *see* cotters
farming, immigrant
  animal husbandry and produc-
    tion, 176–8, 183, 185–6, 187–
    8, 190
  capital for, 168–9, 172–3, 174–5
  crop mix and diversification,
    173t, 176–7, 181t, 182t, 186–7,
    190, 234, 283 n25, 285 n54
  hay production, 183
  vs. American patterns of, 139,
    169, 171
  vs. traditional patterns of, 4–5,
    6, 9–10, 20, 136, 138, 167,
    168–9, 171, 174, 191–2, 233,
    234, 238
  in settlement areas, 175–91
    passim
  wheat production, 178–82, 185–
    8, 188–90, 284 n36

farming, Norwegian
animal vs. crop production, 74,
75t, 76, 258 n70, 258–9 n71
capital for, 73–4
development of and alterations
in, 3, 7, 8, 23, 58–9, 61, 96
and fishing, 2, 13, 19, 20–1
implements used in, 31, 33, 39,
43, 73, 246–7 n25
and market opportunities, 59,
61, 69
mechanization of, 73, 128, 129,
168, 193, 195
outputs of, 57, 58
regional variations in, 18–19,
246–7 n25
specialization of, 59
traditional patterns of, 2, 7, 23–
45 passim, 56, 59, 61, 69–70,
72, 74, 76, 82, 83, 128, 248
n60, 258–9 n71, 273 n47
farms, Norwegian
cost of, 82–3, 261 n103
division of, 25, 27, 28, 59, 61,
245 n9, 246 n21
flatland, 64, 65, 66, 74, 75t, 76,
256 n31
mortgages on, 73, 83
shoreline, 64, 66, 74, 75t, 76,
256 n31
size of, 61, 82, 173, 261 n101,
283 n17
social structure of, 47–8
value of, 126–7
see also land: intergenerational
transfer of
fertility, patterns of
and economic opportunities, 8,
24, 96, 101
among immigrants, 9, 202, 208–
11, 223, 235
and inheritance patterns, 12, 48,
86
and marriage patterns, 53, 93,
94–5
regional differences in, 19
fertilizer, 73, 74
see also manure
festivities, neighborhood, 51–4
Fillmore County, Minnesota, sec-

ondary migration to, 153–4,
155
fishing industry, Norwegian
and emigration, 20–1
and farming, 2, 13, 19, 20–1
growth of, 13, 15, 19, 58
and inheritance patterns, 24
and trade, 16, 17, 59
Fjærlandsfjord, Balestrand
and emigration, 132, 133
and natural forage, 39, 42, 45
folk culture, 18, 46–54, 133, 268
n77
effect of American environment
on, 135–6, 203
and emigration, 21, 134, 135,
150–1, 276 n77
forage, cultivated, *see* hay
forage, natural
amounts needed, 44, 249 n85,
250 n88
collection of, 34, 36, 42–5, 78
sources of, 34, 35–6, 38, 45, 59, 70
types of, 26, 42, 44, 45
forests, 42, 58
see also forage, natural
Foss, H. A., *Husmandsgutten (The
Cotter's Son)*, 232, 233
fruit, as trade item, 76, 77t, 78

gard, see farming, Norwegian, traditional patterns of
grain, Norwegian
and cotters, 65, 69, 77, 79
importation of, 7, 33, 76, 77t,
259–60 n76
production of, 2, 10, 30, 38, 64,
70, 71, 74, 75t, 76, 259 n73
as trade item, 16, 17, 46, 58, 59
see also labor, sexual division of
grain, immigrant production of,
10, 169, 187, 190–1, 234
see also wheat, American
granne, see neighborhoods, ties
within
grend, see neighborhoods, ties
within

Hafslo, Sogn, 17, 33
immigrants from, 279 n33

Hafslo, Sogn (*cont.*)
servant migrants from, 256–7
n42
handworkers, *see* craftsmen
Hansen, Marcus Lee, 138–40
Hauge, Hans Nielsen, 233
Haugean church
and immigrant settlements, 157,
160, 203
and pietistic movement, 155,
207, 217, 233
see also Camp and Bandon
townships, Minnesota,
churches of
hay
harvesting of, 38–42, 65, 234,
256 n36
Norwegian vs. immigrant production of, 30, 38, 183, 184t,
190–1, 234
see also crop production
herring, as trade item, 17, 20, 21,
46, 79
see also fishing industry
høstingsbruk, see farming, traditional patterns of
household formation, patterns of,
235
landed vs. landless, 96–102,
104–5, 263 n46, n51, n54
traditional, 8, 86–7, 92–3
household industry, *see* craftsmen
husmenn, see cotters

illegitimacy
defined, 93t
and landlessness, 8, 265 n46
and night courting, 91–2, 95,
102–3, 109
rates of, 10, 19–20, 95, 102–3,
213–14, 215t, 216t, 221, 237,
263 n27, 266–7 n61, 267 n62,
290 n14
strictures against, 87, 106, 108,
203, 267 n69, 268 n77
see also births, prenuptially conceived; conceptions, prenuptial; night courting
Illinois, Norwegian emigration to,
3, 144, 145

immigrants
American settlement patterns
of, 4, 5, 143–5, 148, 160–1,
163–6, 166–7, 170–1, 278 n27
cultural adaptations of, 6, 9–11,
138–9, 150, 222–3, 230, 233–
9
farming adaptations of, 4–5, 9–
10, 128, 167, 168–9, 172–3,
174–5, 273 n47
see also farming, immigrant; settlements, immigrant; social
patterns, immigrant
implements, agricultural, *see*
farming
imports, *see* trade
industry, 15, 57, 58, 78, 254 n16,
275 n74
see also protoindustrialization
information, about America
and emigration, 115, 123, 124,
125–6, 129–30, 133, 138
types of, 116–17, 130–1
inheritance, patterns of, 8, 12, 59
and emigration, xiii, 121, 124,
271–2 n21
impartability, 13, 61, 83, 96, 97,
251 n104, 255 n21
and marriage, 86, 266 n55
and naming customs, 48, 250–1
n102
regional differences in, 18, 19
and secondary migration in
America, 160, 166, 281 n68
traditional, 24, 26, 47–9, 51, 261
n2
and women, 47–8
see also land, intergenerational
transfer of
innmark, see farming, traditional
patterns of
innhus, see farming, traditional
patterns of
Iowa, Norwegian emigration to, 3,
137, 142, 143, 154

Janson, Kristofer, 140

kårkontrakt, see land, intergenerational transfer of

kinship groups
  and emigration, 10, 115, 130,
    131–2, 233, 274 n61, 275 n69
  and immigrant settlements, 4, 5,
    9, 139, 140–1, 233–4, 277 n14
  and land strategy, 46–51
  role of, 46–7, 51–2, 61, 111, 250
    n100
  see also neighborhoods, ties
    within
Koshkonong, Wisconsin, as immi-
    grant settlement, 140, 142–3,
    145, 148, 170, 221

labor, immigrant
  and adaptation of traditional
    patterns, 233, 235, 236
  collective, 174
  see also family, nuclear
labor, Norwegian
  class division and specialization
    in, 59, 63–9, 254 n16
  collective, 51–2, 252 n119
  cost of, vs. American, 234
  demand for, 26, 32, 54, 57, 58,
    69, 255 n28, 268 n74
  and emigration, 81, 128, 134
  inputs of, by cotters, 62–3, 64,
    65–6, 68–9, 72–3
  inputs of, by farmer and family,
    63, 64
  inputs of, by servants, 64, 65,
    66–8
  and marriage patterns, 263–4
    n31
  regional variations in, 16–20
  yearly patterns of, 28, 30
  see also laborers, wage
labor, sexual division of,
    immigrant
  vs. American, 169, 286 n61
  and animal husbandry, 196–8,
    199
  farm vs. household, 200–1
  and servants, 193, 195–6, 197
  vs. traditional patterns of, 192–
    201, 203, 230, 234, 235, 236,
    238, 286 n62
  and wealth, 198–9, 201

labor, sexual division of,
    Norwegian
  and animal husbandry, 34–5,
    36, 37, 67–8
  and servants, 67–8
  traditional patterns of, xiii, 9–
    10, 46, 50, 58, 85, 88, 247 n30,
    257 n46
laborers, wage, in America
  availability of, 168–9, 171–2,
    173–4, 193, 283 n15
  on immigrant farms, 174t, 235
  immigrants as, 168, 169, 170,
    283 n16
  see also servants, immigrant
laborers, wage, in Norway
  demand for, 63–4, 69
  landless as, 18, 62, 68–9, 74, 80,
    81
  opportunities for, 74, 80, 82
  payment to, 81t, 260 n96
  see also servants
Lærdal, Sogn, 17, 32, 33, 259 n75
  and emigration, 118, 119, 279
    n33
land, American
  availability of, 4, 8–9, 121, 123,
    124, 126–7, 137, 138–9, 142,
    152–3, 170–1, 233, 272 n39
  price of, 124, 126, 129, 142, 234,
    278 n21
land, Norwegian
  division of, 25, 27, 28, 59, 61,
    245 n9, 246 n21
  intergenerational transfer of,
    48–9, 51, 85–6, 88, 96, 262 n6,
    265 n47
  ownership of, 53, 57, 62, 95–6
landless, 6, 8, 12–13, 96, 271 n14
  and economic opportunities, 24,
    57, 62–3, 74, 96, 97
  and emigration, 8–9, 61, 122t,
    133–4
  household formation strategies,
    86–7, 97–102, 104–5, 265 n54
  and illegitimacy, 102–3, 267
    n62
  as wage laborers, 18, 62, 68–9,
    74, 80, 81
  see also cotters; livelihoods

landowners, as emigrants, 119–20, 120–1, 122t, 123, 149t
land use
  alterations in, 58, 69–73, 257 n51, 258 n54
  and emigration, 20, 23
  intensification of, 71–2, 258 n58
  strategies of, 6, 19, 26, 46–7, 258–9 n71
language, immigrant patterns of, 150, 227–8, 233, 236
Leikanger, Sogn, 33, 81, 103
  emigration from, 117, 145, 148, 150, 279 n33
  and immigrant prenuptial conceptions, 217
  and trade, 17, 78
leisure, immigrant adaptation to, 222–3, 228, 233
  see also social patterns, immigrant; bourgeois behavior
"letters home," and emigration, 4, 12, 21, 22, 116, 117, 123–4, 125, 126, 130–1, 133, 145, 170, 272 n26, n39, 279 n37
lineage, and inheritance patterns, 47–8, 49
livelihoods, immigrant
  and marriage patterns, 203–5, 234
  and prenuptial births, 213, 214, 218–19
  and secondary migration, 233–4
livelihoods, Norwegian
  and emigration, 87, 114–15, 124–6, 138
  and marriage patterns, 86, 87, 88, 94, 99, 100–1, 102, 108, 138, 260 n4, 264 n36, n40, 266 n57, 267–8 n69
  and prenuptial births, 104
livestock, see animal husbandry and production
lumbering, 2, 21, 59
  see also wood
Lyster, Sogn, 17, 32
  and emigration, 118, 119, 279 n33

manure, 30, 31, 33, 36, 38, 246 n19
market structures, 4, 26, 57, 69, 169, 176–7
marriage, patterns of, immigrant
  age at marriage, 202, 203–5, 206t, 207t, 217–18, 288 n4
  intrachurch, 164, 165, 281 n72
  and Norwegian regional ties, 150–1, 152t, 279–80 n44
  and secondary migration, 137–8
  seasonal, 207–8
  vs. traditional, xiii, 10, 202, 203–5, 207, 211, 219–20, 234, 289 n5
marriage, patterns of, Norwegian
  age at marriage, 86, 93, 96–7, 98–9, 101–2, 265–6 n54, 266 n55, n57, 290–1 n15
  celibacy, 99–100
  and inheritance patterns, 48, 85–6, 96–7
  farmer vs. cotter, 8, 24, 93–4, 95–6, 96–7, 98–9, 262 n57, 267–8 n69
  regional differences in, 18, 19–20, 94–5
  role of parents, 53, 91, 94, 95, 96–7, 98, 264 n42
  seasonal, 53, 91, 92, 263–4 n31, 264 n34
  traditional, 52–3, 87–8, 91, 92–3, 107–8
mechanization
  and emigration, 128, 129, 168
  and sexual division of labor, 193, 195, 198, 199, 235
migration, immigrant (in America)
  age specificity of, 161, 162t
  causes of, 137–40, 142–3, 153, 159–60, 233–4, 278 n27
  and church membership, 155–7, 161, 163
  and nuclear family, 138, 173
  route of, 153, 280 n50
  and wealth, 161, 162t
  see also settlements, immigrant
migration, internal (Norway)
  alternatives to, 20–1
  causes of, 13, 15–16, 20, 24, 61

vs. emigration, 21, 119, 120t,
    121t, 239
rural vs. urban, 134–5, 275–6
    n74, n75
seasonal, 16, 243 n18
migration, Norwegian tradition of,
    12, 22, 134, 135, 243 n18
milkmaids, 34–5, 36, 37, 43, 45, 72
    see also labor, sexual division of;
    animal husbandry
Minnesota, immigrant settlements
    in, 3, 5, 136, 137, 142, 143
morality
    and courtship and marriage pat-
        terns, 106, 107
    and illegitimacy, 87, 90, 92
    and immigrants, 203, 232
    regional variations in, 19–20
    see also night courting; pietistic
        movement
Mundal, Ingebrigt, 110
Mundal, parish of, Balestrand, 42,
    48, 59, 62
    cotters in, 66, 79
    emigration and internal migra-
        tion, 133t, 135, 276 n76
    farming in, 61, 62, 70–1, 74, 75t,
        76, 82–3, 259 n73
    marriage ages, 99t, 100
    prenuptial conceptions and il-
        legitimacy, 93t, 104t, 105t
    servants in, 67, 257 n44

naming customs, *see* inheritance,
    patterns of
nattfrieri, see night courting
neighborhoods
    and emigration patterns, 132–3,
        275 n69
    ties within, 51–2, 252 n119
night courting, patterns of, immi-
    grant, 213, 232, 234-5, 237
    American opposition to, 213
    attitudes toward, 203, 219–21,
        272
    end of, in America, 221, 291 n23
    moral condemnation of, 203,
        220–1, 229, 291 n18
    and prenuptial conceptions, 217

night courting, patterns of,
    Norwegian
    attempts to reduce or end, 8,
        106–7, 108–9, 114, 229, 236,
        237, 269 n82
    attitudes toward, 88, 90, 102,
        105, 106, 107, 108, 262 n9
    and prenuptial conceptions or
        illegitimate births, 87, 91–2,
        102–3, 104, 263 n24, n25
    variations in, 19–20, 88–90, 94–
        5
Nilsson, Svein, 220–1, 222
North Dakota, emigration to, 3
Norway
    population of, 2, 3, 6
    regional differences within, 12–
        13, 17–20, 244 n29
Norway, regions of
    Gudbrandsdal, 16, 17, 19, 42,
        44, 246–7 n25
    Hallingdal, 17, 18, 22t, 67
    Hardanger, 16, 22t, 141, 258–9
        n71
    Helgeland, 20, 21, 131
    Hordaland, 117
    Møre, xiii, 17, 20, 61, 246–7
        n25
    Nordfjord, 20, 62
    Nordland, 16, 17, 119
    Numedal, 16, 22t, 121, 145
    Rogaland, 117, 140
    Romsdal, 17, 20, 21, 119
    Ryfylke, 22t
    Sunnhordland, 22t
    Trondelag, 2, 13, 18
    see also Sogn; Telemark; Valdres;
        Voss
Norway Grove–Spring Prairie,
    Wisconsin, 132, 160, 170, 173,
    274 n65
    churches, 150, 151t, 152, 280
        n45
    courtship and marriage pat-
        terns, 203–4, 205, 214, 215t,
        216t, 217–18, 219, 220, 288 n4,
        290 n15, 291 n18
    farming patterns, 175–88 passim
    land taking, 170–1

Norway Grove–Spring Prairie,
    Wisconsin (*cont.*)
  non-Norwegian vs. Sogning set-
    tlers, 145, 146t, 147t, 148
  and secondary migration, 5,
    153–4, 280 n47

oat production, immigrant, 32,
    172, 176, 187, 190, 191t, 247
    n41, 283 n25, 284 n33

parents, role of
  as elders, 85, 261 n2
  and marriage arrangements, 91–
    2, 94, 95–6, 98, 232, 261 n2
pietistic movement
  and courtship practices, 8, 87,
    109, 141
  and immigrant settlements, 8,
    115, 152, 153, 155, 157, 203,
    222, 280 n59
  Norwegian vs. immigrant, 10,
    236–7, 238
  and societal divisions, 109, 110–
    11, 114
  and worship patterns, 109–10
  see also reader movement
Pontoppidan, Erik, 90
population growth, 15, 54–5, 252
    n129
  and agricultural expansion, 56–
    7, 71
potato production, immigrant,
    176t, 177t, 181t, 182t, 191t,
    284 n33
potato production, Norwegian, 6,
    7, 23, 32, 63, 71, 82, 259 n73
  and cotters, 65, 79
  and trade, 17, 59, 76, 77t
pregnancies, prenuptial, *see* births,
    prenuptially conceived; con-
    ceptions, pre-engagement;
    conceptions, prenuptial; il-
    legitimacy; night courting
Preus, Herman, 150
prices, for farm and industrial
    goods, 78
production, agricultural, *see* farming
production, nonagricultural, 18,
    19, 45–6, 58–9, 62

protoindustrialization, 58, 59, 254
    n16

reader movement, 110–11, 270
    n87
  see also pietistic movement
Reiersen, Johan Reinert, 123, 125,
    126, 272 n22
religion, *see* churches
retirement (*kår*), see land: in-
    tergenerational transfer of
rites of passage, celebrations of,
    52–4

salt, 17, 46, 58, 78
seafaring, 19, 20, 58, 59
  see also fishing industry
servants, immigrant
  work role of, 195–6, 197, 201,
    225, 228, 287 n70, n72
  see also labor, sexual division of
    (immigrant)
servants, Norwegian
  courtship and marriage patterns
    of, 88–90, 106t
  and farm family, 26, 48, 108,
    268–9 n80
  and illegitimacy, 102–3
  and internal migration, 16, 67,
    129, 256–7 n42
  length of servitude, 66–7, 82
  nonagricultural production of,
    46, 50
  sex ratios among, 195, 196t
  sources and availability of, 66,
    67, 81
  wages of, 39, 67, 81t, 129, 260–1
    n100
  work responsibilities of, 28, 64,
    65, 66–8, 69, 82, 257 n44, n46,
    265 n41
  see also labor, sexual division of
settlements, immigrant
  bourgeois behavior, 200–1, 222–
    31
  colonies of, 4, 5, 137, 138, 139–
    40, 143, 157–60, 166, 233–4
  courtship and marriage pat-
    terns, 141, 207–8, 213–14,
    215–22, 289 n5

cultural adaptation of, xiii–xiv, 6, 202, 230–1, 233, 234–5
divisions within, 141, 277–8 n18
and elderly, 164–5, 166
fertility patterns, 208–11, 212t, 223–4
illegitimacy, 213–14, 215t, 216t, 221, 290 n14
kinship and cultural ties among, 9, 10, 143, 155–7, 158, 160
languages in, 141, 227–8, 277–8 n18
marriage ages in, 203–5, 206, 207t, 288 n4
morality, 220–2
new arrivals in, 142–4
and Norwegian regional ties, 115, 140–1, 143–5, 148, 160, 277 n14
stability of, 160–1, 165–6, 233
sexual relations, premarital, *see* night courting
sheep raising, immigrant, 235
vs. American, 177, 187, 188, 283 n26
sheep raising, Norwegian, 17, 35, 36, 41, 49, 64, 79
shipbuilding, 19, 21
social patterns, immigrant
and bourgeois behavior, 201, 222–31, 235, 236–8
transition in, 202, 203, 236
social patterns, Norwegian
and bourgeois behavior, 10, 11
and class distinctions, 18, 108, 268–9 n80
and emigration, 128–9
and pietistic movement, 110, 111, 114
regional differences in, 18, 20, 46–54, 268–9 n80
and rites of passage, 47, 52–4
Sogn, region of Norway
animal and crop production, 32, 258–9 n71
courtship and marriage patterns, 19–20, 94–5
and emigration, 20, 21, 22, 23, 117–18

and illegitimacy, 95, 266–7 n61
immigrant settlements of, in America, 153, 155, 279 n33, 280 n48
and internal migration, 5, 16, 119
and trade, 17, 74, 76, 77t, 78, 259 n75
Sogndal, Sogn, emigration from, 117, 119, 279 n33
South Dakota, Norwegian emigration to, 3, 137, 143, 160
spinning, 46, 50, 199, 208
Spring Prairie, Wisconsin, *see* Norway Grove–Spring Prairie, Wisconsin
stol, see animal production patterns; farming, traditional patterns of
summer feeding system, *see* animal husbandry and production, strategies of
Sundt, Eilert, 3, 18
on Norwegian courtship and marriage patterns, 19–20, 88–9, 90, 265 n54
on Norwegian morality, 94, 95, 108, 114, 115, 213, 236, 267 n62, 269 n82, 290 n14
on Norwegian overpopulation, 56
Sunnfjord, region of Norway
courtship and marriage patterns, 19–20, 94–5
and emigration, 20
farming, 62, 258–9 n71
illegitimacy, 95, 108, 114, 268 n77
Sværefjord, Balestrand, 132, 133t
Sweden, 2
emigration to America, 209, 271, 277 n14, 279 n38, 284 n36, 289 n10
prenuptial conceptions and illegitimacy in, 263 n25, n26, n29, 266–7 n61, 268 n77
social divisions in, 268–9 n80
swine, immigrant production of, 177–8, 187, 188, 235

Telemark, region of Norway, 16,
18
and emigration, 21, 22t, 121,
131, 140, 145, 273 n47
Thistlethwaite, Frank, 1, 4, 297
timber, *see* wood
Tinn, Telemark, Norway, 274 n60
and emigration, 121, 123, 131,
273 n55, 275 n75
Tjugum parish, Balestrand
communion celebration, 111,
112t, 113t
cotter productivity, 66, 79
and emigration, 120, 133
farming, 61, 62, 64, 70–1, 74,
75t, 76, 259 n73
marriage ages, 99t
population growth, 59, 61
servants, 67, 260 n100
social divisions, 62
trade
by boat, 17, 21, 259 n75
and farm production, 45, 46, 54,
57, 59, 74, 76, 77t, 78, 259–60
n76
regional, 16–17, 18, 23, 26, 30,
58
traditions, cultural, *see* folk culture
transportation
for emigrants, 21, 129–30, 131
and immigrant crop mix, 178–9
and nuclear family, 131–2, 274
n62
truloving, see engagement
tun, see farming, traditional patterns of

utmark, see farming, traditional
patterns of

Valdres, region of Norway, 17, 67
emigration from, 21, 22t
and immigrant settlements, 141,
143
Vangsnes parish, Balestrand, 259
n75
and emigration, 132, 133
farming, 59, 61, 64, 79
internal migration, 135, 276 n76

vårstøl, see animal husbandry and
production
Vienna township, Wisconsin, 171,
282–3 n13
fertility patterns, 208, 209t, 210t,
212t
immigrant enclaves in, 145,
146t, 147t, 148
marriage patterns, 204, 205,
206t, 208
Vik, Sogn, 17, 20
emigration from, 117, 119, 121,
131, 279 n33
Voss, region of Norway
emigration from, 22t, 117
farm size in, 61, 261 n101
and immigrant settlements, 145,
148, 150

wages
American vs. Norwegian, 124,
125, 126, 128, 272 n39, 272–3
n40
of day laborers, 81t, 260 n96
and emigration, 81t, 128, 129,
134
paid by farmers, 63–9
of servants, 39, 67, 81t, 129,
260–1 n100
wealth, immigrant
and bourgeois behavior, 203,
222–3, 224, 226, 227, 231, 236
and morality, 222, 224
wealth, Norwegian
vs. American, 232
as basis of marriage, 87–8
see also livelihoods
Wergeland, Henrik, 12, 23
wheat
as American crop, 9, 10, 168,
174–5, 179
decline in production of, 181,
184–7
harvest of, 174, 179, 180t
as immigrant crop, 10, 167, 169,
176, 178–82, 185–6, 187, 192,
234, 235, 284 n36
price of, and emigration, 127–8,
180

immigrant vs. American pro-
    duction of, 171, 173t, 177,
    180, 284 n33, n36
  speculation in, 181–2, 183–5,
    235
Windsor township, Wisconsin,
    immigrant enclaves in, 145,
    146t, 147t, 148
winter feeding system, *see* animal
    husbandry and production,
    strategies of
Wisconsin
  immigrant settlements in, 3, 5,
    120, 136, 141, 142, 144, 221,
    278 n27
  wage rates in, 126
  see also Camp and Bandon
    townships, Minnesota: Nor-
    way Grove–Spring Prairie,
    Wisconsin
women, immigrant
  immigrant vs. American at-
    titudes toward, 106, 195–6
  domestic work role of, 199–201,
    211, 224, 227, 228, 230, 235,
    236, 238

farm work role of, vs. Nor-
    wegian, 169, 193–99, 234, 286
    n63
  as servants, 195–6, 197, 201,
    225, 228, 235, 238, 287 n70,
    n72
  as wage laborers, 173, 174t, 195
  wage rates of, 126, 272–3 n40
  see also labor, sexual division of,
    immigrant
women, Norwegian
  age of at marriage, vs. men, 99,
    100, 265–6 n54
  and illegitimacy, 105–6
  and inheritance patterns, 47, 48,
    97, 265 n51
  as servants, 67–8, 82, 257 n44,
    n46, 265 n41
  as wives of cotters, 93, 264 n34
  see also labor, sexual division of
wood
  and cotters, 80
  and intrafamily contracts, 49
  as trade item, 16, 17, 46, 59, 76,
    78
  see also lumbering